Aviram Barkai / **For Heaven's Sake**

Aviram Barkai

For Heaven's Sake
The 201ˢᵗ Squadron and the Yom Kippur War

Senior Editors & Producers: ContentoNow
Translation: Jacob Mogerman
Editing: Michael Kadichevski
Cover and Book Design: Benjie Herskowitz

Thanks to Ilan Lazar, Combat Navigator
& Nof Bar Consulting Ltd.
for their massive contribution to the English edition.

ISBN: 9789655503111
International Distributor: ContentoNow
Habarzel 3, Tel Aviv, Israel
www.ContentoNow.com
Netanel@contentonow.com

Aviram Barkai

For Heaven's Sake

The 201st Squadron
and the Yom Kippur War

To my mother, Tamira Burkai, of blessed memory,
who led me into the world hand in hand,
and showed me the way.

TABLE OF CONTENTS

INTRODUCTION

In September of 2009, I published the book "**On the Edge**," which describes the exploits of the IDF's 188th Armored Division during the Yom Kippur War. After a short time, this division and its accomplishments received the national attention it had long-since deserved, and I found myself lecturing about the Yom Kippur War to audiences consisting of all the stratums of Israeli society.

During one of the lectures, someone posed the following question: "Why didn't the Israeli Air Force know what was going on?"

"Why were fighters sent into such chaos?" someone asked during another lecture. "What caused the failure of Operation 'Model 5'—the mission to destroy Syrian Missiles?"

"I haven't researched the matter" and "I don't know" became my standard answers, but these questions sparked my curiosity.

In August 2010, after a chance encounter with a fighter pilot who had participated in the Yom Kippur War, the spark grew into a fire. Three years later, I completed a fascinating, exciting, often painful, and frustrating journey into the incomprehensible events of October 1973.

At its inception, I decided this book would not address all of the exploits of the entire Israeli Air Force (IAF) throughout the Yom Kippur War. Instead, I decided to focus on the decisive events, while touching upon others. I focused on one type of aircraft, and one squadron in particular. The choice of aircraft was obvious.

The close support aircraft, which consisted of the improved Dassault Super Mystère ("Sa'ar") squadron, and the five A-4 Skyhawk ("Ait") squadrons, did their best. However, their limited capabilities reduced them to only one mission: close air support. They were provided very few opportunities to participate in aerial warfare or in preventive aerial depth strikes.

The four Mirage squadrons, which were comprised of the Dassault Mirage III ('Shahak'), and the Israel Aerospace Industries' (IAI) 'Nesher', received most of the glory during the War of Attrition. However, they received far less attention during the Yom Kippur War, despite being crowned "the aces of the skies" yet again, and despite providing the decisive advantage in the battle west of the Suez Canal by shooting down incoming Egyptian airpower.

In October 1973, there was only one fighter aircraft inherently capable of taking center stage in the unexpected role into which it was forced. It was the aircraft capable of performing all of the necessary tasks: air support, preventive enemy infrastructure attack, deep air strikes, and interception—the McDonnell Douglas F-4 Phantom, which the IAF referred to as the "Sledgehammer".

In October 1973, the IAF had four Phantom squadrons. I chose one of them—the 201st Squadron ("The One"). The exploits, which I would report, were based on the experiences and perspectives of its commanders, pilots, and officers during the great upheaval that was the Yom Kippur War.

"The One" was the first Phantom Squadron—the pioneer, though this fact alone would not have brought me to choose it in particular. I needed more and I found it.

In the five weeks prior to the end of the War of Attrition, the heavens had come crashing down on the young squadron; they suffered numerous casualties. Without hesitation, the pilots postponed their mourning and charged forward with full thrust.

During the Yom Kippur War, the brave pilots of "The One" proved that the fighting spirit they had displayed during the War of Attrition was still intact.

Over the course of twenty days of ceaseless fighting, the 201st Squadron was forced to muster all of its strength as it replaced three of its commands and lost more fighter pilots, jets, and POWs than any other "Sledgehammer" squadron. Despite this, the brave members of "The One" forged ahead, taking on the most challenging and dangerous missions of the war.

At the end of the war, when data was collected and relevant tables were created, the IAF discovered that despite the relatively small number of aircraft and air crews, "The One" had shot down more aircraft than any of the other three squadrons.

There was another important factor: at the end of the Yom Kippur War, the 201st Squadron had a total of 52 members, more than half of whom elected to remain after their mandatory service had ended. By the time they had completed their service in the IDF, the members of the squadron's October 1973 model had amassed an impressive and unprecedented record: ten colonels, seven brigadier generals, two major generals, two branch commanders, and one chief of staff.

* * *

For Heaven's Sake is based primarily on the eyewitness accounts provided by members of the 201st Squadron both soon after the war, as well as after 38 years. I utilized research methods that I had developed while writing other texts, in addition to the integration of myriad accounts, and while bearing in mind that memories tend to fade over time and people tend to minimize their failures. In doing so, I have documented what I believe to be an accurate depiction of the events that unfolded in and around the Yom Kippur War.

A few remarks should be made regarding the members of the 201st Squadron as interviewees:

This is not a talkative group.

I had to be relentless.

After breaking the ice and jumping through several hoops for them, they decided there might be some benefit to entrusting their stories with an outsider who has no agenda, preconceived notions, or external commitments. Once they had read *On the Edge*—they were finally willing to lower their guard.

We have been in constant contact ever since.

I came across inconsistencies among the various interviewees. I said, "Please decide whether what you fly is an 'aircraft' or a 'jet.'" "Is the area you fly in called the 'air' or the 'sky'?" "Do you ascend or climb?"

They were also snobs.

They used English terms such as "pipper" (Predicted Impact Point), "pickle button," "throttle," "stick," "hot mic," "drop tank" "oscillation," and "vertigo." Apparently, Eliezer Ben-Yehuda[1] never reached their base.

For Heaven's Sake does not attempt to portray every event in which "The One" was involved over the course of the Yom Kippur War. I have focused on the central and significant sorties—the events that were characterized by some peculiarity, whether military or historic. Even with regard to the selected sorties, I did not turn the spotlight onto every person who occupied a cockpit. When writing a book such as *For Heaven's Sake*, a research project presented in the form of a story, I must redact the text so as to retain the pace, suspense, and pathos I am seeking. As a result, there are individuals whose total contribution to the war effort was far greater than depicted in this text.

The highly experienced pilot, Lt. Col. Levy Zur, an IAF staff member, participated in several sorties throughout the course of the war. Lt. Col. Yigal Bar Shalom, an experienced Weapon Systems Operator (WSO, hereafter: navigator), returned to the squadron after engaging in some ground combat operations in the Golan Heights. From October 14 and on, Bar Shalom participated in every operation in which 'The One' was involved. The young navigator, Lt. Shimon Tzror, and the pilot, Capt. Amiram Shaked, who had served in the War of Attrition, took part in most of the squadron's missions, from the outbreak of the war until the ceasefire. Senior navigator, Lt. Col. Uri Talmor, participated in one sortie. 4th Wing commander, Col. Amos Lapidot, and Head of the IAF Intelligence Directorate, Brig. Gen. Rafi Har-Lev, participated in a few sorties near the end of the conflict.

---

1   A prominent figure in the Hebrew language's revival in the 20th century.

We must of course mention Lt. Benjamin Kiryati. Over the course of the Yom Kippur War, Kiryati, a navigator, completed 51 sorties! He spent every day of the conflict in the air, until his aircraft was shot down. As a POW, entirely isolated from his companions, Kiryati became the focus of the Syrians' attention. He was seen as the key to deciphering the IAF and the changes it had made in the six months since the ceasefire. He endured ceaseless torture; arguably the worst endured by any of the POWs of the Yom Kippur War.

* * *

The text before you is not just about the squadron called "The One." *For Heaven's Sake* is not merely the history of several young men in flight overalls and pressure suits performing aerial stunts.

How could it be?

Between the rocky grounds of the Golan Heights and the sands of the Sinai Desert, the fighters of 1973 lost their innocence and their dreams, not to mention their friends—nearly 2,600 of them.

I was there as well, and the personal anger I felt regarding my friends who were sacrificed, tossed and pushed me far beyond the aerial perspective with which I had begun—all the way to the hallways of the Israeli government; the IDF General Staff; the various intelligence organizations; the Knesset's Foreign Affairs and Defense Committee; and the Israeli Embassy in Washington, D.C.

I wanted to understand what exactly happened to the Israeli people during this historic event, this watershed of Israeli history, during the war after which nothing was ever the same.

Now, we can begin.

PROLOGUE

D amascus, again? I don't feel like it. I really don't feel like it! *Sleep, buddy...just sleep. Stop stirring up your fears. You have to get rid of that image of the aircraft engulfed in flames; close the shutters; lock it down; build a wall around it; disengage.*

The phone rang.

"Are you up?" *Um...um...*

"ARE YOU UP?" *Yeah, yeah. Where am I headed this time— Damascus, right? I'm really not in the mood...I'm really just not in the mood. Relax, man! You earned your wings for days like today.*

He put on his overalls, and slipped his shoes on, lacing tightly. Then it was time for the teeth-brushing ritual, letting the water run, and on and on.

He made his way to the squadron. In the dark, everything looked the same. He entered the briefing room and glanced at his friends. There were some briefing materials in the room, as well as the formation leader, looking quite calm.

Well, at least someone is keeping his cool.

Radio operations; radio-silence protocol; switching from air- ground to air-to-air; he was busy remembering and trying not to make any mistakes. He wrapped himself in the protective cover of familiarity and practice. The heartbeat slowed down—the magic of routine.

The briefing was over. Everyone headed upstairs to the officers' club: breakfast sandwiches and the scent of omelets.

There's nothing new under the sun. They're just a bunch of regular folks... without overalls. There are the squadron's ladies – the aide officer, the driver, and the secretaries.

He stretched out on an orange couch, a sandwich in one hand, and a cup of coffee in the other. A quiet air-conditioner cooled the room, and a different energy, reconciled and peaceful, assuaged any thoughts of Damascus.

"Hedgehog formation, head to the buses." The heartbeat accelerated, and the compulsion to scratch his head returned... as did the thoughts.

Relax, you hear me? Relax!

The bus stopped and he was careful to take his first step with his right foot. The night was quiet, except for the sound of boots echoing on the concrete, all the way to the aircraft.

He entered the underground hangar's office and signed for tail-number 45.

Great! I love this aircraft.

He headed over to it, noticing that the navigator was already in the cockpit, already performing the navigation system alignment.

Good thing I got him, I want someone experienced over Damascus.

He went through the walk-around exterior checks: he scanned, shook, slapped and stroked.

Don't let me down, you hear me? Don't let me down.

He climbed into the cockpit, his legs quivering slightly.

I hope the maintenance personnel technicians below don't notice...

He placed his helmet on the air-intake sidewall, pinned the map portfolio to the forward-left windshield, sat down, strapped-in to seat, slid his head into the white helmet, and attached the oxygen hose to the supply line.

"Do you hear me?" he asked.

"Roger," answered the navigator from the rear cockpit.

"Is the 'eject' light on?" he asked.

"It's on." The navigator answered.

He lowered the canopy, and locked it down.

He initiated the engines start procedure, and began with the left engine. The mobile start-up compressor screamed, and the navigator confirmed he could switch to internal power, hence the cooling system began blowing air.

He started up the right engine and checked flight controls—everything was in working order.

"We've got NAV," the navigator called. They taxied to the outer ramp. The maintenance personnel buzzed around the weapons systems, unlatching the safety catches of the gun and bombs, and presenting the removed safety pins. *We're ready for taxi.*

It was then that his mouth began to feel dry.

They reached the threshold of the runway. "You're good to go," the 'last-chance' technician indicated.

He aligns the Sledgehammer and completed the engines check.

"The air intakes are check," the navigator announced.

He pushed the two throttles forward, running the engines at MIL power setting, and stood-by for the rpm to stabilize. His feet began shaking on the brake pedals... and he released. The Sledgehammer started a light sprint.

Now...now...

He lightly pulled the throttles beyond the MIL power detent and pushed them forward—full to afterburner ("firewall") position. Two huge flames blasted forth from behind the aircraft, and with them came the familiar propulsion that stuck his back to his seat. They reached 170 knots, and he pulled lightly on the stick—lift off. The landing gear retracted to their well, and he heard the hatch lock-up. He turned left and joined the lead formation, flying at low altitude, and maintaining radio silence.

Suddenly there was silence, like a training flight. The Mediterranean Sea was underneath—as was the city of Haifa, followed by Acre. Someone was surfing near Nahariya.

They were three minutes from the border; his heart was pounding.

They crossed the border, flying low—as low as possible, scanning the sky around for signs of the enemy.
We're not going to let those bastards kill us.
"One minute to pull-up," said the navigator. The skies were clear.
At least I won't have to deal with any MiGs.
Focus...focus...three...two...engage. He pulled up, climbing at a 35-degree angle. The target was on the left. Puffs of black smoke dotted the skies.
Ignore them...
At 8,000 feet, he executed a wingover, dove toward the target at a 35-degree angle. Gold and orange sparks streamed from the basalt peaks, but there was no beauty in them, for he knew that every spark represents a venomous tooth seeking to pierce him—and

only him. He needed to continue, despite the series of supersonic booms streaking mere inches from his canopy.

Ignore them. Ignore them and concentrate.

Pipper on target...pickle...4,000 feet...release. The aircraft trembled. At 3,000 feet, he dropped his wing.

Nice hit.

He turned outward, straightened the aircraft, and joined the formation.

Home...let's get home as fast as possible.

The Radar Warning Receiver (RWR) triggered an alert and the indicators on the display lit up. It was a missile!

Where is it? Where is it?

"Break," screamed the navigator. "Break! Missile on the right!"

He broke, and out of the corner of his eye, he noticed a fire trail heading toward them at breakneck speed. He had never actually seen a missile before. Now he had! It was huge, menacing, and close... very close. Suddenly, a massive fireball engulfed Number Four.

"Eject! Eject!" they all shouted.

A lone parachute hovered over the skies, and down below was an enormous blaze.

That's all that remains of the best aircraft in the world.

There was no time to lament, though, and no need for eulogies, as Number Four was on the Guard (radio distress channel) announcing that he ejected.

Yeah...like we couldn't tell.

Meanwhile, everyone was scanning the skies for the other parachute, for missiles and Gundish AAA (Anti Aircraft Artillery) fire. Their limited fuel supply forced them to leave a pilot behind with nothing but his parachute, not to mention the navigator. *Who knows what happened to him?*

"Shit!" he yelled, "Shit, shit, shit!" *Another one bites it! I've lost all my friends from the flight course.*

He hoped that the navigator would not hold his sentimental outburst against him.

They crossed the border.

All the tension was gone now. He climber up to the sky, gliding, and started to sing. The navigator joined in. What a chorus!

He landed, and with legs quivering, deplaned, soaked in his own sweat.

I hope they don't notice.

The navigator came over to him, and they hugged.

Until next time, he thought… *till next time.*

CREATURES FROM ANOTHER PLANET

Mankind is innately curious, and it is that curiosity, that burning desire for progress, which has propelled mankind forward throughout its history.

On December 17, 1903, many years after it all began, Orville and Wilbur Wright managed to add an important facet to humanity's development and its endless journey of exploration and discovery. Over the sands of Kitty Hawk, North Carolina, a 'bird' of the Wrights' own creation ascended to the skies, traveling 120 feet, in history's first powered flight.

With great enthusiasm and inspiration, precipitated by the recognition of the power harnessed by engines, propellers, and an advanced understanding of the secrets of lift, many more inventors would continue to tame the skies. They built wondrous machines that could transport people and cargo, redefining time and space and dramatically shrinking the globe.

In 1915, the iron eagle joined the war effort.

Armed with a piston engine, a propeller, and a machine gun, the first aircraft took to the skies to participate in World War I, greatly increasing the unending dance of death.

By the 1940's, the first jet engines had been developed. A decade later, the machine guns were replaced with cannons, and soon thereafter, missiles were added.

70 years after the Wright brothers' pioneering first flight over Kitty Hawk, the grandchildren of the Wright's inventions had developed far beyond what Orville and Wilbur could possibly have imagined. These "jets" could cruise at 67,000 feet high, at a speed of 400 feet per second, breaking the sound barrier, with precision navigation, both during the day, and in the black of night. They could release weapons directly over a target, diving like falcons toward their prey, waging an aerial war against their enemies.

* * *

At the start of the 1960's, the IAF first integrated the Dassault Mirage III into its fleet. The other jets immediately prostrated before the "king," which proved worthy of the title. Of the 143 enemy aircraft shot down over the next few years, 133 were shot down by "his majesty."

In early 1968, the United States introduced its first strike fighter, the Skyhawk, and around 18 months later, the Phantom arrived.

Until the summer of 1973, the IAF phased out the French-produced Dassault Mystère, Ouragan, and Vautour, and began relying primarily on good old Uncle Sam. The IAF acquired 100 Phantoms, which it designated "Sledgehammer", 165 Skyhawks ("Ait") as well as 65 French-built Mirages ("Shahak" and "Nesher") and 20 of the newly improved Super Mystère ("Sa'ar").

In autumn of 1973, the Mirage was still considered the IAF's premier fighter jet, but it would soon to meet its match.

The pilots of the all-purpose Phantom had scored 32 kills, and two more were credited to the pilot of a Skyhawk, which was an aerial strike and support aircraft not known for having particularly impressive acrobatics.

On a special wall reserved for the decorations given to the fighter-pilot companies hung numerous merit badges, bearing the names of those few, proud, pilots who had scored kills against the enemy, and who would forever remain in the pantheon of aviation glory.

Every pilot wanted to have his name on that wall.

The slogan "the best become pilots," appeared on recruitment posters in the 60's, and then someone added, "pilots get the best ladies." This holy trinity of pilot wings, beautiful women, and the possibility of having your name of the Wall of Glory was too tempting for any young man to resist.

Just about everybody applied.

After 20 months of grueling training and painful sifting, 20 to 30 young men would fling their cadet hats into the air, and celebrate their induction into the most elite and restricted clubhouse in Israel: the pilots of the Israeli Air Force.

Within this already exclusive club, one could find, glimmering like diamonds, the "chosen few" who would become fighter pilots.

About a week after the commencement ceremony, the new inductees began their advanced training in the OTU (Operational Training Unit). Building on what they had mastered in Flight

Academy—flight, navigation, rules of engagement, and the like—the new pilots learned to control jets that could fly faster, higher, and harder. Their expertise increased, and eventually the word "fighter" was emblazoned upon their "combat pilot" seal. Then they were divided into squadrons.

With dreams of enemy aircraft engulfed in flames, the IAF's best and brightest began to settle into a routine. From altitudes high and low, practicing pop-up and loft strike methods, they would "neutralize" missile batteries and airstrips, "annihilate" concentrations of infantry and armored corps, and snipe at the air and at the ground with their canons—day and night.

According to the experts, anyone who would master dogfighting would significantly improve his overall capabilities, and that sounded just right to the new kids. They would make sure to finish their other duties as quickly as humanly possible so they could get back to "the real deal," to the thing that got their hearts pumping: dog fighting—or better yet, winning at dogfighting.

While the whole of Europe was enveloped in the Great War, which would eventually lead to the deaths of millions of soldiers on the battlefield, a new ethos was being formed overhead: dogfighting. A battle to the death, and may the best man win.

The pioneers of aerial combat, the gladiators of the heavens, learned to visualize and assess the situations speedily passing below them, to determine whatever significance the situation below might have, to plan a step ahead (sometimes two), to find the precise location to strike and to kill the enemy, all in the blink of an eye.

Fifty years later, the new fighter pilots of the IAF sought to accomplish the same, only at supersonic speed. This was their dream, and until they were given the chance to prove their mettle in actual combat, they would have to settle with training exercises. However, they fully intended to view those exercises as the real thing.

Dancing the skies on laughter-silvered wings, these young men participated in duels to the death, and for those few hours, the well-being and success of their closet compatriots mattered little, if at all. *Let the bastard crash and burn, for all I care.*

To succeed as fighter pilots, these young men had to be prepared to do whatever was needed to break the glass ceiling.

Safety and security are luxuries pilots must not afford themselves, and in order to assimilate that axiom, and of course, in the name of the holy contest—dogfighting—they would try to find every way possible to bend, or break, the rules, as though they were drawing water from a stone.

Armed with stick and throttle, the heavenly gladiators would redefine the laws of nature: they would climb to unprecedented heights; conduct passes at unforgivable proximities; challenge the minimum (and of course the maximum) possible speeds; fire at forbidden angles; and conquer the limitations of load (g-force).

Let the bastard crash and burn, for all I care.

Aircraft crashed. Pilots ejected. Pilots died. Supervisory officers were appointed and investigations were conducted. Pilots were warned, and reprimanded, and warned again. "Yes, sir!" they would answer, nodding respectfully, "understood, sir." They would then carry on as before.

* * *

The number of pilots who served in the squadron on a regular basis rarely exceeded ten for most squadrons, and 20 for the Sledgehammer Squadron. There were twice and sometimes three times as many jets as there were pilots, and each squadron maintained two sub-squadrons: an emergency assigned team and a reserve serving team.

About one year after arriving at the air base, an airman would be sent to serve his duty as an instructor in the Flight Academy. Overnight, his title would change from "Active Member" to "Emergency Team Member," and he would pass his former title to some young new hotshot.

When their commission was over, between five and eight years after their conscription, some would sign on for permanent duty. Over the years, they would be appointed to various positions at the Flight Academy, to head HQ Branches and Departments, and even to command bases and wings. Wherever they ended up and whatever they ended up doing, however, one thing never changed: they remained a member of the emergency team.

Shoulder to shoulder and wing to wing, the pilots—permanent, emergency, and reserve—were scheduled for practice. They practiced together and fought together, side by side.

"Get yourselves prepped and ready for practice," the commanding officers informed the reserve and emergency pilots that had moved on to civilian jobs, "Come prove you still have what it takes."

They would arrive, don their overalls, G-suits, and life jacket torsos, slide into their helmets, and take off into the skies, activating the afterburners, pulling the stick, and proving, yet again, that they had earned their wings.

Sometimes the squadron leader would go up against a young lieutenant, one of the "regulars" who had just recently completed combat training. Sometimes he would even get shot down. That is just the way it is when you face a young clone of yourself. It was fine to know you are capable of losing to one of the young guns, even if everyone was watching—and yes, everyone was watching.

On a wall in the briefing room hung a plastic laminated board—the "kill board," with the scores of that day's training recorded on it. Even the squadron leader's results were posted. The kill board did not tolerate excuses or delays, and it did not hand out special dispensations. It was a strict, clear, and immediate accounting of each pilot's strengths and weaknesses, for all to see.

Even the Air Force Commander, who would arrive from time to time.

"Number 2," a young lieutenant would snap at the major general, who was, after it all, the commander of all the pilots, "back to position!" The major general had strayed off course during a two-ship dogfight exercise.

Regardless of their assignment, regardless of their rank, including the highest-ranking officer in the IAF, these pilots would take to the skies as equals, bound by the same rules, and battle. They would conquer the forces of acceleration, climbing, breaking, rolling, bombing, and A/G (Air/Ground) strafing—kill or be killed.

* * *

The same approach that had yielded the IAF's unprecedented organizational structure yielded the belief that pilots do not need to have designated aircraft. There was no reason to encourage preference for a particular jet. The jets were merely tools, and no one jet ought to engender much personal loyalty. Jet tail-number 73 handled well around the turns? Great! Now fly tail-number 94.

From time to time, a senior staff officer would observe army operations.

He could immediately recognize the differences. The "greens" (a nickname for the ground military forces) had teams, consisting of one commander and many soldiers.

They trained together and fought together—all for one and one for all.

Compare that with the pilots. Each pilot was an officer, riding his own "horse." They were lone soldiers—teams of one. The commander would contemplate how far the IAF had reached, such that even formation assignments applied to one mission only. It was as though the card dealer changed after every hand, even in the Phantom's twin saddle. Don't look for a Catholic wedding here.

* * *

'You men are capable of doing anything', they were told. You can navigate day or night; you can strike any target; you can extricate yourself from any situation; you can kill the enemy; you can survive the horrors of imprisonment; you can rush a burning building.

Indeed, they did everything, even on the ground.

The intelligence officer was a pilot. So were the officers for training, operations, weapon-systems, navigation, history, culture, and gardening. That's right, gardening.

"The coveted pilot wings that you display on your dress uniforms are a great honor," they were told, "and you must prove that you deserve them on a daily basis. You must apply the same level of diligence that you would when preparing for a dogfight or a bombing raid to all your 'missions', such as trimming the grass, planning trees, hanging curtains, preparing a speech, and organizing an end-of-term party."

* * *

The principles learned in Flight Academy, the operational training and further training they received on the air base turned these young men into highly skilled fighters, characteristically diligent, curious, goal-oriented, and cool under pressure. Ice coursed through the veins, and they feared no one—there was no threat too daunting for them to face head on.

They would allow themselves a 'tender moment' on rare occasions. Sitting with the esteemed veterans of previous conflicts, they would listen and observe, wide-eyed, as their senior compatriots regaled them with tales from famous battles, dogfights, and bombing raids. As they listened, the young pilots of the new generation pictured themselves in the midst of a furious air battle.

Many of their "friends in green" had sworn to protect their tiny country against all enemies foreign and domestic, in Israel's ongoing battle for survival. They swore to do so with all their might, and were fully prepared to pay the ultimate price in serving their country.

Despite the young pilots' extraordinary characteristics—the qualities that had first gained them entry into the world's most elite fighter squadrons; despite the many months of rigorous training they had endured; despite having honed their skills to such an extent that these skills—exactitude, focus, independence, steadfast determination, and an unwillingness ever to cut corners—were now second nature; despite having redefined their very essences to suit their charges; despite it all, one question lingered—when facing the chaos of actual battle, would all of their training serve them? Would they muster the courage, the grit, the determination, the fighting spirit, to face death head on? Would they return home, having succeeded where others were doomed to fail? Did they *truly* have what it takes?

WALKING BLINDLY

When searching the annals of history for the moment that planted the seeds of the Yom Kippur War, undoubtedly Israel's most traumatic experience as a nation, one comes to the date of May 14, 1967.

On that day, unaware of the fact that he was being duped by Syria and the USSR, Egyptian President Gamal Abdel Nasser determined that it was his political and perhaps even moral obligation to assist Syria's ruling military forces, who had lost six fighter jets just two months prior and were now facing a brutal onslaught from the Zionist army. He sent infantry and armored brigades into the Sinai Desert, toward the Israeli border.

The Egyptians soon fell in love with their newfound military prowess, expelled all of the UN observers in the area, diverted more and more forces to the border, closed the Straits of Tiran to Israeli ships, and convinced the Jordanians to serve as the third leg of this alliance of bullies.

The Egyptian radio announced on the "Thunderous Voice of Cairo" program, "We will drive them into the sea!"

The Egyptian commandos shouted, "We will cut off their heads!"

A black cloud descended, casting an ominous shadow over the entire region and the future of the Zionist nation.

* * *

On June 11, 1967, the citizens of Israel awoke to a national celebration. In the course of just six days, the tiny nation—one that spanned a mere 7,700 square miles at the time—had not only successfully repelled the forces of three nations, it had conquered enough territory to quadruple in size. The map of the region was redrawn, and the citizens of Israel could sleep soundly, knowing the distance keeping them away from conflict had increased dramatically. They shed the mourning shrouds of May, replacing them with their best celebratory clothes.

The international community was astonished by Israel's achievement, to put it mildly. The leaders of the free world felt compelled to register their admiration for the minuscule Jewish nation that had pulled off the greatest military upset in history. The Six-Day War, as it came to be known, was the stuff of legends.

"There's no one quite like them," people declared worldwide, and the world's finest military academies began offering courses about the various military campaigns that had resulted in this unprecedented victory.

Israeli pride swelled, and drunk with self-admiration, the nation produced articles, albums, hymns, and even stamps, all depicting Israel's miraculous success.

* * *

On Saturday, July 1, 1967, with IDF forces stationed along the length of the Suez Canal while his army licked its wounds just three weeks after losing the Sinai Peninsula, Egypt's ruler made his first attempt at bursting Israel's Six-Day War bubble.

Just after 19:00, the dogs of war were heard howling to the north of the Canal. A collection of approximately 100 Egyptian soldiers, armed with simple ordinance and anti-tank missiles, opened fire on an IDF patrol that was making its way north, to Ras el-Ayash, near the great swamps. By midnight, the shelling from the tanks and mortars dwindled, but the Egyptians had made their point. They were prepared to reclaim their honor, and were ready for "day seven" of the Six-Day War.

* * *

On August 29, 1967, representatives from eights Arab nations met in the Sudani capital of Khartoum, to discuss the consequences of the Six-Day War for the Arab world.

Three days later, at the end of the summit, the Arab world announced it would follow Egypt's leadership, headed by President Gamal Abdel Nasser. The following principles were ratified at the summit's conclusion: no peace negotiations with the Israelis; no peace agreement with Israel; and no recognition of the State of Israel.

Armed with the full backing of the Arab world, as delineated during the summit in Khartoum, Nasser returned to Egypt. After considering the endless flow of arms Egypt was receiving from the Russians, he announced, "What was taken from us by force will be taken back by force," and decided to intensify the flames of the conflict.

Three weeks prior, the IAF had established its conversion team for the Phantom, which had just returned from the United States, at the 201st Squadron. The team consisted of Maj. Samuel Hetz, who would serve as Squadron leader, Yoram Agmon, who would serve as 1st Deputy Squadron leader, Itzik Fier as 2nd Deputy Squadron leader, Menachem Eini as Chief Navigator, and Yair Rod as Deputy Chief Navigator.

Five elite members of the 69th Squadron who had also participated in the trip to the United States joined the new team: pilots Avihu Ben-Nun, Rami Harpaz, and Ehud Henkin, and navigators Eyal Los (Ahikar) and Samuel Levy.

"Until your aircraft arrive," they were told, "you will all work together. Get started with the first Phantom conversion course, ASAP."

They began by gathering the top young pilots, as well as some seasoned veterans, into the study rooms for initial briefings.

The start of the process was highly disappointing. For one thing, the Phantom was just an ugly aircraft.

"What happened to 'French fashion'?" the pilots chided. Then they took aim at the loss of the simplicity to which they had become so accustomed.

"What did they do to the cockpit?" the pilots objected, "The Mirage cockpit was perfect! Everything was right where it was supposed to be." The pilots found themselves seated so deep in the cockpit that it interfered with their field of view. It was like being in a bunker, looking out through an embrasure. Not only was the

Phantom's cockpit deep, it was huge! Instruments and buttons were all over the cockpit with no rhyme or reason. All of those bells and whistles, and not one of them was in the right place. The angles were weird, things felt out of reach, and in order to switch from one missile to the next, a pilot was expected to flip *three* switches!

When they finally took off and started maneuvering the beast, the pilots started missing the Mirage even more. This U.S. monstrosity kicked, rattled, and tossed, giving the pilots the feeling that they were in an old clunker that had trouble even making it down the road. On top of all that, the engines spat out ugly, black plumes of smoke that could be seen for miles. *Whose idea was this anyway?*

However, then they opened the afterburners. *Wow!*

It was at this point that they realized that thanks to the best weapon delivery and navigation computers in the theater, the Phantom was capable of anything: air ground and air to air, during the day or at night, faster, higher, farther, and loaded with lots of weapons.

From that moment on, the pilots started to love the aircraft—they admired it.

At the beginning of November, the two commanders of the IAF's Phantom Squadron set out on a "show of force." The two were Maj. Shmulik "Mister One-hundred" Hetz, commander of the 201ˢᵗ Squadron, which was already in possession of Israel's first eight Phantoms—a fact of which he was very proud—and Maj. Avihu "Expectations" Ben-Nun, the future commander of the 69ᵗʰ Squadron.

They crossed the Suez Canal at very low altitude, observing the desert and the green valleys and the white sailboats gliding on the Nile. Moments later, they reached the edges of Cairo, the pyramids of Giza now directly below them.

Looks just like in the pictures, thought Yair David, the navigator sitting in the back of the cockpit. He saw Hetz pushed the throttles leftward and forward, and felt the afterburners engage. He could feel the aircraft pushing toward the sound barrier, and knew that while he sat in the cockpit, insulated from the upcoming supersonic boom, the residents of Cairo would be shaken by the supersonic noise, with windows of many homes shattering as a result.

Maybe this little exercise of ours will calm them down a bit, he thought to himself.

On November 11, pilot Ehud Henkin and navigator Eyal Los (Ahikar) were the first to encounter a MiG-21, which they promptly shot down.

Within a week, the Phantom had proven itself to be the "landlord" in the skies above Cairo, and fully capable of taking out enemy aircraft such as the Mirage.

A short while later, the second conversion course began.

Yoram Agmon, Deputy Squadron leader A, began by describing the Phantom:

"At first, it looks like a really ugly aircraft, but after your first flight, your perceptions of the aircraft will change. Pretty soon you'll get used to it, and then it'll look like the most beautiful thing in the world."

"Like a woman, only the other way around," somebody joked.

* * *

In the two and half years after the Six-Day War, the Egyptians suffered severe losses at the hands of the Israelis. Thousands of soldiers were killed or wounded, 70 fighter jets were destroyed, dozens of artillery batteries were taken out, four cities around the Canal became ghost cities, and hundreds of thousands were without homes.

How did the Egyptians respond? They just brushed it off and continued calling for war.

"It's time to start thinking out of the box," Israeli politicians remarked. The only way to convince the Egyptian people that the War of Attrition had to end was to bring the conflict to their doorsteps.

By the beginning of 1970, Egypt's capitol was under siege, blacked out, and fortified with sand bags. The Egyptian people's will was beginning to break.

"Save us!" Nasser cried out. "Save us!"

Within a month, the president of Egypt had handed over the defense of Egypt to the Red Army.

On Tuesday, June 30, 1970, a two-ship formation of Israeli Mirages on a slanted photography recon run approximately 15 miles south of the Canal encountered a big surprise: antiaircraft missiles! Furthermore, these missiles were launched from an area that was supposed to be clear! The two-ship formation landed, and briefed their commanders on the development.

An hour after the Mirages landed, the exploitation personnel viewed the photographs and discovered something new in the theater. In the east of the Egyptian desert was an "Iron Wall" spanning the full length of the Canal, all the way to Cairo. It was a network of ten missile batteries, with Gundish ZSU-23 radar-controlled AAA interspersed among them. The ZSU-23 had a reputation as a deadly system against low flying aircraft.

IAF Central Command declared, "We must strike these batteries immediately!"

Two hours before sunset, the IAF sent a flight composed of eights jets from the two Phantom squadrons to strike the position. On their way back, having destroyed five batteries and severely damaged two more, one of the Phantoms delayed ever so much, and…boom! The Phantom was down.

Before the first flight had returned, a two-ship formation of Phantoms from the 201st Squadron was sent to strike the position again.

"Do not erase," wrote Itzik Fier, the 2nd Deputy Squadron leader and sight-operation instructor for the Phantom conversion course, on the board of the instruction room. "I'll be right back," he promised the trainees, and ran to his aircraft.

About an hour later, the 201st received the news that a Phantom was down—Itzik Fier was MIA. The phrase "do not erase" was left on the board, until his return.

"How do we proceed from here?" IAF Commander Maj. Gen. Motti Hod asked the two Phantom Squadron leaders. Silence.

"And what's your opinion?" the general asked Col. Jacob Agassi, the new Head of the Operations Department, who had only stepped into the role two days earlier, and Lt. Col. Oded Marom, Head of the Strike Branch. More silence.

Suddenly, there was a ray of light.

"I got it! The Americans have a solution," said Lt. Col. Joseph "Yuska" Naor, Head of the Maintenance Department's Electronics Branch.

In the spring of 1970, a close friendship was developing between Lt. Col. Yuska Naor, of the Israeli Air Force, and an American Jew named David Brog.

Col. David Brog, Director of EW (Electronic Warfare) for U.S. Air Force, was a highly experienced Phantom navigator, who had flown missions in Vietnam.

"We have an EW pod, the ALQ-71, which you can load to an aircraft," Brog whispered to Lt. Col. Joseph Naor, a holocaust survivor who headed the IAF's Electronics Branch.

"It's an incredibly advanced system," Brog continued, and began explaining the basic principles of the "wonder pod."

America had come up with so many great inventions, Naor thought, as he set out on a mission to prevent a second holocaust. *America! We need to bring that contraption to Israel immediately.*

"Get the ball rolling," they told him.

* * *

On July 5, 1970, while Naor was still "rolling the ball," another Phantom was shot down. This event illuminated the red warning lights throughout the IAF.

In just a week's time, it became clear that the Phantom, the "most dangerous fighter jet in the Middle East," was no longer much of a threat. Moreover—and this was a major source of concern for those involved— it was revealed that the Egyptians, with the help of Soviet military experts, had constructed an impenetrable "iron wall" of missile batteries near the Canal line. These batteries could provide excellent cover for the Egyptians, were they to attempt any activities in the Sinai.

"We need to strike the batteries with a large force, coming at them from a low altitude," argued Col. Jacob Agassi.

Motti Hod listened, nodded, and promised to consider the idea.

"I have an emergency delivery of the 'wonder pod,'" Yuska Naor announced.

They had brought David Brog in from the United States.

"Using the pod requires a slightly different flight formation," said the Jewish-American colonel at a meeting with top IAF officials as he began explaining the intricacies of the system. "To maximize the pods, which are going to be loaded to the centerline station of the Phantoms, and jam the missile systems so they can't shoot you down, you have to maintain a flight formation you might not be familiar with: the 'Pod Formation'. We're talking about a method that will allow you to approach the target from the ideal altitude to identify the batteries. Just before the strike," Brog continued, "the leader of the four-ship formation needs to get to 18,000 feet, and the other three jets need to straighten their flight path, 550 yards apart, with about 1,000 feet of altitude between each of them."

"In order to sustain the 'pod formation', you must maintain consistent speeds," Col. Brog explained. "You must not, I mean absolutely must not, break formation," Brog emphasized. "Even when the missiles start flying at you," Brog continued, "all it takes is for one aircraft to break protocol and the radars can lock in on him. Then the entire system breaks down and all of you will be sitting ducks."

"Please don't forget," Brog insisted, as he concluded his instructions, "as long as you maintain pod formation, you're in the clear."

Brog's "guarantee" did not exactly calm them down. Somehow they were expected, on a moment's notice, to dramatically change their entire way of flying—to toss everything they had learned until that point out the window. No more quiet approaches from low altitudes. Now they were supposed to start striking the target from so high up that all of them would be detected immediately. Everybody would be fully exposed, and then they were supposed to use some US flight formation that had not been attempted since Vietnam, without maneuvering, without changing speed, without defensive tactics, and without consideration. *What would happen?*

At 06:00, on Saturday, July 18, 1970, at the exact time planned, eight Phantoms from the 201st Squadron, and another eight from the 69th Squadron, entered the airspace over the center of the Sinai Desert, maintaining absolute radio silence. Just short of the Suez

Canal, they increased their speed, engaged their afterburners, climbed to 18,000 feet, and entered 'Pod Formation'.

"Break! Break!" screamed Ron Huldai, Hetz's Number 2, who had just identified a missile streaming toward his commander's jet. It was too late.

"Are you hit?" Huldai asked, his eyes still glued to the red and black fireball that had burst in the otherwise clear blue sky. Silence… As Huldai continued scanning the skies, he noticed Hetz's aircraft emitting a thick stream of white smoke. The aircraft took a nosedive, eventually piercing the sands with a gigantic explosion.

"Can anybody hear me?" They could hear the voice of Menachem Eini, Hetz's navigator, on the emergency frequency, and they could see a single parachute slowly descending into the sands of the desert.

Just as the first sunbathers were opening their umbrellas to escape the hot rays of the summer sun warming the beaches of Tel-Aviv, three Phantoms were landing at Hatzor air base, forced to abandon one jet, destroyed just southwest of Ismaïlia. Menachem Eini, one of the squadron's senior navigators, was MIA, and Maj. Shmulik Hetz, the squadron leader, was KIA.

* * *

From the moment the first Phantom arrived in Israel, the 201st Squadron was asked to juggle two major responsibilities: training the transition teams and conducting missions, sometimes daily. The first required them to focus on the restriction associated with training, while the second required them to toss those same restrictions out the window in favor of the practicalities of real-life battle. This problematic combination of responsibilities required both intellectual flexibility and exceptional maneuvering skills.

The pilots had developed both abilities, and Shmulik Hetz, the commander, deserved most of the credit for that.

Fighter pilots don't usually use the word "love," but that was what they felt for Hetz, their skinny, balding commander, and his mustache. Hetz didn't have any of the features you think of when you imagine a hero, and that's why their love for the commander of the 201st Squadron was so "pure" and deep.

Hetz was quiet and modest, and spoke to everyone as his peer. He never raised his voice, and even though he was not one for physical affection, he had a way of embracing people with his demeanor. Even during the chaos the country and primarily the squadron were experiencing, he always remained professional, responsible, and authoritative, leading all those under his charge to greater and greater heights. Now, suddenly, Hetz was not there.

* * *

That Saturday, Lt. Col Ran Pecker, a war veteran and respected commander who had overseen a Mirage squadron and Flight Academy, celebrated his 34th birthday.

He was planning to travel to England the week after, to enjoy a sabbatical, far away from the tumult in Israel.

"Ran, central command is looking for you!" someone told him.

"Hetz is KIA," Gen. Hod informed him, "I want you to take over his command."

"Yes, sir!" Pecker answered.

The next day, in the early hours of the morning, Pecker arrived at the base.

"We are the State of Israel's support structure," Lt. Col. Pecker told a bewildered group of airmen. "We have missions to complete. I assure you we will move on. Now…get to work!"

Pecker was quite the opposite of Hetz: he was a loud and frightening man who stood out in a crowd. Every time his secretaries would hear his booming voice, they would run to the intercom, certain that he was asking for them. It was not long before everyone discovered Pecker's other side, though. He was true leader, a man made of titanium. He was brave, diligent professional, and never allowed others to fail.

It was August 3, 1970, two weeks since the tragic death of Commander Hetz. Two two-ship formations of Phantoms were sent to the missile batteries that had been discovered near the Suez Canal, and again the Egyptians managed to shoot down a Phantom. This was the fifth one in as many weeks. Yigal Shochat was MIA; and Moshe "Goldie" Goldwasser was KIA.

On Friday, August 7, a few minutes before 20:00, Golda Meir, the Prime Minister of Israel, sat in front of the television cameras of the State of Israel's only official station. She excitedly informed her people that effective at midnight, Israel and Egypt would commence a ceasefire. As she spoke, she tried to block out the frightening truth that IAF Commander, Gen. Motti Hod had told her earlier: there was no clear solution to the issue of the missile battery.

Just after 23:00, Lt. Col. Oded Erez, a highly experienced navigator and the second graduate of the 201st Squadron conversion course, set out on a CAP (Combat Air Patrol) mission that would finally reveal the truth behind the War of Attrition.

"What is that?" he asked himself, as he observed lights moving to the east, toward the Canal. *"Have the Egyptians broken the ceasefire already? Are they advancing the missile batteries?"*

A little before midnight, Lt. Danny Schimmel, the officer on post at the IAF intelligence station known as "The Pit," received an excited message from the surveillance unit in the Sinai, reporting that the Egyptians were advancing the missile batteries toward the Canal. He jotted down the message, and immediately passed the hot potato to his commanding officers.

"We need to strike the missile batteries before the situation gets any worse," asserted the IAF Commander, Gen. Hod.

"Hold off," he was told, "First, let's pass the intelligence about the ceasefire breach to the American and get their confirmation."

* * *

On Saturday, August 8, 1970, the soldiers stationed in the Sinai woke to a quiet Sabbath, their fortifications free of the stench of explosives. They stretched out near the beautiful blue waters, even considering whether to remove their helmets. They remained at their posts, observing the Egyptian soldiers that were bathing in the waters of the Suez with some suspicion.

On September 3, 1970, 27 days after the ceasefire was announced, and 27 days since the Egyptians had begun marching their missile batteries toward the Canal, the US intelligence agencies that had thus far dragged their feet, finally confirmed what the Israeli's had already known to be true from their reconnaissance missions: the Egyptians had indeed breached the ceasefire agreements. Waiting for the Americans had come at a heavy price.

All the IAF top brass had agreed that they should have attacked the missile installment three weeks earlier, when they had first received that data.

"We can still strike now," the officers insisted, recognizing the terrible cost of having waited for the Americans. Forty batteries were now active and ready, spanning the full length of the Canal.

"It's too late," they were told, "Not only would the loss of life be overwhelming, but you told us before the ceasefire was signed that 'the IAF has no solution' to the missile problem. We can earn some political capital by absorbing some missile fire, which we can parley into military assistance."

Meanwhile, the Egyptians were dealing with a tragedy of their own. On September 28, 1970, Gamal Abdel Nasser, the beloved and respected president of Egypt and leader of the Arab world, died of a heart attack.

On October 7, the Egyptian National Council confirmed that Nasser's successor would be his longtime assistant, Anwar Sadat. Three weeks later, Egypt's new president announced at the Pan-Arab Teacher's Association, "We will not forego one inch of land, and we will continue our struggle until we have achieved victory."

* * *

During the month of March 1971, Lt. Col. Ran Pecker proved to the IAF in general, and to the 201st Squadron in particular, that his skills as a fundraiser were comparable to his flight skills, with which he had developed his reputation for excellence.

The 201st received an impressive new clubhouse, the finest anywhere in the IAF, if not the country. It was otherworldly—a bubble of its own. The clubhouse had a wood-paneled ceiling and stunning wallpaper. There were armchairs upholstered with orange corduroy that matched the wallpaper and wall-to-wall carpeting that matched the armchairs. The clubhouse had quiet central air-conditioning, an entertainment system with surround sound, a bar with stools, a kitchenette, and an espresso machine. The guys could make cappuccinos, just like in Italy! To ensure the guys did not lose sight of reality and forget they were still military officers on an air base, there was a huge picture of five Phantoms, with the Jezreel Valley in the backdrop.

This luxury was the result of Ran Pecker's efforts. He had used his extensive social network to provide the men with a standard that was well beyond what was to be expected in a country that had been established just over twenty years prior.

"Every donor that visits the squadron will stop to hear the story of how you were rescued from the Egyptians," Pecker told Yair David, a quiet, introverted man.

"I can't anymore," David responded.

"You certainly can!" Pecker ordered. Then they got the espresso machine and the air conditioner. Then he brought in Moshvitz, one of the most successful businessmen in Israel, sat him in one of the Phantoms, and had one of the pilots take him for a spin.

"Take him around the tracks, and whenever you get to an intersection, open the engines up for him," Pecker advised the pilot. Moshvitz donated.

A few days after dedicating the new clubhouse, five navigators, recent graduates of Navigator Course 29, arrived at the squadron and met with Ran Pecker, their Flight Academy commander. The poor guys thought they had seen the last of the intimidating commander and his forked tongue, but… there he was.

Two days later, he gathered up the young navigators, and with two short sentences, summed up his teamwork philosophy regarding the Phantom.

"Pilots are 'afterburner'," he said, and shifted his hand leftward and forward, as a pilot would with the throttle when engaging the backburners beyond the MIL power detent. "Navigators are 'gain knob'," he finished, turning an imaginary knob in the air with two fingers, as a navigator would when adjusting the radar gain.

The navigators soon realized that everything felt most natural when they were under Pecker's command. Only a commander of his caliber could maintain such discipline within this group of rowdy, Middle-eastern men, which included Deputy Squadron leader A, Maj. Eitan Ben Eliahu, Deputy Squadron leader B, Maj. Ron Huldai, Capt. Adi Benaya, Maj. Eitan "Wild Bull" Peled, Maj. Gadi Samok, and Capt. Amnon Gurion. These were the giants of their generation, veterans of the Six-Day War and heroes of the War of Attrition.

Two weeks later, after the five men had completed the conversion course, they were summoned to a meeting with the Wing Commander, Col. Rafi Har-Lev.

"Don't get married young," he told them, "Do me and yourselves a favor, and hold off on getting married, 'cause I'm the guy that'll have to go tell your families you've been killed."

With their wing commander's warning fresh in the minds, the group made its way to Tehran for a 10-day practice course in a flight simulator. They were barely given a chance to acclimate to the strange contrasts in Iran—a modern military in an otherwise third-world country—and they were already back home. They arrived just in time for the dedication of the new clubhouse.

A list of celebrities and bohemians, including actors Shaike Ofir and Haim Topol, and the singer Yaffa Yarkoni, as well as many other dignitaries, rubbed elbows with the IAF officers, particularly the members of the 201st Squadron. It was crowded, but it was a great crowd.

"Find everybody," Pecker instructed the veteran captain, Amnon Gurion, "and have them make their way to the outside of the clubhouse."

Gurion set out to find his fellow squadron members, as Pecker had commanded. Near the entrance to the clubhouse, he noticed a group of five young men, none of whom he recognized. One of the young men was quite tall, while the others were of average height, and they were just standing there, looking rather out of place. He was about to throw them out, when he realized they must be the band.

"Excuse me, are you guys part of the band?" he asked through pursed lips, glaring at them.

Zetelny, the tall one, and Assael, Lev-Ari, Leif, and Perry, stood there timidly, and explained that they were not part of the band. They were the new navigators.

New navigators needed to prove they were worthy of flying in a Phantom.

It was tough transitioning from the cockpit of the Fouga Magister, the aircraft they had trained in during Flight Academy, to the Phantom. They felt like Alice in Wonderland. They had practiced on scooters, and now they were flying in the Rolls-Royce of the skies.

Soon, however, it was time to sober up.

Their maiden voyages were enough for them to recognize they had a lot to learn. First, this American monster had an endless array of navigation, weapon delivery, and radar systems the navigator was expected to master. Secondly—and this was a lousy thing to discover—it seemed they all suffered from some kind of new ailment. They had all gotten accustomed to the comfortable flight of the Fouga, and suddenly they were being exposed to the mighty g-loads of the Phantom. Apparently that required unique neck muscles, which none of them seemed to have. After they had been smeared across the entire surface of the cockpit, they realized the only way to do their job, or even survive for that matter, was to develop these new muscles, so they did.

A month into the process, they were sure the worst was behind them, and that's when they were introduced to the realities of dogfighting. It was then that they realized everything up until that point had only been preparation.

Harnessed in the front seat of the cockpit, the pilots were not the least bit interested in the suffering the navigators were enduring. The only thing the pilot was interested in was a current "aerial picture" of the skies, and he was not interested in hearing about how he was the one on the controls of the aircraft, which meant he had forewarning about the upcoming turns. That the navigators had to handle a right hand seven-g turns without any forewarning was their problem, as far as the pilots were concerned.

So the navigators learned to deal with it, and continued to focus on their responsibilities: tracking the location of the aircraft and the location of the enemy. They kept their eyes on the dials, tracked their speed and altitude, and even at seven G's they continued to provide instructions: "Increase bank," "Break," "Sharpen your turn."

Between sorties, as they continued training to be elite airmen, the new navigators would meet in the instruction room. On one of the moving boards were notes from a previous class, and written in marker were the words "Do not erase until Fier returns."

"Damn," Assael said, "we missed the action."

* * *

On June 22, 1971, at the Port of Alexandria, Sadat gave an impassioned commencement speech before a group of newly inducted Egyptian naval officers. With King Faisal of Saudi Arabia, Sadat's primary financial backer, in attendance, Sadat announced that 1971 would be the "decisive year."

"I am not willing to wait indefinitely to reverse the results of the Six-Day War," Sadat proclaimed. "Even an Israeli withdrawal to the borders of June 4, will not end the Arab-Israeli conflict! We must continue this fight until the rights of the Palestinian People have been realized. This will be a crueler process than its predecessors, and this will be an unavoidable and unrelenting war."

While the Egyptian president delivered his diatribe in Alexandria, Lt. Gen. Haim Bar-Lev, the IDF Chief of Staff, stood at the podium at the International Convention Center in Jerusalem and asserted to a crowd of 500 assembly members of the Jewish Agency that, "The internal situation on Egypt is not suited for an 'adventure'. Taking on a war requires leadership, and I'm not convinced the Egyptians have a leader capable of declaring war." His remarks were met with resounding applause.

On January 1st, 1972, two close friends, Lt. Gen Haim Bar-Lev, and his lifelong friend Gen. David "Dado" Elazar, with whom Bar-Lev had grown up in Yugoslavia, and who had until recently served as Bar-Lev's deputy and Commander of GHQ, clasped hands, finalizing the transfer of authority and position of Chief of Staff to Elazar.

Long live the new Chief!

* * *

Sometime in spring of 1972, Capt. Meir "Shaniboi" Shani, Combat Manager for "The One" Squadron, was sitting at the wheel of an Autocars Carmel Ducas, traveling down Hatzor Highway. Suddenly, he noticed an attractive, big-breasted lady standing at the side of the road, holding a suitcase.

"Where are you headed, girl?"

"The 202nd Squadron," she responded.

"Minus one! This is the 201st Squadron, pilots, not paratroopers. Come on, get in."

The young lady swiftly fell in love with the squadron.

She was Sima Shavit, the daughter of the famous businessman, Buma Shavit, known for his deep, authoritative voice in the Shavit Ovens commercials. "Simka," as she was called, had a sharp wit and her father's temperament, and she spoke her mind. "Shaniboi," who was the first to recognize her, called her "Bumka," reminding everyone on base of the annoying fact that she was Buma's daughter.

With a month or two, "Bumka" discovered that the squadron followed its own set of rules, and "Shaniboi" taught her which rules could be bent, and which could be broken. "Shaniboi" took a special interest in the lady, and even though one day per week, women were not allowed to leave the base, he set up an elaborate escape: they put "Bumka" into the trunk of Amiram Eliasaf's Peugeot 404, and took her to the beach in Ashdod—and screw whoever was jealous! They didn't always let "Bumka" out of the trunk right away, though. It was just too much fun to hear her begging to be let out.

On May 2, 1972, Lt. Col. Ran Pecker completed his ten-month command of the 201st Squadron, and Lt. Col. Iftach Zemer took his place.

Zemer was a Mirage guy. He had not been in a command position in over two years. Instead, he had spent the last two years teaching at the Flight Academy and then working at HQ. Suddenly, he had been assigned to command the 201st. He was somehow supposed to fill Pecker's shoes.

Zemer spent almost two months mastering the new aircraft, and when he felt ready, he arrived at the squadron. He received a hero's welcome. After all, he was a legendary Mirage pilot and a respected officer. The pilots quickly discovered that he was also a "mensch." He was one of the guys, and he was a deliberate, principled, and intelligent leader. Welcome aboard!

On June 13, a two-ship formation of Sledgehammers from the 201st and a two-ship formation of Shahaks from the 101st accompanied a reconnaissance mission over Egypt. As the mission was coming to a close, the Egyptians scrambled two four-ship formations of MiGs from the air base at the Egyptian Delta. In the first dogfight over Egyptian land, nearly two years since Egypt and Israel had agreed to a cease-fire, over Egyptian territory, the Sledgehammer pilots shot down two MiGs. Adi Benaya, Yossi Lev-Ari, Eitan Peled, and Yoram Romem were the heroes of the day. Their kills were added to the board, alongside the three kills the squadron had collected during the War of Attrition.

Eight days later, in the early afternoon hours of a hot summer day, several miles inside Lebanese territory, the elite commandos of Sayeret Matkal completed Operation "Box Crate." The commandos captured five Syrian assets: two lieutenant colonels, both of whom were squadron leaders, two army colonels, and the brigadier general in charge of territorial defense. The plan was to exchange these prisoners from three airmen held by the Syrians.

While the Syrian Government determined whether to agree to the prisoner exchange, the five Syrian officers underwent rigorous interrogations, intelligence officers on one side, and IAF officers on the other.

"What is the fight squadron's emergency response time?" demanded Maj. Motti Kimmelman, the IAF intelligence liaison at the Ararat Northern Intelligence Base. "Where are the pilots' barracks? Where are the fuel stations? What are the Syrian military's mission plans?" he pressed. Then, almost as an afterthought, he shifted back to the main point: "What is the Syrian air force's signal for war?"

"If the president declares war," the Syrian officers answered, "we will station a squadron of Sukhoi Su-7 fighters at Damascus International Airport, and another squadron of Sukhois at the Bley air base (the air base closest to the Golan Heights). But remember, sir, this is only supposed to happen if the president declares war."

Motti jotted down the intelligence, and passed it on; he also made sure to commit the information to memory.

In August, the IAF Operations Directorate sent a team from the Department of Operations Research, headed by its commander, Gideon Hoshen, to observe the "Battering Ram" training exercise, in which IDF southern forces simulated repulsing an Egyptian infiltration. Throughout the course of the exercise, the team met with several senior officers who repeatedly insisted that an infiltration of that sort would be a logistical nightmare for the Egyptians—it would be a problematic and high-risk undertaking.

"All we would need to neutralize them is some artillery," one of the officers scoffed, "Just ship us a 120 millimeter mortar and we'll be fine."

Hoshen returned to IAF HQ and reported his findings: IDF HQ and Southern Command were completely confident they could repel an Egyptian infiltration on their own. "They don't need our help, so consider the matter closed."

* * *

During July and August, as the searing heat of the Middle-eastern summer was driving the men to the point of madness, two new and very excited pilots, Gil "Ziggy" Zigman and Yossi Eliel, arrived at the 201st squadron for a conversion course.

For Zigman, who had Hebraized his name to "Regev" while in Flight Academy, arriving at "The One" was the achievement of a lifetime—he had reached the summit of Mount Everest.

"Me? Gil Zigman?" he would sometimes think, "I'm just a farmer from Hepher Valley who rolls his R's! Somehow, I made my way through the sifting process, and now I'm part of the most elite squadron in the country, the top of the top, the flagship! I get to fly the envy of every pilot: the Sledgehammer! And not only that, I get to fly one with the 201st Squadron, 'The One'! Wow!"

By the summer of 1972, the IAF had increased the number of Sledgehammer squadrons to four. The 119th Squadron was established during the War of Attrition, and the 107th, still in its infancy, was established a year later. The senior squadrons, the 201st and the 69th, continued to jockey for top position, but everybody knew which squadron was the best.

"Listen," the veteran pilots would say, "you've come to the right place. Here there's no bullshit. This isn't a group of kids playing in the schoolyard. We're real men, professionals, winners. We have no limitations. We are the masters of the universe, the poised tip of the arrow."

In one corner of the clubhouse, where everyone would notice it, Regev located the Kill Board. It served as a constant reminder of the diversity of the Phantom—the aircraft that could do it all. There were five kills: one had been scored by Henkin and Los from the 69th Squadron, so that one, of course, didn't count. The next four belonged to his friends: two in June, and two more from the War of Attrition. Fier and David had scored two kills in Egypt; Eitan Peled and Moshe Goldwasser ("Goldie") had scored two in Syria. Then Regev turned his attention to the cost of these kills. Hetz, the beloved first commander, was dead; "Goldie," as far as they knew, had been killed by villagers; and Fier and Eini were still POW's.

The guys were obnoxious, full of nonsense and *joie de vivre*, frenetic and rambunctious, and they had a killer instinct that could come out at any moment. There were no teetotalers on this air base, and the only tea was "medicinal tea"—whisky. They saw themselves as different, and they were. They were the best-honed yet wildest pilots in the country, and they lived life on the edge. This rowdy bunch had to be kept under control, because the only thing they cared about was dogfighting. They couldn't give a damn about missions and sorties; all they wanted was more kills to put up on the board. If the day's orders included A/G training, they got through them as quickly as possible so they could get back to the "real thing," an improvised air-to-air combat. If the pilots exceeded the g limits, they simply adjusted the high-limit pointer down to five Gs; no one would ever know. It is true that the flight manual instructed that you were supposed to come in for your final approach at a "19-units angle of attack, and at 150-160 knots," but that was for regular pilots, not the pilots of "The One." None of them landed at a 19-units angle. They came in low, just over the power lines of the Kfar Ahim village to the east of the air base, touched-down in the center of the runway, slammed on the brakes, deployed the drag-chute, and prayed for the best. It was group of psychos.

The pilots loved their new quarters. They headed out to the air base at the break of dawn, and they remained there until late at night. Even after they had finished the day's training, the guys would remain on the air base, celebrating in the new clubhouse—a clubhouse right out of the movies.

There was also the "apartment," in the "bachelors'" barracks. Well after "lights out" for their brothers-in-green, who slept in tents, with no privacy, exposed to the elements and the bugs, the pilots of the 201st partied in their tiny rooms. Since two pilots lived in each apartment—God forbid—and they didn't have any keys, just like on a Kibbutz, the rule was that whoever was partying would tie up the doorknob from the inside. If you found the door locked, you simply went elsewhere.

The best thing about the squadron, however, was the camaraderie. There was something so enjoyable about the chaos of the two-seater squadron and its double staff. What a group of guys! There were the three men named Eitan: Ben Eliahu was the most respected. Everyone looked up to Deputy Squadron leader A; it was as though he had the Midas touch. Then there were the other two: Peled and Levy. "Wild Bull," as everyone called Peled, had two kills with the Sledgehammer, and at that time, that was the record for the Phantom Squadron. Levy had his own impressive record: he had made the rank of captain at a very young age, and had earned his stripes during the War of Attrition. Soon after, two more Eitans arrived: Brosch and Shamueli, both of whom were navigators. Regev thought to himself, *"Could five guys named 'Eitan'[2] be some kind of sign as to the strength of the squadron?"*

Eventually, he found categories for everyone. There were the veterans of the Six-Day War: Ben Eliahu, of course, Zemer, the commander, Ron Huldai, Adi Benaya, Eli Zohar, Eitan Peled, with his two kills, Haim Rotem, Amnon Gurion, Uri Sheani, and Gadi Samok. The next generation was headed by Amiram Shaked, Ben-Ami Peri, and Dani Haloutz, all of whom had participated in the War of Attrition. This group also included Eitan Levy, who had gotten a good taste of battle flying a Skyhawk during the War of Attrition, before transitioning to the 201st. Next were the guys that had not fought in battle, but were around for it. There was Yoni Ofir, who had been a commanding officer in the Paratroopers Brigade before becoming a pilot, Meir "Shaniboi" Shani, Itamar Barnea, Amiram Eliasaf, Kobi Hayun, and Yigal Stavi. Then there were the kids, who had not experienced war… not yet. There was Avner Naveh, Doron Shalev, Yossi Eliel, Gideon Eilat, and Motti Redar. Finally, there was a group of guys he had found difficult to categorize. They were older guys, but they were inexperienced pilots: Haim Ram, Moshe Koren, and Ori Shahak.

He then started getting to know the navigators. At the head of the class was Yair David, who had graduated from the mythological "American" team that had first learned to operate the aircraft and were responsible for teaching everyone else. If that was not

---

2   *Also a Hebrew word for 'strength'.*

impressive enough, David also had an incredible story of how he had escaped from Egypt while MIA as a paratrooper. Also in this group were Amiram Talmon and Oded Erez, experienced reservists who were head and shoulders above the others. There was also Yoram Romem, who had received a commendation from the IDF Chief of Staff during the War of Attrition, for managing to land a damaged Phantom after the pilot had lost his hand. Uzi "Shmidko" Shamir, Gil Haran, and Paltiel "Sposh" Barak had all completed the navigation course with Romem, and they had experienced the tail end of the War of Attrition. Then there were the youngsters: "Blumi" Blumenfeld, Yahav, Lezer, Cohen, Barush, and Baram. There was the "Badass Farmer," and there were the "Band Members," "Asa" Assael, "Leibo" Lev-Ari, Leif, and Zetelny, who towered above everybody, physically and intellectually. Yehoar "Rhino" Gal had a solid frame and nasty temper, which made for a dangerous combination whenever he played ball. There was Baruchi Golan, the quiet guy from Ramat Yochanan in the North. Uri Arad, Amnon Tamir, Benjamin Kiryati, Shimon Tzror, Gilad Garber were also in the group, as was Dror Jaffe, the guy who always smiled. Then there were the "babies," Eitan Shmueli, and most especially, Nimrod Amami and Arik Shlain.

* * *

On October 24, 1972, Anwar Sadat gathered the members of Egypt's Supreme Council of the Armed Forces at his home in Giza, and announced to a rather shocked group of officers that because his efforts to jump-start the political process were going nowhere, he had decided to go to war, using "whatever we have at our disposal."

Egypt would not wait for the shipment of long-range SCUD SS (surface to Surface) missiles it had hoped to use to intimidate the Israeli population, as a countermeasure to any attempted Phantom strikes inside of Egypt, Sadat explained. He also informed them that they would not keep waiting for the arrival of new fighter jets with which to strike airstrips and take out the Zionist aircraft while on the ground, even if that was what the Jews had done to them during the Six-Day War. Egypt would attack Israel with whatever it had, and that would have to be enough to win the war.

The generals shifted uncomfortably in their seats. "What will we do, Mr. President, to protect the Egyptian home front?" they asked Sadat. "How will we cross the ramparts along the eastern border of the Canal?" they pressed.

"The point of this war is not to reoccupy the entire Sinai," Sadat explained, taking note of the concern in the eyes of his top generals. "The goal is merely to change the status quo, and in doing so, to restart the political process so we can get back all of the territory."

"If we're going to go to war, it must be an all-out war that includes regaining the entire Sinai Peninsula," said Minister of War, Mohammed Ahmed Sadek, "and we are nowhere near that capability!"

"At this time, it is beyond our capacity to defeat the Israelis in a full campaign and regain control of all of the territory they conquered," Sadat responded. "Let's be realistic," he continued, "and work within our limitations. Let's work to our strengths. We need to construct a new battle plan based on an impenetrable wall of defense, like the one our missile batteries can provide. We will traverse the Canal and shatter the Bar-Lev Line; we will create a defensive line about 10 miles to east; we will position ourselves on both banks of the Canal and reopen it to our ships. We can regain some of the honor we've lost. Now go and create a plan," Sadat concluded, "Prepare a new kind of war."

* * *

In late October, there was not a soul within the Directorate of Military Intelligence (DMI) who was aware of the results of Sadat's meeting; neither was Gil "Ziggy" Regev, the 201ˢᵗ fighter pilot, whose only interest was adding more kills to the board.

Most of the conversations on the air base revolved around dogfighting. Amiram Eliasaf, who had been assigned to the base about a year earlier than "Ziggy," tended to talk the most. Then again, he also tended to produce the most. He was high up on the kill board—a real winner. Amiram had zero interest in flying missions, or even talking about them. Takeoffs and landings were not his thing. The only thing that excited him was dogfighting, and that was the case for the rest of the pilots as well. Nevertheless, the 201ˢᵗ Squadron was assigned primarily to mission strikes. As for dogfighting, that was the Mirage pilots' job.

"Maybe we should just move to a Mirage squadron," Itamar Barnea suggested, "that way we can score some kills."

"You mean leave the 201ˢᵗ?" scoffed Shaniboi. "Not a chance!"

On November 21, 1972, Itamar Barnea's day arrived. By the end of that day, there would be no happier man alive. On that afternoon, a foursome was scrabbled from the squadron, to take on the Syrians. In four-ship formation the tangled skirmish of Sledgehammers, Shahaks, and MiGs, all violently jumbled together, the Syrians lost six jets, two of which were shot down by members of "The One." Amnon Gurion scored one kill, and the other was scored by none other than Itamar Barnea.

Between late 1972 and early 1973, the Egyptians acquired two SA-6 (SA=Surface to Air) missile systems. "What's the point of the new missiles?" everyone at IAF HQ wondered.

IAF officers discussed the matter with their western colleagues. They struggled to interpret the bits of intelligence they received. What they knew was that this missile was affective at surface-to-air kills, particularly against very low-altitude flying jets.

This posed a serious problem: the method of strike used by the IAF was based on low-altitude approaches from which the SA-2 and SA-3 radar systems could not pinpoint them. Now there was a new kid in town, and he was dangerous…and frightening.

Because they were supposed to be maintaining a ceasefire with the Egyptians, the Israelis did not want to risk a reconnaissance mission deep into Egyptian territory, where the missile systems were stationed. So the IAF decided to make do with the intelligence it had, while continuing to hope for an opportunity to perform a proper recon mission and uncover the Egyptians' secrets.

In November of 1972, in the Golan Heights, "The One" Squadron joined its brothers-in-green for a tour of the line, hosted by Lt. Col. Yossi Ben-Hanan, Regiment Commander of the 188th Armored Brigade.

"There, directly across from us, sits the Syrian front-line division, and over there, across from them, sit my two tank platoons. There's also another one behind them for support." Gil Regev thought to himself, *A company versus a division? Do the greens know something we don't?*

* * *

In January of 1973, the Israeli newspaper "Maariv" published a story claiming that British pilots had recently approached the Israeli Embassy in London, asking to join the IAF. These requests, the British explained, were in response to a television interview given by the commander of the Syrian Air Force to British Television. During the interview, he claimed that the only reason the Israelis kept winning air battles was because their Phantoms were flown by American, Canadian, and Australian volunteers who had trained on and mastered the new aircraft. The Syrian aircraft, on the other hand, were not being flown by Russian pilots.

After enjoying a cup of tea with milk with the somewhat surprised embassy representatives, the British pilots, who began to realize they had been misled, were politely sent on their way.

Later that month, in keeping with their president's instructions, the recently appointed Egyptian Minister of War, Ahmad Ismail Ali, and Chief of Staff, Saad a-Din el-Shazly, presented Sadat with "High Spires," the new war plan. For the first time since the Six-Day War, the Egyptians had a viable war plan: cross the Suez Canal, breach the Bar-Lev Line, station in the Sinai from a distance of approximately 10 miles east of the Canal, all the while protected from air strikes by the well-apportioned missile batteries.

* * *

As the British ran around confused by the Syrian reports, and the Egyptian leadership was preparing its new war strategy, "Ziggy," with a new ID card listing his name as Gil Regev, got married to Nurit at the 201st Squadron's clubhouse, him in his uniform; her dressed in white.

They had met in Hepher Valley. She was the oldest daughter of the owner of a huge dairy farm in Kfar Yedidia. They were classmates at the high school in Kfar Vitkin, where he used to cheat off of her math tests, and she used to cheat off of his Bible and literature tests. When he went off to Flight Academy, they had very few chances to meet, but they wrote to each other, and that January, they married.

* * *

By the beginning of 1973, U.S. Secretary of State, Dr. Henry Kissinger had earned the title of "Father of the Deadlock Policy" in the Middle East.

With the backing of the President of the United States, Kissinger managed to torpedo every attempt by the State Department, his bitter enemy, to open channels between Jerusalem and Cairo.

"Any progress toward a solution at this time," Kissinger lectured Nixon, "will only serve to strengthen the Soviet position." Kissinger managed to convince the president that no agreement should be reached until the Arab Nations rejected Soviet support, and embraced the United States.

Near the middle of February, the long-awaited request arrived.

Hafez Ismail, National Security Advisor to President Sadat, informed the Americans that he was on his way to the U.S., and he wished to meet with Kissinger.

Ismail arrived in New York ten days later, sat down with Secretary Kissinger, and dropped a bombshell: Egypt was willing to enter into a peace accord with the Israelis.

"The framework of the accord," Ismail explained, "can be worked out between now and May. The details could be worked out by September, at which time the Egyptians would require a partial withdrawal of Israeli troops from in and around the Suez Canal."

While Kissinger sat stunned, trying to take in the full magnitude of Ismail's message, the Egyptian National Security Advisor slowly brought the Secretary back to earth.

"We will agree to a complete peace and normalization during the second phase," Ismail explained, "after the State of Israel withdraws from the entire Sinai and completes an agreement with the Palestinians—including complete withdrawal from the occupied territories. Until then, we'll settle for a mutual non-combat agreement."

"My advice to Sadat is to be more realistic..." Kissinger interrupted, the last echoes of the advisor's remarks still lingering in the air. "The fact is that Egypt was defeated, so you cannot make demands as though you won the war. How is it reasonable, as the losing side, to make demands of the winning side? I would not advise Sadat to change the current military situation. If he tries, the Israelis will win again, even more decisively than in 1967. Egypt's losses, and Sadat's, will be tremendous!"

Ismail returned to Cairo and proceeded to brief Sadat on the meeting with Kissinger, and how the Secretary had thrown cold water on his offer. He explained that according to Dr. Kissinger, it was primarily Egypt's responsibility to conclude the political process. However, as Ismail explained, Kissinger had thrown them a rope, and had agreed to send the US National Security Advisor to meet with Ismail in April, to continue the discussions.

In his book, **The Watchman who Fell Asleep**, Prof. Uri Bar-Joseph wrote, "There is no escaping the conclusion that the main failure to introduce genuine momentum into the political process, as an alternative to war, was brought upon by the Israelis and Kissinger. Furthermore, it is difficult to assert that they did so unwittingly. With the Israelis, it stemmed from their confidence in their military might and in the ability to end a potential war with results that would force Egypt back to the negotiating table, with better conditions from Israel's perspective. With Kissinger, it stemmed from his confidence in Israel's military might, and because he estimated that the best strategy for advancing the peace process was to lower the expectations of both sides, especially Egypt's hopes for immediate results."

Dr. Yigal Kipnis, author of 1973 – **The Path to War**, takes Bar-Joseph's views one step further. Kipnis points to Israel's political leadership, particularly to the Prime Minister and the Minister of Defense, as the ones directly responsible for the failure to take advantage of a one-time opportunity for peace between the Egypt and Israel.

However, there is another side to the story, and depicting the Israeli leadership as "the bad guys," and the Egyptian leadership as "the good guys" is simplistic and inaccurate.

The Israelis rejected the Egyptian plan because it called for complete withdrawal as a precondition for an agreement that offered neither true peace nor normalization. The Egyptians only offered "a state of peace," which meant nothing more than an absence of armed conflict. It lacked an offer of direct bilateral negotiations, and the timetable presented by the Egyptians for concluding the process was deemed unacceptable by the Israelis.

"We can do this after the elections (at the end of October 1973)," the Israeli leadership argued, "There is no need to back us into a corner."

Moreover, Israel's Prime Minister agreed that Kissinger should continue to examine the Egyptian offer. However, she had little choice in the matter, especially as she needed US approval for the Israeli production of 100 "Kfir" jets (modified Super Mirage jets containing several US-made parts and a Phantom engine) and for supplying Israel with Phantoms and Skyhawks in 1974-1975. As a show of good faith, Golda Meir offered an interim plan that included a phased withdrawal, and allowed Egyptian forces to cross the Canal.

In general, the Israeli leadership, based on the intelligence reports that had been received, believed that Ismail's offer did not represent Egypt's true intentions. It seemed to them that the real purpose of the Egyptian offer was to complicate U.S.-Israeli relations, and discourage the U.S. from providing Israel with more jets. Egypt could not possibly intend to enter into a true peace agreement with Israel, because the Egyptian people would never stand for that.

Sadat's true intentions notwithstanding, the results of the meeting as was reported by Ismail, signified a final straw for the Egyptians: the response they had received was perceived as a direct slight against the Egyptian people and a personal and irrevocable offense directed at their leader.

It is well known that respect is a major issue in the Middle East, and such disrespect was cause for war. It was at that moment, it seems, that the Egyptians unsheathed their swords.

* * *

"M5-series Libyan Mirages, with long-distance deployment capabilities, have just arrived in Egypt," reported Avner Yofi, Head of the Intelligence Section under the Intelligence Department, for the Assessment of Egyptian Air Force Activities, to his commanding officer, Lt. Col. Yehuda "Porty" Porat, Director of Intelligence Research.

"Provide more data," Porat responded.

"Porty" gathered up more data and brought it to Yofi.

On April 18, "Golda's Kitchen"—Israel's premier political and security team—met at the Prime Minister's residence in Jerusalem, to discuss the warning they had been provided by their "Man in Cairo," Ashraf Marwan—a senior advisor to Anwar Sadat, who would often provide the Israeli government with detailed intelligence. According to Marwan, Egypt intended to attack sometime in the middle of May. After enjoying some of Golda's famous homemade cookies, the participants settled in the guest room adjacent to the kitchen. The group consisted of three politicians, Golda Meir, Moshe Dayan, and Yisrael Galili; two military advisors, IDF Chief of Staff David Elazar and Intelligence Director Eli Zeira. Additional participants included the Mossad Director, Maj. Gen. (Ret.) Zvi Zamir, who was not a regular member of Golda's Kitchen, but was a necessary component of this meeting, which was convened specifically to assess the warning from *his man* in Cairo.

"I propose we focus on trying to determine what might happen next," said the Minister of Defense, who opened the meeting. "What are the things we must do?"

"Any logical analysis of the situation," said the Intelligence Director unflinchingly, "indicates the Egyptians would be making a mistake by going to war. If we accept this assessment, there is no purpose to this meeting."

He then proceeded to assess other logical probabilities, and explained that, "As for [the Egyptians] actually crossing the [Suez] Canal, I'm certain we will know well enough in advance to provide warning—not only tactical, but operational; namely, a few days in advance."

"How will we know?" asked Golda

"We will know when there are senior officers touring the area; force deployments; an increase in air defense and other systems; and we will see them clearing all the neglected embankments throughout the canal. Generally speaking, when the entire Egyptian Force is activated, we know about it."

"Would they be able to orchestrate an aerial strike against Israeli cities—especially with these Mirage aircraft that Gaddafi has provided the Egyptians?" asked the Prime Minister, with a combination of purpose and concern.

"They would never be able to reach us," Dayan and Dado assured her, "though we cannot ensure a hermetic seal."

Zeira added, "If the Egyptians enlist mercenary pilots to attack Israel, those pilots better write their wills ahead of time."

Though Golda felt reassured and Zeira insisted nothing would happen, the "Kitchen Crew" decided, in contrast to the Intelligence Director's advice, that the warning they had received from their spy—"Marwan"—as well as several concrete preparations for war that had been observed on the Egyptian side, were sufficient evidence to justify preparing the IDF for war.

The next day, the IDF Chief of Staff declared that over the next two months the IDF would prepare for a two-front war—one that could erupt simultaneously, or in phases—at both the Suez Canal and the Golan Heights. Operation "Blue and White" was initiated.

"Our military preparations," Dado explained, "must be performed in such a manner as to bring the entire force to the necessary state of readiness without raising any red flags, neither here nor in the U.S."

They transferred 10-million Lire to the military leadership, with which they advanced reserve store units to the front lines, bolstered the current reserve units, and established new ones. They also fortified their breaching systems, because they "knew" that soon after the outbreak of the war, the IDF would cross the Canal.

* * *

At the end of April, the airmen of the 201st, having already been impressed by the confidence of the armored corpsmen stationed at the Golan Heights, visited the IDF positions on the Suez Canal. There they encountered some very bored infantrymen.

"Across from us is an Egyptian brigade," the commanding officer explained.

Here we go again, thought Regev. *It's the 188th all over again! These 'greens' really are sure of themselves. A platoon versus a brigade and this kid is totally calm!*

* * *

On May 10, the Egyptians began the exercise "Tahrir-35."

"War is getting ready to break out," announced Capt. Aharon Ze'evi Farkash, Head of the Department of Air Defense, Egypt, at the IAF Intelligence's Research Branch, to his commanding officer, Lt. Col. Yehuda Porat.

Farkash, a redheaded man with the accompanying personality, was the IAF's top man on "Sinai thinking." He was very familiar with the Tahrir exercise series, and he knew this one was different. Alarms sounded in his head.

"In all of the previous exercises," Farkash opened his briefing, "a few regular-service commanders served as the assessment team, while this time all of those commanders are participating, and reserve officers are serving as the assessment team."

"The Egyptians are practicing emergency contact sequences," he continued, "the size of the participating force is much larger than in the past, and the bridging units are positioned on the Canal for the first time since the Six-Day War. I must remind you, Yehuda, that the Egyptians always perform their bridging and penetration exercises separate from their major exercises, either on the al-Balah Peninsula or the al-Fayoum depression. That's not the case this time."

"Based on those facts, and our understanding of Soviet doctrine, which facilitates rapid post-exercise deployment, I estimate that on May 19, when they have completed this exercise, the Egyptians will deploy."

Porat listened and nodded.

While the Egyptians were activating various corps, and Farkash was consumed with concern, an unprecedented event occurred over Syrian airspace.

In April of 1973, at the behest of Syrian President Hafez al-Assad, the Soviets supplied Syria with its first SA-6 missile battery—the cream of the crop—to reinforce their air-defense system, which comprised of SA-2 and SA-3 batteries.

In May, the Syrians began their own military exercises, during which they stationed the SA-6 battery near Damascus. This was the opportunity the Israelis had been waiting for. Aviam Selah and Amnon Factori, from the 69th Sledgehammer Squadron, were selected for the historic reconnaissance mission that the IAF hoped would yield clear data regarding the mysterious and dangerous missile system.

Selah identified the missile system and passed over it at about 300 feet, praying the camera was functioning correctly. He landed and they developed the film… hallelujah!

At that time, Lt. Col. Reuven Eyal was the head of the Technical Department of IAF Intelligence, charged with determining the technical characteristics and military capabilities of enemy weapons systems.

The photographs Aviam Selah captured substantiated what the IAF had suspected: the entire battery system, from radar to launch mechanism, was mounted onto a tracked vehicle, making it easy to transport.

Then they discovered that there were four pipes that extended from the body of the missiles, which they assumed the missiles ramjet propelled. With an engine that powerful propelling the missiles, the SA-6 would have an engagement range of approximately 25 miles, just as their western counterparts had reported.

"That's incorrect," others argued. "A careful analysis of the photographic evidence provides no basis for believing this missile guidance method can reach such distances."

"Not necessarily," others countered. "There are other delivery methods that work within the parameters you've provided, and would be accurate enough at such distances."

"Give us more details," demanded the senior officers of the Operations Department from Lt. Col. Eyal.

"Expect an effective engagement range of 25 miles," they informed the Operations Department. "It's possible we're wrong, but we'd rather err on the side of caution, for the sake of the airmen, until we have hard evidence to the contrary."

On May 14, a meeting was held at the IDF General Staff, with Minister of Defense Moshe Dayan in attendance.

Dayan informed the military staff forum that the neutralization of the Egyptian and Syrian missile systems was a top priority. This meant that from that moment onwards, the responsibility for holding off enemy forces lay entirely with the ground forces. No one asked him what would happen if the ground forces were overwhelmed and in need of air support before the missile systems were neutralized.

* * *

On June 13, Maj. Gen. Benny Peled, who had just recently replaced Motti Hod as the Commander of the IAF, presented his updated battle plans to the Minister of Defense and the Chief of Staff.

With great self-assuredness, and impressive mental organization and breadth, Peled presented his briefing. Upon its conclusion, Peled emphasized that his plan of action could only be realized if the IAF was given permission for a preemptive strike.

Peled also explained that in order for this preemptive strike to succeed, they would have to find the best conditions for success: time, weather, visibility, and intelligence as to the exact location of the batteries.

"You're jumping the gun," the Minister of Defense and Chief of Staff responded, attempting to calm the young general. "We'll definitely strike first, if there's any suspicion they're getting ready to attack."

"Does that guarantee stand regardless?" asked Peled, a true intellectual on all matters of war, who also knew a thing or two about life and the dramatic turns it can take.

"Benny, my friend," Dayan responded, a look of scorn upon his face, "you can take my word for it. If we know they are ready to attack, we will give the go order for a preemptive strike."

* * *

In July, the 201st made its way to the Sinai Desert, to enjoy a third visit with the 'greens'. They observed an exercise by the armored corps. From an excellent vantage point, they observed the desert activity, and were impressed by the firepower, maneuvers, and mobility.

During the exercise, one of the platoon commanders faced an ambush by enemy tanks.

The young officer retreated his platoon to an observation point and called for air support. After around 15 minutes, he got back on the horn:

"Station one."

"Station one, over."

"Resume your mission."

During the debriefing that took place at the end of the exercise, airmen asked, "What exactly happened that allowed you carry on after waiting for 15 minutes?"

"The Air Force arrived and destroyed the enemy tanks," the platoon commander replied, a grin spreading across his sunburnt face.

* * *

At the beginning of August, as the hot summer sun shone over IDF HQ in Tel-Aviv, the Directorate of Military Intelligence's Research Department released a confidential memo regarding four speeches the Egyptian president had delivered over the past month.

"In our estimation," they wrote, "Sadat's remarks indicate he is currently focused on domestic affairs, and therefore, for the near future we need not expect any Egyptian actions that will jeopardize the current deadlock with Israel."

On Friday, August 10, the Military Intelligence memo reached the Knesset Foreign Affairs and Defense Committee.

"The Egyptians are fully aware that the current political and military climate precludes them from taking any reasonable military action," explained Maj. Gen. Zeira.

Lt. Gen. Elazar, also present at the meeting, was pleased to announce to the committee members that the IDF had decided to shorten the mandatory military service, and with that, the meeting was closed and everyone retired for the Sabbath.

Two days later, in light of the indicators coming out of Egypt, and recognizing that all of the estimated dates for the outbreak of a war had passed without incident, the IDF HQ announced the cessation of Operation "Blue and White."

On August 12, 1973, it became clear that the Head of the Directorate of Military Intelligence, Maj. Gen. Eli Zeira, was the HQ's reliable pundit.

He had asserted four months prior that there was no need for war preparations, and though he had met fierce opposition from the leadership, it turned out that he had been right all along.

Zeira was now viewed as the IDF's most promising officer, and not without reason.

He had begun his career as a regiment commander in the Givati Brigade, advanced to the office of the Chief of Staff—Moshe Dayan at the time—and from there he was appointed commander of the paratroopers. Subsequent promotions included Director of the Combat Directorate at HQ, a stint as a military liaison to the United States, as well as numerous positions within the Intelligence community. Wherever he went, he excelled.

Eli Zeira was a brilliant officer with a sharp mind. He was a wise individual, with a broad perspective, an eloquent speaking style, exceptional analytical skills and mental agility, and limitless charisma.

He also had an imposing physical appearance. He had piercing blue eyes and sharp, strong facial features, and he covered his balding head with his red barrette.

On August 12, 1973, he was able to add prescience to that impressive collection of characteristics. At HQ, all debate and discussion at the end of the summer of 1973 ended when someone would assert that, "Eli had said so."

* * *

Over the course of three weeks in August, 15 SA-6 missile batteries systems were positioned behind the three divisions now stationed on the Syrian border of the Golan Heights.

Maj. Oded Plum sported a fine head of hair, to accompany his many other fine features: he was a sober individual, highly curious, with a love for investigation. In the summer of 1973, Plum was serving as the Head of Air Operations for IAF Intelligence Department. It was his job to present updates on the enemy, such as when the enemy positioned 15 SA-6 missile batteries systems along the northern border.

"The implication of the deployment is that the Syrians are preparing for war," Plum asserted to Col. Furman, Director of Operations.

"If that's the case," Furman countered, "why is it that no one over at Intelligence thinks that?"

A few days later, a new officer, 2nd Lt. Yoram Yaron, arrived at Air Operations.

"Welcome," said Plum, and gave him 24 hours to acclimate. Then Plum assigned Yaron to assist Lt. Ben-Yisrael from OR (Operations Research) Branch in investigating the behavior of the Syrian anti-aircraft division deployed next to the front-line divisions.

The two got straight to work. Within a short period, they analyzed material from 20 aerial-reconnaissance missions the IAF had conducted over the Syrian side of the Golan Heights in the past two years.

For each reconnaissance mission, they prepared a separate slide that focused on anti-aircraft deployment for the period in question. Then they superimposed the slides to determine whether there had been any changes in force deployment. The results were clear: the Syrians had made significant changes. The two-ship formation then checked to see whether there was any correlation between the known readiness assessment of the Syrian forces at the time of the reconnaissance mission and the position of the antiaircraft batteries. They found a direct correlation: the greater the readiness assessment, the greater the amount of anti-aircraft batteries and the closer their position to the front line.

At the beginning of September 1973, Ben-Yisrael and Yaron met to analyze the most recent reconnaissance photographs. The batteries were more tightly grouped, and closer to the front line than ever before.

"There is a direct correlation between the Syrian force readiness assessment and the deployment and position of the antiaircraft batteries," the two wrote in their concluding report.

"The current deployment of anti-aircraft batteries in the Golan Heights, unprecedented in its scope, indicates a state of emergency for the Syrian military—a clear warning of an imminent attack or other unusual action."

In the first two weeks of September, the Syrian military unexpectedly deviated from its standard practices. In previous years, with the arrival of fall, the Syrians would thin out the armored divisions stationed throughout the front line of the Golan Heights, and send approximately half of them—three battalions—for training exercises in the deserts of eastern Syria. After three months of training, the battalions would return, and the other half of force would leave for their training. With the arrival of spring, the second half would return, and all six battalions would hunker down for the winter. This was the Syrians' annual process, but...

Beginning on September 4, the Syrians started deploying more forces to the front line. What could this mean? Why were they reinforcing the front line, rather than sending their battalions to their annual exercises?

The IDF took notice of the increase in armored forces and anti-aircraft batteries, mostly SA-6 batteries, along the Syrian front line.

On September 13, they sent another reconnaissance sortie over the area: four clean-configuration Phantoms flying in two-ship formations—one east to west, and the other west to east—photographed the area from 60,000 feet, well beyond the range of the SA-6 or the Syrian Air Force's Soviet-made MiGs.

As the four Phantoms were completing their mission, a flight of MiGs was sent to intercept them. During the dogfight that ensued over Tarsus—Syria's second-largest port city—the IAF shot down 12 MiGs and lost only one Mirage.

"The IAF has proven its superiority again!" was the headline of the morning edition of Haaretz. The story continued, "A new record for the IAF: 13 Syrian MiG-21 jets were shot down yesterday in dogfights." No one seemed to notice the flawed math—only 12 MiGs had been shot down. The thirteenth jet was an Israeli Phantom. Nobody cared. The point was the same: there was cause for celebration.

While the hallways of IDF and IAF HQ's were bustling with the sounds and smells of celebration—wine and song for everyone—far away, on Mount Canaan, Maj. Motti Kimmelman, the senior IAF intelligence liaison at the Intelligence Collection Unit, found himself in an awkward situation. On the one hand, he felt like celebrating with the rest of the IAF, but something was troubling him—a lot. He was intimately familiar with the practices of the Syrian Air Force, and knew how unforgiving it was toward pilots who had failed in combat. Such pilots usually were harshly rebuked, if not imprisoned, and yet tonight the Syrians were praising these pilots for their bravery. *Why,* he wondered. *Something strange is going on…something very strange.*

A few days after the air battle with the Syrians, Col. Iftach Zemer, commander of the 201st squadron, set out with several IAF officers for an educational tour in the United States.

Everything is fine, thought Gil Regev, *otherwise Zemer wouldn't be leaving.*

In the middle of September 1973, the IAF Intelligence Directorate Forum convened.

"What is the implication of the front line deployment of the SA-6 systems?" asked Brig. Gen. Rafi Har-Lev, Head of the Directorate.

"War is going to break out at any moment," answered Oded Plum, armed with the analysis provided by Yaron and Ben-Yisrael. "The SA-6 systems were deployed for that very reason."

"I'm not necessarily rejecting Plum's assertion," interjected Lt. Col. Yehuda Porat, Head of the Research Department, "but if I had to classify them, I'd say they're 'priority seven.'"

On September 17, IDF HQ held a strategy session, beginning with a background briefing by the Head of the Intelligence Directorate.

"The Arab Nations will avoid a decisive campaign, or any attempt to reconquer significant territory; they will not risk a major engagement," Maj. Gen. Zeira began. "That being said, they may decide they have the capacity for a small engagement, or for attrition," he continued. "One way or the other, we do not foresee any conflict in the near future. The main reason is that the Arabs' air power is very weak, and their jets do not have the capabilities needed for an effective strike on our airstrips. By 1975, or at some point in 1976, after an aggressive armament campaign in which they acquire enough long-distance jets to send out 20 to each airstrip, they might consider themselves ready for some minor engagement."

"**All is quiet at the Mouth of the Suez**," was the opening line of a 1973 political poster promoting the Alignment Party for the upcoming election of the eighth Knesset.

"**The Sinai Desert, the Gaza Strip, the West Bank, Judea and Samaria, and the Golan Heights—all the borders are safe, the bridges are open, Jerusalem is unified, settlements are being built, and our political position is strong. This is the result of sound, courageous, far-reaching politics.**" That was the text of the poster, the bottom of which featured pictures of the five leaders of the Coalition Party: Prime Minister Golda Meir, Minister of Defense Moshe Dayan, Deputy Prime Minister Yigal Alon, Minister of Foreign Affairs Abba Eban, Yaakov Hazan, the leader of United Workers Party, called Mapam. Above the main text appeared the words "**The Bar-Lev Line.**" That was their ace in the hole, their trump card: "Our Knesset and government are strong and stable, providing absolute security to our citizens, just like the Bar-Lev Line."

On September 25, the IDF began reviewing the details of the "Tahrir-41" exercise, and Aharon Ze'evi Farkash was not happy.

Something here just doesn't make sense, he thought to himself. *Why are they increasing their bridging and engineering supplies around the Canal? What's with the artillery? Why are they focusing*

so heavily on communications and mission orders? And why the hell
are they calling up all of their regular and reserve units?

* * *

The same week that Farkash was dealing with his sense of impending
doom because of the Egyptian exercises near the Suez Canal, the
IDF journal "Bamahane" published a festive pre-Rosh Hashanah
interview with Lt. Gen David Elazar, the Chief of Staff.

"Our actions against Syria at the end of 1972 and the beginning
of 1973 impressed upon the Syrians the implications and, more
importantly, the price... I suspect they've reached the conclusion
that the price is unacceptable, that it's too high," the Chief of Staff
reassured the reporters of the journal, as well as the employees of
the IDF radio station "Galei Tzahal."

"Israel is strong by any standard; not just ours, but that of our
enemies as well. In other words, even in the opinion of our enemies,
Israel is strong enough to deter them from war; to prevent war."

"We need to shorten the term of mandatory service," the Chief
of Staff continued, "and to reduce the size of the active IDF to suit
a more peaceful era... We will eliminate certain commands and
reduce certain battle units."

* * *

In the early morning hours of Wednesday, September 26, on the
eve of Rosh Hashanah, a letter arrived for the commanders of
the various squadrons of Hatzor Air base, signed by Maj. Gabai
Ramazi, adjutant.

"On Sunday, September 30, immediately following the holiday, we will hold the wing's bi-weekly meeting, at the office of the commander, Col. Amos Lapidot," Gabai wrote. The letter then provided the topics of the meeting: "Irregularities in flight hours; light aircraft for emergency post transport; fueling roster."

In the afternoon hours of the eve of Rosh Hashanah, Yehoar "Rhino" Gal, a navigator in the 201st Squadron, left the air base to pick up his father-in-law, Aharon Davidi, one of the legendary founders of the "Tzanchanim"—the IDF's elite Paratroopers unit.

Gal packed his father-in-law's luggage on top of the car, along with the luggage belonging to Errol, one of his father-in-law's fellow paratroopers, and joined them in the car. He listened to their stories about the wonders of London, and immediately found himself contemplating a stark reality: *hey kid, war is going to break out.*

"What are you guys talking about?" the "Rhino" yawned, as he listened to them discussing fellow veterans, family—they were out in left field by that point.

"Here it comes," smirked Gil Regev, as he sat in a corner of the briefing room watching Ron Huldai, who had replaced the commander, announce that things were heating up along the Syrian border. The man had seen one day of war, maybe two, and he so desperately wanted a kill to his name, like Barnea, like Peled, like Gurion.

* * *

Over the Jewish New Year, the Syrians transferred two Sukhoi-7 squadrons to the air bases closest to the front line: Damascus International and Bley.

Based on intelligence acquired through Operation "Box Crate," Capt. Motti Kimmelman knew this deployment indicated an emergency status from the Syrians. The Syrians were gearing up for war!

Yet nobody would take his calls.

By the morning of Sunday, September 30, all the excitement of Rosh Hashanah had passed, and everyone returned to their normal lives. The entire country had enjoyed three and a half days of rest and relaxation. The beaches of the Sinai and the hills of the Golan had been packed with tourists, and the IDF had scaled back its preparations.

That Sunday, at 18:00, the IDF Chief of Staff held a post-holiday meeting.

"I have no explanation for the Syrian emergency deployment," reported the Head of the Directorate of Military Intelligence. "In my opinion, it must be some sort of internal matter—to keep the army busy."

"Two days ago, on the third anniversary of Nasser's passing," the Director added, "President Sadat presented a speech in which he said, 'We are fed up with talking'. We assume this means he has decided to stop making promises about this being a 'decisive year'. I see no indication in Sadat's remarks that he intends to go to war," the Director concluded.

On Monday, October 1, as the cool autumn winds gusted over the Golan Heights and the Israelis turned their attention to the "Ten Days of Repentance," the Israelis noticed a significant and inexplicable reduction in the number of training exercises performed by the Syrian Air Force.

During the next few days, the intelligence-gathering unit on Mount Canaan collected numerous reports, according to which several, lone Syrian jets were flying over Syria.

What is going here, and how does it relate the decrease in training exercises, wondered Capt. Kimmelman, the IAF representative within the unit Suddenly it hit him! Syrian Air Force Command was trying to maintain the serviceability of its jets, keeping them grounded, while simultaneously putting out maximum effort to maximize the number of jets in the theater. The lone flights must be those aircraft the Syrians had just finished refurbishing—these were test flights. Kimmelman wrote a report and considered emphasizing what he suspected: one plus one equals war! He decided against emphasizing his suspicions, remembering he had not yet received a response to his pre-Rosh Hashanah warnings. *"I guess the geniuses over at research know better than I do."* He stopped short of writing the obvious conclusions.

That same day, IAF Intelligence received intelligence data, sent from Egyptian Air Force Headquarters to the Bomber Brigade in Aswan titled, "Battle Orders," or *"Amar Kithal"* in Egyptian.

"The Egyptians are getting ready for war," said Maj. Avner Yofi, Director of Intelligence for the Assessment of Egyptian Air Force Activities, to his commander, Lt. Col. Yehuda Porat.

"Based on?"

"The standard orders sent out by the Egyptians always say, 'Ta'alimat Amliat' (mission directive)."

"Quit playing linguist," said Porat, "There's no threat of war on the horizon."

"Today the Egyptians began their 'Tahrir-41' exercise, and at the Golan Heights, directly across from the front line, the Syrian Army is stationed in an unprecedented, emergency formation," Rafi Har-Lev, Head of the IAF Intelligence Directorate, informed Maj. Gen. Peled, his commander. "Both of these armies are capable of extracting themselves from an exercise or emergency formation, directly into combat."

"Why are you so certain that isn't exactly what's going to happen?" Maj. Gen. Peled asked.

"The Intelligence Directorate says nothing is going to happen," Har-Lev responded.

On Wednesday, October 3, Lt. Col. Ami "Goldie" Goldstein, the commander of the Skyhawk Squadron, was killed during a tragic aerial maneuver. When Pecker found out about the incident, he recommended that Maj. Giora Rom replace "Goldie."

"So ordered," replied Maj. Gen. Peled.

Giora Rom was not familiar with the Skyhawk. Therefore, the moment he was appointed squadron leader, he invested every waking hour in familiarizing himself with the jet and its systems. During a war, the squadron leader is not supposed to bother with flight problems; he is supposed to lead the men into battle. Pecker, his direct commander, knew this, and so did the IAF Commander, Maj. Gen. Peled.

* * *

That same week, Lt. Col. Yona Bendman, Head of Branch 6 (which focuses on Egypt, North Africa and Sudan) of the Research Department in Military Intelligence, called Col. Reuven Yardor, the Senior Code Decoder in Unit 848. During that call, Bendman demanded that he be read the intelligence information that had recently been received.

Yardor read it to him, in the Arabic source.

"Reuven," Bendman said, "you made a mistake in the translation. You wrote 'with the start of military operations, the Egyptian army will land commando squads near Um Hashiva and at three other locations in the Sinai'. Except that the word *'andah'* is translated more correctly as 'if', rather than 'with.'"

"I wasn't wrong," said Lt. Col. Yardor, the star of the Hebrew University in Jerusalem for Arabic studies, who was transferred from the Armored Corps to the Intelligence Corps on account of the claim that without him, the State of Israel would lack sufficient warning. "I was not wrong. *'Andah nushub al-amilaat'* means 'with the start of operations'."

"*I won't accept it*," Bendman ruled.

"*I've had it with you guys*," Yardor snapped, "*If you insist on proving in every possible way that a war will not happen, and are willing to distort the contents of this information, then write whatever you want.*"

"Wow, Yardor," said the head of the Egyptian Branch on the other end of the line. "What happened? Have you also joined the hysterical establishment that sees war on the horizon?"

During the Days of Repentance leading to Yom Kippur, after knocking on most of the doors in IAF Headquarters, constantly repeating his argument that the emperor had no clothes and that it was not really an exercise taking place in Syria and Egypt, there were those in the IAF HQ who thought Maj. Oded Flum went one step too far.

Since no one paid attention to him—after Yehuda Porat and Rafi Har-Lev said and reiterated that nothing would happen, and shook their heads disapprovingly at his 'doom and gloom' act—he brought his distress to the "kids." Lt. Yossi Boles, the young Section Officer in the Operations Department, was one of them.

"They're crazy," he explained to the astonished Boles, "They don't see, they don't listen. They are blind. You need to go and tell them."

Boles listened to him and thought, *wow, this guy is crazy.*

On the morning of Wednesday, October 3, in light of the Minister of Defense's explicit request, some of members of the "Kitchen Group" met at the Jacobs House, the official residence of the Prime Minister in Jerusalem's Rehavia neighborhood. This group included the ministers Dayan, Alon, and Galili, as well as military personnel - David Elazar, Benny Peled, and Brig. Gen. Aryeh Shalev, the Head of Military Intelligence's Assistant for Research, who filled in for Zeira, who was ill.

"To the best of my knowledge and recognition," Brig. Gen. Shalev concluded his remarks, "and based on our accumulated material, Egypt still believes that it is not ready for war. Therefore, the possibility of a joint Egyptian-Syrian war does not seem reasonable."

"We are not standing in front of a joint Egyptian-Syrian attack," the Chief of Staff said in his turn, "and I don't think that Syria would attack Israel on its own. The deployment and distribution of our forces along the border, along with the small reinforcements already in the field and the Air Force's state of alert, are all reasonable measures for any possible scenario."

"Could there be a scenario in which the Syrians would attack in order to conquer several towns, at which point the Egyptians would settle for limited fire just to harass Israel?" Golda asked.

"In my opinion, Assad is a reasonable leader," Shalev answered. "Although he wants to conquer the Golan Heights and avenge his fallen aircraft, he is a realist. He understands that Israel has a huge strategic and aerial advantage. Therefore, because the balance of power favors the IDF, and out of a concern for the safety of Damascus, he is unlikely to initiate a war on his own."

"It's possible that the Syrians would open limited fire," Shalev finished his learned doctrine, "but that is also unlikely."

"Thank you, Aryeh, you've calmed me down," the Prime Minister said.

On Wednesday, Capt. Yoav Dayagi ("Fishy"), the Assistant to the Head of the Research Department in IAF Intelligence, joined the "concerned" group. On the third day of the Egyptian "Tahrir 41" exercise, stages for dignitaries still had not been placed for the concluding event. In previous exercises, the stages had been set up at the start of the exercise, and based on the locations of the stages, the soldiers knew where it would end. What is going on here?

On Thursday morning, Capt. Aharon Ze'evi Farkash decided that the gut feeling that bothered him throughout the preparations for the "Tahrir 41" exercise was indeed justified.

Something stinks across the Canal, and it stinks considerably. Why are the Egyptians loading trucks with artillery ammunition in the Wadi Hof warehouses in the Nile Delta? Also, why are they bringing hundreds of them, loaded with ammunition, to Ras Safrana in the gulf area, and to the front? Why are they allowing their soldiers to break the Ramadan fast? And why is the radio traffic so quiet now?

He stormed into Porat's office and nervously told his commander, "I think there is going to be a war!"

"Gather all of the material you have on this matter and bring it to me after the holiday," said the Head of the Research Department in IAF Intelligence.

Porty is a very professional man, Farkash thought. An experienced Arabist, he knows how to analyze, how to write, how to summarize, and how to focus. If Porty is calm, who am I to argue with him?

On Thursday afternoon, October 4, news was received that sent right over the Northern Command's Intelligence Officer straight to the office of the Head of the Command.

After the Six-Day War, as the stench of death still stuck to the rocks of the Golan Heights, a Syrian thief was captured trying to find "work" in Israel. He was faced with two choices: spending time in an Israeli jail or becoming a member of Intelligence Unit 154. He chose the latter, enlisted, and received the codename "Kinshasa."

In the years that passed, his recruitment proved that it was worth the price. His focused eye and unconventional ability for chatting up troops in the Southern Golan, his old neighborhood, repeatedly brought accurate information concerning the Syrian Army's movements. In 1973, the flow of information improved, as one of his family members was appointed to a role in one of the line sectors. A direct pipeline from the well.

On Thursday, October 4, "Kinshasa" passed to his handlers the following news:

"Starting tomorrow, farmers and shepherds are prohibited from walking around the border area."

"This absolute prohibition," Kinshasa said, "apparently stems from the Syrian Army's decision to go to war."

"Hakah," Lt. Col. Haggai Mann said to Maj. Gen. Yitzhak Hopi, his commander, "This is the first, absolutely clear indication pointing to the offensive intentions of the 5th Division, located across the border from the southern sector of the Golan Heights. We've identified a problematic sector. We've also received an indication as to the timetable—from Friday and onwards."

"There's one more thing," the Command Intelligence Officer added, "This news is about a specific sector, but it is possible that that is the trend along the whole front line."

* * *

On Thursday afternoon, Phantom jets belonging to the 201st Squadron accompanied the 101st Mirage Squadron on a slanted high-altitude photography flight mission, and headed towards Egypt.

Capt. Haim Ram, a veteran fighter pilot, though new to the Phantom Squadron, recalled the Hanukkah holiday as a fountain of colors adorned the RWR display. SA-2 and SA-3 missile radars searched for them, found them and locked on them. This went on repeatedly. All that's missing is for them to launch.

He returned to land his aircraft. "Something bad is happening on the other side of the Canal," he informed those at the base.

While Haim Ram was concerned in the Sinai, the Second Deputy Squadron leader, Capt. Amnon Gurion, and his navigator, Lt. Paltiel (Sposh) Barak, found themselves on a patrol flight in the Golan Heights sector.

What's the meaning of all this electronic activity on the RWR display? Did the Syrians go crazy?

On Thursday evening, after the updates of missile locks in the Sinai and the Golan, not privy to the evacuation of the Soviet advisor families, nor to "Kinshasa's" alert, Maj. Ron Huldai, Deputy Squadron leader for 201st Squadron and current Acting Commander, was busy trying to find a cure for his private pain—a huge boil above his tailbone. He went to the Wing's clinic, and explained that he was having trouble sitting down. "Help yourself to some antibiotic pills," they told him. "Take a week off from flying. What could possibly happen?"

October 5

Black Flag

On the eve of Yom Kippur, at 06:00, while still not fully awake, Capt. Daniel Schimmel, deputy head of the Early-Warning Section at the Intelligence Department, reported for duty in the Air Force "Pit" in the Kirya military base in Tel Aviv. As always, he began to read the news that had accumulated on his desk. The teleprinter rang in the background, indicating that a new message had arrived.

He grabbed the thin paper that the machine ejected from the tray and read that the urgent evacuation of the families of Soviet advisors in Egypt and Syria was continuing.

06:30. Flight School at Hatzor

As the sun rose in the east and softly stroked the groups of flight instructors on their way to a briefing in the morning, Lt. Avner Naveh made a decision.

The day before, he began to feel an inexplicable tingling down his neck. Now, he felt like he had an explanation—battle day. This weekend, there would be a battle day. For sure. No one had called yet, and no one had said a thing about it. *I don't have a MiG to my name. There's Itamar. He already has one. It's my turn now.*

"I'm going," Lt. Avner Naveh waved his keys in the face of Lt. Itamar Barnea, his friend from the 201st Squadron and the Instructor's Course as well.

"Cut it out," Barnea urged. "Ben Rom (the Commander of the Instructor's Course) will get mad."

"I'm going to the squadron," Naveh snapped impatiently. "Are you coming?"

06:45. Office of the Defense Minister

On the morning of the holiest Jewish holiday, just as Naveh started the engine and Barnea was convinced, Israel's Minister of Defense, a strong man with a rare sense of self-control, found himself reviewing the updated intelligence bulletin that was placed on his desk a short time earlier.

He read it repeatedly. He found it hard to believe it. He reached the final paragraph, and understood that he was not mistaken: "Based on the findings, it can be clearly inferred that the Egyptian army on the Canal front stands at an unprecedented level of emergency preparedness, a level that we have never witnessed in the past."

07:00. Headquarters Staff Meeting in the IAF Commander's Chambers

Maj. Gen. Peled lit another cigarette, piercing through the smoke screen with his dark eyes into the space of the large room, filled with the scent of nicotine, and said, "We'll wait for Rafi."

"Where is he?" someone asked. Someone else answered, "He's at Zeira's."

They waited.

The office door opened and Brig. Gen. Rafi Har-Lev, Head of Air Force Intelligence, nodded in greeting, sat in his chair and with his characteristic gesture, he threw back his shirt collar with two fingers. He said, "I feel terri..." then immediately corrected himself, "Relaxed. I feel very relaxed."

Afterwards, he informed them about eleven Soviet Antonov aircraft that arrived to Egypt and Syria during the night, with no explanation. From the moment that they arrived, they began an urgent process of evacuating the families of the Soviet advisors in both countries, without even giving them enough time to pack their belongings.

"Nevertheless, the assessment of IDF Intelligence remains unchanged," Har-Lev said. "According to Military Intelligence, there is no logical reason for Egypt and Syria to go to war."

08:00. Flight School at Hatzor

An hour after Naveh turned on his car's engine and Barnea was persuaded, a general warning was given in the Flight Academy.

"There's a high level of tension with Syria, and we are missing people," the clerk said on the other end of the line.

Lt. Kobi Hayun shouted, "Start the Peugeot, quickly!"

08:20. Office of the Chief of Staff

The news of the evacuation of the families of the Soviet advisors, combined with the decryption of the photographic sortie of the Canal that appalled the Minister of Defense, led Lt. Gen. David Elazar to hold an urgent discussion in his office.

"I have no good explanation for the evacuation," said Maj. Gen. Zeira.

Attentive to the lack of a reassuring answer from the national assessor; aware of the first crack in the wall of self confidence of the Intelligence Directorate and its leader; and informed of the emergency preparedness of the Egyptian and Syrian militaries along the borders, the Chief of Staff decided that the moment had arrived to change the rules of the game.

"The Air Force will be put under full alert, and all holiday vacations will be cancelled," Lt. Gen. David Elazar instructed. "All of the vacations for those along the northern and southern fronts are also cancelled. We need to bring back all of the tank crews that have gone home for the holiday. The 7th Regular Armored Brigade will strengthen the northern front, and the brigade from the tank school will fortify the southern front."

Then, just before sending the participants in the discussion to proceed with the results of the discussion, he added, "I am declaring State of Alert Level C[3]." Elazar said this while knowing that it was the first time such an alert level had been declared since the Six-Day War.

---

3 State of Alert Level C—In this alert level, all IDF forces are placed in a "primed and besieged" status a moment prior to a potential outbreak of war. From this level, it is possible to return to normal or to go up to Level D (certain war at the gates). Level C calls for the mechanisms for mobilizing the reserve forces to come online and begin the emergency organization of warehouses and storage facilities to prepare for a general mobilization of reserve forces.

09:00-09:30. *The 201ˢᵗ Squadron*

After the end of the gallop, in which the battered Peugeot 404 proved that in the right hands, it was actually a racecar in disguise, Amiram Eliasaf and Kobi Hayun arrived at the gates of the 'promised land': the manning of on-alert interception four-ship formation. *Now they'll come. Syrians. Egyptians. Whatever, as long as they just come.*

At the squadron, they mostly went around in circles, and the air was humming with an eruption of guesses. *We're going on a preemptive strike, we're not going on a preemptive strike; it's serious this time, it's not serious this time; it's only Egypt, no, it's Egypt and Syria; this'll only be a day of fighting at the most, no, this will be all-out war.*

Everyone searched for a responsible adult to come along, lift up the veil, and tell them what was really happening. Since no one came, they lounged on the orange clubroom chairs with cups of coffee from the espresso machine, and started games of rummikub and bridge.

Still no one had come. "Whatever may be, let it come," said the sports addicts, "just as long as it doesn't fall on the Israel-Turkey match of the European Basketball Championship."

Huldai, the acting commander, arrived and gathered the men in the briefing room. He said, "The aircraft are armed to strike, as there is a warning that something may happen." He immediately sent everyone to go check their posts in the operations room. The formation leaders began to dive into the operation orders, and the young guys were sent to draw up maps and bring up intelligence information for the various destinations.

09:00-10:00. Office of the Defense Minister

Like every week, on Friday, the eve of Yom Kippur, the State of Israel's top security brass met in the Minister of Defense's office. The minister immediately began the morning's discussion and discussed the reinforcement of the Egyptian front, as was reflected in the intelligence briefing that arrived at his office. "You could get a stroke just by looking at the numbers," Dayan said, "their artillery has increased in numbers by 300, reaching around 1,100."

"You men are not taking the Arabs seriously," he said, as his one eye passed over the forum in front of him.

Calm, devoid of a sense of being insulted, the IDF Chief of Staff proved that he was, in fact, very serious. He updated the Minister of Defense on the discussions that were held in his office earlier. He concluded, saying, "They are reinforcing their forces on the front, they are removing the families of the Soviet advisors from both Egypt and Syria, and there is a change in the deployment of the Syrian Air Force. All of these could be signs of an offensive. On the other hand, they could also be signs of defensive maneuvers."

"I have no evidence that proves to me that these are not offensive maneuvers," Dado continued, "Therefore, I lean towards announcing a serious state of alert."

"For Yom Kippur, very well," Dayan said, withdrawing his accusations against the IDF, after he realized that he was quick to draw conclusions, and had erred.

"I don't know why the Soviets removed the women and children. I can speculate," Maj. Gen. Zeira said. "The first possibility is that the Russians know that Egypt and Syria are about to attack. The second possibility is that the Russians are afraid that we're going to attack. A third possibility is that there is some friction in the relations between the Russians and the Syrians. Perhaps there is also something in Egypt that we don't know. The bottom line is that I have no explanation as to why the Russians are doing it." He paused, and peered straight into the forum with his piercing blue eyes, and said, "Tzvika Zamir received a message from his source during the night, and it's a good source. He warned that something is going to happen, and asked that Tzvika come to meet him immediately. At ten o'clock tonight, he is going to see him…"

Satisfied with the preparedness measures taken by the Chief of Staff; informed about additional intelligence that was supposed to come from "Tzvika's Man," the most important spy in Egypt; and still visibly troubled by the intelligence gathered that morning and the evacuation of the advisor's families, Israel's Minister of Defense turned to the national assessor, to provide him with the most powerful 'sleeping pill' for the eve of Yom Kippur.

"Eli, in all of the (communications) traffic on the Egyptian lines, is there anything notable?"

"It's completely quiet," Zeira said. "There's a lot of material about the cargo (of the Soviet families) and about the exercise. Even regarding the exercise, I have a dilemma. Is it a tactical exercise without troops? A phone exercise? An exercise for the HQs? Is it an exercise with all of the forces? Until now, we have no indication as to what form this exercise is taking. Forces aren't being moved in most of the locations… I see no change in the basic assessment. I do not envision either Egypt or Syria attacking, despite the Russian exercise. However, it does raise doubts for me, and it is completely justifiable to pursue the course that the Chief of Staff has started with the raising of the alert level."

On Friday, October 5, the eve of Yom Kippur, Maj. Gen. Eli Zeira, the Head of the IDF Directorate of Military Intelligence, knowingly deceived Israel's Defense Minister.

When Dayan asked what he had asked, he was aiming for a unique source, which was referred to as the "special measures." Zeira was aware of its unique yield, more than anyone else. In the mid-1960s, when he was a colonel and the Head of Military Intelligence's Collection Department, it was Zeira who urged along with others for the creation of a new warning source, one that would outshine the contemporary measures. Furthermore, he was very pleased with the praised results that the source provided—"breaking" news about the flow of Egyptian forces into the Sinai Peninsula prior to the Six-Day War.

On Friday, October 5, Maj. Gen. Zeira was aware of the existence of "special measures" such as those that warned of Egypt's military movements in the Sinai, which were sown after the Six-Day War.

He also knew something else. In May 1973, the Egyptians exposed an antiquated "relative" of the "special measures." In light of the fall of the "relative," instructions were given to close down the "special measures" so as to prevent them from being discovered.

In the five months that passed between the exposure and the order to close down the "measures," they were activated every now and then. A "technical test" here, a "test run" there—verification that everything was still functioning properly so that, at the moment of truth, when they would be required to return to full activity, they would be able to deliver results.

In the first week of October, in the wake of the preparations for Egypt's large-scale exercise, alarming indications had accumulated. Given this and the knowledge of what was supposed to be launched in the middle of the exercise according to Soviet War Doctrine, the Collections Department's senior brass pleaded repeatedly that their senior commander, the Head of Intelligence, allow them to reopen the "measures."

Zeira had refused. As far as he was concerned, it was not yet time. The Egyptians did not intend to go to war, and it would be a shame to risk exposing the IDF's best intelligence source needlessly.

On Thursday night, Zeira finally authorized a "test run." Late at night, at exactly 01:40, the "special measures" were activated. At 11:00, they were shut down. A report concerning their activities came out at 14:00. Therefore, when Dayan asked Zeira about the communication line traffic, and Zeira answered as he did, he did not mislead the Minister of Defense on one issue, since the "measures" were actually at work at that exact moment. However, it was apparently the only "ray of light" in Zeira's conduct regarding the "special measures" since the start of the "Tahrir 41" exercise in Egypt.

This "ray of light" is also something that necessitates profound investigation. Where, for example, did the Head of Intelligence obtain the information that allowed him to proclaim at 09:00 that "all is quiet," if the summary report had not been completed before 14:00?

Why did he not bother to update the Defense Minister and the distinguished group that met in his office that it was a one-time "test run" that was underway? Furthermore, why did he not state that Military Intelligence actually had no other indications from the "measures," on account of the fact that they had remained closed until that moment?

Moreover, in the same week, prior to the "test run" held before the Eve of Yom Kippur, Lt. Gen. Elazar - the IDF's supreme commander and the man who was directly responsible for the security of the Jewish state - asked the Head of Intelligence whether or not Military Intelligence was utilizing all of its sources of information.

"Yes," Zeira said, at a time when he knew that the "measures" - Israel's most important collection source in Egypt - was not activated.

On the day before Yom Kippur, the Chief of Staff thought that the "special measures" were operating all week, since he was promised that the "measures," along with other sources, would provide at least a 48-hour warning before fire would erupt. In addition, since Zeira claimed that, "Everything is calm," even on the morning of the Eve of Yom Kippur, there was no reason to panic. It was possible to make do with just augmenting the borders with regular army forces.

The sense of security that emanated from Lt. Gen. Elazar seeped, directly or indirectly, to the leaders of the whole country: Ms. Meir, her Deputy Yigal Alon, Minister of Defense Moshe Dayan, and the legendary advisor Israel Galili. They were all convinced that the "measures" were put to use throughout the first week of October. They were not, and Zeira knew it.

Therefore, on the morning of Friday, October 5, Israel's top decision-makers were not aware of the phony 'sedative' that Maj. Gen. Zeira gave them, which potentially prevented the air raid sirens from sounding and red lights from flickering. Mobilizing the reserves, for instance.

From an analysis of the Chief of Staff's words throughout the day, it is possible to assume that the realization that the "measures" were not at work the whole week would have brought him to call up the reserve forces on Friday, even if only for a partial mobilization, and to spread them in a containment-minded defensive position along the fronts.

Why did Maj. Gen. Zeira mislead?

In October 1973, Zeira felt like the Oracle of the IDF General Staff. That was why he chose not to follow the basic elements of good administration, including not reporting the truth to superiors, for example.

Am I supposed to sacrifice our best warning system due to the quirks of the doomsayers, the laymen who are misinterpreting the moves of confrontational countries and are predicting a war that is not supposed to erupt?

Whatever the arguments may be concerning the conduct of the Head of IDF Intelligence—the man who promised to detect any attempt to surprise us at least 48 hours in advance—Maj. Gen. Zeira did not take the precautions that a person in his position was supposed to take. Thus, he was at the very least extremely negligent in fulfilling his duties.

10:00. Office of the Prime Minister in the Kirya in Tel Aviv

At the conclusion of his meeting, the Minister of Defense, accompanied by the Head of Intelligence and the Chief of Staff, rushed over to the Prime Minister to update her on the essential points.

Maj. Gen. Zeira began by presenting to the Prime Minister the information that had been gathered by Military Intelligence about the evacuation of the families of the Soviet advisors from Egypt and Syria. He also brought up several possible explanations for the actions, and concluded with saying that while an Egyptian-Syrian attack was unlikely, it was possible that the Russians thought it was likely, "since they're not so familiar with the Arabs."

In his book, *The Watchmen Fell Asleep,* Uri Bar-Joseph analyzes the poor statement of the Head of Military Intelligence: "If there is one sentence that summarizes the level of intellectual vanity, the power of self-confidence, and the contempt for other people's opinions—it is that sentence. What Zeira essentially told the Prime Minister, the Defense Minister, and the Chief of Staff was that there was nothing to worry about. Granted, the Soviets maintained a large-scale military training and consultation layout in Syria and Egypt, and Soviet military personnel were regularly present in command and control centers and in all areas of their military activities, particularly in Syria. Granted, Moscow had supplied both countries with all of their armaments for ages, and that in times of trouble, they had and would approach the Soviets to ensure that troops are sent to aid them. Granted, there was a contract of friendship and cooperation between Egypt and the Soviet Union, with a clause that required them to consult with each other in situations that posed a threat to their security. And granted, in light of all this, both client states would need to inform the patron they relied upon about their intent to go to war, as they knew that they would require its help, and might even need its army to ensure their protection. Yet despite all of this, there was nothing to worry about, since we (IDF Military Intelligence) had better information than the Soviets, understood the Arabs better than them, and knew that they were wrong if they thought that Egypt and Syria were headed towards war."

"I still don't think that they are about to attack," the Chief of Staff said, "but there is no positive proof that this isn't an offensive layout. Therefore, measures have been taken to reinforce our preparedness."

"I am still not requiring the mobilization of the reserve forces," Dado continued explaining to the Prime Minister. "In the event that Egypt and Syria decide to attack, I assume that we will receive better indications," he said, thinking of the 'special measures'.

10:00. Carmel Ridge

"Hello Etti, it's Ron Huldai. May I speak with Yair?"

"Yair isn't home," Yair's wife replied. "He'll be back by noon."

"Let him know that if he wants to do what he most loves to do with me, he needs to get to the squadron quickly."

There's nothing better than "father and son" time, Yair David, a veteran navigator of the 201st Squadron, thought to himself, while savoring the cool autumn morning and the pleasures of nature on the hiking path on the Carmel Ridge, with his young son behind him.

A few months ago, he signed up for another stint. He felt that he could not quit the Israeli Air Force as long as Itzik Fier, Menaham Eini, and Rami Harpaz, his comrades from the Endorsement

Delegation to the United States, languished in captivity while the Egyptians declared that they would never be returned.

Who's yelling my name? What is my neighbor doing here?

He was informed by his neighbor, who was sent urgently, and received Huldai's message. *What I love to do the most with Ron, even now, on the eve of Yom Kippur?* Suddenly, he understood.

He apologized to his son, and promised that they would finish their hike tomorrow, the following weekend at the very most.

11:30. Bluza (Pelusium). Sinai

Capt. Adi Benaya, a fresh reservist from 201st Squadron and a civilian pilot for Arkia Airlines, had just landed his Islander aircraft on the airstrip, and suddenly remembered that he had to hurry up and arrive for his holiday duty at the squadron.

"What's happening here?" he asked, in amazement, the lone soldier that climbed into the passenger compartment. "Where is everybody?"

"You mean you haven't heard?" the soldier asked. "There is an alert for the whole military. They've closed the departures."

Wow, Benaya thought, *An interesting Saturday is waiting for me...*

11:30. Government Meeting. The Kirya in Tel Aviv

Five ministers who resided in the center of the country were summoned to the Prime Minister's Office, where they were addressed by Dayan. "The news we received in the last 24 hours has somewhat changed the negative assessment that we had regarding the possibility of war erupting on two fronts, or only on the Syrian front," Dayan said.

"This change is significant enough to warrant summoning you to this meeting," he said to Trade and Industry Minister Haim Bar-Lev, Minister without Portfolio Israel Galili, Police Minister Shlomo Hillel, Social Welfare Minister Michael Chazani, and Transportation and Communications Minister Shimon Peres. He then ceded the floor to the Head of Military Intelligence.

"A strange thing happened tonight," Zeira said, "Eleven Russian transport aircraft arrived to the Middle East: five to Syria and six to Egypt. Our hypothesis," added the national assessor, "is that these aircraft are designed to evacuate something. Obviously not equipment, but perhaps people."

"Furthermore," he continued, "nearly all of the Russian vessels that were stationed in Alexandria have left the harbor. This has only happened once, in 1971, when there were concerns that the Egyptians would engage in the 'War of the Decisive Year.'"

"We still maintain a high probability that the Syrians and Egyptians are on alert out of a fear of us. There is a low probability that the Syrians and Egyptians intend to carry out a limited offensive strike," Zeira assured them, once again noting that "… The extraordinary thing in this whole process, the arrival of eleven Soviet aircraft to Egypt and Syria, still lacks an explanation."

"Military Intelligence's assessment, that we are not facing war and that these are merely defensive maneuvers, is an assessment I find reasonable," said the Chief of Staff, after informing the group of the readiness measures that had already been taken. "However, a layout such as this one is capable of transitioning from defensive to offensive. We do not have sufficient proof that they do not intend to attack, and we have no indication that they intend to do so. I believe that we will receive additional information should they change their intentions. We will wait for more information before we decide whether or not to mobilize the reserves (another reference to the 'special measures')."

"The situation today greatly reminds me of what transpired before June 1967, in terms of the Arabs' messages in the newspapers," said the Prime Minister, her gaze turning serious as she referred to the disinformation campaign waged against Israel in those days, which argued that Israel was the aggressor. "Perhaps this should tell us something."

Then, just before she sent them off while wishing them an easy fast, she turned her gaze to the gathered group around the table and asked, "Is all of that power standing there by the Golan Heights just intended for shelling some town?"

Her question was left hanging in the air.

Other questions hung in the air as well.

How was it possible that nine hours after the Head of Military Intelligence issued a report about the hasty evacuation of the families of Soviet advisors from Syria, not only was the issue not stressed, it was not even mentioned to the security consultation forum that met outside of "Golda's Kitchen?"

Did Zeira, Dayan and Elazar fear the "overreaction" of the former Chief of Staff (Bar-Lev) and the former Deputy Minister of Defense (Peres)? What was the motive behind the concealment of such vital information from a forum that was urgently summoned to make immediate decisions regarding Israel's preservation in light of new, troubling information? Furthermore, why was Deputy Prime Minister Yigal Alon not summoned to a meeting held with the purpose of discussing the alarming regional developments? Lastly, why was there no decision to hold a meeting with the participation of every last minister?

11:40. Office of the Prime Minister at the Kirya in Tel Aviv

"Top Secret, For the Recipient's Eyes Only," wrote Mordecai Gazit (referred to as "Motke" by his boss), the Manager of the Prime Minister's Office, at the top of the telegram that he sent to Mordecai Shalev, at the Israeli Embassy in Washington.

"A telegram will arrive shortly that will require a meeting with 'Naftali' (the code name for the US Secretary of State, Henry Kissinger). Please check to see where he is, either in New York or with you (in Washington). Please alert the Foreign Minister (Abba Eban is currently in New York). If he (Kissinger) is in New York, please accompany the Foreign Minister. If he is in Washington, please set it up alone. The meeting needs to be limited, just you and Eban, and needs to take place sometime today."

Shalev wondered, *What is this? Why the urgency?*

Noon. Refidim. A Man Named Epstein

On Friday afternoon, Maj. Giora Epstein (Aban), the Photography Section Chief in the Strike Branch, an IAF Headquarters man, joined the interception alert at Refidim.

In October 1973, Epstein was inducted into a decorated, limited, and glorified club.

Alongside names such as Ran Pecker, Yiftach Spektor, Giora Rom, Asher Shnir, Avraham Shilmon, Oded Merom, Kobi Richter, Israel Baharav and Amos Amir, the Head of the new Photography Section was crowned as one of the IAF's ten top aces, pilots who had taken down five or more enemy aircraft.

Epstein was a legend, even among the dream team. A pilot whose doomsday weapon, his sharp vision—a necessary tool for a fighter pilot in the 1970s—was at the center of tales that roused the imaginations of all the airmen.

At Refidim, he found two two-ship formations of Mirages and a two-ship formation of Phantoms.

"Comrades, there is going to be war," Col. Eliezer (Cheetah) Cohen, Base Commander, briefed the pilots who had just joined the remote alert post in Refidim.

You must be joking, Epstein thought, grinning and trusting the atmosphere at the IAF Headquarters. *There won't be any war.*

12:30. General Staff Meeting

"The likelihood of a war initiated by Egypt and Syria is still very low," the Head of Military Intelligence said at the end of an intelligence review presented to the IDF General Staff.

"I accept the assessment from Military Intelligence," said the Chief of Staff. "However, since there is not enough to interpret and the General Staff is subject to the heavy responsibility, we will take safety measures."

"The Arabs have the option of launching an attack in a very short amount of time," Lt. Gen. Elazar added, "and I have no conclusive proof that they have no intention of doing so."

"In the event of a catastrophe," Dado added, "we will need to contain them with the Air Force and with all of the forces we have on the border lines."

Just before dispersing the meeting, he fixed his gaze on the General Staff forum and said, "*Chatima Tova* to all of you. We will be ready for every situation. As you all know, we have no interest in a war, and I would really not want one to come our way as a complete surprise. This is not because I'm concerned about the final results, but that this isn't exactly the beginning that we would want. Should we get a warning that something is going to happen after 24 hours, and we will be able to get a little organized, then I'm certain that we will do our job very well. It is my hope that we will fulfill the goals of all of our future plans."

13:30. IAF Command at the Kirya Base in Tel Aviv

They had just finished a round of marathon morning meetings, when a group of senior staff officers approached the parking lot.

Will there or will there not be a war? This was the question that troubled them.

Then came Brig. Gen. Rafi Har-Lev, performing a ritual of his own—throwing his shirt collar up and back—and said, "Friends, nothing is going to happen." He got into his car, started the engine, and drove off.

Every person in that parking lot was convinced that nothing would come to pass. If this is what was being said by Rafi, the Head of the Intelligence Department, the man who knew better than everyone else, then that was a sign that the case was settled.

14:30. Sde Dov Air Base (Air Force 15)

In the large briefing room at the Sde Dov air base, named "the Igloo" due to its shape, there was a hush.

"I believe that there is going to be a war with Syria," said the IAF Commander, opening his remarks to the forum of base commanders, wing commanders, and senior staff. "This might even happen tomorrow." He paused, staring at the band of officers lining the hall, and said, "The armored forces in the Golan Heights are rather sparse. If their line is breached, I may order a strike against the Syrian forces, even before paralyzing their missile defense systems."

Col. Giora Furman, Head of the IAF's Operations Department, was the next person to speak.

"The updated plan, 'Model 5', which is intended for the elimination of the Syrian missile systems facing the Golan Heights sector, was sent to you all about three weeks ago," he reminded the forum, and presented it again with last-minute updates.

After him, Brig. Gen. Har-Lev took the stage.

"All of the signs of war are in the field," he said at the conclusion of his intelligence review of the deployment of enemy forces. Someone in the audience shouted, "Will there be a war?"

"The conditions are not ripe," Har-Lev said, "and because of this, there will not be any war."

"There will be war," Benny Peled repeated his insight during his concluding remarks, ignoring the postscript of the Intelligence Department Chief. "Make sure the aircrews go to sleep early, and get ready."

15:00. Chamber of the Head of the Command Center

Itzchak Zetelny, one of the navigators of the 201st Squadron, hobbled on his foot and passed the guard's check at the entrance to the depths of the Air Force "Pit."

A few hours earlier, he had been summoned from his home in Tel Aviv.

"I can barely move," he informed the clerk on the other end of the line, and touched his aching knee.

"We're calling everyone. Come."

"How will I get there? I don't have a car and my leg limits me."

"Go to the IAF Headquarters. Our Emergency Placements are there. Catch a ride with them."

He went.

This is rookie nonsense. He was angry at himself, recalling the unsuccessful roll he had done two weeks earlier, in an afternoon of sports. "Go home," they told him at the clinic, after wrapping the leg. "You have a problem with your meniscus. You need solid rest."

His accelerated walk down the streets of Tel Aviv did not contribute to his recovery. However, there was something urgent in the girl's voice.

He arrived. He clung to Eitan Ben Eliahu, the Deputy Commander of his squadron until two months ago, who was leaning over the maps. Furman, the Chief of Operations, was also there, and was telling everyone in the room that it was not clear what would happen, but it would certainly be a good exercise for alertness.

15:30. Office of the Prime Minister (09:30 Washington Time)

The buzz that came from the teleprinter sprang Motke Gazit from his seat.

"The meeting is set for 16:00 in New York (22:00 Israel Time)," stated Mordecai Shalev's telegrammed reply. "I've organized with the Foreign Minister and I will accompany him. I am leaving here on an aircraft at 13:00. Please confirm that this telegram has arrived."

16:00. Barcelona-Hatzor

In early October, there was a cause for celebration: the endless celebration of basketball. For the last two weeks, Barcelona, the capital of Catalonia and the second largest city in Spain, had hosted the European Basketball Championship. Just before the pre-fast meal, the Israeli national team celebrated a significant victory over Turkey's national team and finished the championship, honorably, in seventh place.

Nearly 2,000 miles east of the events, as the radio announcer Gideon Hod announced the game's final whistle, a concerto of joyous cries came from the die-hard basketball fans in the 201st Squadron.

"The team brought us a nice gift," someone said, "this is a great way to begin Yom Kippur."

16:00-19:00. Mount Canaan

Maj. Motti Kimelman, the IAF Representative in the Listening Unit of the Intelligence Corps at the summit of Mount Canaan, had already begun to plan his holiday vacation at home when he intercepted the broadcast:

"Four Syrian cargo aircraft about to take off from the Damascus military air base of Al-Mazzah."

Whoa. A flight on Friday, the Muslim day of rest?

While he tried to make sense of the change from the usual pattern, the first transport aircraft rose into the air. *What is this? And why the radio silence?*

Then, the others took off while also maintaining radio silence. They landed in northern Syria, far away from the front line.

Kimelman absorbed everything that he heard, combined it with what he knew, thought of a possible scenario, and was troubled.

He called to Maj. Abraham Benedek (Pat), the Head of the Early-Warning Section.

"Pat, the Syrians are conducting a military plot," he said. "They're afraid of our reaction, so they moved the transport aircraft far from the IAF's reach. Moreover, they left the helicopter squadron in its place. Is it possible that they are planning to land troops into our territory?'"

There was silence on the other end of the line.

"Pat," Kimelman continued, "all four of the transports flew in a state of radio silence. We can find convincing and reassuring explanations for everything else that happened, but radio silence?"

Pat heard him, said "Thank you for the update," and hung up.

17:00. Military Intelligence

As the masses in Israel finished their pre-fast meals, wrapped themselves in prayer shawls and walked to synagogues for the sanctifying *Kol Nidre* prayer, Lt. Col. Reuven Yardor, Senior Code Decrypter for Unit 848, the Intelligence Directorate's Central Collection Unit, cracked a message. According to the message, which was sent by the Iraqi military attaché in Moscow to Iraq's Defense Ministry, most of those in charge in Moscow were not willing to rule out the possibility of a combined Egyptian-Syrian attack in the coming days.

With the decoded knowledge in hand, Yardor raced to the unit commander's office, barged into the big room, waved the piece of paper in his hand and declared, "Casus belli!"

From the head of the table, he briefed the astonished commander, Col. Yoel Ben Porat, and his deputy, Lt. Col. Arie Benatov.

"This is the answer to the Soviets' behavior in Syria and Egypt," Yardor said excitedly. He passed the decoded report to the commander, who put on his glasses, read the report, looked up at the two men, and said, "This means war!"

"Did you submit a report?" he asked Yardor.

"Yes," said the senior decoder.

Ben Porat lowered his glasses to his nose and reached for the encrypted telephone.

He asked Maj. Gen. Zeira, who was on the other end of the line, "Sir, have you seen the news that arrived just now?"

He listened to the answer.

He read the news, then paused and said, "Sir, this is war."

He listened again for an answer.

"What did he say?" Benatov carefully inquired, seeing his commander's face darken.

"He told me to stop messing about," said Col. Ben Porat. The Commander of the Central Collection Unit could barely conceal his outrage. "You will deal with the news, and leave the assessment to me."

There were three factors whose combination set off warning lights for the three experienced intelligence experts.

The first was the fact a message was decoded for the first time since the start of the "exercises" in Syria and Egypt that was neither hesitant nor restrained , and according to it, war was about to erupt. Furthermore, it indicated that the war would involve Syria—whose intentions they had been worried about for two weeks—as well as Egypt.

The second factor was the source of the message: senior defense establishment officials in Moscow.

The third factor was the matter of the timing—the message came only several hours after the start of the urgent evacuation of the families of the Soviet experts from Syria and Egypt as well as the departure of the Soviet naval vessels from Alexandria.

The Head of Intelligence's conduct in light of the message that was received originated, apparently, within the "conception," and perhaps stemmed from more than just that.

The Directorate of Military Intelligence's Research Department tended to consider the Iraqi military attaché as a laughingstock. Several months earlier, he had been asked to pack his belongings and move to the Netherlands to serve in his country's attaché office. It was a significant blow to his stature, and his repeated pleas to have the decision reversed were categorically rejected.

"If the transfer is implemented, I will kill myself," the attaché wrote.

A decision was made in his country's Defense Ministry to avoid a potential scandal, and the attaché was left in his position.

This was enough for the Research Department, which deemed that the attaché was simply not reliable.

While Yardor and Ben Porat were updating the Head of Intelligence, the message circulated, as usual, to the Reporting and Distribution Center of the Intelligence Corps—the crossroads of the various message collection agencies. Maj. Ilan Tehila, Head of the Political Section of the Superpowers Wing (Wing 3), was on duty in the Research Department alongside the Research and Distribution Officer. After he finished reading the message, he started working on exactly the thing for which he was placed on duty: reducing the processes and condensing the knowledge into an emergency bulletin, to be used should the need arise.

The need arose.

He sat down and wrote a "colorful" emergency bulletin, which was supposed to be in the hands of the country's leaders in thirty minutes, an hour at the latest. He finished the bulletin, and was tempted by the 'forbidden fruit'.

He did not exercise the judgment required of an intelligence officer of his level who came across such a message—one that came at the end of a day in which Soviet families were evacuated from Syria and Egypt, and Alert Level 3 was announced for the first time since the Six-Day War. Rather than immediately distribute the bulletin to the places it needed to go, he chose to wait.

As he was among those who trusted in the "conception" that persisted within the Intelligence Directorate, according to which everything that was happening on both fronts was nothing but a false representation without any malice, Tehila was fearful of the telegram he was holding. *What if the transfer of the emergency bulletin to the Office of the Chief of Staff leads to an unnecessary mobilization of reserve forces on Yom Kippur? What will the immediate officers say, those who are belittling the feasibility of war? Perhaps it'll be better if I update them first, move the hot potato to them and leave the dilemma on their doorstep?*

He chose the second option.

17:15. IAF "Pit" in the Kirya in Tel Aviv

A dozen feet from Maj. Tehila, within in the depths of the IAF "Pit," Lt. Yonatan Lerner, the on-duty intelligence officer for the Corps, found himself staring at the teleprinter's tray.

He pulled out the sheet of paper that came out of it, and worry lines formed on his forehead.

"The families of the Soviet advisors are urgently evacuating from Syria and Egypt due to the immanent war," he said, emphasizing every word to his senior commanders on the other side of the line.

Porat inquired, "What did they say about it in Military Intelligence?"

"Let me find out."

"We are in the middle of writing the emergency bulletin," Maj. Tehila said on the other end of the line.

17:30. Ofir Air Base (Air Force 29)

As the sun's last light ran further west, painting the southern entrance to the Gulf of Eilat a vivid shade of red, the wheels of a

DC-3 Dakota aircraft struck the asphalt surface of the air base at Sharm el-Sheikh.

Two minutes later, Col. Yaakov "Yak" Navo (Milner), the base's emergency commander, emerged.

Over a small precast concrete shack, he identified two Sledgehammer teams sent on holiday alert, and they were boasting the most important weapon in the sector—16mm projectors.

"Nothing is really known, but we need to be on alert," Yak updated, and joined the screening of the classic black and white war movie "*Tora! Tora! Tora!*" about the surprise Japanese Air Force attack on Pearl Harbor.

Around midnight, after they finished denigrating the "American fools" for their Intelligence disgrace, they retired to sleep.

18:10. (12:10 Washington Time). Tel Aviv-Washington

Two hours and forty minutes after requesting that the telegram be prepared quickly to ensure its arrival ahead of the meeting with US Secretary of State Henry Kissinger, and six and a half hours after receiving assurances that an urgent telegram was already en route, the long awaited document finally reached the desk of Mordecai Shalev.

"The Prime Minister," Motke Gazit wrote, "requests that the following message be delivered to Naftali (Kissinger). Please deliver the contents in a literal and accurate manner:

1. The information gathered here compels us to consider that the military preparations in Syria and Egypt, the deployment of their forces and the state of alert that their

forces are currently in, especially the increased number of troops along the front lines, can stem from one of the following two possibilities:

a.   The *bona fide* assessment of both countries, or one of them, for whatever reason, that Israel intends to launch an attack against one or both of them.

b.   The intention of both of the countries, or one of them, to launch a military attack against Israel.

2.   If the aforementioned development along the front is a result of their concerns of an Israeli military attack, such fears have no foundation. We want to assure you (Kissinger), personally, that Israel has no intention, of any kind, to initiate a military attack against Syria or Egypt. On the contrary, it is our desire to contribute towards calming the military tension in the region. Based on this data, we hope, through your courteous office, to update the Arabs and the Soviets about our approach, in order to dispel their fears and restore the calm in the region.

3.   If Syria and Egypt are planning to launch a military attack in the region, it is important to clarify in advance that Israel will respond militarily, aggressively, and with considerable force. We would like you to bring this message to the attention of the Arabs and the Soviets through the avenues at your disposal."

20:00. The 201st Squadron

"It still isn't clear what will happen," Maj. Ron Huldai, First Deputy Squadron leader of the 201st Squadron, told the fighters of the air staff gathered in the briefing room. "All twenty-four aircraft are fueled and armed for 'Model 5'. Go to your quarters. Tomorrow morning, show up early to the Squadron. By then, we will be smarter."

20:00. Office of the IAF Commander

A few minutes after 20:00 in the evening, after returning from a commander's meeting at the "Igloo;" after finishing a marathon of conversations and updates with the base and wing commanders; after making sure that they have internalized the commander's spirit; and after convincing everyone to prepare for the following day, Maj. Gen. Benny Peled, Commander of the IAF, retired to his house in the pilots' neighborhood, Neve Rom, in the outskirts of Ramat Hasharon.

20:00. IAF "Pit" at the Kirya in Tel Aviv

For a few hours on the evening of Yom Kippur, the IAF's Operations Department was still in turmoil. The officers repeatedly went over the attack plans, because Benny kept repeating: "War is at the gate."

Except that Rafi said no. Rafi knows better than anyone. Therefore, everything was done with a 'wink'. They did everything possible to further the war plans, but "knew" that, in fact, nothing was going to happen.

23:00. Eli Zeira

Six hours had passed since Military Intelligence received the message from the Iraqi attaché in Moscow. At the end of incessant telephone discussions with senior officials in the Research Department, Maj. Gen. Zeira instructed Maj. Tehila, the on-duty officer in the Research Department, to hold off on the bulletin's distribution, as he was waiting for more information.

The Agranat Commission, which investigated the performance of the intelligence layout in the days that led to the war, later asked Maj. Gen. Zeira, "Why did you not wake the Chief of Staff?"

"I saw no reason to call the Chief of Staff at eleven o'clock at night and say, 'this message arrived' and then to add what we wrote afterwards, that the source was not the most reliable of sources and that there were mistakes..."

Zeira was involved in all of the discussions that day. He had listened as Dado explained that the main reason for postponing the decision about the reserves, despite the uncertainty about the evacuations of the families of the Soviets advisors, was the need for additional indications pointing to a war. This was an explanation that he heard repeatedly—in the meeting with the Defense Minister, in Golda Meir's cabinet meeting, and during the meeting of the IDF General Staff.

Zeira knew that the most important indication, the "special measures," was disabled. Therefore, additional indications could only have arrived from other sources, and there was the Iraqi attaché in Moscow—the place where people knew precisely what was behind the evacuation of the frightened Soviet families—stating that the reason for the evacuation was that Syria and Egypt were going to war.

Yet Zeira stated—"I saw no reason to call the Chief of Staff."

Moments Before Midnight. The 201ˢᵗ Squadron

Capt. Moshe Koren got up from the couch in his living room and announced, "We're going to sleep. Tomorrow there will be war."

The group of airmen, huddled since the early morning hours, thought, *did he go crazy? It's just an alert, like always.*

They held their cards, and continued their passionate game "prayer." They did not understand Koren's sudden whim, nor how he could he interrupt the Yom Kippur evening tradition.

He insisted. *Tomorrow there will be war. We need to sleep.*

Grumbling, failing to comprehend the meaning of the silliness that had taken hold of him, they got up reluctantly and dispersed.

Moments Before Midnight. Chamber of the Head of the Command Center

Lt. Yonatan Lerner, in the duty officer in the Intelligence Department, seized a thin piece of paper that came from the teleprinter tray, and felt the hair on his neck stand up. *The Egyptians plan to transfer passenger aircraft to Libya tonight. Tonight? Why such an urgency?*

A few hours before, the message from the Iraqi attaché was received, and then this. *The Egyptians are planning an offensive,* Yonatan thought to himself. *They know that we'll respond by striking their air bases, which sometimes have civilian airliners parked next to military aircraft.*

He called the lead trio of the IAF's Intelligence Division and updated them

They listened.

"Continue to monitor it," they told him.

Midnight. (18:00 Washington Time). Office of the Prime Minister

Just after a half-moon hung its smiling face in the eastern skies, the Prime Minister's Office received an angry telegram from Mordecai Shalev, the frustrated representative in Washington.

"Due to the delay in receiving the letter from Israel, I had to cancel the meeting that I set up with 'Naftali' in New York. At the suggestion of Rodman[4], I met with Gen. Scowcroft[5] at 17:30 (the telegram was received, in its entirety, at 16:30).

1. I handed Scowcroft the Prime Minister's statement to Naftali, as well as intelligence assessments that I received from Ephraim[6]. He promised to pass both of them immediately to Naftali in New York.

2. I added what was stated in section 4 of your message.

3. Scowcroft noted that he requested and received the US Intelligence Assessment twice today. Their opinion

---

4   Peter Rodman, Special Assistant to Kissinger.

5   Brent Scowcroft, Deputy National Security Advisor and Assistant to Kissinger.

6   Ephraim Halevi, the Mossad official in Washington.

is that these are defensive maneuvers. However, the Soviet aircraft that arrived in Cairo and Damascus have aroused astonishment. Today, they were informed of the Tupolev 22 that is on its way to Damascus.

4. I have established means of contacting him on Yom Kippur as well.

Chatima Tova."

After Midnight. England.

As the sound of the clock struck midnight, and the cool Friday in the British capital passed on to early Saturday morning, Mossad Chief Zvi Zamir understood that he was about to receive something potentially explosive in nature.

Twenty-four hours earlier, around midnight between Thursday and Friday, a lengthy telegram had been received at Mossad Headquarters in Tel Aviv. "Bear," a Mossad official in London, who had been the handler of the spy Ashraf Marwan for four years, detailed the content of a phone conversation that he had with Marwan at great length. "Our man in Cairo" said that Libyan leader Muammar Gaddafi was planning another terrorist attack on another El Al aircraft, this time in France. This was after an attempted terrorist attack against an El Al plane in Rome had been thwarted the previous month, following a similar warning.

At the end of the telegram, "Bear" added that Marwan, who was currently in Paris, would arrive the next day to London, and wished to meet urgently with Zvi Zamir to discuss the topic of "chemicals" (a code word that meant "a war alert").

In the middle of the night, Freddie Eini, the head of Zamir's office, was summoned from his home in Kfar Shmaryahu to the Mossad Headquarters. As he read the last part of the document, he realized that there was something unusual here. Marwan had met Zamir before, more than once, but it was always initiated by Zamir.

Zamir added one thing (war) with another (a precedent-setting request for a personal meeting with the Head of Mossad) and decided to call his commander, despite the late night hour.

This isn't about an alert for an immediate war, thought Zamir, as he fought off sleepiness in his study in the Tzahalah army personnel neighborhood, on the outskirts of Tel Aviv. *Marwan didn't use the code words given to him specifically for that purpose.*

A few minutes later, the phone rang again. It was the Head of Military Intelligence, Maj. Gen. Eli Zeira, informing him about the emergency evacuation of the families of the Soviet advisors.

It's true that I've not received a specific warning concerning a war, Zamir thought. *But this is the first time that "Our Man in Cairo" demanded to see me, the situation is tense on the borders, and now there's this update from Zeira.*

On the morning of Friday, October 5, Freddie Eini gleefully picked up Zamir from his home, drove him to the airport in Lod and accompanied him on the way to his flight, El Al 315 to London.

At 22:00 GMT (Midnight, Israel Time), Zvi Zamir and "Bear" walked to the meeting place, an apartment furnished in a heavy English style.

At 22:30, there was a knock on the door. Ashraf Marwan, 29, wearing a suit, exchanged handshakes with them and sat down in front of Zamir.

Half an hour later, after finishing the "small talk" about the hijacking events in Rome, Marwan stretched in his padded chair, and, getting excited, he said, "I've come to talk to you about war, nothing else."

"I've arrived," Marwan continued, his eyes fixed on Zamir, "to say that war will break out tomorrow, in a coordinated attack involving Egypt and Syria."

"Will the fate of this warning be similar to the fate of the previous warnings that you delivered?" Zamir pressed Marwan, because the spy's previous warnings passed without incident, including the previous one, "Blue-and-White" in May, which had cost the state 60 million Lira.

The spy squirmed in his chair, evidently uncomfortable, paused his display of confidence, and answered, "Sadat could change his mind at the last minute."

Just before 02:00 Israel Time, Marwan left for his hotel, and left the Head of the Mossad troubled as never before—even more than in Munich.

In October 1973, Zvi Zamir, a veteran of the Israel's battles of independence, former Head of the IDF's Southern Command and a man who did not lose his temper easily, was the 'top person' in the secret order of the Israeli Mossad. He received the appointment more than five years earlier, during the period of former Prime Minister Levi Eshkol. The five years that passed under his leadership were characterized by constant dealings with Palestinian terrorism around the world, and the Mossad's constant attempts to locate threats and thwart them. In early September 1972, Zamir was sent to try to orchestrate the release of the Israeli athletes who were taken hostage at the Munich Olympics by a Palestinian terrorist cell. The failure of the rescue operation, which was carried out against his judgment, was still seared into his flesh.

What should we do? Zamir debated. On the one hand, a report on his part about an imminent war towards dusk would have immediate, far-reaching consequences for his homeland. It would cause a huge jolt in every home in Israel: a noisy mobilization of reserve forces, thousands of vehicles pushing down the roads, people being called out of their homes and synagogues—all of it in the midst of the holiest Jewish day.

A memory of the "Night of the Ducks" fiasco passed through his mind—an erroneous public alarm for the mobilization of reserve forces, which transpired in April 1959. He knew that the Israeli elections were about to occur. It was clear to him that a false alarm would result in the dissolution of break up the Israeli government, which announced during the election campaign that "Our situation has never been better." If it would fall, so would he.

On the other hand, he weighed the accumulated information about the intentions of Egyptian and Syrian preparations for war, the update received from Military Intelligence about the inexplicable evacuation of the families of the Soviet advisors, and most importantly, the recognition that this was the first time that Marwan stated the date and time of a war. If his statement was true, Egyptian and Syrian forces would storm the strongholds on the Canal and the outposts in the Golan Heights on the shortest notice that the country had ever had. He considered over and over what he should do, while using everything from his rich life experiences.

A few minutes after 02:00 (Israel Time), the Head of the Mossad entered the office of the London station chief, took a piece of paper and a pen, sat down in a chair, and began to formulate a message.

OCTOBER 6 – MOMENTS PRIOR

For Whom the Bells Toll

At 20:00 Friday evening (Saturday, 02:00 Israel time), while residents of New York City were getting ready for a new night of excitement and fun, an emergency dispatch from Israel arrived to the US Secretary of State.

In the penthouse suite of the Waldorf Astoria hotel, Dr. Kissinger wondered, *What's with all this pressure? The intelligence services keep claiming that the concentrations of forces are part of a military exercise. I've already cleared this evening of any work and now there's this cable.*

He pondered and decided to postpone handling the matter until Saturday morning.

* * *

On September 22, 1973, Dr. Henry Alfred Kissinger stepped into the East Wing of the White House. He rested his right hand on a Bible, swore to protect the constitution of the United States against its enemies at home and abroad, and was appointed Secretary of State of the greatest superpower in the world.

For a Jewish refugee born in Germany, this was the end of a long journey that began 35 years before, when he escaped with his family over fears of the Nazi regime, just before the flamethrowers of hatred were to consume European Jewry.

Kissinger was asked, "Given your family background and your national heritage, how will you calm the Arabs with regard to US foreign policy?"

"I was called to manage U.S. foreign policy, and I will manage it without giving consideration to my personal family roots," Kissinger answered, the first Jew to serve in such a high capacity.

02:40. *Kfar Shmaryahu*

"Put your feet in cold water," he heard Zvi Zamir's tense voice on the other side of the telephone line.

"I'm awake," Freddie Eini, his bureau chief, replied.

"Start writing," Zamir ordered.

Slowly, emphatically, using the code language they agreed upon before Zamir left for London, the Head of the Mossad began dictating to his bureau chief his message:

"The company is still going to sign the contract today sometime around the evening. The contract is being discussed with the same terms that we already know. They know that tomorrow is a holiday. They think they can land tomorrow before dark. I spoke with the manager, but he isn't able to postpone due to the commitment made with the other managers, and he wants to stick with it. I'll telegram all of the terms of the contract. As they want to win the race, they are very worried that the deal will be published before it is signed and that there could be competitors, at which point some of their shareholders would have to reconsider. They have no partners outside of the region. According to Angel, there is a 99.9% chance that they will sign, but in any case, the man is like that."

Zamir asked from London, "Is everything clear?"

"Everything's clear," Freddy answered on the other end of the phone line in Kfar Shmaryahu, as he felt his heart pounding.

"Start passing it on to everyone," Zamir said.

03:00. "The Pit," Israeli Air Force

Yonatan, get up.

Lt. Yonatan Lerner sat on the edge of the bed, still not fully awake.

"848 discovered a tractor in Ismaïlia," said the soldier.

"Okay, okay," he replied to the idiot who woke him up in the middle of the night for a stupid tractor.

03:00. Kfar Shmaryahu

Freddie Eini sat at his desk, "translated" the message that he received from Zamir, passed over his calling list and started dialing.

The Head of the Directorate of Military Intelligence, Maj. Gen. Eli Zeira; Brig. Gen. Israel Lior, military secretary to the Prime Minister; Brig. Gen. Yehoshua Raviv, aide to the Defense Minister; and Brig. Gen. Aryeh Shalev, Deputy Head of Intelligence for Research.

Within an hour and a half, all of the State of Israel's top decision-makers were on their feet, without having to stick their feet in cold water. The content of the message that was read to them did not need further measures to help them get up in the middle of the night—"Our source in London is reporting that today, at sunset, the armies of Egypt and Syria will launch an all-out war against Israel."

04:25. House of the Chief of Staff, Ramat Aviv

"Tzvika's man is reporting that an all-out war with Egypt and Syria is expected toward nightfall," Lt. Col. Avner Shalev, head of the Chief of Staff Bureau, said on the other end of the line of the red telephone.

"Okay, I'm getting dressed and then I will head to headquarters," he said to Shalev, "Call the limited staff to meet at 05:30, and the commanding generals at 06:00," he hung up the phone. "That's it, Thelma," he said to his wife as she roused from sleep. "It's war."

04:35. House of the IAF Commander, Neve Rom, Ramat Hasharon

"Today, at nightfall, we are expecting an all-out war to open up with Egypt and Syria," the Chief of Staff passed the "news" to the IAF commander. "Get your people ready for preemptive action. What do you suggest?"

"I suggest that we go for the Syrian missile layout," the IAF commander responded, "and then move on to their airports."

"Start moving things along," said Lt. Gen. Elazar.

From the moment that the War of Attrition ended, IAF commanders repeatedly stressed to the leaders of the IDF and the Ministry of Defense that the Air Force aircraft would not be able to help the "greens" in the first 48 hours of an all-out war. The reason behind this was that they would first need to eliminate the enemy's missile layouts.

Furthermore, if missiles were the target, then Syria's had to go first. Major Jewish settlements within the Golan Heights, the Galilee, and the Jordan Valley would be close and appealing, targets for Syrian armored forces.

04:35. "The Pit," Israeli Air Force

Again with this annoying soldier?

"Yonatan, sorry to have to wake you up again, but I checked with 848, and 'tractor' is their code word for an SA-3 missile battery. They moved such a battery towards Ismaïlia. But this time it's not because of the tractor. The office of the Deputy Head of Military Intelligence wants you."

"Hi, Lerner," said someone on the other end of the phone line. "Get Yehuda Porat scheduled for an emergency meeting at 04:45."

Yonatan peered through the cabin door towards the big clock hanging on the wall at the foot of the stairway to the room of the head of the control center: 04:37.

Have they lost their minds? Don't they know that Yehuda's back home?

Yonatan called Porat.

"I suggest that I take your place at the office. I'll update you once you arrive."

"Okay," Porat said.

He made his way to the Intelligence Branch of the IDF.

"*Khotel* (one of Ashraf Marwan's code names) is reporting that war will break out today," Brig. Gen. Aryeh Shalev said.

"Launch the 'measures,'" Gen. Zeira instructed Col. Menachem Dagli, head of the Collection Department.

It was five days after he was approached by Col. Ben Porat, Commander of Unit 848, to activate the "special measures" and had refused his request. It was five days after he was asked by the IDF Chief of Staff if he had activated the "special measures" and answered positively. It was twenty hours after he was asked by the Defense Minister in regards to the communications traffic of the "special measures" and he answered that "everything's quiet," without informing about the meaning of "everything's quiet." At 05:00 on Saturday morning on October 6, Yom Kippur, the "measures" were finally activated. The "measures" were prepared for the specific goal that the requesting and inquiring people had intended—to prevent a surprise and to act as a warning siren for detecting the intentions of the Egyptian Army.

05:15. "*The Pit,*" *Israeli Air Force*

A few minutes after he left the office of the Head of Military Intelligence and passed the air force intelligence baton to Lt. Col. Yehuda Porat (Porty), who had just arrived from his home, Lt. Yonatan Lerner found himself in the midst of telephone alerts to officers of the IAF headquarters.

He finished another conversation, stretched, checked off another name on his list and noticed Porty, who just entered "the pit" and announced that "Military Intelligence is still adhering to the prior assessment. There is a low chance of war."

05:15. Office of the Army Chief of Staff

While one man continued alerting IAF officers, and another announced that nothing had actually changed, the Chief of Staff entered his office with a new, grim insight. *The Head of Intelligence was wrong; and he's misled, misled everyone. This is no exercise. This is war, and it is going to fall on the regular forces in the Golan and the Canal in 12 hours, maybe a bit more. The time for deliberations has passed.*

Five minutes passed, and his deputy, Gen. Israel Tal, presented himself in the office. They consulted each other over four issues. They discussed the IAF's preemptive strike, while weighing the method and scope for calling up the reserves. They agreed that if the political leadership would approve a preemptive strike, they would proceed with a covert mobilization. They then began to discuss the level of civilian alert near the country's front and in the homefront.

Ten minutes passed, and the heads of the General Staff, the Israeli Air Force and the Israeli Navy entered the office to join the urgent meeting.

The Head of Military Intelligence updated the expanding forum regarding information that arrived from "Tzvika's man," reported the telltale signs that had accumulated on both fronts, and finished his short review with a statement. "War is not necessary for Sadat, from either political or diplomatic considerations."

"Eli, let's act as if there is a war coming," Dado said to Zeira. "If the Arabs get here, and have left us only twelve hours before the outbreak of violence, then from our perspective that is a complete surprise, which is not good."

06:00. Office of the Minister of Defense

Five minutes after the IDF Chief of Staff finished briefing the commanders in his office, he already made his way to the Minister of Defense's office for an emergency meeting. In the spacious room of the man with the black patch, on the other side of a long corridor separating their two offices, Lt. Gen. Elazar found that the Defense Minister was not convinced that a war was imminent.

* * *

Israel's Defense Minister, a highly privileged former IDF Chief of Staff, a man of brilliant analytical abilities and a first-rate political mind, understood the meaning of the specific warning brought by "Tzvika's man" just in the nick of time. The warning was added to the big question mark that hovered over the evacuation of the families of the Soviet advisors. Yet Dayan had also heard Zeira's assessment that—despite all of the warning signs obtained from aerial reconnaissance missions and intercepted by the listening units—there was no logic in an Egypt decision to enter a state of war. He received the evaluations from the foreign intelligence services that stated, "everything's quiet, there won't be a war;" he remembered the ways that the previous warnings about war had ended—they did not lead to anything; and he internalized the final part of the warning that was received from London, that if Sadat would learn he had lost the element of surprise, there was a possibility that he would cancel, or at least postpone, the time of the attack.

At that moment at 06:00 on Saturday morning, Yom Kippur, two decorated fighters, devoted with all of their heart and soul to their homeland, found themselves in a state of utter disagreement.

"I'm starting to seriously consider the messages that 'Tzvika's man' gave us," said the Chief of Staff.

"Have we received confirmation from the Americans?" the Defense Minister asked.

"They are completely in the dark about this and have reached the conclusion that an attack will not take place," said Dado. He continued, "We can launch a preemptive strike against the Egyptian and Syrian airports, and we can focus just on Syria—the Syrian Air Force and the missile layouts."

"A preemptive strike is not an option," Dayan said, "especially if the Americans say that they won't be attacking."

"The Arabs will achieve a big surprise if they are going to attack tonight," said Dado. "I suggest that we tell the Americans everything that we know. It's possible that they'll tell us that all the information is correct. If the situation arises and the conditions are ripe for a first strike, I favor taking out Syria first."

"If there aren't any unexpected surprises, then that's out of the question," Dayan said. "In my assessment, even if the Americans are completely certain about the information, they would still not allow us to strike first…there will be no preemptive strike. As for a preemptive strike on Syria if the Egyptians start things first—then yes, absolutely."

Afterwards, they spoke about the issue of mobilizing the reserves.

"I want an almost full mobilization," Dado said, "200,000 men."

"In my opinion, a mobilization to that extent cannot be done given the current information," Dayan answered. "The mobilization of up to 20,000-30,000 soldiers is possible...what layout do you want to put in the Golan?"

"I want three divisions...let's say the Arabs attack, I want to proceed to an immediate counterattack."

"If we bring another division to the Golan, that should be enough. A counterattack doesn't seem necessary to me just yet."

"It's possible that a full mobilization would wreck their plans completely."

The Assistant Defense Secretary, Lt. Gen. (Res.) Tzvi Tzur ('Chara") asked, "How would you do that today, given that all of the media outlets are closed?"

"Should I decide right now, then in the evening we will consolidate forces in the evening, and enter combat by the morning," Dado replied, elegantly circumventing the question.

Dayan pressed, "How many tanks?"

"We need another 300 tanks in the Golan Heights. Even if it's just for defensive purposes, I would still call up 50,000 men."

"Throughout the whole country?"

"Yes."

"The question is what's the last possible hour, and I will need to speak with Golda," Dayan said. "We'll talk about the division in the North. What else do you need?"

"I would call up two divisions to the north, a division in the south, and a division in the center that would just consist of General Staff reservists."

"You are approaching 100,000 soldiers. The Air Force will need to mobilize as well."

"Yes, and immediately. That's pilots, ground crews, and anti-aircraft crews."

"A full mobilization for the IAF. A division to the north and to the center (apparently referring to the south)," Dayan instructed.

"What do you have in the Sinai?"

"298 tanks."

"Let's say a division in the north and one more to the Sinai. Regarding the third, we'll review the possibility tonight."

"Chara, are you in favor of this?"

"The political rationale is for it," Chara responded.

* * *

When Chara said "the political rationale," he ostensibly referred to the question of the public. What would the Israeli masses say, the people who had been exposed to the election propaganda of the ruling party from every platform proclaiming since July that things had never been better. Those who heard of upcoming cuts to the defense budget and compulsory service. Those that had already imagined the fluttering wings of a dove with an olive branch. Now this earthquake was about to occur. Suddenly, in the middle of this good life that they were promised, and in the midst of the holiest Jewish holiday, they would be called to war.

I want to be in the best shape possible tomorrow morning, the Chief of Staff explained.

"The Americans know that the Russians are hightailing it to the sea," Col. Avner Shalev, Head of the Office of the Chief of Staff, contributed his part.

"Yes, and they're saying that it's nothing," Dayan replied. "Shuli (Zeira) will come here."

"I'm in favor of requesting authorization from Golda for mobilizing a division in the north, a division in the south, and for mobilizing the IAF. That's 50,000 men," said Dayan, suddenly passing the decision onto the Prime Minister moments after it appeared that he had approved a defensive mobilization.

"I would still start a general mobilization, so that the whole world will know that we are ready for war," The Chief of Staff continued to put pressure on Dayan.

"It's possible to inform the world without mobilization."

"Should there be a war tomorrow, then we will have gained," Lt. Gen. Elazar explained once more.

"Politically, it could be harmful, since it will be said that we were the ones who were about to go to war. This is because the mobilization of reserves is an act of war."

Maj. Gen. Shlomo Gazit, the IDF Coordinator in the Territories, intervened in the debate, "Is someone coming in and counting how many you've called up?"

"I'll bring both proposals to Golda, except the bare minimum that is necessary for defense, the Golan Heights, the Sinai, and the Air Force."

"I'm in favor of a general mobilization," Dado repeated. "I'm in favor of mobilizing the fighting layout, at the very least."

"How many is that?"

"Four divisions."

"Okay, we will go to Golda with these two possibilities. It would be a huge scandal if we were to mobilize everyone. When it comes to defense, we have no choice."

At 06:37, Eli Zeira joined the discussion.

Dayan asked, "Do the Americans know (about the hasty evacuations of the families of the Soviet advisors)?"

"They know, but they aren't reacting. They say that everything is quiet. There won't be a war," Zeira repeated.

They then discussed the telltale signs and their significance, and whether or not to deploy an unmanned aerial vehicle (UAV) over the Syrian deployments. Dayan said that it would be best if they did not, since if the Syrians would succeed in taking it down, they would have an excuse to begin combat. He also mentioned the need to evacuate children from the Golan Heights and Abou Redis. A moment before he sent the negotiators on their way, when the clock pointed to 07:00, he turned to the Chief of Staff and said, "You have my approval for the Air Force, a division in the north, and one in the south."

According to the meeting's protocol, it turns out that as of 06:30 on Saturday, October 6, perhaps even a few minutes earlier, it was already possible to begin mobilizing the two initial reserve divisions that the Chief of Staff and Defense Minister agreed upon. This did not come to pass.

The Defense Minister's communicative ambiguity implied that the Prime Minister had been granted the role of supreme arbiter with regards to the mobilization of the reserve forces and the essential defense layout, on two occasions. This led the Chief of Staff to understand that any sort of mobilization, including the mobilization of the two divisions for the Golan Heights and the Sinai, would require the Prime Minister's approval.

The Defense Minister thought otherwise. He had declared on four occasions that as far as he was concerned, there was nothing preventing the immediate mobilization of the two divisions, and that the discussion in Golda's office would concern whatever would come beyond that. This is evidenced in the summary sentence at 07:00.

One way or another, the two luminaries of the Israeli defense structure, those entrusted with Israel's protection and wellbeing more than anyone else, had already failed in the early hours of Saturday morning to correctly read and understand the crisis that was at their doorstep. Dayan had not verified that the Chief of Staff comprehended the conclusion of their discussion and understood that it was possible to begin the partial mobilization of reserve forces. Dado, the visibly worried man, did not explore the meaning of Dayan's closing remarks, did not repeat his demand, and did not begin the immediate mobilization. Thus they both waited for Golda, for the meeting that was scheduled for 08:00.

06:00. On the Premises of the Flight School in Hatzerim

What's with the siren?

Exhausted from the turbulent card games that they played until the third morning watch, the air crews jumped to their feet, were briefed by the base headquarters about the elevated state of readiness within the Air Force and were tasked with making their way to their Operational Squadrons quickly.

06:05. The 201ˢᵗ Squadron

"Get to your squadrons immediately," the operations secretary's voice was heard, unambiguously, on the other end of the phone in the residential compound. Afterwards, she entered the alcohol-soaked club, a room cloaked in darkness with mattresses strewn about the floor. "Everyone, wake up," she ordered the group of crewmen who were snoring deeply. "Get organized and then get to the briefing room immediately."

06:05. Head of the Control Center Chamber

"Send a Skyhawk to alert all the Air Force crews," Lt. Col. Oded Erez, the on-duty head of the Control Center, instructed Col. Amichai Shmueli (Shumi), the commander of the Hatzerim air base.

A few minutes later, in sharp contrast to the normal, sleepy Saturday protocol, the chamber of the control center was filled with the bustling of the top brass, and Lt. Col. Erez was able to address the issue for which he was at the Air Force HQ—in the capacity of Head of the Defense Branch.

"Engage the 'rock' deployment plan," he ordered the Anti-Aircraft Defense Officer, Col. Meir Shariv, thus preparing the air-surface defense layout for all-out war.

"Raise the readiness," he instructed the Air Force squadrons, and verified that they were all applying the new readiness level—a two-ship formation in immediate takeoff standby, and a two-ship formation in 15 minutes standby.

Finally, he turned to the air control units. He made sure that they received the war alert command, and that they had begun to reinforce themselves with reserve forces and entered a state of high alert.

06:45. *The 4th Wing (Hatzor)*

"The Egyptians and Syrians will start a war at 18:00," Col. Amos Lapidot, Commander of the 4th Wing, reported to the operational forum that had convened in his office. "Golda is pressing to get US approval for a preemptive attack in Syria. We are making preparations to proceed with operation 'Model 5', striking missiles in Syria."

"Engage the siren," Lapidot ordered one of the staff officers.

At 06:52, the wail of the siren tore through the sanctity of Yom Kippur at the 4th Wing.

"We'll go down on foot," said some of the religious soldiers of Capt. Benzi Nahal, Technical Officer of the 201st Squadron. They were reluctant to desecrate the sanctity of Yom Kippur by riding the trucks that showed up to take them.

What should we do with this problematic announcement? Benzi wondered, noting that he was not all that surprised with the siren. After all, he had sensed on Thursday that something strange was brewing. *The work of the righteous is done by rabbis,* he smiled to himself, watching as the Rabbi of the base raced from the entrance of the synagogue. With the veins on his neck swelling and his face flushed, his vocal chords screamed towards the conscientious objectors of the trip. "Get on the trucks immediately and get down there, it's *Pikuach Nefesh*[7]!"

07:00. Office of the Air Force Commander

A few minutes before 07:00, the senior staff of the Israeli Air Force met in the general's office.

"Sometime towards the evening, a war is going to break out with Egypt and Syria," Maj. Gen. Peled updated those present. "I've recommended to the government that we launch a preemptive strike in Syria. 'Model 5', with the H-hour at 10:30-11:00."

During the briefing, he was interrupted by the phone ringing.

"Low morning clouds will cover the area until the afternoon," the on-duty Forecast Officer announced.

"Understood."

"What about clouds deep in the territory?"

"Clear skies," the Forecast Officer replied.

"Stop 'Model 5', let's move to 'Header XI'."

Gen. Peled called Dado, told him about the issue of cloud coverage over the Syrian missile batteries, and requested permission to change priorities. They would start with the Syrian air bases.

"Received," Dado answered.

Why was it decided to attack the Syrian air bases in particular?

On October 6, 1973, the IAF HQ did not attribute any great importance to the Syrian Air Force. It was said that in a war, should

---

7   A Jewish principle that defines the saving of lives as overriding any other religious considerations.

one would even erupt, President Assad's aircraft would play a marginal role amid the numerous threats facing Israel. The missile batteries were the main enemy, and the IAF trained over the course of three years specifically in order to deal with them. The batteries represented the biggest threat to the IAF's aircraft and their ability to affect the course of the battle. Clouds above the missile batteries? It is possible to wait a few hours, delay the H-Hour, and let the morning clouds—a familiar sight at the Golan Heights—fade into a welcoming blue sky. It was also possible to go for a sure thing: the Egyptian missile system. On Saturday morning, the weather conditions along the Canal were gracious and hospitable.

Furthermore, the destruction of Syrian aircraft on the ground would be no small matter: the airports were defended by AAA batteries, and some of them were even defended by missiles. As a result of the lessons learned in the Six-Day War, the aircraft were stored under an impermeable concrete shelter, and the runways—another take-away from Operation Focus (the destruction of Egyptian Air Force aircraft on the ground at the onset of the Six-Day War)—could be fixed in a short period of time.

So why did the IAF Commander decide to attack the Syrian air bases? How was it that the operational forum that was at his side did not try to dissuade him from his decision, nor brought other potential targets to the table?

07:15. Operations Room, Hatzor Base

The 4th Wing commander's red phone began to ring.

"Understood," Col. Lapidot responded, his constantly flushed face a hot crimson. "Yes, we will organize ourselves accordingly."

"IAF Headquarters is reporting that the H-hour for the intended operation is supposed to have heavy cloud coverage over the missile batteries," Lapidot said to the commanders in his office. "'Model 5' is cancelled. We are proceeding with 'Heading XI'. The new task commands are on their way. All wing aircraft are to prepare themselves to participate in the attack. Return to your squadrons and get ready. Let's hope we get the long-awaited approval."

07:15. The 201ˢᵗ Squadron

"Gili, get up, I hear a siren"

"Forget it," Gil Regev urged his new bride Nurit. "It's just the increased alert for the holidays." He went back to sleep.

"Gili, get up, it's serious. There are cars and a lot of noise outside. Maybe you should call the squadron?"

Gil called.

"Everyone's here. Get down here immediately."

07:15. Office of the Chief of Staff

As a soft western wind rolled through the sleepy streets of Tel Aviv, the General Staff gathered in the Chief of Staff's office.

Maj. Gen. Zeira began by describing the latest developments on the border, expanded with regard to the Egyptian and Syrian plan of attack by land and air, and ended with a sales pitch. "While signs on the ground indicate preparation for war, politically it seems unlikely."

Lt. Gen. Elazar briefed the group on the discussion that came up in the Defense Minister's office and presented the stages of the war as he saw it in his mind: the containment stage would continue from Saturday evening through Sunday. These 24 hours would mostly be a war for the IAF. The concentration and organization of the recruited forces would occur Monday, Tuesday, and Wednesday. Afterwards, the IDF would conduct its counterattack.

"We need to check all of the operational arrangements of the regular forces," Dado added, "before calling up the reserves." He then went immediately to a short briefing of two commanding officers. "Fit the operational plans to the current situation," he said to Maj. Gen. Shmuel Gonen (Gorodish), Head of the Southern Command, and to Maj. Gen. Yitzhak Hopi (Hakah), Head of Northern Command. "Get back to me in the afternoon for summary command group."

07:45. Ofer Sharabi

A Skyhawk in the Yom Kippur skies?

Ofer Sharabi, a smiling, observant Yemeni Jew, discharged the prior year from the Air Force, former "child" (Sergeant) in reserve operations at the Routine Operations Branch, stopped at the gates of the synagogue.

Something's brewing, he murmured in amazement. *Why is the Skyhawk in the sky? May God forgive...*

He headed home.

"Ofer, where are you?" the worried voice on the other end of the line asked. "We've been looking for you since yesterday. Get yourself together and get to the 'Pit.'"

07:55. Office of the IAF Commander

"Rafi, I'm sending you to head the Air Force Command post in the North," the IAF Commander said to Col. Rafi Savron. For the last five days, Savron had been the Commander's personal assistant, attending to the budgets and housekeeping, a praised combat navigator in his past, and the Head of Joint Forces Operations Branch until about five months before.

08:05. Office of the Prime Minister

A few minutes after 08:00, in the small, renovated Templar house, a three minutes' walk from the offices of the Defense Minister and the IDF Chief of Staff, the meeting that was supposed to decide the fate of the alert from "Tzvika's man" began.

"We cannot allow ourselves to go on a preemptive strike," the Defense Minister began, "but the moment that they begin, we can immediately attack. Including in Syria, even if the Egyptians attack alone."

"The Chief of Staff wants a bigger reserve mobilization than I suggest," Dayan continued. "I'm reluctant. I am all in favor for a full Air Force mobilization, as well as one division each in the Golan Heights and the Sinai. Fifty to sixty thousand soldiers. If things get worse and fighting intensifies, then we will mobilize the entire system."

"I read the cable from 'Tzvika's Man," Dado said, reacting to Dayan. "It's an authentic message. For us, this is an incredibly short warning. If they attack in ten hours, the regular army is maximally prepared."

"Until now, the reserves have not been called," Dado continued, "I would like to call up 200,000 soldiers. If not, than at least 70,000 to 80,000. It won't matter to the world if we raise 70,000 or 200,000, but perhaps the Arabs will be deterred. Even if they say that we called up reserves in order to start a war, they had better say that we started it and we will win. They will say it anyway. I'm all for the big mobilization."

"A preemptive strike is, of course, a huge advantage," Dado added, "it would save many lives. We are able to destroy the entire Syrian Air Force today at 12:00. We will need another 30 hours to eliminate the missile system. It's a very tempting operation. It's not necessary to make a decision on this issue right now, there are about four hours in which we can discuss the matter with the Americans...Perhaps by noon, the Americans will also say that there certainly will be an attack, so we'd be able to go through with the preemptive strike. A preemptive strike on Syria, today before noon, is what affords us the best chance of winning."

On the morning of Yom Kippur on the Jewish year of 5734, 27 years after his enlistment to the Palmach; 12 years after commanding the Armored Corps; nine years after being appointed as the Head of Northern Command; four years after being appointed the Head of Operations; and 21 months after receiving the title of IDF Chief of Staff, Lt. Gen. David Elazar (Dado) was no novice in understanding political, military, and interpersonal processes.

This is why a short time after 08:00, in the office of the Prime Minister in the Kirya base, the Chief of Staff realized that his chances of obtaining the political approval needed for a preemptive strike were slim. Very slim.

Shortly after 06:00, he had already heard Dayan's opposition; he knew that the Prime Minister and the other senior state officials of the country believed that the Western nations would not tolerate another Israeli preemptive strike against its neighbors. He understood that, in a dilemma between his opinions and those of Dayan, the opinions of the head of the Jewish State's Ministry of Defense would be preferred.

Yet Dado would need that preemptive strike, and desperately.

On Saturday morning, Lt. Col. Elazar's own words were still fresh in his memory; that if we would be surprised without receiving adequate warning, and following that, that the reserves would not be ready at the fronts prior to the eruption of hostilities, then the regular army would have to handle things. Alone. Without any problems. For 24 hours. For 48 hours.

Yet on that very morning, in those very minutes, a chilling realization began to seep into the mind of the IDF's top soldier: that Israel was already in trouble.

Nine Egyptian divisions, with 1,340 tanks and tens of thousands of soldiers, were situated near the Canal, and faced 300 tanks and a few hundred Israeli soldiers on the opposing side.

Five Syrian divisions, with 1,030 tanks and tens of thousands of soldiers, were stationed near an anti-tank ditch, and faced 180 tanks and a few hundred Israeli soldiers. Could the regular army really hold them all back?

"If we act according to the second possibility, that of a parallel (Egyptian-Syrian) attack," said the Chief of Staff, finishing his last attempt to paint a grim future with no preemptive strike, "we will not be able to strike the missiles today. They will be able to land a penetrating attack here and there. There is no seal. They would be able to attack large targets."

"With regards to a preemptive strike, how much warning time do you need?" asked MK Israel Galili, planting a renewed hope in Dado.

Hanging by the end of a rope that was dropped to him by the secret and legendary advisor to Levi Eshkol and Golda Meir, the Chief of Staff tried once more to steer the War Cabinet in his favor. "We will be ready to engage at 12:00. Between the Air Force and the missiles, we would need three hours [to prepare the aircraft after the operation to destroy the Syrian Air Force and the operation to engage the missile systems]. The Air Force will take from 12:00 to 16:00. After 13:00, it will be impossible to make a sufficient strike on the missiles." The selection of 16:00 as the last hour to set out for a strike was a direct result of the total operation time (about an hour), with sunset at 17:15 and the attack aircraft's inability to commit surgical attacks, as is required for such a strike, after darkness has fallen.

"What is our capacity to know what is going on?" Golda asked, trying to gather additional data before having to make a decision.

"We know what is going on," the Head of Military Intelligence explained. "They can go on the offensive at any moment. Their front layout is suitable for both defensive and offensive maneuvers. Right now, there are signs of an offensive. They are technically and operationally ready for war, according to the plan that we are aware of."

Just then, as was always the way of such a national barometer, Maj. Gen. Zeira completed his ordered doctrine and carved his summary into the ears of those present: "Despite the fact that they are ready, in my opinion, they know that they would lose. Today, Sadat is not in a position that would necessitate his going to war. Everything is ready, but there is no necessity."

"Maybe we can influence what Sadat will do or decide," Zeira added, "what will deter him is our reserve mobilization and a dispatch sent to him via the Americans—'We know what you are planning. We are warning you. We are waiting. There are no surprises.'"

Once again, it was Galili that pulled the end of the rope that was thrown In the conference room, this time from the Head of Military Intelligence, and he reminded everyone that "Tzvika's source did say that a war could perhaps be prevented through a leak indicating that 'we know'. Tzvika even supports it."

The Defense Minister, as usual, focused the discussion, called everyone to order, and proposed that they decide on the major issues that the meeting was called to address.

"This [calling up the reserves] will have an impact on the economy tomorrow," Golda said, "if there is war, it's not a catastrophe." She then added, "If there is war, we won't understand why there was a 12 hour delay."

"As for a preemptive strike," Golda added, "the heart desires, but we'll see."

She then returned to the advice given by Marwan, Zamir, Zeira, and Galili, "Why don't we accept the advice of this friend (Tzvika's man), and inform everyone by way of the BBC, CBS, and others that the Russians are vacating Syria and Egypt? Why not give them our assessment as to why they are doing it, and then leak to the news agencies that we know what is happening on the borders, thus destroying Egypt and Syria's illusion of surprise?"

No one answered the Prime Minister, and she did not push it. The question dissipated in the air, and Dayan once again returned Golda to the pressing matters.

"If you authorize a full mobilization, I will not resign," he said, adding that in his opinion, a division in the north, one in the south, and the whole Air Force was more than adequate. "If it seems by nightfall that we need more, we'll call up more," Dayan continued. He then went on to explain that his resistance to a full mobilization stemmed from the apprehension that the mobilization of the entire reserve layout would lead the media to claim that Israel was the aggressor.

"The US assertion is that the situation is merely defensive," Dayan said. "Our assessment changed when we saw the Russians begin to leave. The Americans have no explanation for that. One way or another, it can't be ruled out that if we call up everyone, even the Americans will say 'well, there wasn't going to be a war, but the Israelis pushed it.'"

"It's not like in 1967," Dayan continued his explanation. "The war will begin in Suez and in the Golan (meaning better starting positions for Israel). It's extremely important it will not be said that we started it."

"We'll go according to the *Hashomer Hatzair* book," the Prime Minister said, "in stages. First of all, a mobilization, over which there is no doubt."

At 09:00, Lt. Gen. Elazar ordered his aides to leave the meeting and to begin to put the mobilization of two reserve divisions into motion - a process over which there were no more differences of opinion since 06:30.

"I'm willing to compromise and settle for an incomplete mobilization," Dado said, "on the condition that they will grant me approval for four armored divisions as well."

"Even half of that is enough," Dayan argued again, "it's better to start modestly, with all the difficulties entailed."

"What difficulties?" Golda asked, attentive to the nuances in the Defense Minister's explanation, wanting to know more about the situation.

"That we'll to handle containment on the fronts with fewer forces, and it will be more difficult for us to mobilize more in the middle of a war," Dayan answered.

"I have only one standard," Golda said, "if there really will be a war, we need to be in the best condition possible…It's better if everyone gets angry at us if it means having our situation be better. No one will be able to count exactly how many soldiers we call up…If there will be a war, we really need to be in the best situation possible."

"The 'best situation' means a full mobilization," Dayan said.

"So long as there will not be a situation where the first blow will hurt us more than if we had additional forces at the ready," Golda concluded her insight on the mobilization. "If there is a war, then we must make ourselves the least vulnerable. As for the preemptive strike, we won't be able to explain that one sufficiently, but we will see how the day goes. If the Egyptians open fire, and the Syrians don't join in, we will strike Syria anyway."

They all said 'amen', and trusted what the old woman said, while adding that if the situation were reversed, with the Syrians striking and the Egyptians doing nothing, it would be possible to strike Egypt.

At 09:20, the Defense Minister turned the Prime Minister's words into reality, and determined: "The Chief of Staff is to mobilize the whole layout as he has proposed [four divisions]"

09:00. *The Air Control Unit at Mt. Meron*

In the Air Control Unit at Mount Meron, life seemed sweeter than ever the morning of Yom Kippur. Outside, with the autumn sunshine dotting the October sky, the mountain had just been reinforced with reservists, primarily, and shouts of joyous reunions sounded like the singing of angels, in the ears of Capt. Yair Kafri, the on-duty officer.

Kafri, the veteran fox, assumed that it was one more alert among many, and on that would be cancelled soon, as always. In the meantime, he allowed himself to drift into ecstasy, nostrils flaring and filled with the scent of fish roasting on the fire.

09:00. *Ofira*

The ringing of the telephone startled Capt. Amir Nachumi out of his Yom Kippur nap in his bed, not far from the blue water of the Gulf of Sharm el-Sheikh.

"Give me the person in charge of the 107th Squadron," someone from Air Force's Operations Department requested.

"There's no one here," Nachumi answered.

"Understood," the guy from operations answered, "Take five (five-minute takeoff alert)."

Nachumi called his squadron, updated his commander about the call from headquarters, and he was reminded that he was still not accredited to lead a two-ship formation of interceptors.

"You are now qualified," Yiftach Spector, his commander, answered.

09:00. The 101st Mirage Squadron, Hatzor

"A high-altitude reconnaissance mission in Egypt has arrived to the squadron," announced Maj. Avi Lanir, commander of the first Mirage squadron in the IAF, to Capt. Mickey Katz, who had rushed into his room.

"This is a very important mission. Get organized."

Katz took the task order, settled into the map room, and drew out his flight path.

The phone rang.

"There's been a change," Lanir said, "Syria is the destination. The timetable stays the same." Katz threw out the Egyptian maps he had been working on to the corner of the room, took the updated task order, and began to prepare the maps for the Syrian mission.

Uncharacteristically, he was excited. A veteran pilot, with an impressive track record, on a reconnaissance mission across the Middle East. He knew that the IDF was on high alert, and that the Syrians and Egyptians, with their malevolent missile systems, were poised as tightly-wound springs at the borders, ready to burst forth. He put on his white 'astronaut suit', and got into the Mirage. Shahak tail-number 98, of course.

He rested his foot on the ladder, when suddenly he received a frantic phone call: "It's not Syria," they told him on the other end of the line, "it's Egypt after all."

"Get back to the squadron," he ordered the bus driver. In the photography room, the maps he had thrown away were still sitting there. "Bring them here, hurry, hurry."

He got them. He climbed up. Drove. The runway lights turned green. He set the timer, released the brakes, raced forward, pulled up, folded in the wings, grabbed the map with his left palm and glanced at the creases in the order, while flying with his free hand.

He was calm. He established radio silence, preserved the 98, played the part of the favorite photographer, getting as close as possible to the sands of the Sinai, just under the prying eyes of Egyptian radar.

He hit 420 knots. No need to rush; need to save fuel. At the pre-planned waypoint in the Sinai sands he accelerated up to 540 knots, and kept up the airspeed to the pull-up point. He jettisoned the external drop tanks from the wings; pulled up to increase altitude; and broke radio silence. "Flag One is pulling out," he announced to air traffic control at Refidim. "Copy, authorized."

He pulled the control stick to his belly; 36,000 feet; he leveled out; Mach 1.8, almost twice the speed of sound. South of the Suez Canal, he penetrated the Egyptian border, high above the SAM system and the AAA.

All of the sudden, the center of the RWR display to his right started flashing in strobes, and constant audible warning tones deafened him. *No one in Egypt slept on Yom Kippur*, Katz thought, as he jettisoned the supersonic centerline fuel tank. Now, that the aircraft was clean, he climbed to 60,000 feet, and intercepted the leg start waypoint.

A deep blue sky, with him within it, with aircraft number 98. He knew that he could not screw around. Someone was waiting impatiently for his photographs. He stabilized the aircraft, and maintained a precise route. He got into the routine of high-altitude flying. He enjoyed what the Earth has concocted for him—the Mediterranean Sea; the Sinai; Egypt's eastern desert; the Delta; the Nile. What a beautiful world.

He climbed even higher, to 70,000 feet. His Zeiss camera continued clicking with a dutifully Prussian rhythm. Facing Port Said, he turned off his camera, turned right, lowered the nose, and started to glide in idle engine setting, all the way back to Hatzor.

What's this? He had never seen hardened aircraft shelters with so much equipment and so many people. He opened the canopy and climbed down the ladder. Suddenly, he understood everything: Avi Lanir who emphasized the importance of the mission, all of the warnings during the flight, and now all of these soldiers from the IAF Intelligence Technical Services unit…

"Thank you so much, Mickey," his beaming commander said. "You did exactly what I wanted you to do."

* * *

The photographs that Mickey Katz, his Mirage and his German Zeiss camera brought in the morning hours of Saturday, October 6, left no doubt as to the Egyptian's true intentions—their military forces were outside of their camouflage nets, located at linked starting points at the crossing point of the Canal.

These photographs, which would land in the hands of Israel's leaders within the next few hours, would add another significant pin into the balloon of illusions being held by IDF Military Intelligence.

09:30. *The 201ˢᵗ Squadron*

The briefing room of the 201ˢᵗ Phantom Squadron was packed: regulars, emergency forces, reservists. Capt. Dani Haloutz, a fresh reservist, arrived by hitchhiking, without bringing underwear or even any toothpaste. It was just another day of battle, sure to be finished in the evening. Maj. Eli Zohar came with textbooks from Bar-Ilan University: *between all of the briefings, I'm sure that I'll find time to study for the statistics exam.* Within the buzzing human hive, everyone waited for someone to show up and remove all of the mystery as to why they were called up in the first place. Ron Huldai then walked in.

"We need to hit the Syrian kettle before it boils over," said the acting squad commander. "War is going to break out at some point into the evening." Pausing for a moment, he stared out into the crowd in front of him and added, "we need to get ahead of them, we'll smack them with a preemptive strike. The squadron will strike the T4 air base. Time of arrival over target is 12:00. You will find your placements at Operations. The aircraft are already fueled and armed. Start getting ready."

On Saturday morning, the deputy commander of the 201ˢᵗ Squadron, Maj. Ron Huldai, was sure that the Egyptians and the Syrians wouldn't really start a war, but they would try something. Some sort of clash with all the bells and whistles, an escalation to help their political processes. More than anything, he was sure of his Air Force.

Huldai, the new deputy commander of the first Phantom squadron, was happy. Although Zemer, the squadron leader, was also in the area, Huldai didn't feel pressured. Why should he? He is quite the people-person. He looked around and checked out his men: Amnon Gurion, Adi Benaya, Eitan Peled, Eli Zohar, Dani Haloutz, Yair David, Amiram Talmon. Experienced, calm, and trustworthy. They will be right by his side.

Itzchak Zetelny, young in age but a widely respected pilot, found himself embedded in the combat management team.

He issued the "Header XI" plan from the vault and began to update it with regard to the mission orders he'd received, continually rising out of the teleprinter, the metal fountain flowing in operations.

Arik Shlain and Nimrod Amami, the youngest navigators in the squadron, were sent to the chart room to do what all young navigators are supposed to do: hover over a series of 1:250,000 maps covering the whole floor with like a Middle-Eastern carpet: Israel, Lebanon, Syria, and Jordan.

They pinned the four maps to one another. They placed black carbon paper between them. They began to sketch the path that leads to the T4 air base. First of all, the direction. They navigation route legs according to the required headings. Now they wrote at the top of each leg its magnetic heading in degrees, adding the decreasing distances, and accumulating times, as well as the designated airspeed. Then remaining fuel and altitude AGL (Above Ground Level). An acceleration point. And pull-up point for strike.

The upper map, the most clear of them all, would be given to the four-ship formation leader. Oops. The last copy was hard to read, needs to be sketched again. Oops. The maps did not overlap each other. Again, from the beginning.

"Here are all of the aerial photographs of the attack site," the intelligence officer said. They attached them to the maps. There, all done. Good luck to everyone.

They left the chart room, passed by the window of the operations room, which was in its typical condition: air crew members sitting about and looking at their assignments. A surprise: Amami was assigned. The last convoy of aircraft, but still, he was assigned. Very surprising, as after all, he still was not authorized for flight operations.

He raised his chest, as if an operational flight was second nature for him. But inside, concern bubbled through him. He had never crossed the border. Still, "this thing" seemed as neat and organized as 1967 to him. The confidence of veterans from the Six-Day War and the War of Attrition was exhibited in all directions. This was child's play.

Then Yigal Shochat arrived. A legless pilot from the War of Attrition, he explained that all "senior citizens" in Be'er-Tuvia were taking out their old, rusted farm "recoilless gun jeeps" and recruiting themselves up for reserve duty. He said that everyone's confidence was going through the roof, as even the town elders were getting ready for war.

09:45. Office of the Chief of Staff

"At this juncture, there is no authorization for a preemptive strike," the Chief of Staff told the Air Force Commander as he left the 'war cabinet', "though nothing is final. Continue your preparations."

"The latest time in which we could effectively launch a preemptive strike is 16:00," Peled repeated to Elazar. "The strike alert needs to be in my hands no later than 15:00."

"In addition," Peled added, "if it is decided not to go through with the strike, the Air Force needs to change its aircraft from attack to clean configuration for defense. Notify me by 13:00 at the latest."

10:15. Office of the Prime Minister

Half an hour after the end of the meeting, the Israeli Prime Minister met with Kenneth Keating, the US Ambassador to Israel, who was summoned urgently to a face-to-face meeting (Simcha Dinitz, Israel's Ambassador to the US, who was called back to Israel due to the death of his mother, also sat in the meeting).

After the usual greetings and preliminaries, Golda got to the main point.

"We may be in trouble," she began the monologue, and continued, informing the ambassador about all of the decisions that were reached in her office. "All indications suggest that Syria and Egypt intend to begin a war against Israel," Golda said. "This attack is scheduled for sometime this afternoon, and the IDF intends to ward it off."

"For the last ten days," the stunned ambassador informed the Prime Minister, "there were regular contacts between the embassy in Washington and the IDF, and it had been clear that these were just defensive deployments. Just yesterday," he added, "Washington was sent a list of inquiries. The answers indicated that that was still shown to be the case (that they were defensive preparations)."

"I'll narrow the gap between Israeli and US intelligence," Golda replied. "We also thought that Egypt was conducting a large-scale exercise at first, but according to our sources, it seems that they intend to cross the Canal and launch a general strike."

"On the basis of reports in your hands, will Israel strike before they will?" Keating said, agitated.

"No," the Israeli Prime Minister replied, as she leaned forward, continuing in excellent English. "Even though it would be much easier for us, and despite all of the information that we have accumulated, Israel will not strike first. This is so that the United Stats and the world will not doubt which party started this war."

"Therefore," Golda said, "it is important to us that the US will do everything in its power to prevent this war on both fronts. Israel also requests to inform the Russians and the Egyptians, through your auspices, that we do not intend to start a war, but we are ready to repel their attack. It's important that they know that they can't surprise us, and that we have no doubt that we will win."

"The United States should not take our mobilization of our reserve forces as a sign of aggression," she concluded. "We must take the necessary protective measures. The reserve mobilization is the minimum that is required."

At 10:30. the US Ambassador left the Prime Minister's office, and his face went pale. Right in front of him, in the name of political and state relations, the State of Israel declared, through its Prime Minister, that it was ready to pursue the necessary steps.

11:00. Bunker of the Head of Central Command

What's happening outside? Maj. Eitan Ben Eliahu wondered from the IAF Control Chamber at the command bunker, deep underground in the Kirya base in Tel Aviv.

Suddenly, he thought about the War of Attrition. He recalled his intense frustration at the world on two separate fronts: the home front, which continued living its regular life; and the front in which young soldiers were constantly in the midst of the storm. Here we are again, only this time, someone projected the film backwards: the home front was at war, while everything was relatively calm in the command center. Telephones were ringing, and ringing, without stopping, and with every call was another person volunteering to mobilize with the reserves.

What's going on outside that we don't know about in Central Command?

At 11:00 AM, cut off from daylight, Maj. Ben Eliahu was not aware of the new reality that was transpiring in citizen's homes and synagogues, filled with worshipers, whose calm was interrupted by recruitment squads. Starting at 09:30 AM, the roads of the country were overtaken by the rumblings of noisy traffic, and Yom Kippur, much like Maj. Ben Eliahu, refused to accept the shattering of what was holy in the sand.

11:00. The Senior Command Post ("The Pit")

Buried within tons of reinforced concrete, the "Pit" was the place from which the country's military leaders were supposed to manage the state's emergency operations. And war knocking at the gates was the biggest emergency scenario of them all.

At 11:00 AM, the Defense Minister went down into the "Pit" and joined the IDF officials—the Chief of Staff, his deputy, various department heads and branch commanders. "What can the IAF do tonight?" Dayan firmly questioned.

"If we estimate that the crossing locations are known," the Air Force Commander said, "then we are capable of jettisoning the bombs on the other side and causing a serious commotion."

12:00. The 200ᵗʰ UAV Squadron

A bit before 09:00 AM, a convoy of trucks, carrying 16 decoy UAVs, known by the codename "furrows," (based on the model BQM-74A (Chukar) jet powered target drone), six launchers and other support equipment, went on its way to the Dalton airstrip in the Galilee. Maj. Shlomo Nir, the commander, led in a truck, followed by the rest of the convoy. They were alone on the road, with traffic lights flickering away at them, the whole way to the Galilee. By the midday, they had arrived to the airstrip, high in Ramat Dalton, a stone's throw from the settlement that gave it its name and the picturesque settlement of Gush Halav. On the horizon, about three kilometers away, overlooked Mount Meron, and the antennas of the Air Control Unit sticking out on top.

They placed the six launchers in their positions and connected a field-telephone to the line connecting the field with the switchboard at Mount Meron. Hallelujah.

* * *

The 200th Squadron, a highly classified unit that was known to only a few within IAF headquarters and which settled at the beginning of the 1970s at the Palmachim base, specialized in two fields: reconnaissance UAVs (drones) and decoy UAVs.

In 1972, the unit established three launch sites for decoys: one at the Dalton airstrip, and two in the Sinai.

The tiny decoy UAV, about two meters long, codenamed "furrow," was pre-programmed for each mission, so that the flight profile effectively mimicked that of a real strike fighter. The decoy was meant to mislead the radar of the enemy's missile batteries—to cause them to see the decoy as a strike fighter, to lure the missile batteries to launch at them, thus exposing the positions of the batteries to the real strike fighter, which were supposed to emerge immediately after it.

12:00. Cabinet Meeting

Armed with the photos taken by Mickey Katz in his Shahak 98, which covered the basics—Egyptian artillery units removed from their covering installations; concentrations of life jackets; bridging and fording equipment; APCs and tanks along the waterline—the Defense Minister left the command post. From there he entered into what would be the most exceptional cabinet meeting ever—on the afternoon of Yom Kippur, twenty-one ministers, most of whom were early, saw on their way that their official cars were not alone. Dozens of cars raced on the roads, most of them in Tel Aviv. *What was the meaning of this?*

"Based on a message received from our source in Cairo," Dayan said to the intense group in front of him, knowing that eleven of them were hearing for the first time about the border developments over the last week, "the assumption is that this evening, with darkness falling…maybe a bit before, maybe a bit after, a full attack on two fronts will begin." Seeing the stunned faces, worried, he added, "The Americans are still not convinced that this will occur." Giving them a moment to simmer in the 'news', he continued, "the combined attack is planned for dusk, as the Arabs are concerned with the IAF's abilities." Dayan, continuing, said, "Our military leadership wants a preemptive attack by the IAF, but they haven't pressed the issue, with the understanding that it's impossible. Thus, the preemptive strike was not approved, unless the government says otherwise."

12:00. Hatzor

"In the evening, a war is supposed to break out with Egypt and Syria," Col. Lapidot informed the wives of the air crewmen in the family housing section. He added, "As directed by the IAF headquarters, we are required to evacuate the housing buildings. The evacuation will begin at 14:00. By then, you must be packed and ready to go."

12:20. Office of the Chief of Staff

At noon, Lt. Gen. Elazar knew that the cabinet had convened and realized that the chance to overturn the terrible decree prohibiting the preemptive strike was slim to none. Therefore, he internalized that everything depended on the regular ground forces stretched along the borders. The army alone was supposed to halt the attack; until the reserves arrive.

True, the IAF had a plan designed to address this situation, named "Scratch," but according to the plan, they were supposed to receive attack targets from ground forces. Could the regular forces, which were already busy with curbing a wave of tanks and infantry, provide targets to the aircraft?

Everything depended on Hakah and Gorodish.

He waited for the two command generals. He wanted to know what had occurred in their sectors in the last four hours. To make sure that everything was ready.

The first to present himself was Gorodish.

He informed the Head of the Southern Command about the news that had just arrived, that according to the new information, the Egyptians had begun to deploy networks of artillery batteries. He quickly reviewed with him the readiness plan for defense in the Sinai, "Dovecote," and stated the operational trends for the command—that evening, they will stop. The following day as well. On Sunday night and into Monday, it would be possible to take over Egyptian territory to the north and northwest of the Canal.

"From Monday until Wednesday, forces will continue to accumulate," the Chief of Staff informed him, "and it will enable us to counterattack."

12:30. Cabinet Meeting

While the Chief of Staff and the Commander of Southern Command went over the defensive plans in the Sinai, the meeting at the Prime Minister's office continued with the Defense Minister's updates regarding the main surge of army forces, the mobilization of the reserves, and the evacuation of the families of the Soviet advisors.

"What will happen if they move up their attack?" asked the Justice Minister, Yaakov Shimshon Shapira, lacking a security background, but full of common sense.

"The IAF will be on patrol in the sky beginning in the afternoon," Dayan answered, and immediately informed them about the preparedness of the IAF for an attack on the front starting at 12:00.

"The final decision rests in your hands," he said.

"I've decided that we must prove that we are not the ones who started this," the Prime Minister explained to the agitated forum in front of her. "This time, the identity of who started things needs to be clear and completely transparent, so that we won't need to go all around the world and convince everyone of our righteousness." She then described her meeting with the US ambassador. "I told him that God is witness to the fact that we have decided not to go to war, and if the Egyptians attack, they will get exactly what they deserve."

Around 12:45 PM, the Israeli government approved the series of measures that had been taken so far, as well as the diplomatic steps intended to prevent the war. The government, like the Prime Minister and the Defense Minister, decided that Israel would not be the one to begin a war.

12:30. IAF Commander's Bureau

Upon his return from the "Pit," Benny Peled assembled the officials of the IAF Headquarters in his office. They waited there for the results of the cabinet meeting. It was then that announcement came.

"There is no authorization for a preemptive strike," Benny said. "This time it's final. Everyone must switch to an air defense configuration."

"Why?" asked Col. Giora Furman, Head of the Operations Department.

"That's the directive," the IAF commander shot back at the room.

"We have enough aircraft for defense," Furman insisted. "Let's prepare an organized plan, let's keep some of the planes outfitted with bombs."

"No," Benny growled.

It is possible to assume that there were three layers of thought that led the IAF Commander to decide as he did. These layers are found within the national, professional and personal levels.

At the National Level: The trauma caused by the bombing of Tel Aviv during World War II and the War of Independence greatly influenced the definition of defense as the IAF's central task. Defense, above all else - this was what the country's leaders set for the IAF's commanders, and this notion seeped down from the top and influenced accordingly.

At the Professional Level: Maj. Gen. Benny Peled had been cut off from the cockpit, from leading a squadron, and from direct command of operations for many years. During his brief tenure as IAF Commander, he did not express great enthusiasm for "big operations" proposed by the Operations Department for striking missile batteries. Moreover, Peled was well aware of the problematic SA-6, the new neighborhood bully, and internalized the fact that the regular anti-aircraft layout, and especially the missile layout, had grown to frightening proportions. It is possible that in the moment of truth, he preferred to avoid having to deal with them and decided to "play it safe" with dogfights.

At the Personal Level: "Patience" was not a prominent character trait for the IAF Commander. Brig. Gen. Peled was known for his hot temperament and his short fuse, which eradicated his best men's willingness to confront him. His fuse became shorter whenever he had to accommodate the insights of the Operations Department's men in the field. People such as Giora Furman, for example.

Lt. Col. Yossi Aboudi, Head of the IAF's History Branch, the Air Force's official historian, sat to the side. He listened, he watched and he did not notice any signs of distress amid a normal atmosphere. *Pass me a cookie. Get me a cup of coffee.* Things were calm.

"I repeat, a war begin today at 18:00," Benny stated, "The go-time against the enemy begins at 15:00—until darkness falls."

On Saturday, before the eruption of hostilities, several officials in the IAF HQ heard their commander as he emphatically expressed himself: if war were to erupt, it was unlikely that enemy aircraft would come in the dark. 15:00 was the "H-hour" in which their arrival should be expected.

Why, then, did the IAF Commander give the directive to unload bomb clusters from the pylons of all the Phantoms and Mirages? Peled was supposed to know that it was impossible to change the entire array from strike to clean configuration within a couple of hours, and that those caught in the midst of the configuration change to clean would not be available for any mission type, short of becoming part of a helpless "duck shoot," once they were in the sights of enemy aircraft.

"I do not estimate that the Egyptian ground forces will be able to cross into the East Bank before nightfall," Maj. Gen. Peled continued, "and it is not expected that the Air Force will have to attack down there. My assumption is that we will have to attack any deployment areas that we will discover at night and at first light. I expect that the enemy will try to operate through attack helicopters, and we will need to engage by hunting them down. Tomorrow morning, we will begin with the Syrian air bases, and afterwards with their missile systems. After that, we will move to the southern front, where we will begin to destroy the Egyptian Air Force, and afterwards, their missiles."

Meanwhile, Brig. Gen. Rafi Har-Lev, a senior intelligence officer in the Air Force, still insisted—there would be no war.

At the same time, Lt. Col. Yehuda Porat, head of the Research Department at Military Intelligence, the man who knew better than anyone, focused on the indications that…no war would break out.

How did this come to pass? After one of Israel's best spies in Egypt warned that war would erupt by nightfall; after a reconnaissance photography sortie pointed to the beginnings and certainty of war; after a UN transmission indicated that camouflage netting had been removed from tanks and artillery, while the previous day saw the urgent, inexplicable evacuation of Soviet families from both Egypt and Syria; and when the IAF Commander reiterated, loudly, "Today there will be a war;" how did it transpire that even after all this, most of the commanders of the Air Force's HQ, bases and squadrons were blind to the tsunami that was about to hit them?

The answer is simple, if infuriating. Air Force officials opted to accept the "no war" version of Brig. Gen. Har-Lev, who had not long before been an operations officer—the commander of the Hatzor Airbase—and then headed the Intelligence Department.

As for Maj. Gen. Peled? He had already been gone for a long time. Thus there was no need to panic.

12:45. *The 201ˢᵗ Squadron*

In the Phantom squadron at Hatzor, a series of harassing phone calls sprang up Capt. Adi Benaya, one of the senior pilots in the 201ˢᵗ, leading the alert interception four-ship formation that was not assigned for the strike.

"There is no authorization to strike," reported the urgent voice of Lt. Col. Nissim Ashkenazi, commander of the squadron. "I repeat—there is no authorization to attack. Get everyone back to base. We need to prepare the air defense."

"There is not permission to strike," Benaya informed Huldai. Through the control tower, he contacted the aircraft and told those already settled under their aircraft cockpit canopies to return immediately to the squadron.

"Does what Ashkenazi said make sense to you?" Benaya asked Huldai. "We are going on the defense?"

"Apparently so," said Huldai, and his face betrayed his astonishment.

Capt. Benzi Nahal found it hard to understand as well.

The whole morning, they drove him crazy with Operation Orders. His people worked like never before. They unloaded weapons. They loaded weapons. They matched the bomb fuses. Repeated and refueled. He was proud of them. If the squadron was a fire-producing unit, it was possible to imagine that the Technical Division, which he headed, was the latch—which placed the bullet in the barrel, and allowed the pilot to aim and to pull the trigger. And they actually put bullets into barrel, despite all of the pressure and the changes, and despite Yom Kippur.

Then there was the new order. *Upload the weapons and switch to missiles configuration. What is going on here? We aren't attacking?*

"No green light," Huldai said, "and no governmental approval for a preemptive strike." He added, "We have to deal with it. We'll perform the orders that we obtain. We'll do what they tell us to do, and then we'll send the crew to the clubroom to pass the time cheerfully, between cups of espresso, backgammon, gin rummy, and bridge."

"We're going to the cafeteria," someone yelled.

What a disgrace to Yom Kippur, Gil Regev thought, who, though thoroughly secular, knows a thing or two about the traditions of Israel and their connection to the IAF and the whole army structure. In the army, you just don't eat on Yom Kippur. Ever. And not this, even by command. *We will regret this in the end.*

13:00. Office of the IAF Commander

Brig. Gen. David Ivry, commander of the Air Division and the Number 2 in the entire IAF, also thought that he would be able to spend the Sabbath in his bed. Earlier that week, he suffered an attack of the mumps, and according to his doctor, resting was still "imperative." However, an urgent phone call chipped away his focused mumps-combating plan and there he was, in the commander's office.

He was briefed on the government disapproval of a preemptive strike, as well as Maj. Gen. Peled's orders to unload all strike weapons from all interception aircraft.

He descended into the "Pit" and called Yigal Bar Shalom. "Come quickly, we need you."

Lt. Col. Bar Shalom, a veteran pilot of 201st Squadron and until one month earlier the IAF liaison in London, still felt on his buttocks the vibrations of the boat on the waves during the journey with his wife along the ports of the Mediterranean. He had only returned ten days ago. He was supposed to receive his discharge notice from the IAF and the IDF at any moment. Now this news had arrived.

"Get to Kibbutz Naot Mordechai," Ivry ordered him, his neck bandaged up and suffering a high fever. "Meet up with Maj. Gem. (Res.) Dan Lanner, the commander of our newest division. Join him as an aerial consultant."

He got into a battered Carmel car that he got from somewhere, and traveled to the Dov Airstrip. Overalls, uniform, flight jacket. Pistol. *No bullets,* the supply room told him.

No big deal. What could happen in the Golan Heights?

13:15. Um Hashiva. Sinai

It's too quiet, Lt. Dudi Yaron, the active IAF representative on "Babylon" base, pondered as he settled into his position in the center of the bunker.

Three key IDF positions in Sinai were located on the Um Hashiva mountain ridge, nearly 2400 feet above sea level and 25 miles from the Canal. Three underground bunkers, covered with mounds of earth and a sea of antennas: the front command post of Southern Command, "Debela;" the listening unit of the Intelligence branch, "Babylon;" and the IAF's Electronic Warfare Unit 545.

"Babylon" was established to meet all of the warning needs of the IDF and the IAF, via COMINT (Communication Intelligence), for monitoring communication between people, and via ELINT (Electronic Intelligence), for monitoring energy-emitting electronic sources.

Yaron looked around. The monitoring positions were only partially manned. *Why don't we boost our use of these positions? Why was I summoned from home, when all of these transmitters are idle?*

The silence continued to roar in his ears. Saturday is a day of normal activities for armies in conflict. Yet now the silence continued. *What are they up to? Why is there not a single aircraft in the sky?*

Who is the officer from 848 responsible for the listening positions? It's David David. Excellent. He's a good one, a veteran of the War of Attrition. Glad he'll be by my side.

13:15. Office of the Prime Minister

At 07:15 AM New York time, a full day after the decision to turn immediately to the United States and send an urgent message to the Arab states, a telegram from Mordechai Shalev, Director General of the Office of the Prime Minister, came out of the tray of the teleprinter. The message read as follows:

"Naftali (Kissinger) called at 07:05, and asked to announce:

1. *News arrived to him that Israel will begin operations within six hours.*

2. *They talked to the Soviets and the Egyptians, and delivered the requested message. The Soviets are collaborating, and special communication arrangements have been established between them.*

3. *He, Naftali, is requesting to warn us of any action.*

4. *He says that we will be in contact, and that I send the above messages immediately to the Prime Minister."*

13:30. Air Traffic Control Unit, Mount Meron

With the flavor of sea bass still in his mouth, Capt. Yair Kafri entered the bunker to replace the on-duty Weapon Systems Officer of the control unit. The central screens were black. There weren't any aircraft in the sky. Soon, everything would be cancelled.

13:30. The 201st Squadron

Towards 15:00, an air reconnaissance photography mission was planned to take place by the sister Phantom squadron, the 119th. A four-ship formation of Phantoms from the 201st Squadron was to provide escort.

"I will lead the four-ship formation," announced Huldai, the deputy commander of squadron A and acting commander.

"Roni," urged Gurion, the deputy commander of squadron B, "you aren't fully fit, This injury of yours; how do you expect to sit in a cockpit for so long?"

"I will lead the escort four-ship formation," Huldai stated, "I prefer a safe bird in the hand, given this unclear thing that might happen."

"Join Benaya's interception alert formation. Get yourself a partner for a two-ship and join Benaya's formation."

"I'm on my way to you to pick up the car," Telma Koren announced to her pilot husband, Moshe.

"Faster, faster," she urged Nurit Regev, a new driver, as they leapt to the squadron, and got confused in the tangle of permitted and forbidden roads.

13:30. Office of the Chief of Staff

The Head of the Southern Command left, just as the Head of the Northern Command was coming.

"We need to buffer the attack with minimum losses," stated Lt. Gen. Elazar, after checking with the activation of the operational plans and inquiring about the progress of the reserve deployments.

"The Air Force will attack the Syrian air bases tomorrow," the Chief of Staff continued his credo. "Afterwards, our aircraft will attack the Syrian missiles array. Therefore, ground troops will only provide limited assistance on the first day. Only after we can utilize the full force of our aircraft, we will begin ground attacks on the front."

13:40. Aerial Command Post, Northern Command

Too bad it's over, Sharabi thought, and remembered his CH-53A "Yasur" helicopter ride over the Galilee and the Golan. He saw the helicopter glide down slowly, over dark dust clouds of basalt rising from the earth, its wheels softly touching the helipad.

Together with a group from Air Command, he made his way towards the main command post bunker and found within it a hustle and an intolerable density.

"Where is our corner?" growled Col. Savron, head of the command post.

"Over there," someone pointed to a wobbly wooden table, lacking communication lines.

"I have sandwiches," one of them declared.

They went outside. They found a quiet place to sit, 30 meters from the bustle of the command group and the wrath of their commander, Savron.

13:50. The 201st Squadron

"They spoke to us about evacuating the families from the base," Hava Shahak informed her husband, Uri.

"Nothing will happen," he answered.

"What is that, Uri? What's with the siren?"

"Some Arab is pissing on the border," Ori replied. "It's making everyone panic."

OCTOBER 6

House of Cards

It's already a quarter to two, thought Maj. Motti Kimmelman, a senior IAF representative in "Ararat," the Intelligence Corps's central collection unit at Mount Canaan, as he was reminded of the warning that he had received several hours before, that had stated that war would break out by last light.

Everything is calm, he told himself, as he observed a group of skilled radio operators at their listening stations, and heard sounds indicating "dead lines" coming from speakers of the open radios of unmanned stations.

Suddenly, he heard three words. They were repeating over and over like a chorus, but Kimmelman knew that it was not a song, and the band of radio operators repeating them over and over again were not a choir. The words continued to resonate in the large, open room, and Kimmelman felt the hair on the back of his neck, when he heard them from every direction: "I have clicks," "I have clicks," "I have clicks."

Maj. Motti Kimmelman knew that clicks meant that someone on the other side did not want to be heard. There was no need to have to explain to him the reason why. After all, that was exactly why he was sitting among the women on the mountain, and the clicks would not stop. Kimmelman, who could recite the various types of clicks in his sleep, heard clicks signaling a taxi and clicks signaling a takeoff from the open channels. He did not need to divide attention to understand which air base was being mentioned, because the clicks came at him from every direction, from all the speakers, and from all positions.

He screamed into the receiver of the encrypted telephone, linked directly to the alarm room in the IAF Control Center, "The entire Syrian Air Force is in the air!"

"Pat, come quickly!" Ararat's cry was heard within the alarm section.

"The entire Syrian Air Force is in the air," Kimmelman yelled again. Maj. Abraham Benedek (Pat), Head of the Alarm Section in the IAF Intelligence Division, dropped the telephone, skipped three meters to the small sliding window separating him from the room of the Head of Central Command, slammed it with all his might and yelled in a cracking voice, "They're launching! They're taking off! War! War!"

He then skipped over to the early-warning station compound, pressed the intercom button in the center of the table, connected directly to the office of the IAF Commander, and shouted, "There are sightings from Syria! There are sightings from Syria!"

He took a deep breath, turned to Danny Schimmel, his deputy, and said, "They caught us with our pants down."

"Could this be the beginning of the war?" Maj. Gen. Benny Peled asked Brig. Gen. Rafi Har-Lev.

"I don't know," Har-Lev answered. "Let's go down and see."

13:50-13:55. *Air Control Unit, Mount Meron*

At the peak of the mountain, with the Air Control Unit, a staff file of ten soldiers was stationed. The boys were eliminated from flight courses. The girls were graduates of science-oriented studies. They had a secret chamber called the "Cage." Their objective was to detect Syrian aircraft, if possible from the moment that they took off, with electronic inventions at their disposal. With the exception of the unit's commander and his deputy, no one knew what the "absolutely top secret gang" dealt with.

Lt. Ora Fabian was the Sabbath alert soldier in the "Cage." Everything was calm. She reached her hand to the telephone dial and called Micah, her boyfriend, stationed at the Mt. Hermon Outpost.

"What are you doing at base?" he asked, surprised.

"Waiting at the alert station. I was summoned here."

"The alert station? Everything is calm over here…wait, what's that?!"

"What's happening, Micah?"

"Insane shelling just started," he said, and hung up.

A minute passed…

Suddenly, the screen in front of her was covered with lines and more lines, and all of them headed straight for the Golan Heights. "Kafri," she alerted her ranking officer, her heart strongly beating, "it's possible that I have a problem with my system, but I'm receiving a lot of movement on my device. Dozens of Syrian fighter jets are heading straight for the Golan Heights."

Capt. Yair Kafri lifted his eyes to the screen in front of him: nothing. "It appears to be a malfunction," he said. "Report back to me in one minute." She returned to her screen; the lines kept moving and inching forward.

"Kafri," she called again, "the lines are real." The red-headed weapon systems officer raised his eyes to his screen once more: still nothing. *Wait. What's that?* Dozens of yellow blips suddenly flooded the black screen. He reached to his left and pressed the alarm button that was connected to the base at Ramat David. He heard his assistant ordering someone around, and answered on the other side of the telephone line: "Launch everything we have." He then proceeded to contact the air defense system.

"Fire away at every aircraft that you see," Kafri advised the northern Hawk battery.

The battery operator responded, astonished, "Are you sure?!"

"I'm sure, I'm sure. Our aircraft will not be in the air for another five minutes," Kafri replied. "Every one you see is an Arabic-speaking aircraft."

13:51. *"Babylon," Um Hashiva. Sinai.*

At 723 meters above sea level and 45 Km direct-line away from the Canal, Lt. David David of the Central Monitoring Unit in Military Intelligence seriously grappled with the security alert that he received that morning. Just yesterday, he was still leading a course in the center of the country when a message arrived that told him to drop everything and come down to Babylon. Now, as he carefully monitored the voices coming through the open channels of the communications speaker, he knew exactly where to concentrate his attention.

"Number One, OK," he heard from one of the channels.

"It's starting!" he roared into the room. Twenty seconds pass.

"Repeating, over," another voice added.

He shouted at the top of his lungs, "They're coming! They're coming! They're coming!"

Three meters away from him, on a slightly elevated stage, Lt. Dudi Yaron, the IAF representative within the Listening Unit, jumped out of his seat, stretched his right hand towards the alarm button and pressed it.

The scream of the alarm rose and fell, flowing throughout the roads in the base.

He reached for the encrypted phone and picked up the handset.

"Attack! Attack!" he shouted into the receiver.

From 400 kilometers away, he could hear the siren operator yell something to the Air Force "pit." A moment later, he heard Pat's voice: "Received. We know. They are already attacking in the Golan Heights."

A minute passed, and suddenly the silence was shattered: screams of "*Allah-hu Akhbar*" erupted on all operational channels, and chills streaked sharply down Yaron's spine.

"We are attacking," Yaron told Pat while rubbing his ear. He allowed the main alarm to cover the echoes of the bombs that the Egyptian Air Force's aircraft were launching at the central Intelligence base in the Sinai, in the midst of this most holy day for Jews.

13:52. Air Force Command Post, Northern Command

A group of sergeants was biting into their sandwiches, enjoying the fruits of the small sin of breaking the fast, when the deafening roar of engines blasted into their ears. This was followed by the sight of a four-ship formation of aircraft at a low altitude coming from the west, passing over IDF Headquarters in the Golan Heights and releasing its load of bombs on the camp.

The Syrians, the "*Yekkes*" of the Middle East, had planned the war to return the occupied Golan Heights in an astonishing manner. In the aerial front, they flew in dozens of flight paths in complete radio silence, at a low altitude, while taking advantage of the ground's terrain and completely avoiding Israeli radar. At the very last moment, the interception aircraft pulled high up (only then being detected by radar), and progressed in the best possible shape in order to protect the tails of the strike fighters that on their flight westward identified their targets, retraced their steps east, and dropped their payloads on a series of carefully selected, high-quality targets.

13:52-13:55. Chamber of the IAF Commander

Everyone in the IAF Commander's office sprinted up the stairs of the half floor leading to the entrance gate, and continued running 50 meters to the opening of the underground command post, passing the guard and descending to the IAF Commander's cell.

Almost everyone.

Benny Peled was slower. Incessant smoking had harmed his fitness.

"Giora, launch everyone, whoever can be launched," the IAF Commander said, panting at the chamber door.

"There is no need to unload them all from the bombs," Giora Furman, the Chief of Operations, argued passionately, understanding that the order would eliminate the counter-offensive. "We can still carry out an attack. We have enough unloaded aircraft to provide sufficient interception."

Benny did not reply, and wandered to the front door.

Giora grabbed his commander's arm, "Why do you want all the aircraft in the air? We don't need to just unload weapons, we still have the option of jettisoning them later into the sea."

Benny stared at him intently.

Giora did not give in, "It's a shame, let's just wait a few minutes and we'll come up with a plan." The IAF commander shook his head, released himself from Giora's grip, burst into the chamber, got to the counter in front of him, grabbed Shimon Lasser, the senior control officer, by the shoulder and said, "The war has started, get everyone up in the air!"

"I have a four-ship formation ready with bombs," Lasser said, "should I launch them?"

"Launch them. Let them jettison their bombs into the sea. Launch everyone, even those still loaded with bombs."

"The Arabs are so stupid," Lt. Col. Yehuda Porat (Porty), Head of the Research Wing in the Intelligence Division, said to everyone in the alert chamber, "They are going to crack their heads. They're making a fatal mistake."

Was the immediate launch of all fighters just a shot from the hip, an unnecessary "excessive correction?"

This is a possibility.

First of all, it was those in both the IDF and IAF intelligence bodies who repeatedly said that the Egyptians still lacked long-range bombers capable of threatening Israel. So where did all of this concern come from?

A second point is that the IAF Commander should have known that all of the air defense plans for defending the State of Israel, including those aimed at dealing with this current scenario, included 70 Shahak and Nesher jets, as well as 8-12 modified Phantoms (Sledgehammer). The air arsenal was supposed to provide a comprehensive response to the defensive needs—to close up and seal the skies alongside all of the potential enemy incursion routes, while simultaneously dispatching reinforcements and controllable turnarounds for the dogfights. The Head of the Operations Division, Col. Giora Furman, reminded Maj. Gen. Peled that there were enough aircraft to pursue this course.

Third, the small slice of sky above the State of Israel limits the potential spaces for engaging in defensive dogfights. Therefore, the optimal number of aircraft that can be employed is not so large.

Fourth, even if for some reason a "gap" would be formed during the rounds of defensive and offensive maneuvers, it would be possible to change the missions of Phantoms heading out to strike—to direct them to jettison their weapons in an unpopulated area—and divert them towards keeping the skies clear.

Fifth, dispatching everyone at once is a proven method to prevent an immediate catastrophe—no aircraft would be caught while sitting on the ground. However, it is also a proven means of losing control. This is especially true for the loss of defensive capabilities. What will happen when all of the aircraft that were rushed out in a panic need to return to land at the same time because of fuel starvation? Who will protect them, and who will protect the country's skies?

Sixth, the Phantoms were in our hands. Most of them were still armed, and all of them (excluding those intended for interception) were intended for a strike. Had they been left loaded with bombs, as was supposed to be done and was practiced, there would have been no problem sending them straight into Syria and Egypt— at the same time as enemy aircraft were in our territory—to carry out the preemptive strike. Enemy aircraft returning to their bases would have had to crash land on pulverized runways, or would have been exposed to risk as they approached to land with their wheels down and lacking fuel.

Lastly, there was the matter of the style. A few minutes before 14:00 on Saturday afternoon, on Yom Kippur, it looked as though someone went crazy. Launching everyone to the air? Releasing bombs over the sea? For combat teams, who grew up with the idea of the importance of self-control before anything else, this phenomenon radiated irrationality. Most of all, this was the first crack in the 'genetic code' upon which they were forged.

So what led Maj. Gen. Benny Peled to dispatch everyone?

It could be that Peled knew what Col. Furman and Lt. Col. Oded Erez, Head of the Defense Branch, did not know, did not remember, and did not take into account. Upon receiving the warning of the penetration of enemy aircraft into our territory, the IAF did not have 70 Shahaks for defense, nor did it have 70 aircraft for defense at all, even after considering the Phantoms. On Saturday, October 6, at 14:00, the IAF's Defense Branch only had 57 available aircraft. These included 43 Mirages with different configurations: four in the 101st Squadron, 20 in the 117th Squadron, two in the 113th Squadron, 15 in the 144th Squadron, and two in the Refidim Division. The other 14 aircraft were Sledgehammers: two from the 69th Squadron, two from the 119th Squadron, two from the 107th Squadron, four from the 201st Squadron, two from the Refidim Division, and two from Ofira.

Moreover, if this was just one major attack flight of Egyptian and Syrian Air Forces, then dispatching every aircraft to the sky would prevent them from being caught on the ground.

There is something else.

A few minutes before two o'clock on Saturday afternoon, Israel was surprised as it had never been surprised before, as was Maj. Gen. Peled. 263 Egyptian attack and interception aircraft, and 132 Syrian aircraft attacked Israel, on their way to permanently undermine the defensive walls in which Israel's citizens had felt secure.

Only the Air Force can stop this catastrophe, Benny Peled thought. *Defense. As fast as possible, and with all of our force.*

13:55. The 200th UAV Squadron

It's so beautiful here, the squadron crew thought, admiring the sight of ancient furrows adorning the Ramat Dalton plateau, as a shriek of jet engines interrupted their viewing. *MiGs!*

A four-ship formation of MiG-17 strike fighters, two two-ship formation in a single file, passed low overhead on its way to the Control Unit at Mount Meron. Explosions. Flames. They missed.

In the background, sounds of the rolling thunder of artillery batteries were heard, and the whole eastern horizon was engulfed by black smoke. Maj. Nir, the commander, recognized other aircraft through the windows that were revealing columns of sky pouring through. Based on their wings contour, he knew that all of them, *all of them*, were built by the Soviet Union.

13:55-14:00. The Cabinet Meeting

Israeli government ministers were used to the fact that with the Minister of Finance, Pinchas Sapir, the room's temperament coasted just on the boiling point. They were forgiving; they had to be.

However, even the Finance Minister, with many years of experience in the swamp of economic and industrial leadership in Israel, with unparalleled professionalism, who was crowned the "most powerful politician of the 1970s," understood the limits of power, stormy temperament, and good taste. One example was with his party chairman and Prime Minister, Ms. Golda Meir. No one dared to behave in a confrontational manner in front of the Queen of the Jewish State; not even Sapir.

On Saturday afternoon, the Finance Minister of the State of Israel exceeded the limits of his customary temperament. "How is it possible that the whole thing has been hidden from us until just the last few hours, and now, we are expected to make critical decisions in the face of an unreasonable time pressure?" He raised his voice, his neck veins popping, then paused, pulled back his anger, looked straight into the Prime Minister's eyes and said, "I don't understand why it is difficult to wait a bit, rather than to make a decision at this very moment."

"It is not clear that the war will begin at six in the evening as we have been told. It may begin earlier," the Prime Minister spoke quietly, maternally, trying to take the wind out of the taut, angry sails of the Minister of Finance. "I do not mind," she added, "and will not leave in any case. On the contrary, if my comrades wish to sit a bit and reflect on things."

As her words echoed in the air, a series of sirens suddenly pierced the walls of the conference room. Brig. Gen. Israel Lior, the Prime Minister's Military Secretary, rushed out, while Golda continued, "If they don't begin the war by 16:30, it will be possible to vote again. I want to know what the situation is, if they will attack before then."

The sirens increased.

"What is it?" the Prime Minister asked.

"Maybe the war has begun," Mitka Yaffe, the stenographer, answered.

"*Nar das falt mir* (that's all I need)," Golda said in Yiddish, while the last fragments of the sirens died a slow death, and Brig. Gen. Lior repeated and informed, "Enemy aircraft were dispatched in Syria. The Syrians have opened fire across the entire sector."

13:58. The 201ˢᵗ Squadron

In the clubroom, the squadron conducted the regular ritual: cards, Rummikub, espresso, soft background music, and someone putting a new record on the turntable.

What is that? Everyone leapt in the air. *The fool chose a song that starts with a siren's wail.* They sat on the bar stools and orange corduroy armchairs, when another piercing siren took over the clubroom space. *What is going on with this record?*

"It's not the record!" one of them shouted, and everyone ran out of the club towards the plaza in front of the squadron. *It really isn't the record!* Long sirens squealed from every direction, increasing and decreasing, and the individual siren joined with sirens from all over the wing. This was the strongest siren anyone had heard, while all of the dogs on base, big and small, added to the noise with panicked howls, and the speakers screamed, "Run to your aircraft!"

13:55-14:10. IAF Base 3 (Refidim). Sinai

From the position of the Weapons Systems Officer at the Air Control Unit on a mountain overlooking Refidim, Maj. Yigal Ziv, the unit commander, reported that a rescue helicopter had just taken off to assist with photographic reconnaissance missions in Egyptian territory.

Even before he completed the report, on the "open line," which indicated every operational event, and connected the air traffic control unit directly to the officers at the Air Force "Pit," he heard a cry: "Launch! Launch!"

"Launch what?" he asked.

"Launch, launch!" he repeatedly screamed, "launch everything you have!"

Col. Eliezer ("Cheetah") Cohen was the acting commander at Refidim.

"Odds are that war will break out tomorrow," Benny Peled informed him last night. Amitai Hasson, the Commander at Refidim, was on a tour abroad. "Get to work."

24 hours into his emergency appointment, and someone hysterical was already on the other end of the line connecting his base with the air control base on the mountain.

"Commander, many formations of enemy aircraft are heading to Sinai. Some of them are headed towards you, and others are headed towards us. All of the aircraft on alert in the center have launched. Your aircraft will also need to launch. There is authorization to open anti-aircraft fire on all strike fighters."

"The war has begun," Cheetah informed the control tower, "Within minutes, we'll be attacked. Activate the sirens. Begin procedures for air defense. Prioritize dispatching interception aircraft."

Sixty kilometers from the Canal line, sirens screamed throughout the Refidim Air Force Base, dozens of anxiety-stricken soldiers, received the siren, and ran for shelter; two Mirages and two Phantoms took off, soaring, pulling west, sent to dance in battle against the Egyptian Air Force, and Cheetah, in his jeep, sped on his way to the control tower.

On the mountain above the Refidim base, the control unit was situated a few miles away, and to the left of Maj. Ziv, the commander, was the telephone center, which directly linked the Sinai Division to several isolated and sensitive outposts along the water line.

"We're firing at them! We're firing at them!" the assistant controller shouted to the telephone switchboard. "Aircraft, they see aircraft!" the two air-defense controllers shouted, connected with the Hawk SA missile batteries, adding more black shade to the dark ocean that had erupted in front of them.

Then, and only then, the black radar screen filled with yellow spots; filling every eye yellow. Yigal knew that the entire Egyptian Air Force was actually over the Sinai.

Cheetah climbed up the tower.

"Get me the control unit!" No answer.

"Get me the head of Central Command."

The Chief of Operations was on the other end of the line. "Cheetah, we know of your situation, but we have no time for you right now. The Syrians and the Egyptians are attacking together. You're on your own! Bye." He then hung up.

You're on your own?! What in the world? The war has just begun, and the IAF is already in a panic?

Another moment and his heretical thoughts about the strength of the IDF and IAF were reinforced, as four four-ship formations with swept back wings emerged at low altitude, directly in front of the control tower.

"We have a positive identification," shouted the commander of the anti-aircraft battalion, standing by his side, "Egyptian Sukhoi-7." The first two four-ship formations pounded the runways. The third four-ship formation decapitated the control tower. The last four-ship formation blew the roof off of a nearby bunker.

Where are our aircraft? Cheetah contemplated in horror. *They're doing to us exactly what we did to them in '67.*

14:00. Ofira (Sharm el-Sheikh)

The alert air crew section of the IAF's 29th IAF air base (Ofira) had never felt so calm and peaceful when a siren pierced through the holy serenity of Yom Kippur.

"What's happening?" Captain Amir Nachumi asked the controller at the end of his sprint to his Phantom.

"More than twenty targets headed this way by way of the sea."

"Two, start your engines," Nachumi ordered to Lt. Danny Shaki.

"Don't start!" the air-controller shouted, "I have orders from the top!"

"Two, start them," Nachumi repeated. "We're taking off."

"Climb with your burners towards Sanafir Island," Nachumi ordered Shaki.

"We will head back to base with extra speed and altitude."

"Yavin, look," he said to Yossi Yavin, his navigator, while he detected a series of explosions and gaping craters in the runway from which they had just taken off. "It looks like the war is right down there."

Then it was just Shaki and him, with Yossi and David in the back seats. They did not let up on the Egyptians that attacked them like this at Ofira, and they sped after them, sat on them, waited for the lock-on "beep," squeezed the triggers, and Nachumi, staring at the first MiG like he had never done before, turned the MiG into a fiery mushroom.

Then came others, many others, and Yavin slowly understood that the members of the four-ship formation crews were experiencing their first air combat experience. It is fast; it is scary; you constantly need to protect your tail. The concentration and courage needed for the duel mission, to bring others down while surviving, does not allow any time for combat cries. Suddenly, it was quiet. Seven separate fires were burning on the ground, and the radio was a flurry of Eagles and Phantoms that had arrived as reinforcements, filling the radio with questions ("Where's the fight?"). Nachumi, exhausted but filled with enough energy to send a short answer, replied, "It's finished," and touched down next to a gaping crater in the runway. He was suddenly reminded that only yesterday a "surprise attack" was a fairly distant idea, something related to the Japanese, the Americans, a film projector and an old movie.

14:00. Air Control Unit at Mount Meron

At the Weapons Systems Chief's station, Capt. Yair Kafri had never seen a dotted screen with so many yellow blips. He had also never seen so many network communications filled with screaming pilots who demanded attention, guidance, and advice; nor the chaos in the sky, and on the mountain. They dispatched everyone, even Maj. Yitzhak David, commander of 109th Skyhawk Squadron, from Ramat David, with a four-ship formation surrounding him.

Why are they suddenly launching Skyhawks for a defensive air mission? Maj. David wondered. *And why send Phantoms to the sea to dispose of their bombs?*

14:05. Air Command Post, Golan Heights

The group of command bunker sergeants rushed in the direction of the central command post, found it illuminated by pale emergency lighting, and everything underground looked like the backdrop of a movie, not like life itself. They made their way to a group of terrified soldiers, the scent of sour sweat, cigarette smoke, and blaring radio speakers.

There's no one to talk to, Ofer Sharabi trembled. *How can you talk if everyone's screaming? What will happen with these phones that won't stop ringing? And what is my role? I left without any instructions. They told me to go, so I went. Ten Lira in my pocket. Noblesse cigarettes. A T-shirt. What should I do here, on the side of this small, rocking table that they allocated for us to serve as a command post?*

14:00-14:15. The 201st Squadron

Capt. Amnon Gurion ran to an interception alert jeep and thought, *How is it that when every combat pilot hears a siren, this demon that makes him want to shoot down MiGs suddenly stays quiet and leaves?*

Brakes squealed in front of the underground interception hangar. Connect; start the engines; takeoff.

Capt. Benzi heard the siren and ran to the underground hangars. *Damn. They didn't have time to disarm all of the aircraft. I wonder what they will do with those who are still armed?*

Sima Shavit was in the operations room, and suddenly everyone was rushing to get inside, each taking the note with the roster of aircraft-hanger assignments and running.

Settle down, she thought to herself, lighting her first cigarette in a year. *Calm down. Nothing to get excited about, it's a children's game.*

Air raid sirens still echoed throughout the wing, and Telma Koren and Nurit Regev tumbled their way through a world overturned. Everyone around them was running: bomb loaders with carts, pilots with helmets, and even aircraft taking off as they never had before.

The Hatzor base commander, Col. Amos Lapidot, also ran.

Lapidot was a veteran warhorse: the Suez Crisis, the Six-Day War, the War of Attrition. Still, no one had prepared for this. He had never believed that the base he commanded would be shrouded in siren sounds, rising and falling, indicating that enemy aircraft were on the way. According to the commands, the protection of the base from these aircraft was the commander's responsibility.

So Amos ran. Short of breath, he ran up the stairs leading to the top of the command tower, ordering the controllers to get to the dormitories, and remained alone there, except for one controller by his side.

Then, as he wore a flat helmet, he remembered the movies from World War II. He made contact with squadrons on the base and advised that the Phantoms of the 201st, still armed with bombs, fly to the sea, jettison their load and return quickly, easily and clean to take part in the dogfights that could be expected to take place right there, above the base's area.

14:05. Chamber of the Head of Central Command

A few minutes after everything began, the Head of Central Command's chamber was filled with senior figures from IAF Headquarters. Maj. Gen. Benny Peled was front and center, Col.

Giora Furman to his right, Lt. Col. Ami Ayalon and Lt. Col Shimon Lasser to his left, and Brig. Gen. Rafi Har-Lev just a bit behind him.

"Is it still possible to launch an attack against Syria?" the Chief of Staff asked as he entered the chamber.

"Some of the Sledgehammer aircraft are still ready for this mission," said the IAF commander, "We are able to begin setting up for a launch."

"Do it," Dado said.

14:10-15:00. The 201st Squadron

"Rabbit four-ship formation request to align on two-nine," the interception four-ship formation commander, reserve captain Adi Benaya, called the controller in tower.

"Rabbit, you are cleared," the controller replied.

Engines checks; step strong on the brake pedals; left hand pushing throttles to MIL power setting. First the left engine; left at max power; engine is satisfactory; temperatures okay; nozzle flaps fine, Benaya muttered to himself. *Sets left engine to idle rpm and accelerates the right; right at max power; temperatures okay; nozzle flaps are fine.* He repeated the checklist "song".

"Rabbit, canopies are locked. Takeoff," Benaya called tower.

"Rabbit cleared for takeoff," the controller tower replied.

He increased both engines rpm to maximum throttles range, waited for the rpm to stabilize at MIL power setting, let go of the brakes, engaged the ground steering by holding the button at the bottom of the stick grip, and engaged both engine afterburners by lightly pressing on the throttles to the left and forward beyond the MIL detent to "firewall" position. Full afterburner.

The "Sledgehammer" leaped, slamming the pilot back to his seat.

His gaze was focused forward. With a slight movement of his head, imperceptibly, he caught, in the corner of his eye, the shutter status indicators on the instrument panel.

"They are activated," he noted referring to the afterburners, which burn twenty pounds of jet fuel for every second of work.

"Activated," said Talmon, and added, "the airspeed indicator is responding."

"Airspeed increases," Talmon continued the takeoff checklist "song".

Benaya's gaze switched over between the runway and cockpit indicators.

"80," Talmon said, and Benaya released the ground steering button and moved over to the rudder pedals, keeping the stick centered.

"100," Talmon said, while Benaya pulled the stick back a bit, gently lifting the nose-wheel, and took one last quick glance at the caution lights panel.

"120," Talmon said.

"We carry-on," Talmon called from the rear cockpit, and Benaya knew that at the airspeed already was 140 knots, the point of "no-return" (i.e., must take off). He already had his "head out," and mentally he was already airborne.

150. A gentle pull on the stick. They were up in the sky.

Landing gear retracted, flaps locked up.

"Landing gear up, flaps up," Benaya said.

"Up, up," Talmon responded.

"Rabbit is airborne," Benaya called the Controller at Mitzpe Ramon, and collected the other aircraft of the formation.

"Full power to engagement," the controller commanded, "20 miles. Heading: two-six-zero."

"Drop tanks," Benaya called on the radio, and they all jettisoned their external fuel tanks.

Kobi Hayun was number four. *This is discouraging,* he thought to himself, *I'm heavy, the leader is already far in the sky, and now I need to chase after them.* He pursued and caught up. He joined into formation, receiving the call to engagement and hearing that Benaya was ordered to jettison drop tanks. He jettisoned.

What's happening? Uncontrollable movement took a hold of his aircraft.

"One, I'm experiencing a flight-control malfunction," he reported to Benaya.

"Four, go home," Benaya ordered.

This is a bad beginning, Hayun thought.

The Huldai three ship formation took off immediately after the alert four-ship formation.

"Tiger is in the air," Huldai informed the controller in Mitzpe Ramon.

"Take one-eight-zero."

What?!

"Come here to defend the territory above us."

"Say that again?!"

"Mitzpe Ramon. Hurry!"

"What did he say?" Abraham Assael, the navigator, asked Capt.
(Res.) Dani Haloutz.

"He's heading south," Haloutz answered from the front cockpit.
I don't understand where this controller came up with that weird idea.
What does he mean, that the Egyptians are on their way to him?
An Egyptian "Operation Focus" on the afternoon of Yom Kippur?

Assael calculated the directions in his head in the rear cockpit.
The Canal heading is two-two-zero. The Golan Heights heading is
zero-two-zero. One-eight-zero? Is he serious?

Hayun landed.

"Boy, the war's begun," Yigal the legless told him, "You're on
your own."

Hayun knew Yigal's ethos: a Phantom pilot in the early days
of the squadron, towards was captured by the Egyptians near the
end of the War of Attrition and lost his leg. *You're on your own?*
Like they kept telling us in the Flight Academy when we had to detect
malfunctions in a Fouga? Except we are not in the Flight Academy
now. Nor is this a Fouga. This is probably war. And Yigal knows
better than me about war.

The three aircraft in the Rabbit formation flew into battle and
found nothing, not a trace of enemy aircraft.

"Get over here," the controller yelled.

Burners. They headed to the Mitzpe Ramon sector.

"Enemy aircraft in sight!" the controller yelled hysterically.

They threw their heads around in every direction. Nothing.

Holding a boaring level flight, they exhausted their fuel. They landed at Hatzor.

"What happened?" Benaya asked.

"Everyone took off," the technicians answered.

"How? With bombs?"

"With bombs. With everything."

14:15-14:30. Skyhawks in the skies of the Golan Heights

About fifteen minutes after the start of the big commotion, the 109th Skyhawk Squadron in Ramat David received a directive to send a second four-ship formation to the skies.

Maj. Hanan Eitan, a reservist, led the four-ship formation, still heavily loaded with the bombs for the preemptive strike that never occurred, holding pattern in the Upper Galilee, in front of the Golan Heights.

Just that morning, he left his sleepy Yom Kippur routine in his kibbutz at the mouth of the Jezreel Valley, and now he was high in the sky, trying to understand the meaning of his mission, circling above Safed, and requested from the attack controller at Mount Meron to get a precise target.

"Keep holding in position," they told him, "hold-on for instructions."

The Air Traffic Control Unit is supposed to receive precise instructions from IAF headquarters during an attack: what sort of action is required by strike fighters, and where exactly to send them. However, the officer in the "Pit" had no idea what to tell his people at Mount Meron, because no one in the "Pit" knew. And how would they know; after all, the armored forces of the 188ᵗʰ Tank Division were struggling at that very moment, dealing with the insanity of swarms of Syrian infantry and tanks, attempting to cross the ground obstacle of the Golan Heights, on their way towards the depths of the Galilee and the Sea of Galilee. Furthermore, since the soldiers of the 188ᵗʰ Division were fighting for their lives, as well as for the country that sent them into this inexplicable disaster that came out of the blue, they were unable to report the chaos to the IAF.

In the heavy fog that fell a half an hour after the first shots were fired, when intelligence updated from the ground was wishful thinking, when no one knew where the Syrians were concentrating their efforts, or if their forces successfully crossed the anti-tank ditch—as all of this was transpiring, no one at IAF headquarters was able to send instructions to the Mount Meron air control unit.

Until then.

Someone decided that it was time to activate the Skyhawk four-ship formation circling Safed, and instructed the controller at Mount Meron to send them their task. Hanan Eitan's four-ship formation arranged into a combat formation and headed east.

"Twenty-thousand feet towards Quneitra," the commander of the 109ᵗʰ Squadron, Maj. Yitzhak David, who had just landed at Ramat David, heard the attack controller at Mount Meron direct the Eitan four-ship formation. *Did someone go crazy?!* Thirty minutes had passed since the attack began. Every aircraft in the Syrian Air Force had returned to base, and all of their missile systems were being extremely vigilant, knowing that every aircraft that emerged from the west was an Israeli aircraft. The Golan Heights, nearly to the edge of the western slopes, was under the threat of missiles. *Why send Eitan so high?!* At twenty-thousand feet, he was in the ideal hunting range for the missile battery operators, a practice range for heavy, hideously slow Skyhawks.

Okay, David thought, *the attack controller is merely an extension of the IAF Commander. He and the whole system up there are synchronized better than we are. If the controller is sending Eitan's four-ship formation to locate unknown targets, then that's what they told him. That's what is needed right now.* And finding targets, David knew, can only be done high above.

Yet the feeling in his stomach would not subside.

"The controller is sending my formation twenty-thousand feet above the Syrian missile threat zone," he informed Lt. Col. Arik Izuz, the Wing's Aviation Squadron Leader, who ran the operations of the wing's command post. "I request that you do something to stop him."

"We'll see what can be done," Izuz replied.

In those same seconds, Yair Kafri was replaced in the weapons systems post on Mount Meron and went out to get some air outside of the bunker. He climbed onto the roof, searching for action in the October sky over the Golan Heights and recognized, to his horror, white rocket trails chasing after a slow, silver Skyhawk. So very slow, too slow. Boom. One of the trails united with the aircraft, exploding in the sky.

How is it possible that an armed and heavy Skyhawk four-ship formation was sent on a reconnaissance flight in the Golan Heights at an altitude of twenty-thousand feet, into a territory threatened by prowling missile batteries?

On the one hand, this occurred due to the lingering euphoria following the Six-Day War, in which Israel turned Syria into a joke, as well as the dogfights of 1973, which took place in January (six downed MiGs), and September (twelve more downed). These events increased the disrespect for Israel's northern enemy, as well as the notion that nothing bad could come from the north.

On the other hand, that was the surprise—they were coming, despite what was thought of them, and four hours earlier than what was expected.

These conflicting impulses—the euphoric smugness and the surprised panic — resulted in befuddlement, a lack of understanding of the battlefield situation, and ample room for error, as was the case with Hanan Eitan's four-ship formation.

14:30. Rockets in the sky above Tel Aviv

Maj. Eitan Carmi is a veteran Mirage pilot, reservist, and a veteran of both the Six-Day War and the War of Attrition.

On that morning, just like all of his comrades, he was summoned to the squadron. He was in the air, a part of two two-ship formations above Hatzor meant to circle and secure Ashkelon.

"Take direction two-seven-zero," the controller commanded in an excited voice, and sent Carmi and his partner to intercept an unidentified aircraft, moving high above the Mediterranean, heading straight towards Tel Aviv.

They closed in on the target, and from far away noticed the clumsy silhouette of a Tupolev 16 bomber.

Son of a bitch. The Egyptians aren't discounting population centers, thought Carmi, realizing that the Tupolev was on its way to bomb the first Hebrew city.

While planning the method of downing the bomber, the Egyptian bomber suddenly swung back around, and something else, glowing, small, began to make its way towards Tel Aviv.

"Turn back to the east," the controller commanded.

They pointed the nose on the orientation of the glowing object, closed-in on it and identified the sight of an aircraft and a backburner. *What's this?* Carmi was shocked, recognizing the familiar silhouette, *the Egyptians are desperate enough to start operating the MiG-15 again? Since when do they have an afterburner?*

Number Two shouted, "It's a Kelt," and Carmi flew over it, and saw the truth in what Number Two had said: the cockpit of the MiG was empty. He backed away and launched a missile. The engine flame of the Egyptian unmanned MiG died on its own, as if it felt an approaching Zionist air-to-air missile locking on to its heat source, and "confused" the *Shafrir* missile that crashed between the Mediterranean waves below.

Guns, Eitan decided, knowing that the old air combat method, those that every pilot was taught and grown up on since the dawn of the first fighter aircraft, would be the one that would save Tel Aviv. He closed in and shot. The rounds smashed into the wing root and Carmi saw how the MiG 15, converted into a Kelt cruise missile, spun, lost altitude, and exploded in a fire the likes of which he had never seen before, as the sky quivered.

14:35. *Chamber of the Head of Central Command*

The news did not stop flowing. Egyptian Air Force aircraft attacked Ophir; and Um Hashiva; and Refidim, so far from the Canal. Syrian jet forces hit the Hermon, Tel Abu-Nida; Tel Fares; and Nefah, all the headquarters of IDF forces in the Golan Heights. Even with the difficulty, this news was tolerated.

Then reports from the ground started flowing in, particularly the cries of despair regarding the strongholds of the Bar-Lev line along the Canal, and the calls for help by tank battalions who were making their way into the strongholds, only to be killed by tank-hunting squads disguised by the sands of the Sinai. It suddenly became clear to everyone that it was not just the artillery that launched thousands of shells on both fronts, and aircraft that released their bombs on command, monitoring and control points; the land armies themselves joined in a comprehensive war campaign and opened a massive dual-front assault—without considering the reasoned opinions of the Head of IDF Intelligence and his men, who had said in the morning, that there was no logical reason for a war to break out.

That was precisely the moment that Lt. Gen. David Elazar, still in the chamber of the Head of Central Command, understood perhaps better than anyone the meanings accompanying the state of the fronts. He checked again with Maj. Gen. Benny Peled to see if the IAF would still be able to go out and strike a severe blow against Syria.

"There is no possibility to attack air bases in Syria," said the IAF commander. "The Phantom layout, the main force for that operation, is currently confined to defense missions."

14:30-15:00. Skyhawks in the Golan Heights. The Other Side

While Hanan Eitan, the reservist from Mishmar Haemek, became the first casualty of the IAF and perhaps the whole IDF, another Skyhawk four-ship formation rushed in, led by Lt. Col. Tzvika Hess, commander of the 110th Squadron.

"Takeoff," the control tower told him, "you will receive targets in the air."

"'Hayden' is airborne," Tzvika reported, and obtained a vector to holding pattern about Almagor. It was outside of missiles threat range.

They did not have a chance to hold in position, and they were already vectored to the south of the Golan Heights. They were ordered to search for an enemy tank that was attempting to break through the area of Tel Fares and Rafid, and to destroy it.

It's like a war movie, thought Yanki Yardani, the squadron training officer, and number two for Hess at that moment. Every road from Syria was full of tanks, APCs, and trucks, all moving towards the border of Israel. He remembered the squadron briefing that morning, when there was still talk of a preemptive strike. *After the destruction of the air bases and aircraft,* they had said, *or perhaps at the same time, you might have to knock out some ground tanks.* However, now that they had begun, without a preemptive strike, there was no expanse of parked, stationary tanks; everyone who traveled westward was a Syrian tank that rushed to the line. Very soon they would trample the few Israeli tanks that dared to step in front of them. *This will not end soon,* Yardani thought.

Tzvika descended, but they were still high above the ground, and Yardani knew that it was preferable that they be as low as possible, and gliding at that height, even after their reduction in altitude, was neither good nor recommended for fighting against missiles. He had heard what happened to Hanan Eitan and he knew that the best course of action was not to be there at all, or at least to descend to a very low height.

Everything was still burning below, and columns of smoke merged with dust and haze, together breaking in rays of sunshine that obscured the field of vision.

Then Roni Moses, leading the back two-ship formation, shouted "Missiles!" He then saw Yardani's Skyhawk disintegrating before his eyes, like cotton wool set on fire.

Visibility is really poor, Yardani thought, while dividing his attention between staying in formation and finding targets on the ground, when suddenly, out of nowhere, he was hit. *Damn,* he cursed in the cockpit.

In an instant, the obedient Skyhawk decided to refuse flying, ignoring the pilot's desperate control input attempts and stalls wildly straight up. Through the G-forces that clouded his vision and threatened to cause him to black out, Yardani succeeded in focusing on the mirrors on the canopy—the aircraft was cut through the middle, broken in two. He was controlling its front half.

What remained of the aircraft began rolling by itself with the nose down, and Yardani knew that he needed to eject. The war was then to reach the ejection handles, the high G-force and heavy hands his enemies. He finally reached the handles, grabbed, and pulled.

15:00-16:00. The 201st Squadron

"Burner full to the Suez," the interception controller instructed the four-ship formation, let by "Wild Bull" Peled.

Off the coast of Ashkelon, they jettisoned their remaining bombs into the sea, opened their burners and cut through the air in a mad dash to the Canal.

In the afternoon of Saturday's Yom Kippur, the aerial situation picture started to emerge in the chamber of the Head of Operations, and indicated that like the Syrians, the Egyptians were content with forays along the front lines.

Why not send aircraft to attack targets within enemy territory?

They still have the initiative, the IAF Commander thought. Our mission remains keeping the skies clear. Containment, with everything that we've got. A large air campaign, such as attacking the entirety of the missiles array or air bases in Egypt or Syria, would require nearly every strike aircraft in the IAF. At that time, most configurations were "clean," with their bombs unloaded , either by way of orderly processes or by jettisoning them with panic to the sea.

How will they attack now, when the aircraft need to be reloaded with weapons? With a few aircraft that'll be reloaded in a rush? An attack against a single air base? Against two missile batteries? Which ones will be attacked, and which ones won't?

At the end of such limited missions, the damage would exceed the cost. The IAF would lose aircraft, and many of them: a missiles array, anti-aircraft artillery and interception fighters would await the strike fighters. The results of the effort would be minimal. A few holes in some lanes, and the destruction of two batteries out of a dozen. Would that be worthwhile?

So why not attack at night, after they finished loading the aircraft with bombs? In October 1973, the IAF did not know how to conduct a surgical attack in the dark of night. Thus, a planned, organized and orchestrated attack, the kind that the IAF had practiced dozens of times since the end of the War of Attrition, was possible only during the daylight hours. The following day at the earliest—Sunday.

Eitan Peled and Yair David, in the rear cockpit seat, were veterans of the War of Attrition. They had experienced flames and smoke. But this time it was big. It was much larger than what they were used to three years ago. The eye was filled with dozens of sketches of missile trails, and hundreds of AAA rounds patching the blue Canal sky with puffs of black smoke.

"This is war," David said.

* * *

Within an hour, everyone had taken off. Nearly everyone, anyway.

Gadi Samok, who had returned only a few days before from the United States, after completing a year at a test pilot's course, did not go. Neither did Ori Shahak and Gideon Eilat.

They looked at each other; especially at Samok, who had seniority in the group. *What will happen to us?*

Samok then said, "Okay, we're a three ship formation. Let's get to the aircraft. Keep in contact, and we'll see what we can do."

Haim Ram was the Combat Manager.

He launched and launched, and suddenly was left with three pilots that wanted to go, one of whom was the young Gideon Eilat, who was not authorized for combat missions.

Gadi Samok, leading the three ship formation, pleaded with Haim to find out what could be done for Gideon, 'the kid'.

"What should we do?" Haim Ram asked Nissim Ashkenazi, commander of the flight squadron at Hatzor, head of the post's wing command.

"Do you still not understand that there's a war? Launch him immediately!" Ashkenazi screamed on the other end of the receiver.

Arik Shlain could not believe his luck. He had still not completed his operational retraining course at the OTU, and there he was, already intercepting enemy aircraft that had invaded through the Canal line.

"It'll be okay," Gideon Eilat encouraged him in the briefing room, and on the short drive towards the aircraft, he explained how and why, and lingered describing the RWR display alerting missile threats.

There was the aircraft: heavy, with two external drop tanks, ten cluster bombs, and two missiles. *What is this? Is this prepared at all for air-to-air mission?*

Now they were at the launching position. There were a lot of Phantoms and Mirages, and everyone was waiting for authorization for takeoff.

The controller got on the radio and checked, formation by formation, their weapons configuration.

Samok, attentive to the controller's questions, understood that takeoff approval was given only to those whose aircraft were configured for aerial combat.

The tower: "Are you armed with bombs?"

Samok: "Negative. We are in air-to-air configuration."

The tower: "Copy. Authorized."

Shlain smiled under his helmet. A fighter pilot is born, first and foremost, to take down other aircraft. *But before taking them down, you need to take off,* he thought, as he felt the aircraft, heavy with bombs and fuel, so very heavy, and sat anxiously in the rear cockpit, watching the sluggish acceleration while the runway was running out.

Half an hour had passed since everyone, including the younger pilots, took off.

This was Gideon Eitan's first operational mission in his life. It was pastoral at twenty-thousand feet. The cries of the controller were the only things tearing through the peacefulness. From far away, the Canal front was visible, covered in heavy smokescreens, as the controller's shouts were unending. Formations were sent in every direction, and things were quiet only for Samok's three ship formation.

"To engagement, heading north," the controller said upon their arrival to Refidim. In the rear of Eilat's cockpit, Arik Shlain wondered *"Engagement," what does that mean?*

From twenty-thousand feet, Samok instructed to jettison the bombs.

Eilat pressed the panic button, jettisoning ten bombs and two drop tanks into the sands of the Sinai. The aircraft suddenly shook, and Shlain in the back seat, thinking *What, have we already been hit?*

The three ship formation of lightweight jets galloped with full afterburners on over the dunes of the Sinai.

"Cancel the engagement," the controller alerted, "are you configured for air-to-ground?"

"Positive," Samok replied.

Gideon Eilat then thought, *This is the second time that Samok has cut corners.* There were rumors in the squadron about his militancy. *Damn, just a minute ago, we had everything. With what exactly is he going to hit the Egyptians?*

"Head on to Budapest," the controller called, "attack any movement coming in from Port Said."

Budapest? What in this desert was given the code name of Hungary's capital? They shifted through maps and found it.

There was the post, wrapped in a blanket of dense smoke, surrounded by many Egyptian vehicles that were creating a huge jam crowded at the tail end of Port Said, while driving towards it.

What do we do? All of our cluster bombs were just thrown in the sand, without a trace, Eilat thought. *We're left with guns, for strafe, just like in the Six-Day War. We snipe from down low, under the radar. That's how it is,* Eilat decided, *I'm going to fight the way life has prepared me to.*

Good, Eilat thought. *Those were pretty good strikes. We surprised them. It should continue this way.* They took a second pass. "Strela" (SA-7) missiles started flying in the air, and Eilat knew the aircraft was very vulnerable—it was big, low, and slow. Yet Samok was not worried, he did not quit, and pulled them to another run, and another one.

Eilat dove again, in a single file line. His face was flushed. Just then, to his right, he saw it—a giant ball of fire rushing towards them at breakneck speed. *I've never seen a missile up close,* he thought, but now he saw it. It was huge, fast, aggressive, and extremely close. There was an explosion, and a giant fireball enveloped Samok's aircraft.

Yehoar "the Rhino" Gal was Samok's navigator.

Greatly frustrated, he fired shell after shell from the 20mm gun on his Sledgehammer, merely scraping the Egyptian armor. Suddenly, the red explosion was next to him. The aircraft jumped in the air. Gal looked behind and saw that they were still in one piece, and only the air intake was perforated like a grater.

Eilat gave up on the strafe run hence avoided the fireball, headed south and searched for Samok. He was not there. He called on the radio—nothing. He searched for anyone that would answer him—nobody.

"Everything's alright," said Samok, returning from hell, "continue with strafe."

15:00-16:00. Hermon Outpost

An hour has passed, maybe two, and Micah Landsman called the air control unit at Mount Meron, and urgently requested from Ora, his girlfriend, to connect him to IAF Headquarters.

"The Syrians are beginning to invade this post," Micah passionately reported, "They are pumping gas. Send aircraft. Hurry!"

"Received," a calm voice from the depths of Tel Aviv answered.

"Faster, fast…"

"Micah. Micah."

Silence.

15:00-16:00. Southern Golan Heights

Yanki Yardani identified the stages of ejection: the canopy jettisoned, the windshield, the rocket launching him to the sky and rolling him in it, the parachute deploying, and pyrotechnic cartridges separating between him and the seat.

"I'm drifting eastward," he announced on the SART (Search And Rescue Transceiver). "My left leg is injured, I don't know where I am."

He glanced down at his airman's watch. *It's almost four, and the sun is in the west, pulling on the sky.* The wind drifts eastward, sticking its tongue out, jesting at his life's hopes and dreams. He was struggling in the strings. *Not so far eastward.*

Land. He looked around, in the middle of a thorny basalt field. There were explosions everywhere. *I need to escape.* He lowered his torso. *I'm so thirsty,* he thought. He reached for his bag of water and drank the whole thing. He ran west, his G-suit pressing and his left leg hurting.

Run, man, run.

He saw a sign up ahead. *Just be in Hebrew, please be in Hebrew.* The sign read: "Danger, minefield, leaving the road is prohibited."

He continued onwards. At a T intersection, he saw a sign indicating the direction of the interstate—116. *What is 116?*

I'm on the edge of the grid, he decided. He needed to go further west. At the side of the road, he identified a concrete structure, and within it a metal telecommunications box. He entered and took off his pressure suit. *What now?* He needed to go west. *Shit. It's a boulder area. This limp is going to impede my progress. North. I'll go north, until I find a highway that heads west.*

He found north. *Where is a damn road to the west?* Bullets whistled. *Who is that?*

He hopped back to the concrete structure, his G-suit on the floor giving him a momentary feeling of home.

16:00. Office of the Minister of Defense. Kirya, Tel Aviv

A bit more than two hours remained before the first star would appear in the sky, marking the end of Yom Kippur, just two hours after Israel was struck with the biggest surprise in its existence. The Israeli Defense Minister took a break from the frequent cries for help coming from the soldiers at strongholds along the Canal, the disturbing news of a successful Egyptian effort, and the shock that gripped the leadership following the loss of contact with the Hermon outpost, and convened with Israeli newspaper editors in his office, in the Kirya in Tel Aviv.

"Tonight and tomorrow, we will be engaging in containment and defense," he informed the assembled company, as he headed to his table. "A defensive war has many advantages, even political ones. We have no need for another war, one that we would be accused of starting. By tomorrow night, we will have enough tanks, both at the Canal and in the Golan Heights. If things go well, we will attack at some point thereafter. They will pay dearly for this war."

"Are you optimistic, Minister?" one of the journalists asked.

The Minister stared at the questioner, and a small smile appeared on his face. "The truth? It's very…I'm going to assume that the Egyptians are going on a big adventure here, one that is not very calculated. We will wait until tomorrow afternoon. Afterwards, I wouldn't want to be anyone on the other side…"

16:30. The 201st Squadron

"Watch out for Egyptian helicopters trying to get commando units to our territory," the controller instructed "Wild Bull" Peled, who was running his four-ship formation over the sands of Sinai.

I hope we'll find one, "Wild Bull" thought. *We'll take care of it.*

It's like a painting, Uzi Shamir (Shmidko) thought in the rear cockpit of aircraft Number 4, behind Yigal Stavi. He was enthused by the desert sands, the water canal, the massive lakes, the lazy boats on the water, and the sun that was descending rapidly.

"Eye contact," someone yelled, and everyone faced towards the glimmer that emerged on the horizon, identifying six Egyptian helicopters crossing the Canal, conducting NOE (Nap Of the Earth) flight.

"Single file," Peled ordered, entering first and missing. Koren approached next, and missed.

"Narrow the range," instructed "Wild Bull," and sent number 3 to recover the squadron's dignity.

Ben Ami Perry was the only pilot in the world who could shoot a Vulcan 20mm gun, which fires 1,200 rounds per minute, with bursts of eight bullets, and get them all to the target. Now he proved that his training was not just a fantasy, and planted the first helicopter into the ground.

Then it was Stavi's turn. He approached, and missed.

"Wild Bull" approached again and hit, and Koren did as well.

Again with Perry: another short burst, followed by another flaming helicopter.

Stavi missed again, and "Bull" got another helicopter to his credit, leaving the last one. Perry liked Moshe Koren, but more than anything else, he wanted another helicopter to his name. He found it really difficult to curb his excitement after Koren missed, knowing that the last one was his—there was no other way. He drove the sight pipper on target—and missed. Zetelny, in the back seat, thought to himself, *two is still good*, but it was Perry in the front seat, and to him, there was no way that the helicopter would not be his last. He shortened the pattern and closed in, opened fire on the helicopter canopy, and claimed his third on the ground.

From the lookout position in the last aircraft in the convoy, Shmidko saw a helicopter burning in the air and soldiers jumping from it, crashing to their deaths, as a second helicopter crashed into the ground, soldiers trying desperately to escape with their lives.

Suddenly, everything was quiet. Six large bonfires illuminated the blanket of darkness that was starting to cover the desert sands. Shmidko thought that the Egyptian soldiers were sent only an hour ago to kill Jews, but no one had prepared them to face the angry "Wild Bull" and his comrades, and they were down there, burning in a huge bonfire, in agony. He saw that the fires were situated straight as an arrow, and at equal distances, and thought that someone had decided that death required strict order as well. Stavi then said "Uzi, sorry I couldn't get you a hit too!"

"Wow," Zetelny and Perry call out in two voices on the ICS (Intercom System). "Wow."

17:00. Ofira Air Control Unit

Just before sunset, the Listening Unit of the Intelligence Corps, situated on a mountain ridge above Ofira Bay, reported that Egyptian commando helicopters were operating in the area. "Pay attention," they informed Maj. Avi Amitai, commander of the adjacent Air Control Unit, who was also situated on the narrow cliff above the bay, "you may be subject to attack."

"Organize a defensive perimeter," Amitai instructed, and dug out trenches, lined with sandbags, were filled for the first time since the unit was established, and everyone was told to try to locate helicopters.

17:30. Southern Golan Heights

In the twilight, Skyhawk four-ship formation pilot Yanki Yardani identified four tanks. Tanks that were approaching. Over the cannons, he saw heads covered in IDF issued helmets. "Do not shoot, do not shoot," he yelled in their direction.

After he joined them, they traveled in the dark and turned left. They climbed to the top of the hill. They met paratroopers who were happy to see them. He listened to the communication devices, and heard the voices of war on the ground as it unfolded. "The ammunition is out," "Dozens of vehicles are headed out way."

A few hours later, after being introduced to the world of tank crews and understanding that there were perhaps worse things than abandoning an aircraft, Yanki Yardani was extracted from Tel al-Saki in the southern Golan Heights.

What will happen to them? Yanki thought, clinging to the protective metal of a rescue APC. *Who is going to rescue the soldiers of the Armored Corps?*

16:00. Prime Minister

As darkness fell and Yom Kippur departed, citizens turned on their radios and televisions and received, through the airwaves and on their screens, the Prime Minister, Golda Meir, in a broadcast that had been recorded a half an hour prior.

"Citizens of Israel," the old lady opened her speech, appearing serious and upset, "Today, at two in the afternoon, the Egyptian and Syrian armies launched an attack against Israel. They conducted a series of attacks by air, tanks, and artillery, in the Sinai Peninsula and the Golan Heights. The IDF fought and pushed back the attack. The enemy suffered serious losses…"

"…Our enemies had hoped to surprise the citizens of Israel on the day of Yom Kippur…our attackers thought that on Yom Kippur, we would not be prepared to fight back. We were not surprised."

"…For some days, Israel's intelligence services had become aware that the armies of Egypt and Syria were preparing a joint offensive. IDF patrols found that large numbers of military attack forces were concentrated near the Suez Canal and the Golan Heights.

The findings of the patrols confirmed the news: our forces needed to meet the danger."

"...We have no doubt as to our victory," the Prime Minister continued, "but according to our convictions, this renewed Egyptian-Syrian aggression—it is like an act of madness. We decided to attempt to prevent the outbreak of combat. We appealed to influential political and diplomatic sources in order to prevent the criminal initiative of the rulers of Egypt and Syria...We called on them to prevent the war...Given the gravity of the situation, I was compelled to convene the Cabinet for a meeting on Yom Kippur. The attack while the meeting occurred..."

"Citizens of Israel! This is not the first time that war has been imposed on us...we are confident in the spirit and strength of the IDF to defeat our enemies!"

18:30. Nefah. Golan Heights

As the darkness engulfed the basalt rocks of the Golan Heights, Col. Yitzhak Ben Shoham, commander of the 188th Brigade, left the command post bunker at Nefah, in which he had been situated since his arrival from the General Staff, in order to join his forces with those in the southern sector.

IAF Sgt. Ofer Sharabi saw the enlisted tank division commander of the Golan Heights preparing to leave, and in the background, he heard the army rabbi scold one of his soldiers. "It's not important to me what you'll do. Scrape the soldier off of the tank with the putty knife and get him buried." Sharabi, who had never been under fire, suddenly understood the meaning of war.

18:30-20:20. Commander's Conference of the General Staff

For the first time since the battle erupted, the top staff of the operational forum of the General Staff met. "In the Golan Heights, enemy aircraft encountered our aircraft before they were able to act. The only place where they succeeded was the outpost at Hermon," the IAF Commander informed the group.

If anyone were to look for the first moment in the Yom Kippur War where the IAF's 'genetic code' came crashing down, then this was it.

There are those who would argue that better decisions could have been made. There are others who would argue about the dynamics that led those decisions. You could even raise an eyebrow at the style they took. However, there is one that is inexcusable.

Maj. Gen. Benny Peled, who commanded a corps that prided itself above all else on its culture of investigations and truthful reporting, free of "rounded corners" and shortcuts, in every situation and at any time, shattered the foundations of the temple as Yom Kippur came to its end.

Did enemy aircraft encounter our aircraft before they could act?

In their first emergence into Israeli territory, at the outbreak of war, enemy aircraft had completely dominated the skies of the Golan Heights. Most of their aircraft had not even noticed the tails of an Israeli aircraft until they had nearly finished their objectives and retraced their steps back to their base.

Was the Hermon outpost the only place that they were able to hit? In addition to the "eyes of the country," the Syrian aircraft struck direct hits against Tel Abu Nida, and its communications and intelligence centers. The Syrians also struck Tel Fares, "the southern eyes" of the Golan as well as Camp Nefah, the command center of the IDF's forces in the Golan Heights (leaving the place blown up and pulverized, disconnected from the electrical grid and with two fatalities and six people wounded). An attempt to strike the Air Control Unit at Mount Meron failed: the Syrian bombs struck the mountain slope.

Perhaps the IAF Commander could arise and explain the puzzling difference between his version and the facts on the ground. Is it possible that Benny Peled, the commander of the corps that was in charge of the central command "Pit," was not aware of the facts even hours after they had occurred?

I suppose that the main explanation for the discrepancy between Maj. Gen. Peled's unfortunate description and the actual facts on the ground lies first and foremost in the IAF Commander's need to continue and create a sense that everything was under control, as always. The IAF Commander struggled to understand that the world he had known—with its well-known framework, in which he lived his life, into which he poured his beliefs and insights, and into which he raised generations of fighter pilots—had shattered to pieces.

In light of his statement, as well as other statements that were given, we can assume that as darkness descended that evening, Maj. Gen. Peled was still inclined to believe that, in spite of the failure that shocked the State of Israel, the IAF remained the "neighborhood bully." Therefore, the situation would continue, and the glory of the Six-Day War and the dogfights of the War of Attrition would pave the way, from the following day's morning hours, to a crushing knockout over the "thing" that suddenly occurred. Furthermore, there would be no mention of any failures or complications; and heaven forbid any thoughts about losses.

The IAF Commander continued to brief about the Egyptian attacks in Sinai, and the destroyed aircraft on our side and on theirs. He concluded emphatically, "It's important that the crews be able to arm all of the aircraft for the morning missions, as whatever will happen will be a quick decision. An hour, hour and a half from now. No more."

He then added, "Our work tomorrow is contingent on the weather. According to meteorologists, low-level clouds are expected above Damascus in the morning, making it difficult to strike air bases and ground forces. In the Canal, as well, low clouds are expected until 09:00."

"From what I see at the moment, here are the possibilities for action for the Air Force tomorrow: We go to Syria. Air bases and then missile systems. Later, we will organize strikes against Egyptian air bases, and if the weather is good, we'll go on to destroy the missiles there, either whole or in part."

Tough questions arise yet again.

According to Peled, in the absence of cloud interference affecting his aircraft, it would be a matter of one day before the missile layouts in Syria and Egypt would become dust, along with their air bases. Dirt and ashes, and nothing else but a memory.

Is that so? Every plan presentation that he and Motti Hod, his predecessor, had done with senior IAF officials of the Operations Department described about 24 hours per layout. This was just for the missile layout. However, Benny was arguing that everything—or at least, just about everything—could be destroyed within 24 hours; missiles, air bases, and on both fronts.

Was this a plan that could have been carried out? No.

Operational designs, for better or for worse, rely (almost) entirely on the IAF strike fighters. Those fighters are meant to participate in every activity: everyone here, and then everyone there, and so on. Such an action cannot be carried out in one day, under any circumstances.

Dado concluded, "This is the IDF's first attempt at winning a war while starting on the defensive. This situation, until now, was only discussed in theory…the first part is to contain and let the enemy break his head, and only afterwards to move on the offensive. Regarding the containment phase, IDF forces are in fair condition…regarding the IAF—top priority will be given to fighting the Egyptian Air Force, while providing assistance, to every possible extent, to the ground forces in the Canal."

19:00. The 201st Squadron

The cloak of darkness did not skip over the 201st Squadron's building, and in the briefing room, under the solemn, bright fluorescent lights, the air crew pilots came and gathered.

There's something soothing in inhaling nicotine, Regev thought, as trills of smoke screens made their way to the clubroom's ceiling, and two air conditioners blended them together, while adding noise to the bustle.

In walked Huldai. With an easy step, he ascended to the stage of the briefing room, his pressure suit on his body, his "leadership stick" in his hand. Without further ado, he began the tradition of inquiries and updates of the end of the day. He explained, to anyone who still had not understood, or internalized, or both, that the State of Israel was caught with its pants down, and the IAF was entrusted with containment on both fronts in order to help the enlisted ground forces curb enemy advances until the arrival of reserve forces.

Just before he left the stage, he stopped for a moment, stared straight down at the forum below him, and said, "Guys, look carefully at everyone else in this room. This is a war. Not everyone that is sitting here now will make it to the end of the road."

Regev thought, *War? We're going to die? Where did he get these exaggerations from?*

19:40. A Letter of the IAF Commander

Fifteen minutes before eight o'clock in the evening, the teleprinters began to issue a cable from the commander, Maj. Gen. Benny Peled, in every IAF base, wing, and support unit.

"The ceasefire has been violated. The Egyptian and Syrian enemy concentrated large forces along our border in the Golan Heights and the Suez Canal, and has swung its arrogant arm on our country in the midst of Yom Kippur, in order to eradicate our independence."

"The long assault arm of the IDF was sent to the air again. The Israeli Air Force is taking off for combat. It is directed entirely to thwarting the enemy aggression, and to eradicate, destroy, and smash the enemy's dreams of breaking through our borders. We will cripple the enemy to the bitter end, and defeat its aircraft in the air and on the ground."

"The State of Israel is trusting in all of us to be worthy to proudly bear the supreme mission incumbent on all of us. I wish to all of our IAF fighters the best of luck, and for a peaceful and safe year for the people of Israel in their homeland."

20:00. The 200ᵗʰ Squadron (Dalton Camp)

"What's going on?" Maj. Nir asked the operations officer in the Air Force "Pit," who was on the other end of the line.

"We are moving in the morning on 'Model 5'," said the officer, directing the strike of missile arrays in Syria.

"Go time is 05:45. Follow the prompt that's in your hands. Do not call anymore. If there is a change, we will notify you."

20:30-21:00. Chamber of the Head of Central Command and its Surroundings

In the IAF "Pit," everyone was waiting for an update, for the news from the ground forces that all was well: that we contained them and that we were starting to chase them. As they declared throughout the years. Just as had been promised

In the alert chamber, intelligence officers were in constant contact with their man in "Babylon," and every few minutes they repeated the same question—"have our troops already crossed the Canal?"

However, reports and updates that flowed into the "Pit" showed the apparently feasible crossing of the Canal to be a fanciful fairy tale, as it did not seem to work in the field. Egyptian anti-tank squads, hiding in the Sinai sands, were ruthlessly massacring dozens of tank crews attempting to break through to aid the strongholds on the Bar-Lev line.

Shortly before 21:00 it became clear and certain for the first time that the Egyptians were able to build some initial bridgeheads over the Canal.

On Saturday night, no one could define for the Air Force exactly where was the frontline between our troops and their forces. Moreover, no one could pinpoint the bridges over the Canal either. Thus, the Air Force was not capable of fulfilling the duties assigned to it from time immemorial: to help the "greens" whenever cries of help arose from an area. These screams continued and grew louder.

At 21:00, Peled decided to send fighters to strike, no matter what, with or without intelligence.

Two past Mirage squadron leaders, Lt. Col. Oded Marom, Head of the IAF's Training Department, and Lt. Col. Amos Amir, who was meant to replace Giora Furman as Head of the Operations Department, were requested by the IAF Commander to undertake the project of preparing targets in the Canal for the IAF.

They were upset; they were confused. Both men are products of the Corps assembly line, the one that sanctified the organization, the order, the method, and suddenly, there was this.

Without orderly intelligence; with fragments of information that still made their way to their table; and especially with common sense and the gut feelings of the officers who were among the commanders of the War of Attrition and knew the capabilities of the aircraft and the "scene" itself—they tried to imagine the areas that the Egyptian army would prefer for setting up bridging and crossing points. With every virtual crossing area, on both sides of the Canal, they divided sections of 100 meters each, in which the Phantoms would be able to inflict maximum damage to the forces...forces that may or may not exist there.

21:00. News Conference. Sokolov House Tel Aviv

Accompanied by the Head of Military Intelligence, Maj. Gen. Eli Zeira, the Defense Minister of the State of Israel stood in front of an array of microphones and television cameras, and smiled broadly in front of dozens of journalists and broadcasters. He began his remarks by explaining the strategic outlook that guided Israel's defensive policy.

"For years, we have been confronted by great, many troops," Dayan said. "If it is our desire to live normal lives, then we must refrain from mobilizing the reserves for deployment. We have taken a risk with what has happened, so that in the end, we will be forceful enough against the enemy, and we will control the combat arena."

"We had information about the aggressive intentions of the combined Arab forces, and we suspected that such an attack would in fact take place. We were faced with a dilemma: to shoot first and thus win an important military advantage—or to pass on the first strike, thus losing the military advantage, but winning in clarifying the image of who are the real instigators of this war. We have chosen this latter option."

"We didn't have a bad day," Dayan continues. "In the north, we had insignificant loses. After this first day of battle, we have stood firmly on the front. As for the first day in the Canal, the Egyptians had no serious crossing. Nevertheless, the Canal is a long line, with many possible avenues of infiltration. I would have been surprised if the Egyptians hadn't managed to cross or establish a few bridgeheads. It may well be that during the night we will see more Egyptian forces build on their side, but as of tomorrow, with the arrival of the reserves, things will start to operate according to our plans. In short, there are no significant Egyptian forces in Sinai, and I am not particularly concerned about them."

"In your opinion, do you expect Jordan to intervene in this war?" a reporter asked Dayan.

"Jordan just had the events of Black September, and it is not in their interest to have a 'Black October' as well," he said, to the sound of laughter in the audience.

21:00. Chamber of the Head of Central Command

Under the guidance of the Chief of Staff, the IAF Commander presented the IAF's plan for the following day—the destruction of missiles in Egypt named Operation "Challenge."

Lt. Gen. Elazar approved the plan, ordered a photographic aerial reconnaissance mission prior to striking the missiles. He then informed those present that he would be in the Command Center at 06:00 to make a final decision.

21:00-22:00. *The 201ˢᵗ Squadron*

Mission orders for nightly loft strikes at the Canal were already there waiting for them as they left the briefing room. It was a single aircraft mission, a difficult one. Until that point, only four-ship formation heads had performed them: this was an "adults only" flight. Most of them had never practiced a flight like that.

"There's no choice," they were told. "This is what there is, and this is how we will win."

Amnon Gurion was the Deputy Flight Commander B in the squadron, and he learned that he had seniority over all of the night strike teams. He decided to call Amos Amir.

Amos may have been a lieutenant colonel, but there is no substitute for personal introductions, even in the IAF. Gurion knew Amos from Flight Academy and the Phantom course that Amos passed in the squadron, and therefore he skipped all of the words of courtesy and got straight to the point.

"What you are doing makes no sense," he grumbled. "You are taking 'tiles' along the Canal and requiring us to toss bombs over them without any accurate intelligence. Just a train of aircraft over territory where we don't even know what is contained within it. This is not effective, and this is dangerous."

"Gurion, the situation is a mess," Amos said on the other end of the line. "We don't know our right from our left. This is the situation. There is nothing we can do about it. We are trying to prevent the Egyptians from controlling every stronghold. As you know, the loft cluster bombs have a killing diameter of 500 meters. Our hope is that it will hit them at the estimated concentration points. Perhaps on those that crossed, those waiting to cross. Perhaps even the bridges."

22:05. *Air Control Unit Ophir (Sharm el-Sheikh)*

In Zaferat a-Daika, where the unit was located, Dudi Ziv, the control officer responsible for protecting the perimeter of the enclosure, opened the door of the operations trailer, and in an agitated voice announced that he saw lights of two helicopters, coming up the mountain.

"Two helicopters are on their way to attack us," reported the controllers in the IAF base, located below them, while simultaneously calling to the Phantom patrolling 30 miles from them, urging the pilot to quickly handle the suspecting helicopters.

Another minute passed, and a deafening explosion shook the mountain, the control trailer leapt in the air, landed back on the ground, and a hidden hand turned off their lights and cut their radios. Their screen displays went dark as well. A resounding silence enveloped the mountain.

In the black sky hanging over Abu Redis, Adi Benaya patrolled with Itzik Baram in the seat behind him, peering into the darkness while squinting, looking for signs of hostility in the sky.

Suddenly the controller called in a nervous voice, and ordered them to stop everything and get to the Air Control Unit at Ophir at full speed.

"They took the unit," the controller informed Benaya, "Get to there. Snipe. Spray. Do it without hesitation. The flames will direct you to the place."

"Are you sure?" Benaya asked.

"Yes, fire at everything you see." The controller answered.

They arrived. A huge fire consumed the control unit. Benaya took a burst of shells into the center of the flames. There was a jam. *Damn.*

23:30. Airborne Command Post from Nefah to Mount Canaan (Safed)

Midnight approached, and dark rumors were circulating among the command group.

This is it, decided Col. Savron, commander of Northern Command's air command post, who heard of Syrian tanks moving towards the borders, and knew that this was the pretext he was seeking in order to leave the wobbly table and intolerable crowdedness.

In a van whose darkened lights were making their way down the road, they crossed the Daughters of Jacob Bridge, climbed up Mount Canaan and settled into a new and spacious command center—the kindergarten of the police rehabilitation center on Mount Canaan, where children's toys were still scattered.

22:30-24:00. The 201ˢᵗ Squadron

An hour of red flames flickering throughout the night sky passed, and the loft strike teams returned from the Canal. No one knew if they hit anything there in the dark, and everyone was especially pleased towards one another.

A while later, they sat comfortably in armchairs in the clubroom and heard a Sledgehammer making an emergency landing on the base premises. Someone informed them that both the pilot and the navigator were killed. The Skyhawk squadron at Ramat David lost their senior leader. Egyptian military forces were occupying the Bar-Lev Line, and the Ophir air control unit suffered a direct hit from a missile.

"Why did they leave us in air-to-air configurations all day?" someone asked harshly. "Why did we throw bombs in the sea?" someone else wondered. "Why not let us hit them as soon as this started?!"

And how is it that we've flown so much but did so very little? What is this thing that's fallen right on top of us?

Despite the exhaustion, the questions, and the frustrations, they knew that "everything will be alright." It was a fact. Around the evening time, they put down six helicopters. *We made dozens of strikes, and not a single aircraft could touch us. Okay, so the element of surprise was on their side today. We started on a handicap, but tomorrow morning, the real game will begin. This time, we will dictate the rules; and rhythm; and we'll rule the arena. Those idiots. They have no idea where they've stuck their* heads. *Just suicidal. We'll hit them, We'll break them, and we'll mess them up, just like in the Six-Day War.*

Yair David looked around him and it seemed to him that the young ones, the generation that did not go to the desert, had not yet internalized what befell them. *That's strange*, he thought, because the IAF, and the 201st Squadron in particular, came out of the War of Attrition damaged and in pain. *Do they not know their squadron's legacy? Have they not heard about the final six weeks of the war? About the five Phantoms that fell? About Hetz and Goldwasser, who were killed? About Fier, Shohat, and Eini who were captured? They haven't internalized that we are a bruised squadron, that we were hit by strong ones? Yes, we are the 201st, and, come what may, we always have our heads up, but we don't disparage Egypt. We have a serious enemy. This is not the Hebrew Youth Brigades.*

It's time that the young guys understand that this is a war to the death.

It was almost midnight, and Maj. Huldai, the acting squadron leader, understood that something had gone wrong. He knew that, in fact, he did not understand what was happening, and that most likely, no one else did either.

A veteran of the War of Attrition familiar with war, he knew that there would be war the following day, early in the morning, and that war required troops. How many? How could he know, if he did not even know what was attacking them? However, Huldai was convinced that it would be okay, because the Operations Department had already issued a new order for the destruction of the Egyptian missile array. Members of the Technical Division were working to prepare the aircraft for their mission, and tomorrow morning they would fly over there and knock out the missiles. After that, everything would be easy. As always.

He started turning out the lights of the clubroom, where the floor was full of his fighters laying half-asleep on mattresses. Well, not everyone.

Some soldiers were laughing comfortably on the orange club sofas, watching Dan Shilon, the broadcaster on the television channel (there was only one) announce the final basketball game of the European Cup between Yugoslavia and Spain. It was on a direct transmission from Barcelona. Business as usual.

"Go to sleep," Huldai scolded them.

"Let us watch…" they grumbled.

"Turn off the TV," Huldai shouted. "Go to sleep. Tomorrow there will be war. Tomorrow we will hit Egypt."

Midnight. The 201st Squadron

Maj. Huldai was unaware of the desperate containment war being waged at that very moment by IDF ground troops against the Egyptian and Syrian armies. Far from the threat of tank shells and anti-tank bombs blasting into the blue-and-white dam that a few soldiers in khakis tried to set up in front of them, Huldai relaxed in the chair of his air-conditioned office. He strived to breathe deeply and thought to himself—*calm down, buddy, relax. You're an acting squadron leader. You're the boss. It's cold here at the top, but that's okay. This is the face of command. And probably combat.*

Just before he closed his eyes and the fog of sleep arrived to cover the question marks, he recalled a passed-down story about the squadron leader's conference with the former IAF Commander. In it, at the end of the presentation of operational plans to destroy Egypt's missiles, Motti Hod concluded, a tiny smile shown on his face, "It will be just like 'Focus'. By the evening, we'll already be able to celebrate a Missile Destruction party."

One squadron leader said in his direction, "So maybe it's better if we just celebrate already in the evening before?"

Just before he slipped into the protective blanket of sleep, he imagined the following day's party, and the general weariness that would surround it. He could not distinguish that 'tomorrow' had already turned into 'today', and focused on the promise of "tomorrow"—a new, bright horizon, for him, for the squadron, for the IAF and for all of the people of Israel.

OCTOBER 7TH

Earthquake

By the time the hour hand on the war clock finished its eleventh rotation, thousands of young men in khakis were paying the price of the lawlessness that their leaders had them pursue. These leaders had not prepared, had underestimated the enemy, had not respected the harm inflicted on Arab dignity. They did not internalize the anger of Egypt and Syria for having taken their lands, nor their determination towards building new strength, nor that the enemy soldier was a much more worthy opponent than his absurd characterization.

An hour after midnight, the seam between Saturday and Sunday opened an imperceptible crack in Israel's security; and it was growing.

In the Sinai Peninsula, surrounded by strongholds on the Bar-Lev Line, eleven bridges spread over the Canal, and five Egyptian divisions passed over them on their way to establish an outpost in the monstrous sand dunes. In the southern Golan Heights, Syrian tank, anti-tank and infantry forces conducted themselves like patrons on their own estate, and there was no one to obstruct them on their way to the Jordan and the beaches of the Sea of Galilee.

"I don't have enough troops to hold back the Syrians," the Head of Northern Command reported to Senior Command, "I need immediate air support to close the continuously expanding battle near Post 116."

"Aircraft will be sent your way," the IDF Chief of Staff said encouragingly, though informing him that the IAF was not capable of pinpoint strikes at night. "Air support will come to you in the morning."

Weighing the balance of forces on the ground, and knowing that part of the Syrian armored vehicles were heading towards Nefah, the Head of Northern Command, from IDF headquarters in the Golan Heights, realized that a good commander is first and foremost a living commander. He rose slowly from his chair and announced into the air, "We're moving."

Afterwards, he approached Brig. Gen. Rafael Eitan, shook his hand and said, "I'm heading to Mount Canaan. Uri (Simchoni, an Operations officer), Hagi (Min, an Intelligence officer), Kaimu (the Communications officer), and Bar David (the Head of Artillery Command) will stay with you in the meantime. I wish you all the best."

Raful, a man of few words, straightened his Australian hat, pulled the map with a blank expression, and concluded the ceremony for transferring control of the Golan Heights.

00:25-01:00. Senior Command Post

"What needs to be done most urgently on the Egyptian front," the Defense Minister suggested to the Chief of Staff, "is to change the balance of power between our armor and theirs. We could cancel the operation to destroy their missiles meant for tomorrow when we get more tanks in the area, and instead go right now, at night, and obstruct the Egyptian crossings; even if we lose a few aircraft."

"An attack in the dark would not achieve the needed results," Dado said, "and in the meantime, there hasn't been any meaningful crossing yet by the Egyptians."

In the middle of Sunday night, the Defense Minister was not convinced.

Moshe Dayan still believed that the IDF soldiers possessed the "quality" advantage, but he knew that however great the advantage, it could break down in the face of highly unbalanced power. It seemed to him that this was exactly what was happening on the eastern side of the Canal, as Egyptian military forces continued to flow to the sands of Sinai, with the advantage of darkness. It was necessary to unravel the link between the exploitation of night and crossing.

"Around 5 AM, I'm going to sit down with the IAF Commander, reassess the situation, and then we will decide accordingly," Lt. Gen. Elazar said, attentive to the responsible minister's distress.

"Okay," Dayan said, "but if the situation with regards to tanks and bridging is not good in the morning, it's preferable to attack them than to attack air bases and missile batteries, regardless of whether or not they have anti-aircraft capabilities. This is because the latter will have no real effect on the course of battle."

01:00. Air Control Unit Ophir

An unidentified, muffled noise rolled up the steep access road coming to the gate of the Air Control Unit.

"Tanks!" the two guards, older reservists, shouted, as they recognized the familiar silhouettes emerging around the last bend of the road. No one knew who they were or where they came from, and there was no time to wonder, as the tanks lined up in front of the unit's gate and opened machine gun fire.

The two reservists yelled and fell silent, as the tanks trampled the gate and continued their fire.

Maj. Gen. Avi Amitai was not far from the remains of the gate when the treads of the lead tank screeched to a halt five meters beside him, and as the horror seized him, he heard speech from the turret head. Hebrew.

Amitai jumps with all his might from the position on the side of the road, holding a white tank top, and yelled: "Stop, you are killing us!" He climbed up the tank and continued to scream at the commander, so hard his vocal chords nearly exploded, "You psychos! You're shooting at us! There are no Arabs here, we're all Jews!"

"We were told that this mountain had been conquered," the dazed tank commander apologized, "'Get up there and liberate it,' is what they ordered us to do."

The fiasco at the Ophir Air Control Unit Base occurred because of three factors.

The first factor was arrogance. In 1972, Egyptian forces trained in launching Kelt cruise missiles in the area of Aswan. The IAF Intelligence gathered the layout of the drills, and among other things, identified attacks directed against radar installations stationed as targets..

"Egyptian Kelt missiles have the ability to home in on radiation from the radar apparatus," Maj. Avner Yofi, Head of the IAF Egyptian Air Force Activity Division, wrote.

"You are mistaken," replied the professionals of the Technical Branch, "the Kelt does not have homing capabilities."

The second factor was chaos. No one bothered to update the IAF's control units about the Kelt missiles that were launched on Saturday at several targets within Israel.

The final factor was the "domino effect." The Control Unit was warned of a possible commando attack involving the use of helicopters, and Lt. Dudi Ziv saw two lights and was convinced that they came from the helicopters they were warned about. The update from the control unit to the IAF base informed them that two helicopters were heading to the mountain. It was at this point that contact was lost.

Someone reached the conclusion that Egyptian helicopters probably landed their commandos, who then took over the control unit. As a result, an armored division was immediately sent to retake the base.

One way or another, by the end of the long night, it became clear that two Kelt missiles were in fact launched by Egyptian Tupolev bombers towards the control unit, and their lights were confused for helicopters. The first of the missiles missed while the second hit, killing five of the unit's soldiers.

01:30. Chamber of the Head of Central Command

"The problem will be how to get through the next thirty hours before the reserves are deployed," the Chief of Staff said to the IAF Commander.

"The IAF is prepared for 'Challenge 4', the operation to destroy the missile batteries along the Canal," Maj. Gen. Peled answered, pretending that he had not noticed the distress of the ground troops that Lt. Gen. Elazar was throwing at him.

"We will start the morning at 06:45 with the first strike run to hit the anti-aircraft weapons. Forty minutes later, at 07:25, eight air bases in Egypt will be attacked, with the aim to paralyze them... four hours afterwards, the Egyptian missile system will be attacked."

"It is possible," Peled continued, connecting for a moment to the distress signals from the Chief of Staff, "that even during the second flyover, while attacking the air bases, the destruction of missile systems could be implemented, and immediately afterwards, we would be clear to attack enemy targets on both sides of the Canal."

03:51. Northern Command and Senior Command Posts

"The situation is not good," Hakah reported to the Chief of Staff, waking up from a brief nap. "To the south, enemy forces are flowing in towards the 188th Brigade, and are harming it. At the Rafid intersection, the Syrians entered from the west. They've approached near the city of Quneitra. Outpost 110, on the highway, was ordered to evacuate all the men still in the communities. A few other positions surround them, but there is doubt as to whether they can be evacuated or not. Tank reinforcements are likely to come only later. If they won't receive significant help in the morning, the situation could be severe."

"How can you aid in the north?" Dado asked Peled.

"A Skyhawk squadron is nearly complete."

"Good," Dado said.

04:15-04:45. The 201ˢᵗ Squadron

Nimrod Amami reluctantly lifted himself up from the mattress spread on the floor in the Squadron clubroom.

In the navigation room, he met with Shlain, the second "child." Map preparation was always the work of the "children" of the squadron, and particularly at that time, now that Huldai forbade them from flying until further notice.

Under bright florescent lights, they studied the master map of Operation "Challenge 4" that a senior pilot and a senior navigator prepared during the night. They counted the number of planned formations in the operation, checked how many aircraft would be in each formation, and prepared as many maps as there were aircraft in the formation, and shared in the sorrow of the young guy who would receive the bottom map, the one whose course was marked with carbon paper.

04:45. Briefing Room

"Today is the day," Col. Amos Lapidot, the Wing Commander, said as he joined the briefing. "In two hours, we launch the first of four fly-overs to destroy the missiles in Egypt, just like in the Six-Day War."

Ron Huldai, who took over the briefing, specified, "the first sortie is designed to 'cut off the head' of Egyptian anti-aircraft capabilities along the Canal, while simultaneously attacking eight air bases, those closest to the Canal, with the intention to allow our aircraft to do their work uninterrupted."

"Our squadron's mission is to attack the Lakes region," Huldai continued, pointing out the attack site on the map. "Executing a loft strike, we are supposed to hit the bridges being used for crossing, as well as the defensive AAA batteries array around them. In addition, we are to attack, in passing, the Tanta air base runways."

"Afterwards, the most important rounds will come," Huldai added. "Actually, three of them, during which the Egyptian missiles array will be destroyed."

We're returning back to ourselves, Gil Regev thought. *Ordered commands, known methods, self-confidence. An end to this loss of control.*

04:37. Office of the Chief of Staff

Lt. Gen. Elazar took a break from polluting the command post with cigarette smoke and visited the Defense Minister's office, where he needed to provide an update on the situation.

"They have penetrated in three sectors of the Golan," Dado said. "The most serious of the three is Hushniya sector. The number of invading tanks is unknown, but it is estimated that there are dozens of them."

"Has there been a change in the southern front?" Dayan asked.

"From everything we have gathered, there is a change for the better," Dado answered.

"Is there a possibility for air support on the northern front as well?" Dayan wondered.

"We could use a squadron of Skyhawks," replied the IAF Commander, who had just arrived to the room, "but if the weather forecast is correct, it could be impossible to engage in the action."

"How significant is the Syrian incursion?" Dayan asked.

"It's a dangerous one," Dado answered.

Suddenly, perhaps due to the intimacy of the Chief of Staff's office, perhaps due to the disturbing news from the Golan Heights, the Defense Minister wondered aloud, "Will the commanders in the Golan Heights, Hofi and Eitan, who are not members of the Armored Corps, be able to manage the containment battles effectively?" Before anyone in the room had a moment to take in the embarrassing inquiry, he completed the rhetorical question, "I have great doubt."

"Given the situation," Dayan continued, "I want to get to Hakah (Yitzhak Hopi) and see what's happening up there; if we are actually going to lose the Golan Heights." He noticed Dado shrinking in his chair, and added, "I'm not going up Mount Canaan to give him orders, but to see and understand the situation."

05:10-05:30. Chamber of the Head of Central Command

"Everyone," Benny Peled said to those sitting in his office, "as the Defense Minister has said, everything depends on us now. Get to work."

Col. Giora Furman was the head of the Operations Department, and was supposed to be able to provide operational answers even to changing situations; Giora knew that this was exactly that type of situation.

"Prepare the 'Model'," he instructed Lt. Col. Ben-Nun, Head of the Attack Wing. He was convinced that the issue was time, a very little bit of time and that "Model 5," the operation to destroy the Syrian missile systems, would be launched, and hoped with all of his heart that it would take place after "Challenge 4" was concluded. A feeling in his gut bothered him.

"Northern Command needs help," said the Chief of Staff, who suddenly appeared in the Central Command chamber. "The situation up there isn't good, Hakah is shouting for air support."

"Sir, we are doing things one at a time. We still have not concluded one thing like we need to," said Brig. Gen. Rafi Bar-Lev, Head of the Intelligence Department,

"Sir, we are going with 'Challenge'," Ben. Peled said assuredly.

"If we go with 'Challenge', would we be able to do 'Model' in the afternoon?" Dado asked.

"Not on the same day," the IAF Commander replied.

"And if we do 'Model' instead of 'Challenge', what is the last possible hour to decide?" Dado pressed.

"07:30-07:45," the IAF Commander said.

05:20-05:40. Skyhawks at Ramat David

"I spoke with Dayan on the phone," Arlozor Lev (Zorik), Commander of Wing 1, informed two commanders of the Skyhawk squadron under his command. "The front in the southern Golan Heights has collapsed. The 188th Division still remains in the area. It will take one or two days before serious reinforcements arrive. Two Skyhawk squadrons from this wing have to secure that line at all costs!"

A total catastrophe in the Golan Heights, the air crews were informed as they were urgently summoned to the squadron. *We need to contain the breakthrough. Syrian armor is approaching the steps of the cliffs of the Sea of Galilee.*

This was another war on our home.

05:30. "Yedioth Ahronoth" Print House in Tel Aviv

The night print workers were happy. The big printing system put out more and more sheets on Sunday, October 7. Although the main headline was about the heavy fighting in the Golan Heights and the Sinai, immediately under it, another headline appeared, with the usual, familiar details—"Hundreds of Columns of Fire from Syrian Tanks and Vehicles Burning Through the Night in the Golan," reported their northern correspondent Emmanuel Elnekaveh. "This is the most beautiful fire I've ever seen," a senior officer waxed poetic in the journalist's ear.

05:00-05:45. The 200th Squadron

The first plume of light caressed the Dalton Airstrip and softened the surrounding excitement. The system of "furrows" (decoy UAVs) had never been tested in a real operation. This moment would be the first launch of its kind in the country; and in the world.

The first six decoys were loaded on their launchers, and everyone was dashing around, connecting pre-launch checks and launch umbilical cables, taking cover, and moving away from the exhaust systems. They turned the switches to ON, started the engines, and increased thrust to maximum rpm.

Three, two, one. Launched. The two launch assisting rockets attached to each furrow's wings ignited and launched it into the air with a big explosion sound and two large flames burning behind the rockets.

Maj. Shlomo Nir, commander of the squadron, glanced at his watch: 05:40:30. Just in time. He moved his eyes to the sky. Two seconds have elapsed. The launch assisting rockets separated from the six furrows and glided on their way to the ground in the Galilee, while the six decoy "fighters" continued to carry out their mission, according to their preprogrammed commands, crossing through the Galilee skies at 5,000 feet and 300 kilometer per hour, approaching the line of cliffs, and spreading out as a fan, with each one headed to its sector.

Four minutes and twenty seconds.

Nir knew that just about now, the furrow UAVs were supposed to be crossing the line of barrows along the border, pitching up their noses in a fake attack profile and starting a circular holding pattern with a purpose to attract as many possible Syrian SA missiles—which would reveal the location of the batteries while wasting the already-primed missile—before the real fighters arrived to destroy them.

A stripe of pale light painted the eastern sky.

Suddenly, the dark sky was adorned with silver pipes, with trails of white smoke from behind, refracting the sunlight into a shining, multi-branched menorah. It worked!

Roars of joy were heard along the airstrip at Dalton Airstrip, joined with the count. 10 missiles. 12. 14. 20. 26.

Twelve minutes passed since the first launch, and six more furrows were sent on their way. "Veterans" of the operational launch waited expectantly for the "menorah" of missiles. There it was.

Major Nir knew that the first "menorah" served the early fighters attack mission, which was supposed to strike the anti-aircraft artillery employing an offset loft strike method, while the current menorah served the primary attack fighter formations, which were supposed to destroy the missile batteries and their radars employing a close pop-up direct strike. *What was the meaning of the delay? Aren't the Phantoms supposed to attack right now, after the missile batteries are misled by the decoys, and have exposed themselves and emptied their launchers?*

He dialed the Control Unit at Mount Meron, that linked him to the Central Command chamber in the Kirya.

"Avihu, it's Shlomo Nir from Dalton Airstrip. The principle works. Why haven't the aircraft arrived?"

"Oy," he heard Avihu on the other end of the phone, "we forgot to inform you that operation "Model 5" was postponed, because the center of gravity has moved to Egypt. The whole Air Force is in the south. You are on your own in front of the Syrians."

06:00. *Skyhawks in the Golan Skies*

The lessons of the day before were seared into the flesh of the Skyhawk pilots.

At a high altitude, the missiles could take them: they were faster and maneuvered better. A predictable loss, as what happened to Hanan Eitan and Yanki Yardani. *Come lower*, they were told. *The lowest…all the time, low.*

At the beginning of 1968, the U.S. aid promised to Israel with the end of the Six-Day War began bearing fruit, when the first Skyhawks began landing inside the Green Line. Very quickly, pilots were handed the "gray" aircraft, which did not have the dogfight "aura" like the Mirage and was without the flashy fitness of the Phantom.

The aircraft placed in your hands is designed for close support of ground forces, they were told. They understood.

Afterwards, as they examined it more closely, they began to smile. In the Mirage or the Phantom, if one bullet hit a hydraulic pressure tube—there would be no aircraft. With the Skyhawk, that damage was laughable. It's a hard worker, tough. It came to do the job, like a big, hearty tractor for the field crops. It's impossible to kill it.

Now they were flying with napalm loaded to their weapon stations. Dropping other types of bombs at a low altitude endangered the pilots. The last time they trained with napalm was half a year, maybe a year ago, at the shooting range near Mount Gilboa. There was no other choice, so they chose napalm, a cumbersome "bomb"

that creates a large drag while loaded onboard and was only great
for setting fire to oil wells—but not tanks.

They were sent on their way with urgency, without a planned
route map and with no defined goals: *fly to the center of the plateau
and then south,* the air controller told them, and sent them to
Nefah; Petroleum Road; Hushniya; Tel Fares; Ramat Magshimim;
to everywhere. Search, locate and destroy. *Shit,* they complained
among themselves under the aircraft's canopy. *Instead of arriving
at a specific target, in secret, to dash through as fast as possible, and
finish things quickly, they are sending us out with no intelligence on
tank positions between all of the basalt boulders.* They were heavy,
slow, and their airspeed indicator would not get to the 400 knots
tick, and all the while, Syrian anti-aircraft awaited them below,
especially the murderous ZSU-23 "Gundish" AAA. However, they
understood that the Golan Heights region was nearly lost. And after
that, the whole country would follow. It was time to report to work.

The Golan Heights was bright in the first rays of sunlight,
and all the Syrians below were shooting at them with yellow and
orange beams of light, making their way out of the black rocks.
They knew that each beam represented a bullet or shell trying to
hit them, and supersonic booms that passed centimeters from the
cockpit confirmed it.

Overlook it. Ignore it. Yet the Golan Heights on Yom Kippur
afternoon appeared like the sentence awaiting a sinner—at odds
with the chaos of morning mist, black smoke, red fires and dusty
muddy trails. It was within this hellish kingdom that they tried
their hardest to locate its hidden subjects, lower again, lower still,
until the enemy was located; they put their noses on the center

of the identified tank, and at 35 feet deep within the gates of darkness, just a moment before shattering from the fire coming from its guns and those of its comrades, they released the napalm bombs—cumbersome, elliptical eggs filled with 300-400 liters of flammable, gelled petroleum. They dropped down a wing, and looked to see their private bonfires fanning the flames of Hell.

06:05-06:45. Forward Command Post, Northern Command

The Defense Minister's helicopter hovered in the airstrip on Mount Canaan.

Dayan fixed his one eye on the cinema house that has been repurposed as a forward command post, and he knew that Hakah didn't exaggerate.

The three senior commanders—Maj. Gen. Yitzhak Hopi of Northern Command, his assistant, Brig. Gen. Iska Shedmi, and the Reserve Division Commander, Maj. Gen. Dan Lenner—were combat veterans, Palmach fighters who did not blink when facing six armies bent on destroying the little state. They were all withdrawn, with body language signaling defeat. Dan Lenner muttered quietly, "The situation is extremely serious. Fighting in the south has ceased. We've lost. We have nothing left there to stop them."

The State of Israel was desperate, Dayan understood. The hourglass was running out in the southern Golan Heights, signaling the future of the Galilee, the valleys, and Israel itself. The IAF was the only thing that could stop this avalanche. Only the IAF.

Just an hour and a half ago, he had told the Chief of Staff that the purpose of arriving at Mount Canaan was merely for the purpose of a ministerial impression, but the picture that had emerged changed the nature of that promise.

"There are IAF aircraft at your disposal to send to the southern sector of the Golan Heights," the Defense Minister instructed the General of Northern Command, "that will be used until we can build strength with reserve tank forces."

"If our aircraft identify any enemy movement in the Yehudia axis and Johader intersection," Dayan added, "we will strike with our tanks in the field as well."

At 06:40, after trying unsuccessfully to reach the Chief of Staff, the Defense Minister, the head of the command, and several more senior officers passed the doorstep of the kindergarten on the way to the command post, ignored the dozens of glass eyes of dolls that were fixated on them, stuffed in the corner of the room, and stepped directly to the table of the command post.

Sergeant Ofer Sharavi noticed the array of senior officials and yelled, "Attention!"

One of the officers said, "Get the IAF Commander on the phone."

Sharavi lifted the telephone receiver linked directly to the IAF "Pit," and requested that they find the IAF Commander: "The Defense Minister would like to speak with him."

Another minute passed, and the IAF Commander, Maj. Gen. Benny Peled, got on the line. "You need to stop them," Dayan said, "if there won't be a ready four-ship formation until the afternoon, they will break into the Jordan Valley. The IAF is the only factor that can really shut them down, until the tanks get here in the afternoon." Dayan paused for a moment, he listened to Peled respond, and continued. "In the southern sector, only the IAF can handle the movement, otherwise, not only will we lose the Golan Heights, but we'll lose the Jordan valley as well." Again, Benny said something on his end, and Sharavi wished he could be a fly on one of the walls of Central Command, to hear how his commander was answering to the "news" that was falling on him. Dayan then held the receiver, as if it were the last refuge of a safer world, his wrists and hands turning white and face heating up. He said, "Benny, stop everything in the Sinai and bring everything up here. We are standing before the destruction of the Third Temple."

I'm not a great strategist, nor a tank person, Sharavi thought from the road, *but in order to understand the meaning of what my Defense Minister said, I don't need to be one. The Syrians are sitting on Israel's fence, and in a moment they will trample it and trot to Tiberias. Only the Air Force can do it. It's just like Dayan said. Only the IAF can do it.*

06:45. Chamber of the Head of Central Command

"The Rafid Junction is full of Syrian tanks," Benny Peled addressed those present in the chamber with a sense of emergency.

"There is not a single tank that stands against them...if we don't stop them, they will get to the Jordan Valley. Just now, the Minister said that only the IAF can stop them. I request that you all start streaming our forces to there...Let's go, get going, let's move everything up to Rafid Junction."

A moment afterwards, the IAF Commander turned to Giora Furman, Head of the Operations Department.

"Furman, after we fly this 'challenge', we are arming immediately for the Golan Heights, to destroy the Syrian tanks. 'Let's go.'"

"We're not doing the second "challenge" fly-over?" Furman asked.

"No secondary fly-over."

"Perhaps it's possible that we can do both?" Furman tried.

"No, we won't succeed."

At 06:45 Sunday morning, the pressure from the Defense Minister's call gave the IAF Commander the signal. The IAF Commander decided that the second "challenge" fly-over would not take place. The emergency situation in the Golan Heights required that every possible aircraft take to the north urgently, to blow up the Syrian forces that threatened the existence of the Jewish State.

The Head of the Operational Division was still holding onto a shred of hope. Perhaps the problems in the Golan Heights would stabilize, and the panic will smooth over, and maybe someone would settle down a bit and allow them to destroy the Egyptian missile system while also giving air support to ground forces in the Golan?

Stopping "Challenge" is a terrible decision, Furman thought, first and foremost from a mentality perspective. *Yesterday, the first crack was opened. IAF crewmen began to lose their trust in our guiding logic, after we switched their missions and weapon configurations, while in the end, we sent them on a fool's errand to wander around in the skies, with no specific targets and no defined objectives, mostly with no effective results, against the world view and methodology upon which that they had been trained. This morning, they were relieved: the frustration had dissipated. We merely had a temporary setback, a momentary disruption. But now, we are again wavering. The IAF is operating in an orderly way, on their assigned mission, by the book. Just like we have learned countless times: accurate intelligence; a cloudless sky; the electronic warfare unit; the "Challenge;" the operation to destroy the Egyptian missiles. And what is this now?*

06:20-06:55. The 201ˢᵗ Squadron

Eleven Sledgehammer aircraft gathered at the takeoff waiting post, at the aircraft threshold runway.

The first ones, those intended to attack first, or that had a longer flight range, were given the takeoff signs by the flagmen. First, they obtained clearance to align on the runway, aligned. Radios were off, and no words were shared. True, the war already had started last night, but if it was possible to create some sort of minor surprise against the Egyptians, why not take advantage of it?

They quickly checked the engines, activated the burners, lifted off and joined together in the sky. There were five two-ship formations, with one as single. It was time to teach them a lesson, just like they had been trained for three years. Just like they knew how to do best. Okay. They were organized. They were systematic. The IAF at its best.

Amnon Gurion was in the lead.

The Split point. A signal tower with a height of five meters, with painted red and black panels, and with air cadets running along with identification smoke candles.

They split. Each two-ship formation continued to the respective planned checkpoints.

"Pay attention, SA-7 Strela missiles," warned Dani Haloutz.

Hey, Danny, what happened? The navigator Gilad Garber thought. *A few "cigarettes" in the air and you get all excited? You should have been with us yesterday.*

Haloutz pulled-up, released the bombs in the estimated direction of the gun battery, pulled up back in a looped, and felt a sense of missed opportunity. *Instead of hitting them "between the eyes," in direct pop-up and focused strike, we are doing loft strike runs with a high probability of hitting outside of the CEP (Circular Error Probable). In general, in order to take advantage of their head being down momentarily, damaged or not, we need to strike again, near the first attack. But we are the second wave as well. The same aircraft are used in every wave. That means that the second wave is happening two whole hours from now, maybe more. By that time, they will recover, and will be waiting for us.*

Eleven Sledgehammer jets looped back, descended low, and in the midst of fire from the "Gundish" AAA of the Egyptian divisions that were flowing east over the bridges over the Canal, they made their way home.

Over the Rafah Crossing, they saw dust trails stretching from horizon to horizon, with a second look revealing dozens of tanks heading westward.

Why are our tanks traveling on tracks towards the Canal? What is this, is there no one down there capable of stopping the Egyptians?

06:50. Chamber of the Head of Central Command

"Is it possible to switch the decisions?" Dado asked. "Can we decide not to go with 'Challenge', but with 'Model'?"

A few moments before the emergency situation in the Golan Heights, he rushed to leave the command post, raced down the short hallway that separates both "Pits," and now his question resonated in the air of the command chamber.

"I need to decide whether or not to cancel a big part of 'Challenge'," Benny answered.

"In the Golan Heights, small forces are not tipping the scales," Dado said. "What can tip the scales there is 'Model', followed by a massive operation. Together, that can break the Syrian army."

"'Model' will take me four hours [of preparation]," Benny said, "and I cannot save the Golan after the Syrians already get to Ramat Magshimim."

"So what do you propose?" Dado asked.

06:50. Northern Command Central Command Post

The Defense Minister, having just finished his telephone conversation with the IAF Commander, turned to Maj. Gen. (Res.) Hod, the Air Advisor for Northern Command, and stressed his perspective, which had taken over the Command Post for the last thirty minutes.

"The key is in the IAF's hands," Dayan said, "it is the factor which can determine the battle, and therefore it's necessary that they engage Syrian ground forces now, even if, following that, we will not attack their air bases today."

Afterwards, he turned to Col. Rafi Savron, Commander of the Air Command Post, and told him, "I'm giving you a directive to attack everything that moves in the Golan Heights."

"With all due respect, sir," Savron answered, surprised, "I am not able to fulfill an order like that. I have no way of differentiating between our forces and the enemy."

"You have nothing to worry about," the Defense Minister responded, "we have no forces left in the southern Golan. You can attack every tank that you see."

06:52. Chamber of the Head of Central Command

Maybe Benny will now adopt my decision, Furman hoped. *Maybe he'll convince the Chief of Staff to allow us to continue with "Challenge" while simultaneously providing air support to the ground forces in the Golan? It's a shame to stop an orchestra in the middle of their performance. We are able to hit both fronts at the same time.*

"I propose to take a significant portion of the forces that are returning from their fly-over," the IAF Commander told the Chief of Staff, "to arm them quickly, and send them up to the Golan for air support."

Dado: "Maybe I will push everything a few hours back, and then give them [the Air Force] the option to eliminate this army. How much time would 'Model' take?"

Benny: "I would not be able to launch 'Model' before 12:00-13:00."

Dado: "So let's do both things [support and "Model"] in place of the second 'Challenge' strike."

Benny: "It's already approved. Let's go. We're giving them a strike time of 11:30."

06:57. "Stop 'Challenge 4', begin 'Model 5'," the commanding officers instructed the IAF base commanders and all the squadrons under their control.

Furman did not give up. "Let's go on at least one more strike into Egypt," he pleaded to his commander. "Let's at least postpone go-time in Syria."

After already agreeing to stop "Challenge" and to proceed with "Model," Benny slammed his fist on his table.

"Challenge" was halted, and "Model" would proceed.

In the chamber, the IAF Commander's decision was received with astonishment.

First, there was the Minister of Defense. Although he sounded worried for the fate of the State of Israel, at no point did he instruct Maj. Gen. Peled to stop the "Challenge" operation in Egypt! The Minster merely requested air support in the Golan Heights, and that was it.

Second, there was the Chief of Staff. In the early hours of Sunday morning, Lt. Gen. Elazar understood that the more pressing mission was to provide air support for ground troops in the North. Without the IAF, the dam would be breached. Dado also understood from Maj. Gen. Peled that if the aircraft intended for the second strike of Operation "Challenge" would be sent north, he would allow the implementation of two urgent missions—immediate support for the ground troops and the destruction of the Syrian missile layouts ('Model 5'). Led by common sense and a clear picture of the grim situation, the Chief of Staff instructed the general to stop Operation "Challenge" and to go north with full force.

However, it could have been different, and it was all in Maj. Gen. Peled's hands. A few minutes before 07:00, the IAF Commander could have pressed the Chief of Staff to change his decision. *"Commander, let's wait just a bit more. We just started in the south, let us finish. It is a shame to stop now. Right now, we have an immediate solution to the catastrophe in the north."* Had this been said by Maj. Gen. Peled, it is likely that Dado would have agreed. However, Benny Peled did not fight the Chief of Staff's directives with all his might. Therefore, he did not provide a proverbial ladder that would have let the Chief of Staff, as well as himself, climb down from the tree branch that was the wrong decision.

The immediate solution that the IAF commander could have offered was called "Scratch." In the operational planning that occurred before the war, there was an aerial answer to a need for providing emergency support to ground forces in a situation where Israel would find itself in the midst of a sudden attack, before achieving air superiority and before clearing any missiles.

The "Scratch" order defined known stationary targets: artillery batteries, and anti-aircraft guns. Data on the other targets would be provided in the heat of battle directly from the field to the IAF Operations Department, and from there to the cockpits.

On Sunday morning in the southern Golan Heights, there was a dense fog of war, and the field intelligence that arrived, which was essential for the utilization of a "Scratch" order, was weak, confused, and scant.

Still, this was a national emergency. That was, at least, how Israel's top security officials saw it. It was precisely for such a situation, with intelligence reports from the field being as they were, that two Skyhawk squadrons from Ramat David were allotted. They were meant to carry out a "Scratch" mission in the North, in order to assist ground forces even before the skies were cleared, or help with that at the same time.

On Friday night, Lt. Col. Avihu Ben-Nun, Commander of the Strike Branch of the Operations Department, updated IAF commander Maj. Gen. Benny Peled, of the intricacies of Operation "Challenge" in Egypt. He added and emphasized that a "Scratch" order would be activated at the Golan Heights from the early hours of the morning—just before Dayan yelled that "the Third Temple is in danger." The Skyhawks at Ramat David went out on successive sorties in the Golan Heights. Ben-Nun received his commander's approval for allocating two squadrons towards curbing the Syrians, despite the tight missile defense, while "Challenge" was underway.

On Sunday morning, despite the sense of catastrophe that still gripped the Defense Minister, the Chief of Staff, and the IAF Commander, only two Skyhawk squadrons were needed to deal with the Syrian tanks that attempted to head to the eastern side of the Sea of Galilee. The field also could not have accommodated any more.

A few minutes before 07:00, under pressure from the Syrian sword that threatened the continuation of the Zionist enterprise, Maj. Gen. Peled forgot about the "Scratch" order. He forgot what he heard from Avihu, and decided to pursue "Model," alone.

It would have taken him half an hour, maybe less.

It would have been the most worthwhile thirty minutes for the IAF, the IDF, and the country, and throughout all of the Yom Kippur War.

If only the IAF Commander had sought the advice of his staff. "We understand that the Defense Minister is saying that the 'Third Temple' is in danger, and we understand the urgency in the Golan Heights. However, there's another way. It can be done leisurely, in an orderly, methodical fashion, like the IAF knows best. To prevent the catastrophe in the Golan Heights? A 'Scratch' order with the squadrons in Ramat David. Operation 'Model'? Only after we've concluded 'Challenge'. All in an orderly manner, with aerial photo reconnaissance, and with an electronic aid envelope." Had he sought their advice, this is surely what they would have told him.

However, such a discussion never occurred. Therefore, on Sunday, October 7, at 07:00, Operation "Challenge"—the response that was meant to destroy the Egyptian missile defenses, an objective which, if achieved, could have changed the campaign situation in the southern front and changed the whole war as a result—was stopped.

The surprise in the IAF Headquarters was huge, since it was Benny Peled, their commander. The level-headed, opinionated, man who was said to walk with a "titanium-cast spine." He was not afraid of anyone, and he never had a problem standing up to his superiors. However, it was him of all people, and then of all times, who could not stand the heat, who did not stop the tide, did not lower the panic, and did not decide and direct things in the direction that the nation required: the correct one.

"How much time will it take us to switch from 'Challenge' to 'Model'?" Peled asked Furman and Avihu, while ignoring the signs of discomfort from his subordinates.

"Three hours," Avihu answered.

"To my mind, we will need more," Furman added.

"If Avihu says it, then it'll be three hours," Peled followed.

"It's unlikely that it will take three hours," David Ivry joined the conversation.

"If Avihu says three, it'll take three," Peled repeated.

"What about the time it will take the helicopters equipped with Electronic Warfare (EW) systems from Um Hashiva?" asked David Ivry.

"We'll do it without them," Peled said.

The IAF Headquarters staff also had issues and did not come out clean at the end of the chain of events.

Those who surrounded Benny were not terrified rookies. Sitting next to Maj. Gen. Peled were none other than the IAF's topmost officers. These officers, in combination with their characteristics that are supposed to aid them at every moment, especially in critical moments such as that one, were meant to stand by their opinions, in the face of everyone, including their commander; especially in front of their commander.

Yet no one stood up, except for Giora Furman, who did not exactly stand firmly by his opinions, but was extremely hesitant.

Thus, instead of shouting what everyone was thinking—"Benny, it's impossible this way, don't stop 'Challenge', and if you've already decided to switch to 'Model', then wait for the photo reconnaissance, and take the needed time,"—all of the IAF idols vaporized in the face of their commander's short fuse. They clammed up and vanished for fear of his loud, enraged voice.

07:00-07:25. The 201ˢᵗ Squadron

With the IAF commander calling for the end of "Challenge," and their comrades returning from destroying Egyptian anti-aircraft guns, others in the 201ˢᵗ Squadron were making their way for a simultaneous attack against eight air bases, designed to throw off the Egyptian interception jets from hitting the next three sorties.

Huldai led, as five Sledgehammer jets accompanied him, leaving trails of black smoke behind him. *Here's the delta.* Sailboats sailed below in freshwater canals. 540 knots. Flying at a low altitude, on radio silence. *If only these low clouds would disperse.*

Like in the Six-Day War, Huldai pondered, as a sense of I overtook him. *It's a replica of "Focus." Here's the pull-up waypoint.* In the gaps of the low cloud layer, the squadron's target was seen: Tanta air base, located two miles ahead, to the left. *Pull-up. Sight on target. Release. Good results. Disengaging contact.*

"There are MiGs coming from just south of the air base," "Wild Bull" Peled reported.

"Leave them," Huldai ordered, knowing that they needed to return to base. The fuel meter was starting to inch to the left. Mission accomplished. There were other things to do, so he needed everyone with him.

Leave the MiGs? Peled moved restlessly in his chamber. *Why have I been training as a fighter pilot? Why else have I been developing this hunter's instinct?*

Then it was Avner Naveh who was requesting permission from Peled to intercept the MiGs.

"Leave them," Peled conveyed Huldai words.

Everyone then gathered together, overcoming the sense of a missed opportunity, and returned home.

Haim Ram landed from the loft strike mission, taxies down the runway and saw that aircraft tail number 61, which landed just before him, had a gaping black hole in its tail, and both the r rudder and elevators looked like a Zionist piece of art, intertwined as if they were a Star of David.

The 61 needs some major body work, he thought.

In the 201ˢᵗ Squadron there was a general feeling of elation. After Saturday's panic, when every pilot ran to launch their aircraft, and their controllers sent them in every direction, here, they had regained their control and composure.

It needed to be like that. Preparation. Briefing. A formation departing. Striking. Avoiding complications. Having everything in order. Then it was the time to end the issue entirely: the complete destruction of the missile batteries.

The IAF trained for two and a half years on striking SA missiles arrays, reflected Meir Shani (Shaniboi). The "pop-up strike method" was set up by the Operations Department, and the squadrons adopted it. *We practiced these 25 seconds for two and a half years. Where to pull-up, how to gain height, how to dive on target, how when to release bombs, and how to return to NOE altitude on the way back home. It's time to get a return on the investment.*

A Bit before 08:00. Senior Command Post

"We cannot dilute our strength," the Chief of Staff instructed the Head of Northern Command. "We will not conduct advanced strikes. We will contain them and keep the front in good standing. If a need should arise, we can move the front back a bit."

On Sunday at 08:00, another crack developed in the pyramid of the all-capable army. The IDF Chief of Staff authorized the withdrawal of the forces on the northern front. The policy of "no leaving the border line" was no more. No more strict defense, but static. It was now allowed to skip backwards.

Hakah reported that the Northern Command was preparing to lay mines at the four bridges over the Jordan.

"And another thing," the general added, "while the Syrian armored divisions push through to the Sea of Galilee, Division 1, under the command of Col. Tawfiq Jinny, is making a two-headed effort to break through the defenses of the 188th Armored Division on its way to Nefah. As a result, he skipped over the division command post from Nefah to Allayqa."

Only the Air Force can do this, Lt. Gen. Elazar thought to himself. *Okay, let the excellent boys in the sky go knock out those missiles already. It's time to change the course of this war!*

08:35. The Senior Command Post

The Defense Minister, just returning from his inspection in the north, entered the "Pit" and requested an update on the southern front.

"It's still alright," Dado answered him. "It hasn't fallen. We have an infantry presence. Tanks are here and there on the line. The IAF took care of the anti-aircraft guns, and they say that it went very well. We've lost two aircraft."

"It's possible that the Syrian assault will break overnight," Dayan said, informing those present about his visit to Mount Canaan. "In order for the air support to be effective, it's preferable that our forces not press into the enemy. They need to leave empty space between them and the Syrians, so the aircraft will have space to operate."

Afterwards, he told them that he suggested to the Commander of Northern Command to engage the aircraft in areas in which our forces were deployed, even those areas in where it was difficult to distinguish between our forces and the Syrians. He advised to the Chief of Staff to weigh the possibility of replacing command staff, including the Commander of Northern Command.

"They seem tired to me," Dayan suggested.

08:15-09:00. The 201st Squadron

In the middle of a parking lot, outside of the squadron's buildings, they set up a breakfast table.

Hands, tucked tight in a pressure suit, were taken out from semi-open coveralls, creating a visual demonstration that life was returning to normal.

"Wild Bull" Peled muttered to himself: *I've already been to war. In a real war, they tell the operations clerk 'take this down from the board, and put it in the 'drawer'. "This" is still not a real war.*

The speaker screamed out, "Get down to the briefing room!"

Huldai stepped onto the stage, made sure that everyone had arrived, and without any delay, he announced, "'Challenge' has been discontinued. The tech crew has already begun working on the aircraft to prepare them for the new mission. Syria; 'Model 5.'"

* * *

Something bad is happening here, Shaniboi thought. *Something very basic is going wrong in the methods that we're applying.*

First of all, we need to finish with Egypt. "Challenge" is a continuous process, and its success hinges on us not stopping it. Every section depends on the one before it. You can't move on to stage two if step one hasn't already been fully completed.

* * *

"You're not heading out for 'Model," Huldai informed Capt. (Res.) Adi Benaya. "Stay here and act as an operations manager."

Benaya wanted to get to Syria. He wanted to get there so much. As the second Deputy Squadron leader and the squadron's readiness officer, he was of course capable of commanding the squadron. He could not just avoid this duty. It was a fact.

As a disciplined soldier, he returned to the operations room.

"The situation in the Golan Heights is the most difficult," Huldai continued. "During the night, the Syrian army successfully struck at the defensive structures of our forces in the southern Golan Heights. At the moment, the Syrians are pushing towards the cliffs and the shores of the Sea of Galilee. Since the early morning hours,

Skyhawk squadrons from Ramat David have been trying to slow down their advance. In order to change the face of this battle and push the pressure back on the Syrians, we need to destroy their SA missile batteries. We need to destroy the Iron Curtain."

"The batteries are still in place?" asked a few pilots in the back of the room.

"When was the last photo reconnaissance gathered? What is the situation of anti-aircraft guns there?"

"As far as I know," Huldai responded, "the latest photographic findings that we have are from Friday. That's just what we have. As for the flak, consider every area as if it were covered in flak. We have no real information."

Yair David was not calm.

On his way to the briefing room, he took a quick look at the map of Maj. Sami, the AGCO[8] in charge of transferring intelligence from the ground forces, and his heart skipped a beat. Red arrow heads, indicating the enemy's position, were deep inside the southern Golan Heights.

"Ron," he asked, "On my way here, I passed by Sami's map. The Syrian army, with flak attachments with the infantry divisions, are located just under the area we are planning to strike. Is it possible, perhaps, to move the flight paths?"

Huldai was not able to reply before the veteran Lt. Col. Guri Palter, the oldest pilot posted in the 201st Squadron, who had already seen two wars in his lifetime, joined in and said, "Ron, we need to change these flight paths. I know the Arabs' flak well. If we fly low, as we're supposed to fly, all of them could hit us.

---

8   AGCO: *Air-Ground Coordination Officer*

Especially the 'Gundish' system with its four gun barrels crazy rate of fire and radar. The squadron's ingress waypoint is at the Rafid Intersection, located just above the Syrian division sitting on our territory. If we go through there at low altitude, we'll be badly hit. We will have heavy losses."

"We will check with the mission management team," Huldai said. "Yair, prepare the master map in the meantime."

09:00. Chamber of the Head of Central Command

"So far, you've saved us," Dayan told Benny Peled. "Still, the situation in the North is not good. We need to direct all of our aerial efforts to the Golan Heights. Syrian tanks are at the fences of Nefah. As I told you before, if the IAF doesn't do anything about it, it will be the destruction of the 'Third Temple.'"

Afterwards, he added, shocking everyone in the room, "Hakah is not handling the issue over there. He needs to have his spine straightened out."

09:10. The 201ˢᵗ Squadron

"There is a problem with the flight routes," Yair David told Benaya, a moment before he began to convert the mission order onto the master map. "The routes now pass directly over land that the Syrians have captured."

"Get Lapidot on the phone," Benaya requested from the operations assistant.

"Sir, it is not possible to start the mission like this," Benaya explained to Col. Lapidot. "Give me authorization, and I will change the routes to meet the current needs. There is still some time before the mission launch. Everyone is still back at the squadron."

"Wait," Lapidot said on the other end of the line. After a brief pause, he returned to Benaya, saying, "It's not possible to change it. They are orders from above. Under no circumstances will they be changed."

"But sir," Benaya tried again, feeling heavy distress sitting on his chest, "It's not possible to just leave it like this. I will change it, as my responsibility."

"Absolutely not, under no circumstances" the Wing Commander answered.

09:10. The 200ᵗʰ UAV Squadron (Dalton Airstrip)

Two hours had passed, maybe three. No one had gotten back to Maj. Shlomo Nir.

"What can I do?" Nir asked the operations department representative on the phone.

"Get back to Palmachim," he answered Nir.

He returned, convinced that his men were on their way after him.

"Stay where you are," he instructed the squadron operations commander, just before hanging up and following his commander to, "at 11:00, launch the remaining four decoys."

09:10. Office of the Chief of Staff

How can we describe the situation to the Americans? How can we ensure enough time to take out the enemies in our territory before

*a ceasefire is called? How can we ensure a U.S. veto, if such a decision
arises before we have a chance to remove them?*

Golda Meir was preoccupied: her body language betrayed her
distress. She was surrounded by years of experience: the man of faith
Israel Galili, who had been the Head of the National Command in
the Haganah, as well as "Defense Minister" for the critical years
of 1947-1948; her deputy, Yigal Alon, the former commander of
the Palmach; the former head of Military Intelligence, Maj. Gen.
Aharon Yariv, and Yitzhak Rabin, the Chief of Staff of the Six-Day
War. All of them were respected defense veterans, and she expected
them to scatter a pinch of the magic dust of experience over "this
thing," and make it disappear.

"If, God forbid, we stand in this situation again," Golda
concluded with a serious face, "we should ignore what the world
has to say, and let the army to engage. We were all of one mind
yesterday: no preemptive strike."

"Dado said, 'Give me a chance,'" she continued, regret coming
through her voice. "In the end, and this is important to remember,
we gained goodwill will only from America. Despite this [that
we've been avoiding a preemptive strike], Kissinger cannot recruit
another two or three countries to call for a ceasefire and return
to their places."

09:30. *The 201ˢᵗ Squadron*

Col. Amos Lapidot was not calm. Capt. (Res.) Adi Benaya
is a respected, level-headed pilot. If Benaya sounded distressed,
it seemed that everyone in the squadron had the same problem.

"Syrian armored forces have broken into the Golan Heights," Lapidot said to the air crewmen as soon as he entered the briefing room, joining Huldai on the stage. "No one can contain them. Once we destroy the missiles, we will stop the Syrian armor."

As if they did not already know.

Huldai, in a straightforward manner, brought up the issue of the flight paths: "It's like running your head into a wall," he said. "The Syrian army is spread all along our ingress routes."

"Wild Bull" Eitan Peled, one of the planners of Operation "Model 5," a veteran of the Six-Day War and the War of Attrition, raised his hand. "This program is not designed for the current situation," he warned, contradicting the Wing Commander. "'Model 5' is designed as a preemptive strike scenario. It is an operation meant to land on the Syrians with a complete surprise. Now, Syria is already in our territory, and outfitted with mobile SA-6 missiles. We don't know anything about them."

Eli Zohar, of the same age as Peled and a veteran of the same wars, needed to know exactly where Syrian forces were located in our territory. "We are supposed to fly at a low altitude," he said. "It's not necessarily just the missiles. Every weapon that a Syrian soldier shoots in the air could harm us, especially the 'Gundish' systems."

"We do not know their exact position," Lapidot said. "There aren't any recent photographs taken by our spy aircraft. There is no choice, you have to go out and destroy them. This is war. There is no one else that can contain them."

Noises of "opposition" echoed in the briefing room.

"To change the paths," Lapidot said, attentive to the distress among his people, "I need approval from headquarters," retiring to the Operations Room.

"I checked with Headquarters," he returned to the briefing room with a grave look on his face. "I'm sorry, they won't authorize any change. The entire Air Force is supposed to attack there. It will be very crowded in the air. The operation will involve additional units— chaff dispersing artillery [to jam the radar] and others. We are not given a chance to break up this coordinated, complex framework. You cannot change or delay it."

"Guys, remember, he who doesn't hit his target, will help his comrade get toppled," he said, "You all depend on each other. Hit the road. Good luck."

Eli Zohar caught him at the exit.

"Amos, the path is very dangerous."

"Eli, I checked it out with Headquarters. Like I said to you, it is not possible to move the entrance path of the 201st Squadron. Squadron leaders should move a bit to the side, if it looks dangerous. That's the best we can do."

In the Navigation Room, Yair David continued to plan. Outside of his door, he heard noise and bustle. Everyone wanted to see the problematic routes that David had prepared for them. *You're all right,* the veteran navigator thought, *preparations that have been made on the ground have a considerable impact on what happens later in the air.*

For the moment, he put down his ruler and his pencil, approached the Navigation Room door and found Col. Lapidot, his wing commander, standing in the doorway, blocking his comrades from coming in.

"Don't bother David," the Wing Commander said, "let him concentrate!"

Something is resting heavily on Lapidot, David thought, as he continued delineating the track based on the mission checkpoints.

This order is dense, Lapidot thought. *It simultaneously sends an armada of aircraft that are supposed to arrive at specific times to their targets. A command that is not flexible to last-minute path changes. The crewmen of the 201ˢᵗ are right, these are dangerous paths. But war is also dangerous,* he finished his internal debate.

09:25-09:40. Senior Command Post

"There's a catastrophe in the South," the Southern Command headquarters at Um Hashiva reported. "Egyptian forces have made it to the Artillery Axis (Central Longitudinal Axis about ten kilometers east of the Canal, so-called because of the arrays of artillery installations set up on it). In the area of the Jidi intersection, tank combat is occurring. Strongholds are continuing to fall. The Egyptians are injecting more and more troops into Sinai. In divisions 14 and 401, only around 30 tanks remain, and Division 460 has even less. Urgent air support is required."

Ten minutes passed, and the Head of Southern Command ordered the placement of ambush bazookas to prevent the Egyptians from getting to Refidim. He asked again, "What about the Air Force?"

09:45. Chamber of the Head of Central Command

Following Gorodish's update, the IDF Chief of Staff went down to the Central Command chamber to inspect every option available to send emergency support to the south. He instructed the Air Force to coordinate efforts against the three intruding Egyptian columns that were heading east.

What do they want from us? Maj. Gen. Peled thought, confused by the swing of the IDF's changing needs. *Decide already, do you want the whole air force in the north or the south?*

A few minutes passed, and the IAF Commander internalized what this update meant. *I may have to split the Skyhawks between the two fronts. We cannot lose any aircraft.*

"Savron," he turned to the commander of the Air Control post at Mount Canaan, "I want to warn you, for the next two hours before we launch 'Model', do not lose any aircraft!"

"Motti," he turned now to his predecessor, the current advisor to the Commander of Northern Command, "you put my aircraft in this situation without any preparation, and now I am losing some to missiles…I request that you proceed with caution. 'Model' is slated for 11:30. Please, be cautious."

10:00. Government Meeting at the Kirya in Tel Aviv

A governmental meeting took place with the participation of nearly all the ministers, save for Knesset ministers Evan (who was abroad), Givati (who was sick) and Defense Minister Dayan (who was at the front). The meeting was supposed to serve as an opportunity for the ministers to hear their leader, the Iron Lady from Ramat Aviv, discuss what exactly went wrong for the people of Israel, and why.

"The main reason that we've reached this situation," Golda explained to the ministers, "is that we did not take preemptive action. We explained that to Kissinger. The U.S. Secretary of State understands that and appreciates our restraint. Our advantage, now that there is no dispute as to who started this war, is that America is with us, and is actively working to prevent the push to a ceasefire so that we will be able to push the Egyptians and Syrians back out of our territory."

"The military situation is not so good," she finished her statements, "but I would prefer to let the IDF Chief of Staff explain that."

Fifteen minutes after the meeting had begun, Lt. Gen. David Elazar entered the conference room, and surveyed the faces of the ministers, to whom just last night he had explained the relatively good position the army was in, considering the deterioration of the fronts.

"The situation is difficult," Dado said to the stunned ministers, "There are ups and downs, especially in the Golan Heights, where the situation is very serious. The Syrians were able to penetrate into the southern sector of the Golan Heights, with 400 tanks and ten thousand soldiers." He saw the ministers' jaws drop in disbelief. He continued, encouragingly, "we estimate that approximately two hundred were destroyed."

"Overnight," he added, "we believed the situation was actually more dangerous in the Canal, and therefore we planned to use our air power against the Egyptians, in an operation that was meant to strike a heavy blow and destroy their missiles and paralyze their air bases. However, due to the deterioration in the north, the plan in the south was only partly completed, and the main efforts of the IAF were directed against the Syrians."

"I hope," Lt. Gen. Elazar continued, "that tomorrow it will be possible to perform counter attacks, both in the Golan and at the

Canal, with the destruction of enemy missile systems by the IAF. It is possible that the attacks will not occur simultaneously on both fronts. In light of the relatively serious power balance stacked against us, a lot of our efforts will depend on the IAF, which is now filling a crucial role, both in containment and in opening up the possibility of a counterattack."

"The situation is fine at our strongholds," he finished. "I gave an order that, in the event that a stronghold is in danger of being encircled, Southern Command will evacuate it. The trouble is that it is difficult to evacuate due to the active fire. Within the strongholds, the fighters are protected."

* * *

The strongholds were fine?

On Sunday morning, the IDF Chief of Staff was still unaware of the real situation of the strongholds? After all, every simple soldier in the Sinai sector knew, and actually, one did not need to be a soldier in a stronghold to know. It was enough to hear the anguished cries on the communication networks.

10:30-11:00. The 201ˢᵗ Squadron

It was for these exact situations that they invented the phrase 'cut through the air with a knife', thought Abraham Assael, the navigator. *"Model" is a dangerous mission due to the problematic flight paths. It's like trying to maintain balance while crossing on a narrow beam over crocodile-infested waters. There doesn't seem to be any other choice. Headquarters must have considered it once or twice. Maybe they know something that we don't.*

This mission, the likes of which has never been imagined, sits on the shoulders of the Air Force, and on all of our shoulders. Saving the Homeland, thought Shaniboi, the pilot. *It'll be alright. We are the 201ˢᵗ. We stride with a knife between our teeth. "Model" suits us.*

"Your aircraft is still not ready," the pilot Haim Ram was told in Operations.

Ten minutes passed. Bravo. There was an aircraft.

Wonderful, he thought, *Benzi and his people worked fast to set up the 61, the aircraft with all of the holes from "Challenge." Statistically, I should be okay. In all likelihood, the aircraft won't get hit twice in a row.*

This is going to be the squadron's first encounter with the Syrians, the navigator Yitzhak Yahav thought. *Syria is always scary. Repress it.* The stories of Syrian prisons were wrapped in their minds with a thick, isolating cloak.

Despite everything, there is order in this chaos, thought Capt. Ori Shahak, who converted just a year ago to the Phantom after many, many years on the wings of a Dassault Super Mystère.

Here we go, the navigation route is set on the map, the target is on the aerial photograph and there is a reasonable amount of time to memorize the navigation route and study the target. There is order in madness.

"Uri, this is going to be serious," Maj. (Res.) Eli Zohar said, as if running calculations in his head. "This business is dangerous. We have to do evasive maneuvers all the time, with all of our strength. The anti-aircraft guns and the missiles in Syria are on a different scale from what we know from earlier wars."

"It's all going to be alright," Uri answered.

Maj. Uri Sheani, the senior pilot of the squadron, the commander of the preparatory stage in the Flight Academy, joined the group.

"Regev, Shani is going to replace you," they told Nurit's new husband.

"Why?" He asked, full of resentment. Afterwards, he calmed down. *It's Uri, you cannot say no to the straight, quiet, sincere Uri.*

Anyway, he thought to himself, *I'm not missing anything dramatic. After all, despite all of the concerns, it really is a pretty simple task. A quick fix.*

10:50-11:00. Wing 1 (Ramat David)

In the heart of the Jezreel valley, not far from homes of the worker's town of Nahalal, the 109th Skyhawk Squadron and the 69th Sledgehammer Squadron prepared for their operation, "Model 5-B."

The density of aircraft on the solitary runway forced the Skyhawks to take off earlier than needed, and now they were 'wasting time', zigzagging over the trees of the Jezreel Valley and the Mediterranean waves.

Turn around. Round over the sea, to the direction of the Golan Heights.

What is that? Alon Givoni, the young Skyhawk pilot, wondered, as he saw dozens of tanks through the aircraft's canopy, seeing dust clouds following them on the endless dirt roads of the Zevulun Valley, between the white cotton fields. *Wow, do we have a problem!*

11:00. The 201st Squadron

"There's a malfunction in your aircraft," Capt. Moshe Koren was told. "Stay at your aircraft's canopy. It's possible that by the time "Model" starts, we should have this ready to go."

"Faster, faster," he pushed them.

Takeoffs.

"What's going to happen?" Capt. Dror Yaffe, the navigator, asked.

"Everything is from above," Koren answered. "It's a sign that we weren't meant to take off for this mission."

Capt. Amnon Gurion, the second deputy commander of the squadron, was supposed to lead a three ship formation.

"What is this? The aircraft isn't even armed!"

"Amnon, we are friends, I took care to prepare an aircraft with no bombs for you…" Captain Adi Benaya, combat manager, tried to calm the upset Gurion. "Come, join me in managing the battle."

Shaniboi was happy. The time had come to beat those bastards. His optimism, mixed with a cynicism about life and everything around them, stuck comfortably and well to Assael in the rear cockpit, as well as to Haim Ram and Yitzhak Yahav in number 2, who were rolling down the taxiway to the runway threshold with him.

Amiram Eliasaf was number 2 of the couple in front of him, and something was bothering him about the starting position of his Sledgehammer. He pointed his index finger to the nose landing gear energy absorber, which was completely sunk, indicating to him that there could be a problem taking off.

The senior technician of the "last chance" post checked the energy absorber and signaled Eliasaf to get back to the squadron.

You blew it, Amiram, thought Shaniboi. *You won't be joining us in the missile destruction party.*

It's true that this is war, and it is not possible to surprise the Syrians like we were planning to do yesterday, thought "Rhino" Gal, sitting in the rear cockpit of the first aircraft in the convoy. *Still, every surprise, even the smallest ones, will aid our survival. Radio silence is okay with me.*

"Hey, what's this?"

An American Valiant car, painted army brown, began braking and stopped suddenly in front of the aircraft. Col. Lapidot, the Wing Commander, leaped frantically from the vehicle while holding a cardboard sign, and waved it in front of their eyes.

"We can change the route!"

Amos Lapidot's cardboard sign is an outstanding symbol of the chaos of the memory. The Rashomon effect at its best.

I interviewed 25 crew members regarding Operation "Model 5."

Twenty of them have said that this never happened. The wing commander never came, there was no Valiant, and no cardboard sign. One said, "Now that [you] mention the event, I have a faint shred of a memory." Four others said, "It happened, all of it. We remember that as though it was yesterday." The wing commander also contributed his part to the issue, and stated, "I don't recall such an incident."

So, did it happen or not? It did.

In the experience I've accumulated in interviewing fighters, I have realized that the human mind tends to forget events more than it invents them. When I discovered stories that were "invented," there was always a clear agenda behind them, of quieting the speaker's conscience, an attempt to shed a correcting, compassionate light on an incident that bothered the speaker.

That is not the case with the launch of "Model 5."

None of the four needed the sign held by the wing commander to cover their shame and soothe their conscience. This is why I state with a high degree of certainty that the story happened.

Why is it that not everyone remembered it?

First of all, the memory plays tricks. Secondly, it is possible that some of them missed the incident, as they were concentrating on the "inner-world" of their minds—relearning the route to the objective while detached from the outside world, focused on their mission.

There are surely other explanations

Why did those who claimed to have seen the wing commander not change their paths?

The pilot Yigal Stavi and the navigator Yehoar Gal, the first in the group, saw Col. Lapidot and his sign. However, their mission to drop their bombs in a loft strike demanded that they arrived at a specific waypoint. This was set on the computer, at a certain pre-programmed angle, and at a preset heading and airspeed. Any change would have scrapped mission's feasibility.

What about the others who claimed that they saw?

They were not excited about it either, which is seemingly strange. They were just released from the most dangerous part of the mission, and they did not take that opportunity with both hands?

Apparently not. For them, it was a meaningless act, and there was nothing substantive in it, other than the goodwill of the wing commander. The message arrived too late to the platform, and the train that had already left the station could not alter its course.

Was that really the case?

In order to fulfill the mission, the targets needed to be destroyed. This could not have been changed.

In order to destroy the targets, it was desirable to arrive at the pre-planned pull-up waypoint, increasing the chance of locating the target and minimizing the risk to the striking fighter.

It was also preferable not to change the selected targets pull-up waypoints. So what could have been changed?

The ingress waypoint, from which pilots start their navigation leg towards the pull-up waypoint, was set for them at the border line at Rafid intersection, which forced them to fly over a seemingly endless arms depot of two Syrian divisions that controlled the southern Golan Heights. This was the reason for the loud opposition in the briefing room.

In the navigator course, they trained on performing mission changes in the air in aircraft that lacked an INS (Inertial Navigation System). So why not then, when the wonders of 1970s technology were at their disposal? It was supposed to take them 15-20 minutes from the moment of takeoff until their arrival in the Golan Heights, over territory free from threats, over the sea, over the State of Israel. It was an amount of time that was supposed to allow navigators to locate a new ingress waypoint, which will be located a kilometer or two north of the center of the simmering pressure cooker.

It was supposed to be simple. "I'm in head-down state," the navigators would say, disconnected from the outside world, while locating landmarks on the map as a new and more secure "ingress waypoint." They would enter the new waypoint coordinates into the computer, and obtain a new heading and distance. That would have been it.

True, sometimes the INS drifted, and additionally, there would not be a prominent "ingress waypoint" tower that could be used for INS update, but so what? This is what the navigators were trained for. As required, they could correct their flight path with respect to the pre-planned route by employing the good-old time-map-terrain navigation (also designated Contact-Nav) method. They did not do so. Why?

The central argument, the one that convinced the 201ˢᵗ Squadron to adhere to the problematic flight paths, was the knowledge that the entire IAF would be up there in the sky, and that everyone was supposed to descend on their targets together. Thus the skies of the Golan Heights would be crowded with IAF jets.

Some of them recalled that the 119ᵗʰ Squadron was the one just to the north of them, but none of them had a flight map in their cockpit that marked the flight paths of their sister squadron. As a result, they had no indications as to the borders of their sector, nor how spacious it was. Furthermore, there was no way at the time to find out, as everyone entered radio-silence a moment before takeoff. Therefore, there was no choice. They could not alter any paths and they were determined to win with what they had.

The red light turned green, and Lt. Yigal Stavi was in the front cockpit of the "Rhino," the first in a long line of heavily armed Sledgehammer jets. He identified the green glitter from the control tower and started pushing down the runway.

Four hundred meters behind him, Lt. Motti Reder saw two orange flames protruding from the jet engines of Stavi's Sledgehammer. He knew, from a safe distance, that many pollutants were being released into the air, though he especially knew that it is time to release his brakes.

Stavi retracted his landing gear, turned off his burners, and saw Reder joining him from behind. He knew that, in a few minutes, at fifteen second intervals, fifteen additional Sledgehammer jets would join them and organize into their formations in the blue October sky.

A few minutes after 11:00, 113 aircraft from most of the IAF's combat squadrons were sent to participate in Operation "Model 5-B"—the destruction of 25 surface-to-air missile batteries in Syria.

No aerial photo reconnaissance jet was sent in front of them to locate the missile batteries. The radar-jamming system was not being used (which would limit the capabilities of enemy radars and missiles to lock onto the attacking force). The number of aircraft at disposal for the operation did not exceed 76% of the number specified by the command. Despite all of this, and primarily because of the sense of emergency that had taken hold of the captains of the Jewish State, the Israeli Air Force jets took off on their way north, as the words of their commander from the night before strongly motivated the pilots of the attack force: "...eradicate, destroy, and smash the dreams of our enemy to smithereens."

11:15. Skyhawks in the Golan Heights

At 11:15, dozens of Skyhawks, the first wave of "Model 5," threw dozens of tons of explosives at Syrian anti-aircraft artillery batteries. Alon Givoni saw strike fighters all over the sky, and recalled the large Allied bomber formations aircraft from World War II. Now, after finishing, he looked down to see what was happening, and saw a world of flames and smoke. He saw a convoy of Phantoms passing under him and muttered under his helmet "Good luck, guys, good luck."

11:20. The 201ˢᵗ Squadron

It isn't spring, the "Rhino" pondered to himself in his rear cockpit position, *and we are not flying to nesting places in Europe, and yet, after the Skyhawks, we are the first swallows. We are continuing the softening pretreatment, but this time using Sledgehammer jets. In another moment, we will fall upon the Syrians. We will teach them a painful lesson about their audacity and arrogance.*

Sami didn't exaggerate, the "Rhino" thought, identifying silhouettes of Syrian tanks filling the territory of the southern Golan and the burning border, with curling black smoke towering hundreds of meters in the air, creating a wall of foul air, mixing with the morning mist that refused to fade away.

11:20. The 200ᵗʰ Squadron (Dalton Runway)

While Maj. Shlomo Nir, their commander, made his way south as IDF forces flew to the north, and as aircraft engaged in Operation "Model 5" passed over him without his knowledge, his soldiers, those remaining at the airstrip, were preparing to submit the last directive that remained in their hands. Small. Condensed. Coincidental.

The four remaining "furrows" deployed at the Dalton airstrip launched on their way, serving the original attack wave, which was postponed since dawn of the same day.

11:25. Lanner Command Post

Up the road that leaded from the north end of the Sea of Galilee to Katcha's farm on the outskirts of the Yehudia stream, aircraft decorated with the symbol of the 201st Squadron passed over the head of Lt. Col. (Res.) Yigal Bar Shalom (Barshi).

I should be there, Barshi thought as he counted them. *What do I have to do with this ground command post?*

11:25-11:30. The 201st Squadron

It's not good to be Syrian right now, the "Rhino" thought, seeing Skyhawks returning and Phantoms going, and he knew that the time had come to cut the heads off of the bastards, before the main gang under Huldai came to knock out the missiles themselves. He felt a slight bump as Stavi, in the front cockpit, released in loft strike the bombs on the artillery batteries and turned around to return to base.

Here is Rafid Junction, thought Maj. Ron Huldai, leading a convoy or fifteen Sledgehammer jets, and knew that exactly at this point his aircraft would spread out into six formations, each one with a designated target.

11:30. *Here is the Sheikh Maskin radar*, Huldai identified the target, exercised a wingover maneuver and dove towards it. A prolonged press on the pickle (weapon release) switch. The aircraft shook. The bombs were released. They descended, lower, lower. A glance behind them. *It's a shame it wasn't destroyed*, Huldai thought. *I wonder how the others will do.*

Maj. Uri Sheani was Huldai's Number 2. He pulled up, inverted, dove, locked on his target, pressed the pickle on the stick grip and... nothing. The bombs were not released. He made a 270° turn to make another pass, switched the controls to "direct mode," and released the payload on what looked like a Syrian force. He broke out, low. The lowest possible level.

A shame it didn't get destroyed, Lev-Ari thought in the navigation cockpit. *I wonder how the others will do.*

Capt. Eitan Levy and Capt. Yair David led the second formation.

"Let's bypass Tel Fares from the north and the west," David suggested, and Levy agreed and broke to the left.

A single Skyhawk cruised a few hundred feet above them, its "body language" suggesting that "everything is alright, comrades." Rafid Junction. Burners. The ground passed at 1,000 kmph. About a kilometer every four seconds.

What is that? Through the pilot's cockpit dividing the blue sky, cruising more or less at the speed of sound, Levy identified a Syrian tank division below on the rocky basalt soil. The tanks were lined up, and the Syrian tank crews, with their leather helmets, gathered for a briefing. *That density is tempting,* Levy thought. *Should we continue to the radar, or attack and destroy this tank division, with 11 360-kilogram Mark 117 bombs?*

Two seconds of hesitation were cut short in a flash by the words of their wing commander at their departure briefing: "Guys, in this mission, you are dependent on one another." *We'll continue to the radar.*

Pull-up. A flash inside the mosque. Boom. Something shook the aircraft. He ignored it, completed the climb-out, aircraft wingover maneuver, and released bombs. Bull's-eye. The Zamarin radar went up in flames.

He pulled-out from the bombing dive. The engine's fire warning, light indicator was ominous. He shut-down the engine, pointing the nose westward, on one engine. With afterburner off, low airspeed, and the sky was full of exploding cotton balls.

Lt. Kobi Hayun was Levy's number 2. He pulled-up, rolled, dove, and the sky in front of him was full of pops and booms from flak. *Concentrate on the target. Ignore the little angels of death.* Boom. The aircraft shook. *Ignore it and continue.* He depressed the pickle switch. Release. Nailed it.

He broke strongly to the left. The cockpit warning lights flashed brightly. *Is the "Test" button broken?* Reset. *It's not the button.*

From the rear cockpit, Lt. (Res.) Shmidko shouted, "Break left, missile!" Doron Shalev, Number 3, also shouted, "Number 2, break, break, a missile is heading towards you!" Hayun broke from side to side, repeatedly. *There's Petroleum Road. Israel. We're saved.*

"Levy is hit," Lt. Doron Shalev, Levy's Number 3, reported to Lt. Uri Arad, who sat in the navigation chamber.

Three seconds passed. "Hayun is hit."

Now it's our turn, Arad thought. *Our turn...*

* * *

The aircraft is still responding, Levy thought as he gained altitude on a single engine. *Don't give up. Carry-on, carry-on.*

Here is Safed. Here is Ramat David. He landed. He lowered the arresting gear like on an aircraft carrier. He got to the mid-runway cable. He stopped. Only Yair David remained apathetic in the rear cockpit, as if nothing happened.

"Get down fast," Levy screamed, as more threatening thunder pounded in his ears.

Everything's alright, Hayun thought. He shut-off the burners, and heard a hissing sound from the right engine. Hayun said to Shmidko, "I'm pulling up." He sailed. Damn, the right engine has failed.

Shalev then said, "Number 2, there's smoke coming from you."

Here's Hula Valley, Hayun thought, *we'll attempt an emergency landing in Rosh-Pina airport.* The aircraft halted in mid air.

"Both engines are gone," Hayun reported to Shmidko as he looked at the altimeter: 9,000 feet.

He attempted air-starts. Nothing. Altitude, 7,000 feet.

"Get ready. We're ejecting," Hayun said as he pulled the handle.

Lt. Col. Guri Palter and Lt. (Res.) Ilan Lazar led the third formation. They were the first in the squadron who were supposed to actually hit missile batteries. However, there were no missiles in the area of the intended attack. They located an anti-aircraft artillery battery situated nearby and released their weapons on it. *Such a colossal waste*, Palter thought.

Lt. Gideon Eilat was Palter's number 2.

He could not seem to find missile batteries as well, and also dropped his ordinance on whatever he could find.

They began to head back. Suddenly, the sky filled with angels of death, both small and large. Gideon flew lower than any Phantom had ever flown, and darted around like a madman, thinking that it was not possible to do more than that. Amnon Tamir, in the rear cockpit, did not know what would happen. A parachute was deployed in the sky and the radio was filled with distressed calls. Amnon felt that something bad was happening.

In the Kunass jet that led the fourth formation, things had never been so entertaining. Shaniboi and Assael goofed around loudly, and here and there sang a variety of duets.

Rafid Junction. *Are they crazy?* Assael thought, *why are they shooting as us?*

Suddenly, there was a slam sound, a light hit. *Poor bird,* Shaniboi thought as he continued to the pull-up waypoint.

Haim Ram was Shaniboi's number 2. *The Syrians are smart,* he thought, as he saw unending amounts of flak in the air. *They've learned quickly. At first they were hiding from fear of the first aircraft, they saw that they weren't the target, pulled themselves together, laid on their backs, lifted barrels to the sky, and now seem as though saying 'Alright, celebration time'.*

Suddenly he thought about the ejection lever. *If I eject, both of us are outside. If Yahav ejects, it'll be just him outside. If Yahav turns the lever 90°, he'll eject us both.*

"Even if we get hit and go up like a torch, don't turn the ejection lever to your control," he said to Yitzhak Yahav in the rear cockpit, "I'll do whatever it takes to get us back home."

Yahav suddenly thought about Uri Ilan, who was captured and committed suicide in Syria.

Enough with these disturbing thoughts, Ram thought, seeing Shaniboi accelerate to the 'ingress waypoint'. He identified and passed it. Ninety seconds to pull-up. *What is this?* Fireballs erupted in the air intakes of Shaniboi and Assael's aircraft, which was thrown back with a huge, uncontrollable flame.

Tick, tick, he suddenly heard a small knock on his fuselage.

* * *

Dani Haloutz and Eran Cohen led the fifth formation.

"Check out my house down there" Navigator Eran Cohen said in the Sledgehammer, full of bombs and fuel, as it passed over the palm groves of Kibbutz Degania.

This was supposed to be simple, Haloutz thought. *Like an air show pass on Independence Day. After all, we've practiced all of this many times. The 'ingress waypoint' towers are scattered all over the Golan Heights and draw the right strike leg for us. At the last tower, I'll start my stopwatch. Continue with the speed I've accumulated, 600 knots, and I know that in another minute, ten miles beyond the Purple Line, I'll identify the pull-up waypoint, and Eran will tell me two, three, and release. Then we'll pull up, keep the correct angle, perform a wingover maneuver onto the target, release our bombs and head out at a low altitude, until we reach the cliffs again. Then we'll let out a sigh of relief and sing the whole way home. But something isn't working today.*

First of all, those flames down there won't stop. We were supposed to come in as a surprise, not like this. Everyone says that we'll win with what we have. But how can we win if we can't identify the target?

Haloutz released the payload on something unidentifiable, and with a sense of disappointment, he descended to a low altitude for his return westward. Itamar Barnea, his Number 2, joined into formation. Haloutz urged him to climb a bit higher; Eitan Shmueli, who had already imagined them planted in the ground, breathed a sigh of relief when he saw that Itamar finally ascended a bit, and was still only slightly above the ground. It was the lowest they had ever flown.

* * *

"Wild Bull" led the sixth formation. It closed the convoy.

"Tree-two-one, ready pull up" Blumi said, and Peled pulled up.

"The battery is empty," Peled called on the ICS.

"We're going to get them," Ori Shahak said to Gilad Graber in the rear cockpit, hoping to make it up to himself for missing the morning strike, having had an aircraft malfunction that prevented him from striking Egypt with the squadron.

The last of the group, they climbed from south of the Sea of Galilee to the Golan Heights, discovering the Heights covered in black dots. Tanks, almost at the cliff line, with artillery, heading to the west. *What? The Syrian army is this deep in our territory? We need to inform Sami the AGCO. His maps have them located much farther to the east.*

Missiles. This is good. They fly up, we fly low below.

We're returning, Blumi thought.

It's not with Peled. It doesn't make sense to call him "Wild Bull," this obstinate person, that's continuing to the pull-up waypoint, wingover maneuver, diving. The computer in the rear cockpit is beeping out loud.

Cramped in the rear cockpit, Blumi understood a few things about bombing computers. He knew that a constant beep indicated that the bombs were not able to be released due to a steep launch angle, very steep and… *We will not get out of this dive.* Peled pulled the stick. There was no response. Faithful to his nickname and his survival instinct, "Wild Bull" Peled did not give up: not on aircraft, not on a destination, not on their lives. He pulled the stick again to his stomach, the most he could pull; the strongest. He continued pressing the button to release the bombs with his right thumb.

At a low altitude, so low, clearly lower than the safe levels set by the aircraft's manufacturer, the computer gave in. Perhaps out of fear, perhaps it just gave up to this stubbornness, it reached a strained solution and agreed to release the bombs, which voiced their blunt protest by releasing a dose of shrapnel that shook the aircraft as well as Bull and Blumi, who felt like he received his life as a gift.

"Where's the target?" Shahak asked. Graber could not identify it either.

The RWR display indicated that a missile was launched. *We are going in at any cost,* Shahak decided, dispensing chaff from the speed brakes. He recognized the hits caused by "Wild Bull" and Gadi Samok that entered the strike before him, and assumed that perhaps they identified the target, executed a wingover maneuver on target, and aimed at the bonfires of "Wild Bull" and Samok. The radar locked. He pressed the pickle button and aligned with leveled wings to release the bombs. Nothing happened. He switched to "Direct Mode." The bombs were released. He pulled-up to recover, while breaking left westward.

What is that? High in the sky, he saw something in the color of bright orange. It was not an orange ceiling lamp in the blue sky, Shahak knew, and realized that the orange object was a parachute hanging near Samok's aircraft. *What is happening here? Gadi's aircraft seems intact and is continuing to fly. Did Leif only eject himself?*

"Let's stay in the area," he said to Graber, "We'll see where he lands. Maybe we'll organize a rescue operation for him." Just then, the aircraft received a small knock.

11:45. Lanner Command Post

"Barshi, what happened, where are all the aircraft?" wondered tank and infantry officers. They knew nothing about aircraft, but saw them enter the zone and watched them come back, and knew a thing or two about basic accounting.

"They're surely on different flight paths," answered Lt. Col. Yigal Bar Shalom, who, two hours earlier, started the climb to the Golan Heights in a shaky half-track. He took off his cumbersome helmet and replaced it with a baseball cap with the emblem of his squadron, standing tall in the fighter's chamber so that they could see that the IAF made it as well.

"When we return from attacks, they split into different flight routes," Bar Shalom continued, trying to reassure them, as well as himself.

11:45-12:00. The 201ˢᵗ Squadron

That's not a bird, Shaniboi was alerted, as the "Master Caution" light burst with bright light before his eyes, and the fire warning light broke into a flashing dance.

"Asa, see anything?"

"Yes, there's fire from behind us."

They got rid of the bombs, pulling left to the north. Pressed "Panic" button to jettison all external loads. The aircraft shook after vomiting its load. *At least we won't get blown up in the air. But Haim Ram will!*

"Ram, eject! Ram, eject!" He shouted to the Phantom above and to the right of him, wholly swallowed in flames.

Now we need to take care of our little problem. First of all, pull the aircraft back to our own forces side. Here's Tel Fares on our left. Easy, boy, easy, do this for me and for Assa.

The aircraft starts rolling to the right, and Shaniboi saw that all of the indicators and gauges winded down. He knew the significance: no hydraulics. Nothing was under control. "Help me with the stick," he said to Assael.

They pulled and pulled; nothing.

Damn. A moment ago, I was on the top of the world, sitting up there in the biggest monster all tough and strong. I was the king.

Now, a fire. My aircraft is out of control, and I'm sitting in a useless hunk of junk.

I'll shut one engine down. The important thing is to not let more fuel get in this fire.

Slam. The aircraft developed an uncontrollable yaw to the right. Shaniboi pulled the stick to the left, tried to roll back. There was no response: no flight control.

He took a quick look outside. There was an inflamed aircraft cruising at a low altitude. Not anymore. The nose pointed itself sharply towards the ground.

"We're ejecting," Shaniboi shouted, pulling on the main ejection handle.

Assael flew into the air, spinning and rolling in his ejection seat, and was suddenly silent. His parachute deployed above him.

A hundred meters to the west, he saw Shaniboi, hanging on the cords of his own orange parachute.

But now, he heard the whistling of bullets. He looked down. Two Syrian armored vehicles were situated on a strip of road, and everyone in them or in to the side of them held a gun and was shooting up at them. Assael wondered: *What is this? The Syrians have never heard of the Geneva Treaty?* He looked up and saw his parachute full of holes.

"Pull towards the west!" Shaniboi yelled, who actually was a paratroopers unit officer disguised as a pilot.

Survive, survive, sirens in Assael's head shrieked at him. *Get ready for the next step, like they taught me. The task now is to get to the ground, preferably far, far away from these mental cases. Watch out for the jagged rocks.* He prepared for landing, holding onto the cords of the parachute and… he stood on clear land. *Thank you, athletic legs.*

Tel Fares is to the left and south. I'm in the Israeli Golan Heights. I've got a good chance to get out of this nightmare in one piece.

He disconnected his parachute and took out his microphone: "Can anyone hear me?"

"Huldai hears you. Continue," answered the acting squadron leader that, just a moment before in his cockpit, concluded that the Syrians had no idea from where the operation had gotten to them, and understood that Assael was just about to ruin his celebration.

"I've ejected," Assael said, holding up his head, and saw Shaniboi spread along the rocks a hundred meters away from him.

He headed in his direction, but heard voices. He stops in his tracks.

Two vehicles moved along the road nearby. *They are searching for us,* Assael thought as he found a place to hide behind a pile of stones. The vehicles stopped. *Drive, drive, please don't stop here.* He glanced nervously from behind a wave of black rocks, gasping Five Syrian soldiers, with steel, dish-shaped helmets on their heads, moved towards his direction.

With one hand on the SART and the other pressed against his upper lip, he whispered, "I'm going to be captured. Syrian forces are closing in on me." Yosi Lev-Ari, who was already making his way back home, for whom Asa was his smiling colleague from the squadron and from flight course, heard everything live on his headset in the navigator's cockpit on his aircraft. Suddenly, he could no longer hear Asa.

Assael put his hands in the air, and someone who looked like a commander said, in broken English, "Don't you to be worry," approached him, removed his aircrew watch, and moved calmly away to the side. Nothing in the body movement of the soldier standing next to him revealed the long burst heading directly to Assael's strong leg. His body leaked below.

It doesn't hurt, Assael thought, *just a great emptiness, and my whole life is flashing before my eyes.* He was unsure by now what would happen to his life, and the "commander" who took his watch yelled at the soldier who shot, then loaded Assael on his back. *First he wanted me dead, and now his job is to scare me to life*, Assael thought. Suddenly, it started to hurt. It was very, very painful.

Shaniboi woke up and found himself tied to a rope on the floor of an armored personnel carrier, and on his shoulder was a dead Syrian soldier, his head blown off and half of his brain missing. He saw another injured soldier, still alive, moving on the floor of the APC in agony, blood pouring out of his leg.

"Asa! What happened?" he asked his favorite navigator.

"They killed my leg," Assael answered. "Killed my leg…"

They stopped, and were thrown into the trunk of another vehicle.

Overcome this, the tormented Assael gnashed his teeth in the face of the upheaval, threatening to crush the rest of his dignity. *Get over this, man. Get some air. Another. Close your eyes. Relax, relax.*

Enough with all of this pain. Enough. It can't go on like this. He shouted, so very much.

Shaniboi was by his side, holding his hand.

* * *

Haim Ram jettisoned his bombs, broke to the left, and tried to roll back to the right. The aircraft would not cooperate. He tried to the left. The aircraft still refused and continued to roll. He tried to pitch up. Nothing. Flying inverted, he pushed the stick. The aircraft rose a bit. He saw basalt rocks and thought *Yeah, those are their natural sizes*, and allowed the aircraft to roll once more. Ten meters above the ground, he understood that this is it, and pulled the ejection handle.

Yitzhak Yahav hit the ground and was unable to break free from his parachute. He was pulled and dragged by the parachute, and hit his head on a basalt rock.

Haim Ram also hit the ground, released his parachute, and saw a bomb crater near him. He jumped in and took out his headset. Everyone was talking about ejections.

He lifted his head and saw a Syrian soldier with a Kalashnikov, its barrel sniffing the rocks, headed towards him.

He took a handful of his papers and concealed them under some black stones. He left the crater and walked towards the soldier with his hands raised. *That's it, another moment and I'm dead.*

Get over here, the soldier signaled him.

He stepped towards him, his hands raised. *Is he going to shoot me in the back?*

He did not shoot.

Suddenly, out of nowhere, a child appeared, holding a large stone and running towards him.

The soldier bypassed Ram, and swiftly and strongly kicked the child, throwing him in the air.

Don't shoot me, don't shoot me!

Then it was like a small encampment, and soldiers surrounded Itzik.

Captive protocol. Remember what they taught you, Haim Ram prepared himself and decided that it's time. *"Let them think that you have a much bigger problem than you really do,"* they were told. *"Make it seem like you are hurt, ill."*

He did it. He remembered that his sister once got a concussion in his presence, and remembered that she panted like a dog. Now, he began as well. *Dog pants, don't stop, don't stop.*

What happened to Haim? Itzik wondered through screams of pain. That was also just what the Syrian doctor was wondering as well, asking Itzik to clarify with Haim what was this strange thing that had a hold of him.

Itzik asked. Haim did not answer.

An injection, the confused Syrian doctor thought, proceeding to stick a needle into Ram's arm muscle, who continued panting like a dog.

Gilad Graber heard a little bang.

He casually glanced at the side mirrors and the rear mirror, and suddenly saw that their aircraft was sitting on a ball of fire.

"We're hit," he yelled. "The aircraft is on fire. We need to eject."

Ori Shahak glanced at the indicator light and saw that the left engine was on fire. He shut down the engine and pressed the "Panic" button to jettison all loads.

"Wait a minute," he said to Gilad. "I'm trying to point us westward."

He pointed the nose to the west. The line of barrows, home, was getting closer.

The aircraft was not responding. The second engine failed as well.

Five hundred feet in the air, a burning Phantom lacked any engines.

"Dog 3 is ejecting," Shahak transmitted and pulled the ejection handle.

Graber saw a hole in his parachute, and suddenly another, and another. He looked down and saw a group of soldiers, all of them with rifles pointed to the sky and firing.

It's just a bad dream, he decided. *Just a dream. Right now you'll wake up. Another moment and you'll find yourself in the backseat.* There was a huge explosion.

Under his feet, he saw the remains of the Phantom explode, like a torch shooting to the heavens.

He hit the ground, trailing on the wind. He detached himself from his parachute and remained lying down. *Get up, get up fast.* He rose. *Soldiers.* Everyone was shooting at him. *Think fast, think of a solution...* He raised his hands above his head nervously as bullets flew past his head. *Bastards, stop it. You'll kill me.*

In the middle of a rocky field, Ori Shahak fainted.

There was a handkerchief over his eyes, hot blood trickling from his head. He was thrown into a vehicle. He landed on someone.

Soldiers sat on both sides of him, their legs stomping on two human sacks of potatoes. The second sack was alive. Gilad. *He's alive, he's alive. I'm not alone.*

12:00. Ramat David

"He'll hit you, he'll hit you," Samok heard them shouting from the control tower. He saw a Phantom standing in the middle of the runway and thought: *Hey, I'm the one who is about to hit it.*

He stepped down on the brake pedals, blowing up the main wheel tires that were burning like torches, turned his Sledgehammer sharply to the side and stopped.

Only Samok can do it, Levy and David thought. They saw the big, strong guy, fresh from a test pilot training course in the United States, slide down the ladder, as if his tires had never blown up, a moment before catastrophe.

"Where's Leif?" Samok asked. "Where is my navigator? When did he eject?" The three of them were trying to come up with some kind of answer. "Maybe he panicked and ejected? Maybe there was a short circuit that activated the ejection system, out of his control?"

What happened to the others?

12:15. Wing 4 (Hatzor)

Col. Lapidot saw them return.

From the top of the control tower he took account of all of the fragments of the formations. *There is one missing here. Two over there.* He was thirty-nine years old, a Wing Commander, veteran of the Sinai Campaign, the Six-Day War and the War of Attrition. *You can't look back,* he told himself, *only go forward. This is a war, and war has casualties. You cannot turn back the clock. It was hard today. We will move on. This is how we are.*

12:18. Senior Command Post

"'Model' is fine," the IAF Commander reported to the Chief of Staff, "We've lost five Sledgehammer jets. We've taken out seventeen batteries."

"Model" was not fine. It was really not fine. It was absolutely terrible. Even if, today, we ignore the other Sledgehammer aircraft that were lost and not reported, there is still the matter for which everyone was sent out: the destruction of all of the batteries. Even if we close our eyes and cut corners, there is no way to turn the number one into seventeen.

Who was responsible for reporting to the IAF Commander that we had blown up seventeen batteries, whereas in reality only one was destroyed, with another battery being partially damaged? How was it possible that in the Air Force, which was entrusted with an investigative culture, no one checked, and made sure what were the actual results of the operation?

In the chaos and confusion that occurred with the targets not being where they were supposed to be, the rockets being launched, the thunderous flak, and the competitiveness of the IAF pilots themselves, in the name of personal excellence, they took advantage of big fires and "made" them into the target. Someone reported to someone else, who in turn told someone else, so the number became seventeen. A fact.

12:15-13:30. The 201ˢᵗ Squadron

Control Tower: "Mouse 3 has landed."

Sima: "What about numbers 1 and 2?"

Control Tower: "They haven't arrived."

Afterwards he continued: "Crocodile 1, 2 are not arriving. Neither are Dog 2, 3."

"The tower says that six aircraft are not returning," Sima informed Benaya, "What is going on here?"

Benaya understood exactly what was going on there, and also understood that everything suddenly depended on him. Therefore, he walked to the operations board, and without any signs of distress or hesitation, he took the plates from the board, held it in his hands, gave it to Sima and said, "Take this. Just put it in the drawer."

Her face went pale. "What?!"

"Everything's fine," Benaya replied calmly. "I'm going to prepare the next strike. Meanwhile, put this in the drawer. We have no use for it at this time."

Pilots don't cry, especially not in front of a sobbing girl, Benaya reminded himself. He later reflected on how, in just one moment, a man can become just a placard in a drawer.

Just then "Wild Bull" returned from his canopy, passed by the operations room, saw the poster removed from the board and quietly said, "The war has begun."

The steps at the entrance of the squadron are used like a reception line for pilots returning from combat training. Descending from the busses, one could see from their body language exactly how it went. Beaten down like losers, for example. A stubby smile doesn't brighten their faces.

Now the bus arrived from the underground hangar, and Gil Regev remembered the loser from training. Except that this time, they all lost. What a loss.

It did not make any sense to him, a damned dash ten miles into Syrian territory. What else could have happened there? And what is the meaning of these new words—ejected, lost. Hit. Downed. Captured. *These words don't stick.*

There was also the confusion. *Who is missing? Who was killed? Where is Shahak? Has someone seen him? Did anyone see him get hit? Samok landed? In Ramat David? So where is Leif? And where is Ram? Have you seen him? Yes? Are you sure? Yes, I heard him on the radio. Shaniboi and Assael? Did you see Asa at the underground hangar? He said on the radio that they were capturing him.*

"Everyone to the briefing room!" the speakers boomed.

Huldai called out, "Sound off." *Like in basic training*, Regev thought.

On Sunday afternoon, October 7, the squadron fighters landed on a bloody reality. They never imagined that anyone would smack them into a knockout in ten minutes, before even twenty-four hours had passed since the outbreak of the war. 34 pilots departed; 22 returned. 17 aircraft were sent out; 11 returned.

Until now, everything was easy, Regev thought. *Yesterday we were messing around, we didn't do anything. We were the kings of the skies. That strike in Egypt this morning, we thought we were once again on the familiar track of the Six-Day War. Suddenly, this thing fell into our laps.*

Shaniboi hasn't come back. How could that be? Shani isn't the type to get shot down.

Gil, you can't fall in this war. He made a mental switch in his head. *You save yourself. Concentrate, don't do any nonsense, don't lose sight of it. If Shaniboi, who taught me to fly low and over the border, if he didn't come back, then all of us could fall.*

Huldai, the nervous redhead, now revealed his greatness. He began lifting people up. The atmosphere was difficult and sad, but Huldai made it clear, very clear, that they needed to get back to how they were before. Mission-oriented. *It happened, it's over, there were injured people. Get out of this damn distress. Do not let impotence run the show. Do research. Let's see how we can do this better. We must continue. Move forward, come what may. Enough with this soul-searching. Continue to get out and fight and fly without "ifs and" or buts." Keep going. Raise your head. We are* the 201st.

There aren't enough people, "Wild Bull" thought, *and there aren't enough aircraft. The biggest concern now is that they will ground us. The 201st Squadron will not be able to take such an instruction. They just need to let us continue. Without delay, without stopping.*

This is not just a day of combat, Dan Haloutz thought. *There is no quick fix, this is not the Six-Day War. Not even the War of*

Attrition. This will be difficult, much more difficult. We need to be sharp. We are dying here. This will be costly up the road as well.

Eli Zohar, a veteran of the War of Attrition, remembered the old days, when everyone said that a 0:1 score was a better than 1:10, and any losses, captured or killed, should be avoided at all costs. But this was war. *We need to defend our country at all costs. Even if Phantoms are taken down; and killed. There will be prisoners as well.*

Afterwards, he heard that Shahak ejected and he grumbled quietly, *he didn't hear me.*

14:00. Chamber of the Head of Central Command

Into the afternoon, an hour after the gong was heard, aircrews returned to their bases.

Two hours afterwards, the final result was revealed.

One hundred and thirteen aircraft participated in Operation "Model 5-B," the operation to eliminate missiles in Syria.

At 11:20, 50 of them, the first attack wave, began dropping their loads—cluster bombs—on anti-aircraft artillery batteries that were supposed to defend missile batteries. They completed their mission, and returned safely to their bases.

At 11:30, the attack of the main wave began, as 62 aircraft from five squadrons, four squadrons of Phantoms and one squadron of improved Skyhawks were sent to destroy three radars and 25 missile batteries.

By 11:40, the IAF was licking its wounds.

Six Phantoms went up in flames, while ten other Phantoms were hit and subsequently grounded. Nine airmen replaced the warm beds of the officers' quarters for the dungeon cells of a Syrian prison, and two airmen—from among the best of the best—were killed.

One could suggest, why was there such a great lament over this turn of events? Is a pilot's blood thicker than those in the other corps? This was war, and the achievement of goals is often accompanied by casualties.

That is true, of course. The IAF is prepared to pay the price to achieve critical objectives.

Yet that is the point—the achievement of the objectives. Or the inability to achieve them, to be more precise.

At 11:40, only one missile battery was destroyed, and another was partially damaged.

The fiasco of "Operation Model" is considered one of the most painful failures of the Yom Kippur War, and as far as the IAF is concerned, the most painful of them all.

There is no doubt that the effect of the failure deviated from the dry summary of the results.

"Model" was supposed to be the light at the end of the tunnel, the operation that would bring about a change in the Syrian front, would contain the collapse, and would turn the wheels of war in the opposite direction. Without missiles defending the Syrian forces, they would be doomed, and the country's leaders would fall to their knees, desperate for a ceasefire. The realization concerning their northern ally's terminal situation was also meant to serve as a warning to Egypt. It was intended to urge Sadat, the sooner the better, to withdraw his forces before the IDF would have a chance to concentrate on one front, his, and to obliterate his forces in the manner that Israeli troops have been known for over the years. However, that did not come to pass, because "Model" failed.

Did the failure of "Operation Model" stem from circumstances relating to time, or could things have been done differently?

One figure pertaining to "Model" skips over the number of question marks involved in its implementation. The operation was not launched by the book!

According to the "book," the operation was to begin after a fresh aerial reconnaissance run, assisted by a full backing envelope (most of it electronic), and with the number of aircraft determined in the order. These three conditions had not been met by the time the bell sounded.

Would "Model" have ended differently with optimal starting conditions?

Let us begin with an examination of the photography mission.

The last effective photography sortie for detecting the missile battery arrays in the Golan Heights was on Friday morning, October 5, more than 48 hours before "go-time." Another sortie was carried out on Saturday morning, October 6, but the cloud coverage made it impossible to locate the missiles and obtain an updated picture. The area was not photographed on Sunday, October 7.

The classic "Model 5" is identified as "5-A"—a strike against the missile array on the front from a state of complete surprise. A preemptive strike. For 5-A, a photo from a few days before was enough to assume, with a high level of likelihood, that the missile battery layout would be in this position as our aircraft pounced upon it.

On October 7, the boys were sent on "Model 5-B"—an attack on the missile layout on the front after hostilities had erupted; a big difference.

There are those who argue that there was no point in a photography mission on Sunday morning, as the cloud coverage would have rendered the mission impossible. Moreover, let us assume that the photography sortie went out after the clouds cleared up and returned with clear, updated shots of the missile batteries. What then? By its very nature, such a flight would have been detected by enemy radar. The operational-intelligence round that would have been required—a few hours between the sortie, the decoding and the arrival of the updated aerial photography to the strike squadrons—would have provided a window of opportunity to allow the mobile missile batteries (most of which were on the front) to move to a different area altogether.

The IAF's Military Historian, Ze'ev Lachish, who has explored the subject of the intelligence used for "Model," holds that Syria's familiarity with the SA-6 missile system was still in its infancy in October 1973. That is, they still had not understood how to utilize the advantages of a portable system, capable of quickly jumping around and misleading the enemy intending to destroy it. Therefore, they probably would not have devised some ruse involving a change of location and deception, had they identified a reconnaissance sortie .

Why, then, were IAF aircraft incapable of locating the missile batteries in their pits? This was because the batteries skipped to different pits, perhaps even to those that had been prepared beforehand. They were moved, not due to any deceptive moves on the part of the Syrians upon the detection of the recon sortie, but due to the course of events on the ground.

On Saturday night, after nightfall, the Purple Line was breached in the southern Golan Heights, and Syrian armored and infantry divisions made their way towards the Sea of Galilee. According to Soviet combat doctrine, which was passed on to the Syrians, the role of the mobile missile batteries, along with Gundish AAA batteries, was to protect ground forces against IAF aircraft. Therefore, most likely, the batteries were moved as the ground forces pushed forward.

Another issue remains. Supposing that Lachish is mistaken in his assessment, and another reconnaissance mission would have brought the Syrians to move their batteries to other positions. In order to solve this issue, the IAF could have sent the reconnaissance aircraft, after the Sunday morning clouds, on a diagonal flight path (which would have been harder for Syrian radar to pick up), or an UAV earlier in the morning, flying low under the clouds (a UAV flying at a low altitude is even harder to detect).

Would a more up-to-date photo have changed the outcome of the operation? Of course.

The lack of an updated photograph is at the heart of the operation's failure. The absence of targets means that none will be destroyed. It is so simple, and so unfortunate. If only a reconnaissance aircraft had been sent out on Sunday, decryption crews would have discovered the empty pits and would have prevented the failure of the operation.

Moreover, it is possible that the photo development would have revealed the updated locations of the missile batteries, which probably would not have been moved yet again and, according to Lachish, the operation would be on the road to success.

We will continue with a review of the back-up system.

What coverage was supposed to stand alongside of Operation "Model 5-B" if it had departed with time constants intact as had been prepared by prior orders? An impressive one. What was available for the actual operation? Mere fragments.

The Hermon outpost, and its network of electronic-jamming tools from the ground, was destroyed on Saturday by the Syrians. The EW system-equipped "Shoulder" helicopter array, which provided electronic jamming from the air, had remained in Sinai-waiting for "Challenge," which was interrupted, to resume. Artillery guns did not shoot regular shells to "cut the head" off of the batteries, nor did they shoot chaff to disrupt Syrian radars (the few artillery batteries that were still active on Sunday were fighting for their lives on the front). Of the nine Skyhawks and Super Mystére aircraft that were supposed to fire rockets and dispense chaff cartridges, only one was launched. Of the array of decoy UAVs, which were supposed to deceive Syrians in the skies of the Golan Heights—to attract missiles and leave the batteries empty—most (twelve of them) were wasted in the embarrassing, careless mistake at 06:00 in the morning. Four other decoys, launched ahead of the operation, were unable to make a significant difference.

Would delaying the operation by a few hours have led to stronger coverage of the fighter jets?

An ordered launch of the operation would have enabled an immeasurably better preparation. Besides the post at Mt. Hermon and the artillery, most of the support pyramid would have come from the Air Force, reporting on time and fully supplied.

We will conclude with the aircraft and the pilots.

According to the plans of Operation "Model 5-B," there were supposed to be 235 launched aircraft, consisting of an initial wave to eliminate artillery (60); a main wave to attack missile batteries (87) employing a pop-up strike method; assistance aircraft (8); and a final wave to complete hunting the missile batteries (80). In the actual operation, 113 aircraft participated: 50 in the first wave, 62 in the main wave, a single aircraft as an assistant and... zero aircraft on the final wave. Is this difference meaningful?

If we look closely at the cluster bombs, which were supposed to take out the enemy anti-aircraft artillery, ten aircraft were missing from what had been planned (17% less). Is this significant? Maybe.

If we judge the operation by the number of aircraft in the main attack wave that were supposed to participate, we will find that 25 aircraft were missing (29% less). Significant? Perhaps.

One thing is clear: the planned operation provided for a longer period of time in order to refuel and rearm, and would have sent a larger force in both the initial and main waves.

Moreover, the air crew, as excellent as they were, also needed specific time intervals to switch modes from each leg of the operation. This is especially true for the destruction of the missiles in Syria, the most difficult task of all. The time allotted to them in the actual operation was lacking, and could have affected their performance.

So why did "Model" turn out the way it did?

This was due to the fact that Maj. Gen. Benny Peled was sent to save the country, and the general sense of panic, which had a hold on him as well, made him forget two important things. First, the missile batteries created no immediate existential threat to Israel; however, the rows of tanks making their way to the Sea of Galilee and the Jordan River did, and they could have been stopped by strike fighters designed for "scratch" orders. Secondly, missile batteries in Syria, mostly SA-6's, the most threatening type, were packed densely in Syria. It was not a situation in which corners should have been cut.

In the end, it turned out that it was not the missiles.

Towards the late afternoon hours of Sunday, October 7, with the failure of Operation "Model 5-B" seared into their flesh, IAF leaders suddenly realized that the worst part was not just that pilots were lost, killed and captured. It was not even the unthinkable outcome. The failure of "Model" was accompanied by a systemic effect that transcends the specific operation and its consequences.

Analysis of the results of the operation shakes the foundation of the attack methodology, the training of the IAF pilots, and seriously undermines the self-confidence of the leadership staff and the pilots. It is suddenly clear that the combat doctrine, based on low-altitude penetration and minimal exposure to evade enemy radar and missiles, may not have been suitable for the conditions of the Yom Kippur War—hundreds of radar-guided anti-aircraft guns. Five of the six aircraft that were lost in Operation "Model 5" were shot down by guns! Not a single one was shot down by missiles!

14:30. Senior Command Post

"I'm worried," Dayan said, having just returned from checking the Forward Command Post of the Southern Command at Um Hashiva, and began sharing his feelings with the Chief of Staff.

"This is a war for the Land of Israel," Dayan continued, "it is best to stabilize a wide road and consolidate there. It would be a shame to erode the forces with repeated attempts to get reach strongholds. Who ever can forge his way back will do so, and those who can't will stay there and get captured."

"In the Golan, we need to hold the line no matter what," the Defense Minister said. "To do so, we need to invest more and more tanks and aircraft. If our tanks withdraw there, it's possible that the Syrians will follow them into the valley or to the communities inside the Green Line. A second line of defense needs to stabilize there to guarantee the protection of Israel's northern border."

"We need to consider the possibility that Jordan will join in the fighting. The military administration, the police forces and the border police need to organize for the possibility that Arabs living within the borders of the country will begin hostilities. What am I most afraid of? That Israel will eventually be left without weapons to defend itself. It's not important where the line is, but if there are not enough tanks, or aircraft, or people trained to defend the Land of Israel… no one else is going to fight this war for us."

"I still have one hope," Dado answered, trying to soften the Defense Minister's apparent befuddlement. "The Egyptian army. They've already fought for so long… if they try to attack tomorrow, we will try to hold our positions, break their attack, give a lot of space and undermine them. If we succeed in destabilizing their forces, we have two divisions, Arik's and Brenn's, to try a massive counterattack."

"We still need to get there," Dayan said eagerly, "I'm currently worrying for the State of Israel over the next fifty years." He turned around, announcing that he needed to meet with the Prime Minister, and left.

"Moshe here was more optimistic than at the Dov airport," said Maj. Gen. Rehavam Ze'evi (Gandhi), the minister's personal advisor, to a gang of shocked officers. "There, he was talking to me about the destruction of the Third Temple and other, frankly unpleasant things. Meetings with the heads of various commands left him feeling pessimistic. Me too," Gandhi added. "In the south, Gonen told us that fifty percent of the tanks were taken out. In the north, his mood was very somber, as Maj. Gen. Dan Lenner told us that fighting in the Golan Heights was over. We've lost."

"We think the minister's assessment is too pessimistic," the Chief of Staff and his assistant said.

"I don't think his is too pessimistic," Gandhi said, "I think that yours is too optimistic."

14:45. *The 201st Squadron*

Capt. Benzi Nahal knew that in war, not everyone returns.

The squadron took a hard beating, its technical officer thought, *but this belligerence, the leitmotif that characterizes it since the days of the War of Attrition, makes it keep fighting without stopping for soul-searching. Men. Get up and carry on.*

He was preparing aircraft for an attack on Egypt. He looked at the underground hangar chiefs with great admiration. Sergeants. Children. Suddenly, all of them had a hundred men under their command, some of them their father's ages, all of them sounding like child tyrants, conducting the technician's orchestra.

"Why don't we have more aircraft?" grumbled the flight division members.

As if he was personally responsible for the five downed aircraft. However, Benzi knew that it was not the time to get insulted, and the task of the hour was to finish turnaround as quickly as possible. This was what the flight division needed, and that was what they would get.

"Reduce the time required for the aircraft serviceability turnaround," he ordered his men, who installed the fuzes on the bombs, although it was strictly forbidden. They cleared the malfunctioned aircraft for the flight, which in peace time no one would dare to do.

He was personally moving between the aircraft, rolls of sticky aluminum foil on his hands, and pasting. Never ceases pasting. A hole was discovered in the fuselage? No damage to critical systems? He pulled out another cylinder and seals the hole. Another one was ready to go.

14:50. Dan Lenner Command Post

What is this? Yigal Bar Shalom peered over the side of a half-track sitting on a hill on the side of the road and remembered "Geva's Diaries"—short movies in theaters, which came before the feature films. The ones following the Six-Day War were shown over and over again, mocking the rows of defeated Egyptian soldiers—soldiers who were crushed, crouched, wrinkled, begging for water.

A movie, just like this, was unfolding right in front of his eyes, live. In reality. Soldiers in khaki, their faces turned down, came to the hill and begged for water and food. To his horror, he understood the difference immediately. Hebrew. They all spoke Hebrew.

14:50-16:20. Office of the Prime Minister

Three hours after the failure of Operation "Model," a few minutes after the 188th Armored Brigade fell in the Golan Heights, a desperate attempt was made to protect the house. National leaders wearing shrouded, black glasses, viewing the situation, and the sense of gloom overtaking those sitting in the Chamber of the Head of Central Command, jumped out of the command post and knocked on the doorstep of the Prime Minister.

"We must pull back in the southern area and establish a new line based on the Egyptian Mitle and Hajidi lines (about 35 kilometers from the Canal)," Dayan said to the Prime Minister, her deputy Yigal Alon, her advisor Israel Galili, and other senior officials. "We need to abandon the Canal and the strongholds."

"In areas where it is impossible to evacuate, we will leave the wounded," the Defense Minister continued, "Whoever arrives, arrives. If they decide to surrender, then they will surrender. We need to tell them that we cannot reach them. Try to break out or give in… We need to evacuate the Canal without hoping to return to it, but to hold the Egyptian line. The war will continue. The Canal line is lost. Neither I, nor the IDF Southern Command, nor the General Staff, see any possibility to get them over the Canal, even if we are provided with more forces."

"I am certain that Jordan will join in," Dayan added, pouring more hot oil into the present ears, "therefore, the troops need to be prepared for a Jordanian strike on the West Bank."

"I did not appreciate the enemy's strength," Dayan apologized, "I didn't fully appreciate their combat prowess. The Arab fighters are much better than before, with more weapons. They hit our tanks with personal, hand-held weapons."

He paused, stared his eye at the Prime Minister, and added, "I also exaggerated the strength of our own forces."

"What you are offering," Golda said, "is to pursue a ceasefire where we stand?"

"We are not standing," Dayan answered.

"Perhaps we should involve Kissinger on the ceasefire matter to finish where we stand?" Golda suggested.

The Defense Minister of the State of Israel, the brave warrior, whose defense doctrine was memorized by generations of fighters and commanders, replied, "I'll take it." He then added an element of apocalyptic teaching: "The Arabs will not stop the war. They want to conquer Israel, to finish off the Jews. If they stop and agree to a ceasefire, they will likely start again anew."

After the ceasefire agreement with Egypt, the Prime Minister of Israel believed whole-heartedly that she was leading her young country into a golden age, and despite the repeated echo of war drums in Cairo, returned and heard countless calm refrains of military experts, who said, "It's a bluff, don't worry, even if they dare, we'll hit them and make the Six-Day War pale in comparison." Now she heard the Defense Minister, no longer a beacon of strength, nor a provider of security. She said, "There is no reason they shouldn't continue. They have tasted blood. This is the second round since 1948."

Israel Galili was a confidant of Golda's. Perhaps more than anyone else, he understood every fidget of body language that the Prime Minister had. She was distressed.

This meeting cannot be locked in this atmosphere, Galili thought, *it's bad for Golda, and it's bad for the country. We need an alternative to Dayan's black glasses.*

"Call Dado, tell him to leave the "Pit" and join the meeting," he wrote on a note to Brig. Gen. Israel Lior, Golda's military secretary.

Shortly after 16:00, the Chief of Staff joined the meeting of government ministers.

"I support the installation of a 'stopping line,'" Lt. Gen. Elazar said, "but one from which it would be possible to counter-attack and to restore the prior status quo."

"Moreover," the Chief of Staff continued, slightly improving the gloomy atmosphere, "division commanders and the GOC are beginning to push me to attempt to cross the Canal."

"On the Golan front, the situation is better," Dado continued, "Our forces are succeeding in establishing a line of defense, which will be possible to stabilize with forces already deployed in the area. We have already pushed them out of Nefah."

Afternoon. Skyhawks in the Golan Heights

Aircraft are immediately required. Company commanders requested from battalion commanders, who passed the message on to division and brigade commanders. The Chief of Staff instructed the IAF Commander, "Get aircraft out and send two-ship formations of Skyhawks to stop the avalanche."

Imbued with a sense that their nation needed them, and knowing that the failure of Operation "Model 5" could not be an excuse for losing the Golan Heights, the Galilee and the Jordan Valley, Skyhawks crossed the lower Galilee on their way to the Golan. They soared over the Sea of Galilee, while the attack coordinator said, "Sorry, I have no information on what line our forces stand." In the absence of such a line, they needed to find their own "permitted hunting areas," and they understood what that entailed—a long stay over enemy forces with divided attention, minimizing their own chances of survival.

Yet orders were orders, and especially those that they received just then, which called out "help us, help us." They were going to fight by what the area had arranged for them.

Thus they were searching. In Nefah; Tel Fares; Tel Magshimim; they pulled up in altitude and found the Syrian army everywhere. They lowered their noses, dove, level up at bush-top height, and shared sectors between them—"I'll take the chunk to the west," the leader announced, "take the eastern side." With racing hearts they locked onto their targets. They shot at artillery, just scraping the armor of the tanks, threw napalm that filmed beautifully amid the flames, and immediately raised their eyes and searched for the ones that were coming to kill them. There were a lot of those. They knew that their Skyhawk was heavy and slow. They knew that they had only one engine, and lacked a bit of maneuverability. Nor was there any afterburner to pull them out of the inferno. They knew that they weren't surprising anyone. They were going to the most expected places. They did not have the privilege reserved for those who attacked at depth and arrived in a flank. They knew their aircraft's operating configuration in the battlefield—low dash—made them more vulnerable. And they knew that the enemy was waiting for them in the very places they were being sent to, again and again, from mission to mission; all the enemy nests, and especially the terrifying Gundish. Indeed, everything below them shot at them; just at them. They shrank in their cockpits, when bullets and missiles shot past, more and more, on both sides of their aircraft, and continued when number 2 gets hit and number 1 ejected.

And the Syrians were stopped.

There are those that say that it was Soviet doctrine that held that ground troops should advance under an umbrella of missile defenses. What if the troops step out of the missile's umbrella? They stop in place. Indeed, Syrian ground troops reached the edge of their defensive barrier in the southern Golan Heights, and stopped.

Yet military leaders know, from only a brief skimming of the pages of history, that every battle plan that is pulled from a door and exercised by operational forces can change in the face of reality on the ground, in the outbreak of live fire.

Commanders of determined Syrian fighting forces reported that they saw the Sea of Galilee and Tiberias. Despite the time disruption, they strived to follow the battle plan "Mashrua 110." In the order, it was written that the Syrian forces would stop at the border, the eastern coast of the Sea of Galilee. *Another small push, and we are there.*

Was the knowledge that they were beyond the range of the missile defense area the only thing keeping them situated there? I doubt it.

Several factors that combined prevented the Syrian armored forces from pushing all the way to the Sea of Galilee, and from there down into the valleys and the Galilee proper. Firstly, 65 tank crews under the command of Col. Ben Shoham, Commander of the 188th Brigade, courageously disrupted the schedule of the Syrians, who were planning to make it to the shores of the Sea of Galilee by 06:00. Secondly, by Sunday morning, the reserve forces, which had shortened the recognized organization practices, had already begun sending their own armored forces to stem the threatening Syrian tide that threatened to burst into Nefah, the Jordan River, and the Sea of Galilee.

The Air Force aided as well, especially the Skyhawks. They were sent along with a squadron of improved Super Mystére jets to stop the tide of the Syrian advance. They flew against the odds and broke the array of Syrian armor in the missile-destroyed area, under the threat of artillery guns, machine guns, and personal weapons of the infantry forces of two Syrian divisions that were dominating the southern Golan Heights. They continued unrelentingly, dropping bombs, most of which missed, some of which scratched, and some of which scored direct hits. Yet, they were in the sky, producing a shock effect on the ground, demonstrating to the Syrians that leaving the umbrella of missile defenses was not worthwhile. The Syrians stopped.

16:10. Chamber of the Head of Central Command

According to the instruction of the Defense Minister, Maj. Gen. Peled ordered Furman, Head of the Operations Department, to pursue the bridges that the Egyptians established over the Canal at all costs.

In those same minutes, the IAF Intelligence Division brought a summary forward. The summary included inter-Arab activities up to 00:15 of the same day, which showed that Egypt and Syria were attempting to drag other countries into the fighting arena. Algeria, according to the write-up, promised to deliver a squadron of MiG-21s.

Habib Bourguiba, President of Tunisia, announced that he would symbolically support the effort. Gaafar Nimeiry, President of Sudan, announced his willingness to transfer forces. Iraq announced that they would move three jet fighter squadrons, and possibly ground troops, into Syria. Yemen and the Gulf states also expressed some willingness. The only country in the region that had not come forward and announced a statement of support was Jordan. With this, the Intelligence officers wrote, there was a possible erosion of the Jordanian position, if the Egyptians and Syrians could demonstrate outstanding achievements against Israel.

16:30. Chamber of the Head of Central Command—Senior Command Post

"In the first fly-over, we have managed to hit seven of the fourteen bridges that Egypt placed in a strip between Crocodile Lake and the Great Bitter Lake. All of the bridges (the seven) are null and void," the IAF Commander reported to the Chief of Staff on the telephone. "The rest of the bridges," Peled continued, "will be destroyed after dark."

"Get here quickly and you will get a kiss," Dado said, enthusiastically, feeling how one report scattered the clouds of doubt regarding the IAF's abilities, which began covering the command post with the end of Operation "Model." *There, the excellent boys in the sky are returning to themselves, and following them, so will the rest of us.*

One of the generals in the "Pit" called out enthusiastically that "This (the move) is changing the war." Another one said, "Now the IAF will do everything—they will blow up the bridges, and then everything will look differently."

"By nightfall and into the night," the Chief of Staff informed the Prime Minister of the first positive report since the outbreak of war, "we will finish the bridges in the Suez."

16:30. The 201st Squadron

In the afternoon, Kobi Hayun and Uzi Shamir (Shmidko) returned to the squadron, after they were rescued following their ejection, underwent medical examinations, and hitched a ride.

Half of the guys are missing, Hayun was amazed, *and those that are here are wearing an unfamiliar cloak—gray faces, dull eyes. It's impossible to get any lower. We can only go up from here.*

18:05. Senior Command Post

"The Egyptians are repairing a few of the bridges that the IAF hit, and they are already crossing over some of them," said the Chief of Southern Command, Maj. Gen. Shmuel Gonen, adding that, in his assessment, the IAF bombing of the bridges was the most effective means of breaking the momentum of the Egyptian advance.

"We need to resume attacks on the bridges," the Deputy Chief of Staff, Maj. Gen. Tal, instructed the IAF Commander.

"We will renew attacks," Peled said.

18:45-21:00. Southern Command Post at Um Hashiva

"If, in the morning, we had only a hundred tanks in the whole sector, we now have four hundred and sixty tanks, divided into three sectors," Maj. Gen. Shmuel Gonen informed the pair of Chiefs of Staff: David Elazar, currently in the position, and Yitzhak Rabin, the Chief of Staff during the Six-Day War, who had joined the conversation.

Upon further discussion, they decided that the time had come for a counterattack. Very early in the morning, our forces would roll over the sands of Sinai and wipe out the four hundred Egyptian tanks that were stationed, arrogantly, on the eastern bank of the Canal.

19:00-21:35. Soldier's House in Tel Aviv

The Foreign Affairs and Security Committee of the Knesset convened to hear the latest news from of Maj. Gen. (Res.) Aaron Yariv.

"The IAF not only provided assistance today," said the former Head of Military Intelligence, who under special circumstances was made the Chief of Staff's special assistant, "but they have attacked thirty-six missile batteries, twenty-seven of which, according to reports, are completely out of commission."

Seven hours after Operation "Model," which was an utter failure, the former Head of Military Intelligence was reporting fictitious stories to the distinguished members of the committee. What was the reason for the fabricated report, which seemed as though taken from recruited journalistic practices found in third-world countries?

Nighttime. The 201ˢᵗ Squadron

During Sunday night, navigator Yoram Romem situated himself in the squadron, and immediately entered Huldai's room.

In August 1973, Romem was discharged from the IAF. As navigator, he led a four-ship formation. He gained rich operational experience during the War of Attrition. Quite enough. A post-discharge trip was all he needed to start on the civilian track.

He took his new bride Esti and they traveled. *Europe is a beautiful continent*, they told them.

On the evening of October 6, they were enjoying a walk through the streets of London. They walked past a newsstand, and took a quick glance at the headlines, which read: "Israel Attacks Syria and Egypt."

It's probably just a small incident. He called the embassy anyway. *Come*, they told him. In the morning, he got a call in their hotel room. *Get to Heathrow Airport.*

He peered down from his seat through the window while the jetliner is crossing the coast of Israel at night. *What is happening that is making them so scared down there?*

At the airport, a taxi driver was waiting with a list of names of the aircrew as well as Yigal Shochat, the legless POW, who emotionally recited the names of those who jumped, those who ejected, those killed, and those with unknown fates.

"They caught us with our pants down," Huldai informed him, and briefly told him what has occurred. Afterwards, he went to the map and saw Sami the AGCO's red arrows illustrated deep inside Israel. *I left Israel at its strongest,* he thought, *and now there's this catastrophe.*

Nighttime. Office of the IAF Commander

Base commanders and their secretaries gathered at the office of the IAF Commander.

"He's gone mad," the commanders whispered, shocked by the unrestrained rage against the senior staff, absorbing the constant barrage of fire and brimstone from the volcano's center.

"We have a problem in this headquarters," they agreed with desolate faces.

Nighttime. The 201ˢᵗ Squadron

A moment before Sunday moved into Monday, Lt. Col. Iftach Zemer presented himself in at Hatzor.

Towards the middle of September, after downing twelve MiGs, he went to the United States as the head of a delegation of three representatives of the IAF. On Friday, October 5, the tour ended.

"There is fighting in Israel," the assistant air attaché informed him on Saturday. "Get me an immediate flight to Israel," Zemer said.

"Don't worry," he told him, "by the time we get there, the fighting will be over."

He landed in Israel on Sunday night.

"This is a real war," Lapidot told him. "The Six-Day War was just an exercise compared to what is happening here."

He descended to the squadron's quarters, glanced at the mission board, said hello to the girls and to whoever else was still awake. Then, Huldai.

"Has anyone spoken with the families?" he asked his deputy.

"We have not," Huldai answered him, proceeding to update him on the war and the fighting.

"I'm tired," Zemer said, "my head is killing me. We'll talk tomorrow."

22:35-00:35. A Soldier's House in Tel Aviv

After an hour-long break, the Foreign Affairs and Security Committee reconvened.

Minister Haim Landau asked, "Perhaps we can put a few dozen Jewish Phantom pilots into battle?"

The Defense Minister wondered aloud. "Should we look for Jewish pilots abroad? Perhaps we hadn't considered the possibility."

He then added, "To be honest with myself, I hadn't expected such a constant and persistent war on their part..."

A Few Minutes Before Midnight.
Office of the Prime Minister

"Our lost child returns," Golda stopped the special session in her chambers in a voice imbued with authority, affection and wisdom, aimed at Zvi Zamir, Head of the Mossad, who had just arrived from London.

"Tomorrow, the IDF is pursuing a counterattack in Egypt," the former IDF Chief of Staff Yitzhak Rabin, who had just returned from a trip to the southern front, informed the group. Zamir, hearing the details of the program, said, "The Egyptians are just waiting for an attack like this on our part."

A Few Minutes Before Midnight.
The 201st Squadron

"Sami, stop drawing the Syrian red arrows so large and our blue ones so small," said Yossi Eliel, the squadron's resident clown, who had just returned a few hours prior from a ski vacation in Italy, and now stood directly in from of the giant mission map.

"I have a son serving in the Golan," Sami, like a gullible man, spilled his heart in front of Eliel. *A Phantom pilot must never play his cards openly in front of him.* Sami pointed to the position of his son's unit and shared his concerns with Eliel.

At midnight, they were still awake.

No one in the "Number One" Squadron knew already that at that time, a little over thirty hours since the eruption of hostilities, IDF losses were approaching 500. Therefore, they agonized over their private traumas, openly, and thought that the sky had fallen on top of them that day, just like that, with no warning. They thought particularly of Shaniboi, Asa, Shahak, Graber, Itzik, Haim and Avikam.

In a bachelor pad belonging to Eitan Shmueli, who had managed to survive Operation "Model," stood Revital, Gilad Graber's girlfriend, waiting. Deep in the night, Shmueli woke from his nightmarish dreams of flaming missiles and aircraft, and Revital was still there, standing at the window. Waiting.

OCTOBER 8TH

Broken Dreams

As the sun's first rays dawned in the East, carrying with them the brightness of a new day, taking the place of Saturday's shock and Sunday's gloom, and replacing them with a self-assured battle cry—the eclipse of the light was about to end, later today. Both the Northern and Southern Commands were preparing to counterattack. Reservist armored divisions stabilized the fronts. All that remained was to guide them and release them to establish a new order. The reserve division in the General Staff of Musa Peled would repel the Syrians in the Golan. Bren and Sharon's reserve divisions would pound the Egyptians in Sinai.

06:00. IAF Headquarters

In the hours of Monday morning, Lt. Col. Amos Amir, the designated replacement as IAF Chief of Operations, was sent to the forward command station of the Southern Command in Sinai.

"The IDF is about to go on the offensive," Benny Peled informed him, "our forces are standing just a moment before crossing the Canal. You will be my guy in Um Hashiva. Good luck."

With the failed attack on the Syrian missile system still searing their flesh, the attack wings of the Operations Department were sitting to figure out "where we went wrong." Despite the initial fragments of information, still no one was sure about the real reason for the fall of the Sledgehammer jets. One thing was clear: it was all because of the rockets. The fiasco occurred on the way to destroy them, on attempts to locate them, and on the way back. They were the core problem. Until they healed their wounds and a real solution was found for the "monsters," we could not wake them.

It was a defensive decision, the headquarters staff knew, and members of the air crews do not like to live on the defensive. *Let's find some other targets. We cannot rest our initiative. It is important to continue to breathe life into our fighting spirit.* The Air Force had enough potential and mental strength to continue to cope with this issue. *Perhaps air bases in Syria, away from the missile threat? Maybe attacking the sparse missile batteries north of the canal?*

06:30. The 201st Squadron

Zemer has arrived, and the squadron fighters were being briefed. Right now, he was at home.

Everyone was waiting for the mature, level-headed figure to come and take over the reins of command.

Sami, the Air and Ground Coordination Officer, was beside himself.

During the few hours of sleep that were not accompanied by a map, something changed in the Golan Heights. An incredible new image was forming, and shaking him. Before him, hard to take in, were three red arrows—Syrian forces—surrounding his son's field unit.

Another moment passed and he thought he was hearing voices. Through his blurred consciousness, his tear-filled eyes caught Yossi Eliel, holding his stomach, his body twitching, uncontrollable laughter erupting from his mouth.

Suddenly he understood, as did Eliel, who ran for his life.

On Monday morning, Yoram Romem found that the squadron that he left in August no longer existed.

Just before the morning briefing, he noticed a lot of empty chairs, and someone found the postcard that he had sent them from a trip to Switzerland, which was read with a certain pathos. *How beautiful it is there. How high the peaks are, how white the snow, and how green the meadow.* No one said "wow," or chuckled, or made a nasty remark. It was as if a giant hand crumpled his friends, shrank their presence, and silenced their pounding steps.

There was Ezer.

The towering figure of the mythical commander filled the entrance of the briefing room.

Hello guys; hello commander, he immediately sat in the front row, attentively, just like everyone else, for the morning briefing.

"The IAF will take out the Syrian air bases this morning," Huldai said, "Our mission—attacking the air base at Hulhula."

Like a paratrooper whose parachute cables got tangled and is sent back immediately for another drop, thought Romem, as he saw everyone shrink in their seats, and then heard the calming comment from Huldai. "We will do it through deep flanking, far away from the missile batteries stationed at the front."

There was Ben Eliahu.

Huldai's predecessor as deputy commander of the squadron after forty eight burdensome hours at headquarters, apologized for being late, shook Ezer's hand and sat down. Like everyone else, he understood that the operation for which he was assigned would act like a correction, raising the bar. An experience that would raise morale.

Huldai finished.

Ezer rose from his chair with his typical nonchalance, sat at the table at the front of the briefing room, and in a sudden shift from the adversities of the "Number One" Squadron, cracks a bunch of jokes, eliciting a roaring laughter, the first in twenty-four hours.

Maj. Ron Huldai was the first to take off into the sky, leading a four-ship formation. Maj. Eitan Eliahu led the second formation, with six aircraft behind him. Capt. Adi Benaya, who experienced the severe consequences of combat in "Model 5" the previous day, closed the convoy as head of his own four-ship formation.

We hit them, they were happy in their cockpits, seeing the runways and control tower absorbing direct hits and disappearing in a storm of flames, left as fragments of concrete, asphalt, and steel. *Give us targets, and leave everything else to us!*

This time, unlike the "Model 5" fiasco, they hit their targets. It is difficult to move an air base from its position. However, it was not a knockout victory—points were barely awarded. The Syrians had learned a thing or two from their defeat in the Six-Day War—an hour after the last of the bombs fell, aircraft were again taking off from Hulhula. Three hours after the attack, the air base was fully functional again.

10:00. A Governmental Meeting

If one word could define the feeling that enveloped the Israeli government ministers in their meeting at the Kirya in Tel Aviv on Monday, October 8—"euphoria" would be the correct term.

We had two difficult days: we cancelled the preemptive strike, and the warning we were given was short-lived. That was it. It's over and done with. The big "welcome" was behind us.

Less than a day after the atmosphere or despair, the gloomy mood, and the "need to defend the land of Israel," the Chief of Staff informed the group, "I assume that by tomorrow, the IDF will already be standing on the ceasefire line in the Golan Heights, and that if the government approves it, perhaps, we shall penetrate Syrian territory."

"In Sinai," Dado continued, "we are weighing the possibility of crossing the Canal today, using the bridges that the Egyptians built, to get to the western side."

"We need to conquer vast areas of Syria," said the Deputy Prime Minister, Yigal Alon, "We need to threaten Damascus."

"I support the IDF crossing the ceasefire lines in order to place Israel in a more strategic position, as well as to teach the Egyptians and the Syrians a lesson, to show them that every action has a consequence," the Prime Minister said.

"Apparently the first IDF force is on the western part of the Canal," Lt. Gen. Elazar was told outside of the meeting room, and he immediately informed the emotional forum.

That's it, the enthusiastic group of ministers waxed poetic, *at this very moment, the regular order is returning, and with it the reality of the Middle East: we win, the Arabs lose.*

11:00. Hatzor

On Monday afternoon, the combat paper 'Wing Leaves' was distributed throughout Wing 4.

"At the last moment," the headline screamed across the top of the page, with two rows of text underneath: "Beginning in the early hours of the morning, our forces reached the water line, and have begun pounding the enemy." Another one read, "The Golan Heights region has been swept up all the way to the ceasefire line"

This statement was not accurate. In the sands of the Sinai, despite the optimistic morning news, the Egyptians schooled us in a cruel fashion and were in complete control of the battlefield. In the southern Golan Heights, far from the border, Syrian armored forces were still crushing the basalt rocks, acting as masters of their new-old estate.

Was this a correction of reality expounded by Col. Lapidot? Regardless of whoever was responsible for the transfer of this information to the commander of Wing 4, who continued to convey it to his soldiers, these two sentences mentioned above are proof that during the state of deep distress that took hold of the leaders of the Jewish State, there were those who decided to distort the situation picture and present it in a false manner.

11:00. The Kirya in Tel Aviv

In the midday hours of Monday, the Number 2 soldier of the Air Force, Brig. Gen. David Ivry, participated in the Deputy Chief of Staff's forum. General Tal's office took account of all of the tanks and artillery: how many were mobilized, how many had arrived at the fronts, and what was expected upon arrival.

Afterwards he heard, and found it hard to believe, that tanks were rushed to the front by way of chain tracks. Crews were armed with tanks that were not affiliated with them. There was a shortage of shells and necessary equipment.

What happened to planning ahead? Ivry was appalled. *When will ground troops be able to regroup and be able to move on with our mission? What about the series of their repeated declarations—"the regulars will contain" and "friends in blue, do not worry, when the dirty business starts, you will get 48 hours to handle your tasks?" The regulars are not containing, and we cannot stop worrying, nor can we concentrate on what we were promised.*

11:00. The 201st Squadron

Sami, the Air and Ground Coordination Officer, heard footsteps behind him, and once again it was Eliel, who felt that the danger has passed, and that Sami, a good man, was not vengeful or vindictive. Eliel said that this time he came up with a proposal similar to the one that had been given the night before. This time was about the huge arrows that were marking the settlement of the Second and Third armies in the Sinai desert.

"For goodness sake, Sami," he turned to the compassionate side of the Coordination Officer, "You are the person with the greatest impact on the morale of the squadron. Perhaps you could put small arrows for the Egyptian forces and big arrows for our depleted forces? Switch it, buddy, switch it."

Towards Monday afternoon, the 201st Squadron set out to repay the deed of honor. To prove to itself, and to anyone who thought to mourn it, that it was capable of dealing with missiles, even without Iftach Zemer, the squadron leader. Though he had returned the previous night, his presence was not yet reflected in the squadron.

A group of eight from the squadron, divided into two-ship formations, were sent with other Sledgehammer squadrons to destroy the stationary missiles array at Port Said—two SA-3 batteries and three SA-2 batteries, which protected Port Said and the surrounding area, as well as the northern entry route to Egypt. The missile array was isolated from the primary array along the Canal, hence it lacked the characteristics of a more fortified missile umbrella. The opening conditions improved the attack, certainly compared to yesterday.

Yoram Romem knew that the missile array at Port Said was detached from the primary array, lacking the characteristics of mutual defense which were common among the rest of the missile batteries deployed along the Canal. The opening conditions improved the attack, certainly compared to twenty-four hours before in Syria. *Could this go wrong as well?* He wondered, leading the octet from Adi Benaya's backseat.

"Three, two, one, pull-up!" Romem told Benaya, knowing that they made it to the strike pull-up waypoint, and the battery was now two and a half miles to the right and in front of them.

Benaya pulled up. The Phantom raised its nose at a 35° angle and found itself above the layer of clouds that covered the target. Suddenly, the sky became a fireworks show and Romem, who only yesterday returned from London, knew that they were not really fireworks. "Stay low," he quietly instructed Benaya and the rest of the squadron formations, adorning the sky with brown-and-green camouflage. "Stay low…"

Only Benaya was high in the sky, maneuvering the aircraft through waves of flak on the right and missiles on the left.

"Break right," Romem shouted. Benaya pulled right.

"Break left," Romem shouted. Benaya pulled left.

Once more to the right, and once more to the left.

Where now? Romem considered the options, moving his head from side to side, with the unending torrent of missiles continuing to tail them.

This was the exact moment when Benaya, in his irritating quiet voice, said, "Yoram, I can't break anymore." The aircraft hit a slight bump.

This isn't the War of Attrition, thought Romem, who has already passed a thing or two in his life, *this war isn't like anything else. If only this aircraft will keep flying…*

"What is happening in the squadron?" Zemer's voice was suddenly heard on the other end of the telephone line.

Finally, Amnon Gurion, Combat Manager, thought cheerfully, and shared a brief history with his commander in short sentences.

"I'm still sick," Zemer said on the line, and hanged up.

What's happening? The high school students of 1967, the youngest in the squadron at that moment, were delaying Ben Eliahu, who was removing his pressure suit overalls at the end of another successful attack that he had led. "In the end, we destroyed the radar at Damietta, hitting the Egyptian's ability to detect aircraft on the penetration path into the Delta."

"What's happening?" they repeated again and again.

Ben Eliahu understood the meaning of those two words well. "What were you doing down there," the young, confused faces wanted to know. Most of them were his subordinates just two months ago. "When will what needs to happen, happen?" When will we hit them like we used to; in your days.

Even Ben Eliahu lacked answers. So he just smiled, tossed a few soothing words into the air, and spread a small feeling of relief throughout the clubroom, before his second sortie.

12:00-17:00. The 201ˢᵗ Squadron

They landed. They gathered in front of the window of the operations room, discovering that, despite their vulnerability, the batteries at Port Said were still alive and kicking.

We're getting ready to do it again, they told them. They were not surprised: partial success didn't count, and certainly not with them. It was not in their mentality. It became clear that it also was not in that of IAF headquarters, which ordered them to strike again at 15:30.

The strike included the same formations, the same missiles, the same airmen, and Benaya and Romem in the aircraft that was bandaged with Benzi's insulated films.

They pulled up and located targets, as the sky around them raged with puffs of black smoke and missile flashes. They ignored and attacked, performing perfectly.

As some returned, more were sent out.

The mission was to attack the bridges of the Canal. Two two-ship formations led by two commanders—the current commander, Huldai, and his predecessor, Ben Eliahu—jettisoned their bombs due to a sea of shoulder-launched air-to-air missiles that was launched at them. *Damn.*

Frustrated by the undershooting, they were sent to address the Egyptian MiG-17 aircraft that were flying around the Sinai launching rockets, bombing and strafing, as if there was not an Israeli Air Force in the world.

"Full thrust," a sudden call from the Southern Air Control was received, sending them to Um Hashiva.

The bastards are trying to knock out our forward command post, Ben Eliahu thought, locating the bug cliff, and... eight MiGs were flying all over the sky. *Bad luck for them,* Ben Eliahu smiled, maneuvering to gain an advantage on the first one. Ten minutes later, he counted his first two downings of the war, learned from Huldai that he brought another down, and heard from Eli Zohar that another MiG flew straight towards the afterlife.

Like that, just like that. Another and another, until we've finished all of their aircraft.

Just then his navigator, Paltiel "Sposh" Barak, announced in the cockpit, "We're short on fuel." They changed direction towards Refidim, finding the main runway full of holes. Someone in the tower directed them to land on the parallel runway, and in the interception underground hangar, they found Michael Zuk, from the Mirage squadron, sitting on the cabinet, gripping a Kalashnikov in his hands. With a stiff face, he informed them that an Egyptian commando force was expected to attack them at any moment.

Sunset. The commandos did not arrive. Nor did Zemer.

Huldai returned from the Canal, gathered that Zemer was still at his house, and proceeded to consult with the wing commander. "I'll handle it," Col. Amos Lapidot said.

Amos was debating.

Last night, he had already picked up on the distress. Zemer's face, the face of the best man and commander in the 201st Squadron, said it all. *Give him a few hours of rest*, he thought. *He'll rest a few hours, gather his strength, regain his will, and come back fresh for the tasks of the squadron.*

However, it was now dusk on Monday. Zemer needed to get back. He had to.

"Take command of the Squadron," he told him.

18:00. Press Conference

The large hall on the second floor of the Sokolov House in Tel Aviv was packed. From the side door, the Minister of Defense, the IDF Chief of Staff, and others entered and took their seats in front of the large crowd of local and foreign journalists.

"First of all, I would like to say that the Chief of Staff recommended a preemptive strike," Dayan said, opening his remarks, "but the political leadership—including myself—were against it... If we had pursued a preemptive strike, they would have said that 'the Israelis have started a war'. We would never have been able to prove that someone tipped us off that a war would break out in five hours."

"The intelligence assessment was that, with a high probability, there was not going to be a war... Even on Saturday at four o'clock in the morning, there was no absolute knowledge. Yet due to other signs, particularly the evacuation of the Russian advisor's families as well as our analysis of aerial reconnaissance photographs, we decided that this time, it looked like war."

"...On that very morning, we reached out to the appropriate channels, the Americans, and requested that they pass a message on to the Arabs to tell them, 'we know that you are planning to start a war, we have no intention to do so. If you do, you will find us ready and you will pay dearly'. Their plan was based on surprising us. We said, if Sadat realizes that he lost the element of surprise, he may decide not open fire... now, this is a point of speculation, but the speculation is fairly solid. They were going to open fire at dusk, and not at two in the afternoon. But when they received our message, they decided to attack immediately."

"When will it be over?" the minister was asked.

"At least another twenty-four hours," he answered.

After the Defense Minister finished, Dado rose to the stage. "I want to turn to the people of Israel and to the soldiers of the IDF who are now in the midst of war," he began, looking straight into the television cameras. "This is a war that erupted by the initiative of Egypt and Syria, and began with a coordinated attack, with both of their armies striking at the same moment. We prepared with the regular army, we were on war alert and we began on the defense, hoping to contain the onslaught."

He then proceeded to detail the sequence of events of the last 52 hours, and finished by saying, "This is a serious war. This is a serious fight. However, I am happy to tell you today that we are already in the midst of turning this around, and we are already progressing."

"Do you foresee a short war or a long one?" journalist Dan Shilon pressed him.

"I predict only one thing now," Dado said, staring into the camera lenses surrounding him. "We will continue to strike, and we will continue to attack, and we will break their bones."

19:50. Office of the Prime Minister

Lt. Gen. (Res.) Haim Bar-Lev, who was sent yesterday to delegate the Northern Command post, with his cool-headedness and his quiet authority, returned and reported to the Prime Minister about the situation. "It is improving and moving ahead."

"What is happening in the Canal?" he asked.

"At the moment, Bren is heading south," Brig. Gem Lior, the IDF Secretary to the Prime Minister, reported, and told of the

Egyptian infantry division that was destroyed on their way to the water line by our excellent men. He then added, "Albert is now sent off, the Egyptians heard about it and started to pressure him, but he has stepped back…"

Deputy Prime Minister Yigal Alon, who accompanied Lt. Gen. (Res.) Bar-Lev for a while in the North, informs that both of them reached the conclusion that it was time to begin the next step in the IAF activity—the systematic bombing of strategic targets. "We should bomb the power plant in Damascus, or the fuel depot, or the Syrian General Staff building, and then maybe the civilian airport in Damascus. Afterwards, we will expand to nearby cities, hitting hard around Damascus. The capital will shake. The government leadership will be rocked. Motti Hod said that they are capable of hitting targets pretty precisely. It's possible that it will help soften the Syrian intransigence, because in the meantime, they are showing tenacity."

20:00. Office of the IAF Commander

It was the second night in a row that the IAF Commander was meeting with base and wing commanders in order to be informed about what was happening in their sectors, and to clarify together the operational plans for the next day.

"This is the news that I've heard from the 'greens' (the army)," Benny reported. "The army has managed to reach the bridges. Everything will work out very shortly." As he continued his updates, he was summoned urgently to the Senior Command Post, leaving behind a curious forum of commanders.

20:00. Senior Command Post

"Nothing in the Southern Command is working according to plan," reported Dado, returning from the press conference where he publicly promised that "we will break their bones."

The IDF counterattack in Sinai, the great hope, proved nothing of the sort. Hundreds of scorched khaki tanks remained in the sands of the Sinai, a silent testimony to the great failure. Inside them and thrown around them were many dozens of dead and wounded. The Egyptian army crushed the IDF, leaving it defeated in the battlefield as it had never been defeated before.

Benny Peled now arrived.

"So far," he informed Dado, "the Air Force has lost 44 aircraft. There are also many other aircraft that require repairs before they would be able to return to action."

Dado reacted with astonishment. At this rate, the IAF would erode its power in a couple of days, and would get down to the red line—after which the IAF would only be capable of defensive maneuvers and attacks with assured air superiority.

"The IAF will do its job," the IAF Commander added, quick to weaken the breeze of pessimism that was enveloping the army's supreme commander. "The corps is in good condition. I'm optimistic, I want you to know."

"So am I," Dado said, who quickly returned to his stony disposition, "Everything will be fine."

He then looked at his watch, and the time is 21:00. "Excuse me, I have to go run the weekly cabinet meeting."

21:00. Office of the IAF Commander

45 minutes passed, and Benny stormed back into his office. "Everything that I told you before? Everything is a lie. It's all a bluff," he shouted into the air of the room. "We did not cross. The Egyptians built fifteen bridges on the Canal. I promised that by tomorrow, we will knock them out."

21:00. Cabinet Meeting

"We have not passed anywhere over the Canal," Dayan said to the group of stunned ministers, who had already begun sewing victory outfits. "On the contrary, the enemy is currently facing us on our side, and the bridges that have been built and set up continue to bring reinforcements to the east."

The Chief of Staff, who, since the morning, thought that the worst was behind him and that the armored forces, along with the infantry, were pushing the Egyptians to the west, and that it was only a matter of time before the crossing command would be given, knew that something fundamental had gone wrong. However, he still did not know just how wrong.

"The stage for counterattacks is still in its infancy," Dado said, "My impression now is that the turnaround will come soon."

Nighttime. Chamber of the Head of Central Command

In light of the distress calls from the Canal, the 201st and 69th Phantom squadrons were sent with loft strike mission on the estimated locations of the new bridges and enemy troop concentrations.

It's stupid to send out aircraft right now, "Wild Bull" Peled pondered, sitting in to help at headquarters.

With a loft strike in the daytime, it is possible to fly low, as there is no concern of CFIT (controlled flight into terrain), and it is also possible to clearly identify the pull-up waypoints and to avoid missiles. In contrast, a loft strike at night is very dangerous: one wants to fly low to avoid the missiles, but the darkness lying on the ground threatens to grab you in a giant flame.

Moreover, the "Bull" thought, *it is impossible to identify the pull-up waypoints using eyesight at night, making the pilot rely entirely on the INS computer. What about the INS drifting, which can get you off-course by a hundred meters?*

"Are the aircraft being sent to strike specific targets?" He asked.

"No, they will scatter bombs at random points along the Canal," they answered.

A few minutes passed, and the Chief of Staff returned from his cabinet meeting, entered the chamber, and said quietly, "It just didn't happen today. But we shall overcome."

These Yugoslavs are exquisite products, thought Col. Shimon Lasser from Air Control, recalling stories of the cool-headed behavior of Bar-Lev, a childhood friend of Dado's, and about his success in stabilizing the mood and the state of the nation at Northern Command, surveying the tiny chamber of the Head of Central Command and seeing another retired Chief of Staff, an archeologist and presently a representative of the Prime Minister, biting his nails to the end.

362 | For Heaven's Sake

Night. The 201ˢᵗ Squadron

"I'm collapsing," Yoram Romem told his commander. "I haven't slept for two days, and today I've done three sorties. I need two hours of sleep. Please take me out of this sling mission tonight at the Canal."

"Who's the pilot?" Huldai asked.

"Uri Sheani," Romem replied.

"Go to sleep," Huldai said. "We'll assign Dror Yaffe in your place."

* * *

"We have no contact with Shani and Yaffe's aircraft," they reported from IAF Headquarters.

They switched the radio over to the "Guard" (distress) channel, as someone from IAF Headquarters would not stop calling them. Nothing.

The telephone in Operations rang.

"Just a moment," the clerk said, putting her hand on the mouthpiece and turning to Sposh, the on-duty manager, "It's Shani's wife. She wants to talk to him."

"Tell her to call later," he said, "tell her that he's still in the air."

Half an hour passed. They continued searching on the Guard channel. IAF bases in the south reported that Shani's Phantom had not landed on their runways.

The phone rang again.

"What's happening with Uri?" Shani's wife pressed.

"He left for a very long flight," Sposh said, "you should wait a few hours before you call."

Except that this was Uri's wife, who knew that her man, the broad, strong nature-lover, was also one to stand by his word. In the evening, before he left, he told her when he was supposed to return, and that time had passed a while ago.

So she insisted and pressed to know exactly where her Uri was and what exactly happened. Yet Sposh could not say, he really could not, and he eventually convinced her to call back. He hung up and prayed that, if there is a God in heaven, someone would come and bring back Uri and Dror.

* * *

At night, Haim Rotem reported to the Squadron.

He was discharged from his service in November 1972. He felt that he had run his course.. He was the first reservist from the Sledgehammer layout.

In early October 1973, he flew to the United States. He set up a road trip for himself from coast to coast.

On Saturday, he heard on the radio that something was happening in far-away Israel.

He stopped on his way and called Shaike Barkat, the Air Attaché in Washington.

"Continue your trip," Shaike said, "It will probably end by the time you get here. Stay in touch." Half a day later he called back. "Is there anything new?"

"I spoke with my squadron," Barkat informed him, "The mood is good. I still don't know what is happening."

"There's a good mood?" *That's a problematic sentence*, Rotem thought, *one that people only say when something goes wrong.*

He left his car in the middle of the way. He flew to New York.

"Come to the airport," Shaike said, sounding less relaxed, "There's an El Al flight at midnight."

He arrived and met with Mirage pilot Gidi Livni and his wife. He was able to get on the flight. Livni was not.

"I can't believe that I'll remain stuck here" Livni grumbled, when suddenly he noticed a familiar-looking man with an average height, dark eyes, and a mustache, with his wife by his side. He kept watching the mustached man, and in a split second, he realized he was the man from "the unit," the one who gave them the survival course at the squadron.

He approached him. "Do you have any idea how we can get on this flight?"

"Come with me," the mustached man answered.

You'd think that he was the CEO of El Al Airlines, Livni chuckled.

They went to a tall man who introduced himself as the El Al station manager at the airport.

"Set up four tickets for us on this flight," the mustached man said.

"In a little bit."

"Not in a little bit," the mustached man ordered, "right now."

"Wait patiently," the tall manager barked from high above.

The mustached man grabbed the manager by his tie, pulled his startled face closer, and held him close in front of his dark eyes.

"Okay, okay," the manager groaned, his face gradually turning blue.

He released his grip on the tie.

"Anything else?" the terrified manager asked.

"Send an attendant to help with the ground arrangements and with our luggage," the mustached man answered.

"Okay, okay."

He loosened up.

Ten minutes later, the Livni couple, Ehud "Mustache" Barak and his wife Nava joined Haim Rotem, the Sledgehammer pilot, on their way to a country at war.

He was killed, another is missing, and this one was captured. He was updated on the steps to the entrance. *Okay,* Rotem thought, *this isn't the Six-Day War. It really isn't.*

"Bring Amami and Shlain up to speed on all of the missing literature," Huldai ordered Zetelny.

Zetelny knew that in order to pass on the amount of material to which the two young pilots had yet to be exposed, they would require a few days if not weeks in normal times, in the old world that disappeared somewhere in the back of the mind. However, it was a new world. This world demanded quick solutions, fast authority and Zetelny was the right man for the job. The tall man crouched towards the two young pilots that he received under his wing, and, step by step, showed them why he was considered the man who possessed the Philosopher's Stone in the Squadron..

As the clock struck midnight, Zetelny reported to Huldai that two new operational navigators had just joined the ranks of the 201st.

Night. Chamber of the Head of Central Command

From his place in the control chamber, Benny Peled sensed, saw, heard, and sometimes smelled, the responses of IAF Headquarters staffers and their fighters.

True, Benny Peled thought, *something very basic in defending the land of Israel went bad. We lost aircraft. Many aircraft. However, the armored corps also lost tanks. Hundreds of tanks. And everyone expects us to pay the bill. Justify their budgets that they were injected with all these years. Only the Air Force can. Our headquarters, with all the fighters in the sky, needs to convey confidence and strength, to be determined and mission-minded. We cannot deal with yesterday's disasters, but instead, we need to focus on tomorrow's designs. Particularly those of today. Of right now. To broadcast an offensive initiative. Only offense.*

Yet how can we do that? How to we bond the cracks and create a new front, a fresh one, immune to crises?

Intelligence officials show distress. They don't understand why there is no flow of information from the army and no targets for the aircraft. When there is, they aren't in place. And when they are in place, we don't always know the results of the strike. And the operations planners are stressed. Their behavior is erratic, they are stuck in an unfocused gaze. They are unsure of the orders that they pass down to the squadrons, with no consideration to time constants.

The worst are these squadron and combat commanders, wondering aloud about the meaning of task orders that come down to the field, and arguing with the staff about attacking the same targets over and over, when according to the old rules of the game, they are supposed to wave white flags.

Since when do field commanders argue with staffers, Benny wondered, *have they still not internalized, in the bases and the wings, that this isn't a matter of a few border incidents, but about saving the people of Israel?*

OCTOBER 9TH

Bewilderment

In the early hours of the Tuesday morning, a day about which Jews have a traditional saying that it is "twice as good," it became clear that reality was breaking from tradition.

It began with information that reached the Senior Command Post, according to which a fresh Iraqi tank brigade was making its way westward in order to reinforce the Syrian forces on the front.

Afterwards, especially following the return of the Defense Minister and the Chief of Staff from their check of the Command post in Sinai, it became clear that the reports that they received on Monday evening were just the tip of the iceberg of an unbelievable reality. The counterattack failed, the Egyptian bridgehead was stable, and there were heavy IDF casualties. Egyptian forces in Sinai were still holding essential areas, and nothing loomed on the horizon that would seem to push them out.

The recognition that nothing in the Sinai went as planned, combined with the knowledge that the Iraqis were coming to reinforce the Syrians, who were still ruling the southern Golan Heights, led to the realization that the enemy was not even afraid of the Israeli Air Force; their aircraft still took off from bombed-out runways and their ground forces shook off the fragments of bombs dropped upon them as if it were nothing, and kept fighting.

On early Tuesday morning, the leaders of the State of Israel internalized, for the first time after the outbreak of hostilities, exactly what it was that they were facing. This was not the seventh day of the Six-Day War. Yesterday, they still believed that. *We had a mishap. The Egyptians and Syrians came as a surprise. They broke through the front lines. They inflicted losses on us, but our counterattacks in Sinai and the Golan will bring the expected change in this arrangement, to the normal "setting" of the Arab-Israeli wars. Another moment and we will pursue, obtain, and distribute the spoils of war.* Just the day earlier, the Israeli government decided that it would be possible to use the bridges that the Egyptians set to allow our excellent forces to cross, the sooner the better, to the other side of the Canal and change the image of the campaign.

The shock was primarily mental. After the existential panic on Sunday, October 7, it was clear that the Egyptian and Syrian armies did not merely surprise us, but they also defeated us on the battlefield.

Before dawn of Tuesday morning, the inhabitants of the underground bunkers at the senior command post comprehended that what began on Yom Kippur was a different war. A completely different war.

At 04:45, the Defense Minister of the State of Israel sat in the office of the Chief of Staff and peeled back the layers of defense covering his listeners.

"We are in distress," Dayan said, laying down his difficult insight to Lt. Gen. Elazar, Maj. Gen. (Res.) Rehavam Ze'evi, and former Chief of Staff Tzvi Tzur. "Larger nations than us—the English, the French, the USSR—have found themselves in distress in times of war. At a time like this, we must consider and decide what is the best thing for us—both the army and the people—to do. A difficult crisis is expected when we tell the people of Israel that we are not able to throw the Egyptians across the Canal and the strongholds of the Bar-Lev line have fallen. However, there is no escaping it. We need to tell the people the truth, so that they will understand the situation."

"In the north," Dayan continued, "We need to give the Command an instruction—do not withdraw at any cost. If we lose all of the tanks in the Golan because we stood rigidly—they will be lost, but so will the Syrian power. If there are commanders, at any level of command, that are not capable of following the task, then they should be replaced. We must strive to end the war in the north, or at least to reach to a decision, in order to only fight on one front. We need to check every option to reach this point, including bombing Damascus."

"I'm speaking without etiquette," Dayan continued, "but we need priorities. We are not able to knock out the Egyptians. Everything that happened in Sinai today, the assault, was not necessary. We need to prepare deeper withdrawal lines."

Then, just as the confidence of those listening evaporated completely, and the feeling was that a greater evil could not have been brought up by the minister in front of them, Dayan dropped the bomb—"We need to mobilize everyone not currently recruited and equip them with anti-tank guns, lest they breach the defense lines, and enemy tanks invade the heart of the country. We need to begin an emergency recruitment of the elderly, those released from the draft for various reasons, and boys under recruitment age."

A few minutes after 05:00, dawn of Tuesday morning, October 9, after 63 hours of absolute tension, Dayan left the Office of the Chief of Staff, leaving those behind in a spirit of Masada, standing on a mountain against the Romans.

05:00-06:30. Skyhawks above the Mediterranean Sea

A rough night passed over us, thought Maj. Avraham Vilan, First Deputy Commander of the 110th Skyhawk squadron in Ramat David, on his way to the Director of Combat Operations. *Of all the places in the world, this shitty rocket had to fall on my pilots' quarters?*

He knew Dudu Dimant (Dotan), who was killed when a piece of shrapnel fell and sliced open his throat. He knew the others who were wounded. They were his own, his squadron, and he knew that they needed to go on.

"Bombing missile batteries at Port Said" was written on the operations board.

"I want to join the mission," he heard a familiar voice from over his shoulder, turned, and saw Col. Arlozor Lev (Zorik), the wing commander. "Put me in the place of the pilot who was killed."

"Look, Zorik," Vilan politely pleaded, "you haven't flown for two months, you don't know the Skyhawk, two hours ago a rocket sprang you out of bed, you didn't sleep at night, nor the night before, and I think it would be a mistake if you flew right now."

Zorik insisted. So did Vilan. Zorik didn't give in.

A three ship formation sets out. Zorik was Number 2.

They passed over the marshes, in the haze of morning light. The water looked like the sky, and the sky like water. Vilan pulled up, released bombs, turned sharply to the right, shot at the direction of the Egyptian outpost revealed below, changed heading around again and again, and an unfathomable image scorched his cornea.

"Number 2, pull up, pull up!" he shouted at Zorik, whose aircraft then plunged towards the rippling Mediterranean.

Nothing.

"Number 2, pull up, 2, pull up!" he shouted again from the top of his lungs.

Nothing.

Boom. Number 2 hit the surface of the blue water.

He circled around the point. No aircraft, No Zorik. No parachute. Just the Mediterranean continuing its pace from time immemorial, sending wave after wave to the coast of Sinai.

06:00. Hatzor and the 201st Squadron

"Uri Sheani and Dror Yaffe haven't returned from their night mission," they told Yoram Romem.

"Why hasn't Uri called?" his wife asked, standing at the entrance to the wing.

Sima Shavit was the on-duty operations clerk, the girl that was on the other end of the line. What could she say?

"Has Uri returned?" his wife pressed. "Has he landed?"

Sima did not answer.

"Hey, answer me! Has Uri returned? Has he landed?"

"Wait a minute," Sima said, frantically pouncing towards the Combat Manager, "What can I tell her? What can I say to her?" Finally, someone agreed to go to be the messenger and go to the gate, to tell her that Uri was gone.

* * *

On Tuesday morning, Lt. Col. Iftach Zemer arrived at the squadron.

He was lagging. He still did not realize that this was a different war, and that the squadron that he left was another squadron--scarred, surviving, with two people killed, seven POWs, and six missing aircraft. Most of all, he had trouble accepting the depth of the crisis that devastated its solid world of values and its doctrine of strong identity, the weakness and the results meeting between them.

"Zetelny attests that throughout the night, you received the stamp of approval for operational qualification," they told Amami and Shlain. "You are qualified for nighttime operations. You will be joining a formation that is leaving on a run to attack the Katameya air base in Egypt."

At 07:00, fourteen Phantoms, laden with bombs, set out to destroy the air base.

I'm not the lead navigator, Amami thought, who until that point fed on the heroic stories of my friends. *Still, I can't screw up. Certainly not now. Accurate navigation, Nimrod,* he told himself, *accurate navigation.*

It was six minutes to pull-up time.

"Another minute until acceleration," Amami warned Hayun, harnessed in the pilot's seat in front of him.

It was five minutes to pull-up. MIL power. 540 knots.

"Switches," Amami called, and Kobi Hayun sets the switches to "ARM."

Head up, Amami reminded himself, *keep us in formation, keep an eye on the tail, and don't forget to continue to call-out run-down times.*

One minute to pull-up.

Thirty seconds.

"Three, two, one, go."

Hayun opened the burners, and the bomb-loaded aircraft pointed its nose at 35°, climbing up into the sky and Amami stretched his neck and identified the target below.

Ten seconds of climb and Hayun rolled over the aircraft to inverted flight, diving to the target, and Amami "put the head down" and locked on a "Ground Echo" with the radar.

Once again, Amami's head was up. *They love to come when we're busy with the attack*, Zetelny warned. But everything was calm in the sky, and it was time to put his head back down and call out the altitude to Hayun. Hayun released the bombs, the aircraft shook, and Hayun broke, dropped, and broke again.

Very simple, Amami concluded to himself. *We came, we located, we attacked, we bombed, we hit, and we left.*

Suddenly Hayun got on the hot mic, and said, "Good work, Nimrod! I didn't feel like I was with a young navigator."

Amami smiled a big smile under his goggles. *That's it*, he thought, *I'm on the team.*

07:00. Office of the Prime Minister

While Amami was spending his time with insights and smiles, those in the Kirya in Tel Aviv were beginning to understand the extent of the failure of the counterattack more clearly.

"We have no chance to cross at this moment," the Defense Minister said, beginning his report to the Prime Minister, ministers Alon and Galili, the Chief of Staff, the current Head of Military Intelligence, Eli Zeira, as well as his predecessor, Aaron Yariv.

"For the time being, we should not try to cross, or even get close to the Canal line. All of the strongholds, except for Budapest, are surrounded. The tanks cannot reach them. Both attempts by Bren to cross have failed. He is left with fifty tanks and their crews."

"I propose that we make a maximum effort to take Syria out of the war," Dayan continued, "The forces in the Golan are fighting well. There is a command not to withdraw. They are fighting to the death, just not moving. A considerable effort now is being placed on the destruction of Syrian forces. I suggest, and request, approval to bomb inside Damascus."

"Inside the city?" Golda asked.

"Inside the city as well as its surroundings, to break the Syrians," Dayan said. "They have been firing rockets at us for two days already. We need to get out of the situation that we are in. Dado does not have the forces necessary to attack Damascus on the ground. The tanks are eroded. We will hit Damascus, take out all of its power, command posts, electricity. The goal is to finish this front. We've hit their air bases enough. There are no more meaningful objectives there. The most significant target right now is Damascus. It's not possible to say that the population will not be affected. We need to approve this now."

"Our situation in the Canal is difficult," Dado reinforced Dayan's words. "Our situation will only get better there if the Syrians will have a more difficult time. Attacking Damascus is essential to breaking Syria."

"Why would this break them?" the Prime Minister urged, "If they bombed us here, would that break us?"

"A heavy bombing on the 'Pit', on Reading, and Ramat Aviv would be very disruptive," Dado answered.

Golda: "If we bomb Damascus, won't they try...?"

Dayan and Dado: "Let them try."

Dado: "Our Air Force is controlling the sky for the most part. They can take care of them."

Golda: "Aren't there any things that we can start with around Damascus?"

Dado: "I'm looking for the 'Breakthrough'. The dramatization of the turnaround. A turnaround is achieved by pressure, whether it is the headquarters, the presidential palace, Assad."

Golda: "What is the situation of anti-aircraft defenses in Damascus?"

Dado: "There are missiles, flak guns. It's possible that we will lose aircraft."

Golda: "It's clear that if they don't get a hit that will knock them, they won't agree to a ceasefire."

Dayan: "Iraq and Jordan are also joining. Meanwhile, they are stronger than us at the Canal."

Dado: "There is an Iraqi column that is making progress."

They then discussed what would be said about them and how the Russians would react, and the Americans. Golda leaned on a map showing a number of potential targets to attack in Damascus, and asked, "How large a radius would be affected?"

"It depends on the attacks, but not a large radius," Maj. Gen. Zeira said.

"Yesterday, President Nixon decided to send the Phantoms (as well as other arms). I don't want that to stop," Golda said, still uncertain.

"We will not be the first ones," the Head of Military Intelligence refreshed the Prime Minister's memory, "they shot rockets last night."

"I would want to start with other targets first," Golda said.

"Moshe, isn't it true that if we began with the General Staff, it would be more surprising than if we started with other targets?" Alon joined the conversation, and not waiting for a reply, he said, "We need to start with army targets in the headquarters."

"Hussein is swinging," Zeira added his weight on the balance, leaning towards military action. "This is what will affect him. Oil refineries will not affect him."

"They've launched rockets for the third day in a row," Dayan said, adding his weight as well.

"This can be done," added Galili, Golda's confidant.

"The line is correct," said Alon, putting his weight of the scales, in case she did not understand.

"I approve," Golda said.

"If we will have a problem, we'll deal with it." Dayan concluded.

09:00. Hatzor

On Tuesday at noon, the Hatzor combat paper "Wing Leaves" was distributed again.

The wing commander summarized the fighting of the previous day, Monday, October 8.

"…On this day, we've made tremendous achievements: Egyptian armored forces were given their due, and the hundreds of tanks that succeeded in crossing the Canal were destroyed or were pushed into a trap that could not be escaped."

If there is a perfect example for the IDF's bewilderment and for the expression "the opposite is the case," it is this unfortunate phrase, quoted from Col. Lapidot, in the bulletin of the wing that he commanded.

The IDF forces in Sinai made no achievements, but rather suffered resounding failures. Egypt's armored forces were not destroyed nor pushed into a trap. On the contrary. Those who were destroyed and found themselves in a trap were the IDF forces.

09:40. Office of the Prime Minister

Half an hour after the meeting in the Prime Minister's office had concluded, Mordecai Gazit, the Office Manager, sent out an urgent telegram to Simcha Dinitz, the Ambassador in Washington.

"The Israeli Air Force is going to bomb various strategic targets in Syria, inside, I repeat, inside Damascus. This will be done in the afternoon. The decision to act was taken after an analysis of the entire military situation, in an attempt to break one front, and it appears possible to do so on the Syrian front, which will stop the attack on the Golan Heights. It is essential to deter Iraq and Jordan from entering the war. We are ascribing the utmost importance to the bombing of selected, strategic targets."

09:40. IAF Headquarters

"Activate 'Dominique'," Lt. Col. Avihu Ben-Nun was told.

In August 1972, Lt. Col. Avihu Ben-Nun finished his stint as commander of the Second Phantom Squadron of the IAF (the 69th) and was appointed Head of the Offensive Operations Department of the IAF.

He then had a short time to get acquainted with the existing plans and check the feasibility of others. "Dominique," for example, was a plan for attacks on strategic locations in Egypt and Syria: command headquarters, electricity, water, sewage, fuel reservoirs, and ammunition dumps.

Would it be right to cut off the power supply to the whole civilian population in Syria? In the name of affecting the front, was it okay to critically strike the home front? Which objectives would undermine the Syrian fighting spirit the most?

Whenever "Dominique" was discussed, a big question mark hovered over the conversation—would anyone ever give the green light to send war aircraft to these targets?

The writing is on the wall, Avihu thought. *Twenty-five missiles were launched from Syrian territory. Here is a direct hit on a children's house on Kibbutz Gvat. There at Machnaim Airport, here at Northern Command Headquarters in Safed, there at a playground in Migdal Haemek. No casualties. A great miracle. No more. Dudu Dimant, an IAF pilot at Ramat David, was killed by a missile in the family housing units. The die has been cast. We are hitting Damascus. It's his idea. His push. The attack can change the picture of the whole war, with a clear signal to the Jordanians and the Iraqis to stay out of the fighting.*

10:00. Senior Command Post

IAF aircraft that were attacking isolated Syrian missile batteries in their territory returned at 10:00. *Excellent hits*, the pilots reported.

"The barrier of the anti-aircraft missiles on the Syrian front has been torn down," the IAF Commander informed the Chief of Staff.

Dado did not hold back his emotions. "There are no missiles, simply no missiles," he announced to the people around him and promptly updated the Head of Northern Command. "Listen, Hakah," he said to his friend from the days of the Palmach, "If the Air Force really finished off the missiles, we'll give you a free hand with the aircraft."

Only six hours ago, the "Pit" was ruled by a 'Masada'-style mentality, and now everything was possible. Without anti-aircraft defenses, the Syrians were in a very difficult situation. Dado knew that in the noontime, they were planning to strike strategic targets, and in his mind he was already imagining the Syrians begging for a ceasefire.

11:00-12:00. The 201st Squadron

"Today, we are attacking deep inside Syria," they updated the men in the briefing room. "Every Phantom squadron will take part. This may be the breakthrough we were waiting for."

At 11:20, two Sledgehammer four-ship formations from the squadron leapt into the sky.

The weather over the sea was welcoming. *Let's hope it stays this way*, thought Ron Huldai, leading the first four-ship formation. The Lebanese coast. Cruising. The sky was covered with black clouds. They turned. Heavy clouds closed the sky and covered the top of Mount Hermon.

What's going to happen, thought Col. Oded Erez, Head of the IAF Defense Branch, and now the navigator in the rear cockpit of a strike fighter on its way to Syria. *What is winter's rush that it sees the need to push autumn away, perhaps along with our ability to perform? Sunshine, give us sunshine.*

War isn't a picnic, the Deputy Commander of the 201st Squadron thought. *Let's continue.*

At a high airspeed, he entered the clouds, knowing that the high terrain conditions of the territory and the clouds covering it could lead them right now to an encounter of the 'crushing' kind.

"Climb," Huldai instructed his four-ship formation, starting to climb above the blanket of black clouds, knowing that at this moment, they were exposed to early-detection radar screens, and he understood what that meant.

Amiram Talmon was the lead navigator. He knew that they were half a minute away from the turn to the last leg of the route to the strike, and another half a minute to the pull-up waypoint. The worry that he might make Huldai, and the whole formation, miss the right waypoint, brushed aside any thoughts of radars, missiles, or fear.

Two minutes before 12:00, four Phantoms emerged out of the cotton-colored layer and discovered a piece of dark blue sky. Below was the Damascus basin, and it was clean, not a sign of clouds. Talmon and Huldai identified the power plant, the target, pulling everyone behind them, commencing the strike and turning it into rubble.

Eitan "Wild Bull" Peled led the second four-ship formation.

How can I blend into this war after a three week absence? Lt. Iftach Zemer, deciding to take a "warm-up round" before taking the reins of the command, resigned himself to be Peled's Number 2.

While they were in the air, the air controller cancelled their mission.

"There is heavy cloud coverage over the target, come back to Safed," he instructed them, "Stay in a holding pattern. Wait for an alternative target."

While they were waiting, a formation of Skyhawks were sent to aid the tank forced in the Golan. "I've been hit, I'm getting out," one of the pilots announced."

"I'm on the parachute," he continued to report.

"I've gotten to the ground, but they are shooting at me."

"I'm closing," and that's it.

"Now it's your turn," the controller informed the four-ship formation. Someone from the Air Command Post at Mount Canaan gave them a direction, time and speed, saying that this was how they would arrive at the proper point, just above Syrian armor.

They pulled to there. Nothing. The controller made a mistake.

Iftach Zemer performed two passes over the area: nothing at all.

This isn't a trip, Zemer thought, *nor is this the War of Attrition, and I have to make up for the days that I wasn't here.*

A third pass. He identified the target and released the bombs. Short on fuel, he landed at Ramat David.

Well, Zetelny thought in the rear cockpit, *this is how a squadron leader needs to behave.*

"Where is the place that you wanted us to go?" Cap. Eli Zohar, leading the rear two-ship formation, asked the Mount Canaan Command Post.

"A large tank force is located a few kilometers southeast of Tel Fares," replied the command post.

"Obtained," Zohar answered, recalling that the strip of maps that he had in his hands did not cover the southern Golan. *We'll manage.*

"Stick with me," he said to Eliel. *Stay linked up.*

Near Tel Fares, he pulled up for bombing, and identified dozens of tanks advancing to our territory.

He set the Pipper at the center of the enemy force. Eleven bombs, Mark 117, 360 kilograms each, made their way down in a row.

"Great, wonderful," someone from the battlefield below called out to them, "Thanks a lot."

By 11:30, by virtue of the "Dominique" master command and task orders that flowed to them, 39 IAF Phantoms were scrambled on their way to strike quality targets in Syria.

Twenty of them were forced to quit the strike due to heavy clouds on the flight path approaching the target. Those remaining destroyed a power station near Damascus (the 201st Squadron, led by Huldai) and a communications relay station between Egypt and Syria, partly damaged oil refineries in Homs, the radar station in Jabal el Barouk in Lebanon, and most importantly—smashed the

General Staff building and the Syrian Air Force Headquarters in Damascus (the 119ᵗʰ Squadron).

An octet of Sledgehammer jets, led by Lt. Yiftach Spector, commander of the 107ᵗʰ Squadron, turned back without carrying out their mission in Damascus. The slightly adjusted flight path did not allow them to emerge through the cloud cover. "Turn back," Spector ordered. He informed the Air Command Post in Northern Command that he was still carrying a full load of bombs, and they would do well to find him an alternative target, another chance.

"Syrian tanks on the Navva-Rafid axis," Col. Rafi Savron, Commander of the Air Command Post at Mount Canaan, instructed him.

A remarkable coincidence led Spector and his men, as well as Eli Zohar and Yossi Eliel, to a major turning point in the counterattack in the southern Golan Heights. Just a moment earlier, as fresh Syrian tank forces advanced in the face of the exhausted reserve forces, ten Sledgehammer jets dropped forty tons of bombs on the concentrated forces of Tank Division 1. Their magic powder was needed by the worn-out IDF tank divisions in the Golan Heights. Syria's counter-offensive came to a halt, and the campaign picture returned to a blue and white smile.

At 13:00, still exhausted from his trans-Atlantic flight from New York, and the terrible, familiar migraine that was shattering his head, Lt. Col. Iftach Zemer returned from his first mission in the war. He understood that there was no choice. He shoved the physical distress aside, and began to impose order on the Squadron.

In the early afternoon, representatives of the Fourth Estate arrived.

"Cooperate," Zemer instructed.

They cooperated, in their way.

"The real reason that we were sent out today was to bomb a nearby power station in Damascus," they explained to a bunch of stern-looking journalists, "was that we wanted to end the electric shocks that our POW comrades are experiencing in Syrian prisons, once and for all."

14:00-17:15. Meeting of the Foreign Affairs and Security Committee

"Our mission is to make it increasingly difficult on the Syrians until it is unbearable to them," Lt. Gen. Elazar said to committee members that gathered in Tel Aviv. He then informed the participants about the strategic assaults in Syria.

"The weak point in this war," Dado continued, "is Syria, which is why we are pushing our main efforts into grinding their army to a halt."

"Regarding the Egyptian front, we are preparing a final stopping line, with pits, infantry, and landmines. I hope that we will not need to use that line. It is a final option. If we withdraw to that point, we will be forced to give up the use of the Refidim air base. With that, this line is meant to stop everything from getting passed."

"Publishing policies are not random," Dado added, answering a question that was asked about the subject, "I think that, in war, it is impossible to tell the truth... Anyway, the IDF Spokesperson didn't publish anything wrong, he just made a headline from the fact that we were attacked."

"This also applies to the announcement, 'We are pushing out the Egyptian Army, and chasing after the Syrian Army and destroying it'?" Begin pressed.

15:45. Office of the Prime Minister

Once again, Office Manager Gazit sent a telegram to Ambassador Dinitz in Washington, this time apologizing that there was not a blitzkrieg.

"It's not possible to formulate an estimation of the requested times," he wrote. "We are in a war that is still based largely on the initiative of the enemy... It is worth mentioning to 'Naftali' (Kissinger) that this may not be a short war," Gazit continued.

"More will transpire," Gazit concluded, "and this containment step that we have stood in will join with the most wonderful phenomena in the history of our people."

18:30. Editorial Committee

On Tuesday evening, a group of senior media people in Israel were horrified to discover that their Defense Minister, the man who had seemed magical since the Six-Day War, was crippled by a great, infectious anxiety.

Until that moment, they had known another Dayan. Brave, determined, and optimistic. Five years earlier, he dealt with the collapse of an archeological excavation site that almost cost him his life, and his one eye kept smiling from his hospital bed. Most knew of the pain caused by his empty socket, the result of an injury in World War II, but he insisted. Smiling, ignoring the pain.

"We do not have the power to throw the Egyptians across the Canal," Dayan said to the stunned group in front of him, his one eye closed. "We have no choice but to withdraw and organize a defensive line between the Canal and the mountain ranges. There are implications to all of this. It has been revealed to the world that we are not stronger than the Egyptians."

"Tonight, at 21:00, I am going to announce what I have just told you to the nation," Dayan concluded.

"If what you've just told us is heard on live television," warned Gershom Schocken, the editor and publisher of the *Haaretz* newspaper, "it will shake the people of Israel to the core."

Evening. IAF Headquarters

On Tuesday evening, unaware of the earthquake that had shaken the Israeli newspaper editors, Lt. Col. Oded Erez, Head of the IAF Defense Branch, stripped off his overalls and pressure suit, and went down to the corps HQ in the Kirya in Tel Aviv. A few hours earlier, he rejoiced at the sight of rising orange flames and black clouds of smoke coming from the direct hit on the target of his Sledgehammer four ship formation, led by Huldai: a communications cable northwest of Damascus.

The former Chief of Military Intelligence, Maj. Gen. (Res.) Aharon Yariv asked, "Were you in the four-ship formation that went to strike the communications cable near Damascus?"

"Yes," Erez answered.

"You've done a great thing," Yariv said, "You hit the communications traffic between Syria and Lebanon and between Syria and countries overseas. The hit has forced the Syrians to 'go on the air', making it possible for our intelligence to receive their communications."

Evening. The 201ˢᵗ Squadron

Without anyone indicating it to his face, the arrival of Lt. Col. Zemer, perhaps alongside the unique position that Tuesday has in Jewish tradition, signified the turning point in the squadron's battles. A perfect day. There were no losses. Everything clicked. Excellent hits. Missions were carried out as planned, and those that weren't were replaced with alternative ones.

Did Tuesday's results signify a change to come in the following days?

Night. Senior Command Post

"Did we lose any aircraft today in the bombing of the Egyptian bridges?" Benny Peled was asked.

"Yes, my son," Peled uttered through his teeth, "they picked him up."

"To this day," the IAF Commander informed, matter-of-factly, ignoring the hissing from those around him, "the IAF has lost 52 aircraft."

"We went to battle with 360 aircraft," Peled continued, "and today, taking away those that have fallen and those craft still being repaired, we are left with 220. We need to preserve the force and reduce risks, or within four days, we will no longer have an Air Force."

"Despite the promises," Dayan said, "the Americans still haven't approved the delivery of Phantoms to replace those that were lost."

"Tomorrow, the Air Force will reduce its activity," the Chief of Staff concluded, internalizing the pair of announcements that he had just heard. A moment later, he was unable to hide his frustration with the IAF's performance. "We destroyed seven of their bridges… and the next day? All of them were operating like new. We've destroyed all of their bridges, twice, and right now, there are eleven bridges over the Canal."

23:40. Office of the Prime Minister

At the end of a successful day of fighting in the Golan Heights, and a less successful one on the Egyptian front, the Office Manager sent another message to the Israeli Ambassador in Washington.

"It is almost needless to say, once again, how much the renowned US resupply is needed… The IDF was set up for a short war. The extent of the enemy's attack and the ammunition needs in the defensive battles far exceeded expectations…"

Night. The 201st Squadron

As everyone returned from their nightly patrol missions, the deep night enveloped in a thick, dark blanket, studded with stars in the skies about Hatzor, Iftach Zemer retired to his room.

His head hurt. His body ached. He had a sick stomach. The migraine did not stop either. He did not eat, or drink, all day. Physically defeated, he rested on his bed.

Late in the night, unaware of the urgent demand for ammunition supplies by the Prime Minister's Office, or even of the plight of his commander, Yossi Eliel called his mother. "Hello, Mrs. Eliel. I am calling from the Casualties Section. I am calling to inform you that your son has been taken captive by Syrians..."

"Madam, this isn't a joke, you should take it seriously," he interrupted the choking laughter on the other end of the line.

Again the laughter emanated from the handset, and everyone who was still awake joined the party. If Yossi's mother, the one who gave him his sense of humor, thought that nothing substantial has cracked the Old World and one could still laugh, and crack up, then everything was still okay.

OCTOBER 10TH

Watershed

G il Regev curled in his comfortable sleep.

Yesterday, administration staff set up a large tent in the parking lot in front of the Squadron. Someone said that the tent was intended for those who want to steal a few more minutes of sleep between shuttles from the living quarters. This fit with Regev, who by the time the little hand hit four, he was supposed to be in the sky, patrolling along the Canal.

"Gili, get up."

Did someone go crazy?

"Gili, get up."

"Let me sleep!" barked the charmer of the squadron.

"Get up, Gili," she continued, softly, as all voices are heard at three in the morning.

Then he remembered. *Patrol, man, patrol. But I want to sleep. Who's the madman who decided that aircraft should fly at night?*

Grumbling, he sat on the edge of the bed, threw on his g-suit, tied his shoes, and stumbled over the beds of his comrades, some of whom were still immersed in their own comfortable dreams.

Just before 04:00, Regev and Tamir cut through the black sky in a boaring level flight. There and back, there and back. The guardians of the State of Israel. Next to the town of Ismaïlia, beams of light swept the dark sky. Evading, continuing, there and back, round trip.

Early Morning Hours. Office of the Prime Minister

"I knew, that in Israel's desperate hour of need, I could turn to you and rely on your deep support and understanding," Golda Meir wrote excitedly in a dispatch of special thanks to the President of the United States of America, in response to a pile of telegrams that she found on her desk, describing the positive turnaround in the United States for Israel's requests for military equipment.

The promise of U.S. aid, and other updates flowing to her desk, according to which IDF forces in the Golan finished pushing Syrian forces back beyond the ceasefire line, and forces in the south were holding up all along the front, greatly improved the Iron Lady's mood. For the first time since the outbreak of hostilities, she felt that it was possible to let out a sigh of relief, as a better future was coming.

07:45. The 201ˢᵗ Squadron

It's pretty down there, Zetelny thought, in the back-seat with Eitan Levy on the controls. *This is my first mission on the delta, and the first time I've experienced what the old timers described—green from horizon to horizon, studded with freshwater canals, crisscrossing the whole area.*

In the seat in front of him, Levy took the aircraft down low, very low, occasionally bouncing it off of the high power lines that interfered with their altitude. *There's the abandoned air base. What is its name? Manzala.* At the briefing in the morning, they were told not to deal with it, to pass it like it was nothing. "Bypass the field!" Gurion suddenly shouted, leading the strike four-ship formation in front of them.

Amiram Talmon was the lead navigator, and at the air speed at which his Sledgehammer was piercing the sky, Manzala was already forgotten, and he was concentrating on the task for which he sat behind Gurion—to bring everyone to the exact pull-up waypoint.

Maj. Talmon is a veteran navigator, who started out in the cargo aircraft array and was converted into the fighter aircraft array. He did not need to have the meaning of a pull-up waypoint explained to him. An early pull-up would cause the dive angle to be too shallow, creating a long, slow strike pass that would impair their survivability. A late pull-up would create too steep an angle, making it difficult to locate the target and will make the recovery at an altitude harder, and, in extreme cases, preventing the release of their bombs.

"Thirty seconds. Three. Two. One. Go." Talmon said.

A few seconds before 08:11 on Wednesday, October 10, Maj. Amnon Gurion pulled up, exactly at the pre-planned waypoint, feeling the correct angle in the nose of his aircraft.

He has his "head up", he identified the target—Abu Hamed Air base, below and to the left. He drew an imaginary circle in the air, which will provide his aircraft with the best point for executing a wingover maneuver and to dive on the target, and he pulls up to that imaginary point.

10,000 feet.

Wingover maneuver towards the target, rolling the aircraft to inverted flight. Ten seconds. He aligned. There was the target. He cleared himself from all other stimuli and environmental hazards. Talmon ensured that there was a lock and took a peek outside—he kept eye contact with the target while checking for enemy aircraft on the tail. With his "head down" again, checking the weapon delivery computer to see that everything was okay, and enabling Gurion to finish at a height of 6,000 feet final aiming, he pressed on the pickle button to release the bombs.

Iftach Zemer led the second four-ship formation.

Abandoned?! He chuckled under his white helmet, understanding that they would not be able to get around, and he continued in the field of AAA flak that was dotting the sky above Manzala. *Boom.* The left engine FIRE light came on.

"We're hit," Zemer informed Sposh, who was sitting in the rear cockpit. Zemer set the left engine to idle rpm and continued heading to the target on a single engine.

On Wednesday morning, they covered the Abu Hamed Air base and the surrounding batteries with a barrage of bombs that slid from the bellies of eight Sledgehammer jets. The bombs collided violently with material that absorbed their heavy attack, sending a mixed pulp of steel, asphalt, and concrete into the air.

They headed home.

Stick to my stomach. level up, buddy, level. Great. Now lower. Lower. More. Gurion was leading, and Zemer was behind him. After experiencing Manzala, they skipped over the abandoned airstrip, and breathed a sigh of relief in front of the Mediterranean Sea, just as Hayun's aircraft got hit with a strong bang, and an AAA round breached the cockpit and stuck next to his left leg.

Hayun thought, resentfully, *what is this? The statistics forgot to write me in after I had to eject during "Model?"* Maybe, he contemplated, cooled down, *maybe the statistics are on my side, and here they are preventing me from sustaining an even more serious hit?* He glanced in the mirror and caught the "Rhino" in the back seat, sitting with calm body language, and something in his serenity took hold of him too. He smiled to himself about his excessive worries. *This war will end, Kobi. Everything will be fine.*

09:50. Northern Command

"I'm happy to inform you that after four days of fierce battles, the Northern Command has managed, with the incredible assistance of the Air Force, to break the Syrian army, which has lost hundreds of tanks in battle."

"The ceasefire line in the Golan Heights is in our hands," the Head of Northern Command continued, speaking excitedly to the Chief of Staff, "We are taking advantage of our success and attacking across the ceasefire line."

11:50. Office of the Prime Minister

"Today, the fourth day of warfare," Mordecai Gazit, the General Manager of the Prime Minister's Office, wrote to Simcha Dinitz, the Israeli Ambassador in Washington, "We sense the success of the containment and stabilization of the fronts. The moment is soon approaching that we will have the initiative in our hands, and we can dictate the next moves at the proper pace."

"Our policy aims at toppling Syria with the forces on the front, the destruction of their strategic inventory, and breaking the country's will to fight. This morning, the first signs of Syria's collapse appeared."

"With regards to the Egyptian front," Gazit continued, "The policy is to continue curbing the Egyptian army… as long as our main efforts remain on the Syrian front."

"…Distress in the Sledgehammer forces is considerable, so it is essential that you find a way to get these fast. The quick arrival of the aircraft will return the Air Force to its initial intensity. The rate of aircraft losses is so high that it is impossible to delay this matter."

13:30. The 201ˢᵗ Squadron

At the end of a light lunch, navigator Nimrod Amami headed out on his first operational mission in Syria—the highway leading to the Damascus International Airport. The goal—to prevent replacement aircraft from landing on an alternative runway.

"Check the RWR display," Eli Zohar, the pilot, requested.

"What?"

"The RWR display!"

Amami rummaged through his memory, compressed with the results of the nightly lesson from the rapid certification course. *What did Zetelny say concerning the RWR?! Is it the thing that warns about missiles? Where is it supposed to be, where?*

"Um, remind me, where's the button for the display supposed to be?" he asked uneasily.

"Down and to the left," Zohar answered, patiently, as though he was giving out a court sentence.

He fumbled. Found it. *Something was lit. What am I supposed to see now?*

They took off.

At 14:10, a four-ship formation of Sledgehammer jets attacked the freeway. In the seats of the leading aircraft were Gurion and Zetelny, Amami's instructor, who was unaware of the dilemmas his apprentice was facing in the aircraft that was closing the formation, and only saw the results of his bombing—a smashed freeway and columns of smoke rising up into the sky. However, celebrations would have to wait, as they needed to get back before the anti-aircraft missiles woke up from their slumber.

They activated.

Zetelny in the first aircraft, and Amami, his student, was in the last. Both saw missiles and heard the RWR warning go off, as clouds of flak decorated the blue sky. Zetelny shouted, "Lower, Amnon," and Gurion answered, "It's impossible, the cypress trees on the side of the road are already taller than us." Somehow, everyone got out of the turmoil intact and climbed over the mountains of Lebanon and returned home.

Now Amami knew what he was supposed to see in the RWR display.

Afternoon. A Man Named Epstein

In the early hours of Wednesday afternoon, Maj. Giora Epstein left his desk at IAF HQ and headed out on his first mission with his favorite interception aircraft.

Patrol in the Sinai, they told him, *until sunset.*

He started the Mirage, took off, flew out to the Canal, and cut through the sky back and forth in a boaring level flight. Nothing.

Giora was a superstar. All of the members of the crew thought so, not only because of six downed enemy aircraft, devastated by his guns' fire, nor even for being a rough kibbutznik, nor due to his famous cool-headedness during events that leave others shaking to the bones.

Giora was the interception idol of the IAF primarily because of his hawk-like eyes. Some even said that the hawk should come to him for an enrichment course. Giora's eyes left almost no chance, up front, to those who tried to confront them in air combat. Certainly not enemy pilots.

Avner Seplak, a contemporary of Giora, and one of the best of the best himself, remembered the War of Attrition and patrolling the Canal with Giora Epstein.

"Twenty miles from you, nine o'clock, enemy aircraft," the controller said.

No normal person can see an aircraft from that distance, not even from half that distance.

"There's nothing there," Giora replied.

A moment of silence passed, and then the controller returned to the radio: "Sorry, you're right, it was just a radar glitch."

Downing enemy aircraft was Giora's purpose in life. They were all knocked out right here, around the Canal. He then searched all over the sky, and no one vectored him for an engagement.

Where are you? No one came.

Disappointed, he headed back down to the Air Force HQ. *What's going on with this war? Did someone up above decide that I've already had my fair share of enemy aircraft?*

15:40. *The 201ˢᵗ Squadron*

Sometime in the morning, an intelligence report arrived at IDF Senior Command, according to which the Russians had begun a massive flow of supplies to Syria. That was a problem. The Americans, despite their promises, had not yet sent so much as a single screw to aid the blue-and-white war effort, while the Russians were acting in a manner capable of preventing, or at least slowing down, the collapse of the Syrian Army.

IAF HQ decided to send a four-ship formation of Sledgehammer jets on the longest mission of the Yom Kippur War so far—50 minutes and 45 seconds to the pull-up waypoint. A Flight Academy in Aleppo, near the border with Turkey. It was one of those missions that one was to suck in, even the last fuel vapors that remain in the fuel tanks. The 201ˢᵗ Squadron was chosen to execute it.

"It is essential to take this air base out of commission for a prolonged time," Lt. Col. Iftach Zemer, the leader, briefed others in his formation. "It is used for Russian airlifts. A fatal blow will delay the flow of supplies to the front and help in the overall effort to eradicate the Syrian army."

"One more thing," Zemer added, "Twelve Russian Antonovs are sitting in this air base. Leave them alone."

At 15:40, the four-ship formation took off.

What a breathtaking view, the "Rhino" thought, overwhelmed, lugging a camera along with him. He was filming, taking pictures, and almost forgot that he was not on a guided trip to heaven, but no one was waiting for them and it really was beautiful, so beautiful. He continued to film, and in this heavenly peaceful atmosphere, they emerged this high blue and entered the attack. *Here's the air base, and there are the aircraft.* Just then, Number 4, Guri Palter, informed the four-ship formation on the radio, "Wherever I place the crosshairs there is an Antonov," and Number 3, Rotem the Ginger who returned from a vacation in the US, said, "Number 4, set the pipper a bit forward, in front of their nose."

Palter acted, and from the navigator's seat,, Amnon Tamir saw an Antonov leap into the air and crash into the runway. *Ten meters isn't a wide enough safety margin*, he thought. Palter then said, "Don't worry. So some Russians will die…"

Rotem the Ginger, who has just created a new safety margin, got excited from what his eyes beheld, and requested authorization from Zemer to hit it himself.

"Stop-stop," Zemer said.

"An external drop tank failed to transfer fuel," Number 2, Yigal Stavi, informed the four-ship formation lead.

Damn, Talmon thought in the leading aircraft.

"Head south," he offered to Zemer, knowing it was the shortest way, however not the safest.

They all headed to the south.

"My fuel is beginning to run out," Stavi reported.

"Pull higher," Zemer instructed him.

"There are MIGs on the way to intercept you all," the controller informed the group.

No one had enough fuel to open the burners and run away, or to take them, and everyone was at 30,000 feet in altitude and 350 knots airspeed, the most fuel-efficient condition.

We're sitting ducks, Zemer knew. "Send some aircraft to handle these MiGs immediately," he told the control officer of the air traffic control unit.

Huldai's four-ship formation, which kept a distance, approached the scene, and the MiGs, perhaps because a rumor reached them about the nature of the redheaded deputy commander of the squadron, broke contact. Far away, in the pale horizon, they were captured in the intentions of a prowling four-ship formation of Mirages.

The eight airmen of the 201st Squadron stretched their necks to the horizon, watching the battle take place like excited fans in the bleachers. Rooting for the Mirages. Even though they were Mirages…

Then everyone, even the charming child Stavi, landed safely.

The success of the attack on Aleppo did not end with the runway strikes and the destruction of the Antonov that entered under Palter's pipper.

First of all, it turned out that the USSR's Air Defense Commander was killed in the attack.

Secondly, there were the Americans. Before the attack, the US Secretary of State was against the airlift to Israel. In its wake, Kissinger understood that the crazy bunch in Israel were fighting for their home, were not going to give up, and were willing to do whatever it took to win, at whatever cost. He also understood that they were moments away from further complicating the US's Cold War with the USSR. So Kissinger ran to Nixon in order to speed up the airlift to Israel.

Thirdly, there were the Russians. After the attack on Aleppo, the Russians stopped their airlift to Syria, and continued while sending their supplies to Syria at a slower pace, using only the naval port at Latakia.

18:00. Office of the Defense Minister

"The Syrian system is alive and fighting," the Chief of Staff informed the Defense Minister. "Progress involves fierce fighting. The troops are tired, at every stop they are falling asleep. I gave the order to cut off all contact with the enemy, to give troops time to rest and organize."

Evening. The Prime Minister's Speech to the Nation

"With the holiday of Sukkot knocking on the door, and the tail wind blowing once again into the sails of Israel's security and belief in the power of its army, we are retaliating harshly against those who have come after us," Golda Meir decided to break the self-imposed silence that she followed since the outbreak of war.

From an improvised studio in the Sokolov House in Tel Aviv, the Prime Minister was facing the general public, informing them about the displacement of the Syrians from all areas of the Golan Heights and the substantial improvement in the Suez Canal region. Looking directly into the eyes of the camera, she explained that this was a different war, a longer one. "We should be prepared to pay a heavy price, so that we should be able to justify the sacrifices that have been made by the victims." Her face was haggard, with a heavy sadness in her eyes.

Evening. The 201ˢᵗ Squadron

She came to congratulate but only cursed in the end, Gil Regev thought, relaxing on the orange couch in the clubroom, watching the Prime Minister's speech and greatly missing Shaniboi and Assael.

We're returning to our old selves, navigator Uri Arad thought. *Here's what the Prime Minister said on television, and now for two days we haven't had any casualties, wounded, or captured. We're coming back.*

Then he left the clubroom and sat on the curb, in the Squadron's parking lot, with Bilha, his girlfriend, at his side.

Suddenly he was speaking fluently, perhaps because darkness was falling, or maybe it was another long night. At 22:00, he went out to patrol again, in the great darkness of Sinai.

"The scariest thing for me is the idea of getting captured," he told Bilha, throwing open the drawer of secrets and lowering his eyes. "It's scarier than dying."

Bilha was silent. Then she said, "It won't happen to you, Uri. It won't happen to you."

23:30. *Office of the Prime Minister*

"We are in the midst of the most decisive day of this war," the Chief of Staff said, opening the War Cabinet meeting that was called at the last minute in the Prime Minister's Office. The meeting was meant to reach a decision about the need to launch an attack towards Damascus, or to fortify the defense lines and to send a division from the north to the front in the south.

"The IDF has reached the ceasefire line on the Syrian front," Dado continued. "We need to decide whether to continue or to stop at this line, which is the most comfortable place to establish a defense, and then send a division to the southern front at the Canal."

"The distance from the ceasefire line to Damascus is sixty kilometers, but Syrian forces may continue to fight and win with the aid of Iraqi forces. If that's the case, then the IDF will be forced to stop after fifteen or twenty kilometers without the benefit of a ceasefire, and on a line that would be very difficult to defend. In other words, it would be a more difficult situation than the one that we are in currently."

"However," the Chief of Staff added, "although the Air Force has lost its intensity, it could still coordinate efforts and possibly bring down the Syrians like in 1967. It is important for us to display to the Arabs the reliability and the strength of the IDF, and therefore we must determine, even if only on one front, the prospects of a ceasefire after this decision. Otherwise, there is a concern that Hussein and others will join. Therefore, when I consider what is at stake, I recommend attacking Syria, until the end."

"I am actually all for going on the offensive on the southern front," the Deputy Chief of Staff said. "Indeed, it is impossible to cross the Canal. However, we can still destroy the hundreds of enemy tanks on the East Bank."

"The decision on Syria, and even the conquest of Damascus, will not require the Egyptians to stop fighting, so it will not stop the war," Maj. Gen. Tal continued. "Moreover, such an attack could further expand the war, requiring Jordan to intervene."

"I side with the Chief of Staff," the IAF Commander said. "We can coordinate efforts tomorrow in Syria, after exhausting their missile system."

"The Syrian Air Force is in a panic," Peled continued, "Just today, we have taken down seventeen of their aircraft."

"I think," he continued, "that breaking ground troops deep into Syrian territory will deter Jordan, Iraq, and the Soviet Union from interfering in combat."

"Another thing," Peled said, concluding his sequence of insights, "We cannot wait four more days to attack the south. During that time, the number of available combat aircraft may fall below the critical level."

"The forces are tired," Dayan said, "I agree about the attack, if they have the ability to give one, good blow."

"Don't wait," the Prime Minister concluded, "We must win, at least on one front. Our forces must threaten Damascus. Decisions about the conquest or the bombing of the city will receive authorization. Moreover, the attack may well deter the Jordanians, or it will make due with a limited intervention on the Syrian front."

Galili, sitting next to the Queen of the Jewish State and knowing the strength, determination, and courage that she has as his Prime Minister, perhaps not yet internalizing her final words, added some concluding remarks. "It is already midnight," he said, "we need to release the senior command in order to line up the angels." Since no one in the country's cabinet, nor the Commander in Chief of the State of Israel, asked what was meant by "angels," it was clear to him, and to them, that the die was cast. Tomorrow, they were going into Syria.

The decision on the night of October 10 regarding the attack on the northern front, only after which the IDF could attack in the south, indicated for the first time the taking of the strategic initiative, and especially the ripening of the assessment that the war could be extended, and that logistical perseverance was essential. The die was cast. Nothing then or afterwards would go according to the 'quick-fix' method.

In the night hours of Wednesday, October 10, the political and military leadership of Israel moved to another step in understanding the current reality, and finally started playing with the right cards.

Midnight. The 201ˢᵗ Squadron

It's still not over, Uri Arad pondered as he hung up his pressure suit and helmet. *After all, what have we done? A routine patrol along the gulf, and suddenly two MiGs appeared out of nowhere, and were not afraid to approach. Despite the darkness. They are not afraid of us,* Arad thought. *They are determined, they are brave. This is not a quick solution. It's just not in me.*

OCTOBER 11ᵀᴴ

Toward Damascus

An hour after midnight, as Thursday emerged, Lt. Gen. David Elazar translated the government's decision into practice, updating the Head of Northern Command and sending his forces, spread out along the Purple Line, to settle accounts with Syria.

"At five in the morning, perhaps before, I will arrive at your headquarters for the final approval of the plans for attack," Dado informed him.

The IDF Chief of Staff examined Northern Command's attack plans in the operations room at Mount Canaan, telling those listening about the supreme strategic importance of the attack, which held the key to the entire war. Meanwhile, two hundred kilometers south of him, in the IAF Command Chamber, the feeling that the IAF was indeed Israel's biggest asset once again solidified in the mind of Maj. Gen. Benny Peled.

True, "Model 5" was a disaster, Peled thought, *because on Saturday they did not allow us to attack preemptively, and on Sunday the world was topsy-turvy, and Dayan was talking about the Destruction of the Third Temple and all the pressure of immediately preserving the Land of Zion and Jerusalem, so what happened, happened, and we performed as we did.*

True, the air support missions could not deliver the goods for the ground troops because of the unending enemy anti-aircraft defenses that prevented the option of swooping in, locating a target, and returning for an attack.

Yet, we are still maneuvering inside the new rules and the bewilderment among the ground forces, and we are succeeding. We have taken down 118 enemy aircraft. Only two of us were shot down in aerial combat. We are fine, just fine.

I must protect our aircraft, so that there will be something to rescue the State of Israel. You cannot rely on the Gentiles. They said that they would help. So they said. Until now, I have yet to see a shred of an edge of a replacement aircraft that has arrived beyond the sea. Yesterday I lost three more aircraft. To date, we have lost 55 outright. Another 45 are undergoing serviceability repairs. Soon, the Air Force will be finished. Today, we are going to pour our wrath on Syria. These are missions that come with a high risk factor. They are not good for the aircraft, but vital to the people of Israel. It's possible that after the sixth day of fighting, after coming from above on their armored reinforcements rushing to the frontline (by employing a preventive enemy infrastructure attacks), will provide a close support against the intruders, and we will attack command centers, parked tanks, artillery batteries, posts, access routes, while keeping the number 55 intact.

Morning. IAF Headquarters and Squadrons

At dawn on Thursday morning, as the first sun rays on the eastern horizon are received by those yawning awake, and exhausted tank crews spread out along the barrows line along the Golan Heights border woke themselves up and began their routines, the Israeli Air Force headed out on its way.

Again and again, strike fighters on the ground at air bases across Syria were pounded, forcing the Syrian Air Force to stay and exercise territorial defensive operation, close to its bases, rather than applying its harmful effects on the IDF's armored divisions, flexing their muscles for their counterattack, which was supposed to depart at 11:00.

Morning. The 201st Squadron

"We're going to Hulhula," they told the guys in flight overalls and pressure suits, a return visit after the violent encounter on Monday. "The Syrians reestablished the air base, and the octet sent today will destroy it, preferably entirely."

"Forget Syria," grinned Motti Reder, a fresh Phantom pilot but a veteran combat pilot, "Come hear about what the Garden of Eden is like."

"You know how to fly? Well, now you will learn how to get laid," the Tel Aviv playboy opened his only appearance, running his hand through the part in his hair meticulously, and on his broad Slavic face with his familiar, eternal smile spread.

"Listen well," he continued, launching into a description of the things themselves, not saving the angle, position, and sound, proving that even the clouds of war were unable to shake his reputation.

He then paused a moment, and in a burst of generosity, revealed the seduction techniques themselves.

"It should be emphasized that this is their last chance before we depart to the mission, from which we might not come back," he said, and a great heaviness settled on his face. "In the case of stubborn resistance," Reder continued, "you need to activate the doomsday weapon—'If I survive the war, I will marry you.'"

Everyone in the briefing room, married and single alike, agreed that women are a great thing. Some missed their wives. Others, their girlfriends. Everyone yearned for a woman who could console them, help them to unload their worries and connect to one. To be with someone who had nothing to do with fighting and operations, with whom they didn't have to think about what 'the guys' would say. *Just you and me. This really might be the last chance.*

They crossed through Jordan.

I wonder what the Jordanians think about all of this commotion around them, Second Lieutenant Yosi Lev-Ari thought in the rear cockpit in Gadi Samok's aircraft, closing the convoy. *Here is Jabal ad-Druze on the right, so we've made it to Syria, and the beeping RWR system also confirms that it's true, beeping unconsciously, reassuring its serviceability with the large fire trails, indicating missile launches.* The missiles crashed somewhere in the sky, having trouble dealing with the eight Sledgehammer jets that were passing at the height of the treetops.

"Yosi, look," Samok said, "Look at that beautiful sand cloud that we raised from the red clay underneath us."

Beneath them, Syrian villages situated at the foot of Jabal ad-Druze passed by, and from every window, sparks of shooting were seen. Yossi tensed up in his seat, Gadi continued to ignore the warning tones and enjoyed the scenery. They passed Lake Halaja, and Yosi saw the desolate volcanic rocks that protect Damascus to the south, not knowing that it is the land of Oz from the biblical book of Job. At a distance, flames were visible reaching to the sky, and Yosi knew that the Syrians were on alert and that all available weapons down below awaited just them, and in a moment, they would be there, inside this fire. Thus, it was the moment when they would have to bolt-lock their will to survive, which screamed "run, baby, run," and dive into the fire instead.

Zetelny and Zemer led the forward four-ship formation.

The last ingress waypoint *is at the seasonal lake in Halaja,* thought Zetelny, *why did I have the silly idea that after six dry months there would still be a lake here?* Now Zetelny was doing what a navigator is supposed to do when nothing works: he tried to find another reference point. But this was Halaja, and all of the basalt rocks looked identical. *That's it,* he decided, *this is the place, there has to have been a lake here.* He pressed on his stopwatch, and at exactly 15:07, at the time designated for pull-up, he said, "Three, two, one, pull-up!" Zemer pulled up, and both of them search for the target. *Where is Hulhula?* 7,000 feet. They needed to enter into the attack. Nothing. They continued to climb. 9,000 feet. Their speeds increased and decreased, and missiles were shooting in their direction. Zemer rolled the aircraft once to the right, once to the left. Nothing. Hulhula was not here. Another sharp banking, and Zetelny stretched out his neck and identified the air base. It was directly below them. That is not how you strike an air base.

The whole four-ship formation released their bombs anyway, while once again descending down to treetop level, and they began to make their way home, as a sense of indignation took over them. *We fly all this way only to make a mistake in the last leg? We pull up for the strike at the waypoint, only to find that it doesn't allow us to dive towards the target? Damn.*

Now the last four ship formation, that Benaya was leading, was unable to locate the pull-up waypoint, and did not quite hit the target. They made their way back, and the feeling of a missed opportunity overtook the sixteen men under acrylic glass canopies.

As these aircraft made their way home, disappointed by the results of their strike results on Syria, seven other crews crushed Egyptian runways. The objective: El-Salhiya, East Delta. Located near the Canal, the air base and its aircraft sorties were a constant irritation for the IDF ground forces in the northern Sinai.

What is going to happen with these missiles? Capt. Yair David, the navigator, thought, battling pulling forces, centrifugal forces, and forces for which names have probably not been invented, and was pleased that his pressure suit was keeping at least some blood cells in his brain, those that were transmitting to him that it was all because Ben Ami Perry was on the controls. A second before he yelled to everyone "Break!" and he had taken it upon himself to break from right to left, avoiding the missiles from the batteries at Port Said.

In his rear seat, David knew that he did not actually know where they were. This was a problem, because he was the lead navigator of his four-ship formation and needed to lead everyone to the pull-up waypoint, and if he did not find it, then they might not be able to perform their mission, perhaps exposing them too long to enemy defenses, who were already giving enough signs that they were ready and eager to fight.

"Are you figuring out the navigation?" Perry asked.

"Yes," David replied, looking through the glass canopy, and identified below a monotonous marsh from horizon to horizon. He knew that he had deviated from the pre-planned flight route that was entered into the INS computer, hence he had to give up on the computer and switch over to the good-old manual navigation method designated Contact-Nav (time-map-terrain).

"Yes," he said again, encouraged by his self-imposed repetition.

When Ben Ami shouted "break," his call got mixed up with shrieks from air control, "Hail-Hail" (a code name for enemy aircraft), and no one was sure what Ben Ami was referring to or where the enemy aircraft were. "Wild Bull," who was a bit ahead of everyone and led a three ship formation that was supposed to take out the anti-aircraft defenses at the air base with bombs from offset, also broke, and immediately ran right in the middle of several MiGs. He jettisoned his bombs, but the bombs remained loaded on one side of the aircraft, so he had to struggle with keeping the wings level while combating MiGs that were trying to check him off the list.

But the "Bull" did not give in. Especially not to MiGs. He did an exercise in the air with his heavy, unbalanced aircraft, and settled behind a terrified Egyptian pilot, who went lower and lower until planted into the ground. "Wild Bull" once again proved his namesake, forgetting the over weight of his aircraft and the lateral balance problems, and pursued another MiG, strafing the gun, but the guy refused to explode. Just then, Haim Rotem and "Rhino" made a pass of their own, and "Rhino" shouted, "We downed him, we downed him!" and Rotem, with fire in his eyes said, "It wasn't us, 'Wild Bull' got him before us. There's no pilot in the cockpit."

In the strike four-ship formation, it was clear to Perry, the leader, that "Wild Bull" and his three ship formation have abandoned the loft bombing run and were fighting for their lives. Someone yelled on the radio, "Dog 3 break," and Perry knew that "Dog 3" was Rotem and it was apparently difficult back there. He knew he could forget about the final suppression of the AAA batteries that would be waiting for them, armed, alert, and laden with bombs. In another minute, all formations were supposed to pass below the currently engaged aerial combat sector, becoming sitting ducks for the MiGs. It was tempting to jettison everything out and forget about the damn air base, to break out and join the aerial combat, because this was really the essence of everything: shooting down enemy aircraft. It was not clear to him at all how, in the middle of this mess, David would succeed in bringing everyone to the pre-planned pull-up waypoint.

"Are we continuing?" He asked David.

The most veteran Phantom navigator in the Squadron, and a former paratrooper, David knew that this, precisely, was the moment of truth, and that everything rested on his shoulders alone. He took a second or two to think, and said, "Yes."

Perry was calm, because Yair David was behind him. *Yair will surely be fine*, he thought to himself, *the work of the righteous is done by others*. In the midst of the mists of the Delta, with identical towns passing below, he saw trap balloons, anchored to the ground. He squinted his eyes and saw that the El-Salhiya air base was there between the balloons. Now he was sure that Yair would find the right point for pull up. Yair was able to find it, and said, "Three, two, one, now," and Perry pulled up, and after him so did the three ship formation. The hits were good. Rotem escaped the MiG. No one even had a scratch.

"Operational orders must be fulfilled," smiled the tribal elder, Yair David, under his white helmet.

Afternoon. Wing 4 (Hatzor)

"…It's difficult to assess how long this war will last. What is clear is that this will not be a short war." The soldiers of Hatzor who were reading the wing's bulletin realized that their commander, Col. Lapidot—whose remarks, until now, had only brought a sense that, really, only a tiny mishap was being spoken of, and we are just about to break into the dawn of the seventh day of the Six-Day War—had grown new insights and was hesitant. The victory celebrations were ahead of their time. There was no quick fix.

Afternoon. The 201ˢᵗ Squadron

Kobi Hayun saw a mysterious lieutenant colonel, with the red beret and red boots of the paratroopers, standing on the stage of the briefing room, as well as Eitan Ben Eliahu, who came especially from headquarters. He also saw Col. Lapidot, the Wing Commander, and understood that the following mission will be a significant one. Though he did not know what would be called for, he was excited. Very excited.

"Hello, my name is Sami," the paratrooper said, "Sami Nahmias. I'm the head of the Special Operations Branch in the Intelligence

Directorate's Collection Department. I didn't come here just to chit-chat. The fate of the war on the Egyptian front may depend on your mission here today."

"Over Damietta, the eastern branch of the Nile in the direction of Port Said, in the heart of the Egyptian Delta, and just north of the town of Banha, is a large freeway bridge, with two lanes in each direction, as well as a railway path."

"Inside the bridge, hidden from view, is the target of this mission," Nahmias continued, "A giant cable that transmits all of Egypt's communications to the outside world, as well as those between the air bases in the Delta."

"Your mission," the paratrooper paused for a moment, "Your task is to hit the bridge and cut off the lines of communication. This will force the Egyptians to transmit via radio wave, and allow us to intercept their transmissions."

"I have no doubt that there will be enemy aircraft that will attempt to interfere," he paused again and stared at the Great 16 at his feet, "You probably know that the location is situated close to three enemy air bases."

"We understand, that not everyone will return," Amiram Talmon, the lead navigator, said defiantly.

Sami from Intelligence noticed Talmon from the Air Force, broke his stare, continued and briefly looked into the eyes of everyone in the room and said, "Listen to me carefully. The IDF is entering this mission with open eyes. We are aware of the risks and the costs. We are ready to take it. I hope that the job will get done without casualties, and yet, if you destroy the bridge and no one gets back home, the price was worth it." He stopped for a moment and said, "I hope to see all of us in here for debriefing after the mission."

"Good luck," concluded Col. Lapidot, the Wing Commander, who was present at the briefing. "And another thing, the wing is experiencing a significant shortage in centerline drop fuel tanks. If you get into an aerial combat, make an effort to jettison only those loaded to the wings. Good luck to you again. Good luck to us all."

"Watch out for the high power line poles that rise to 300 feet," the veterans, alumni of the Six-Day War, warned. *The columns will fall in line*, thought Kobi Hayun, the Number 4 of the interception four-ship formation. *But what about the air bases in the Delta?* There was a nine-minute flight distance from crossing the coast line to the pull-up waypoint for the target of the strike four-ship formation. *That's enough time for the MiGs patrolling the air, and those on alert, to organize and get to us. There will be dogfights, for sure. Who's going to watch my tail?*

Is the number 4 good or bad for Jews? Hayun continued to reflect while making a quick visual inspection of the aircraft's airframe, scanning, shaking, slapping, and towards the end he strokes the nose. He lifted his eyes and whispered, "Don't let me down, okay? Don't disappoint me."

Eight Phantoms stopped their taxiing and parked at the threshold of the runway.

A maintenance personnel crew member checked the underbelly of the aircraft. He then gave a thumbs up for approval.

The strike four-ship formation that Gurion was leading was already in the air. Now, it was their turn.

Ben Eliahu, the leader of the interception four-ship formation, was in the air, as was Yoni. Haim accelerated. His turn had come. Hayun aligned the aircraft on the runway, and finished his engines test, "Air intakes are okay," Arad said. He ran both engines at maximum power, waited a moment for the rpm to stabilize, his foot shaking on the brake. He released. The aircraft started to roll, and he knew that it was the right moment. He punched in both throttles with a slight push to the left and then forward beyond the MIL power detent to "firewall" position. Full burners. Two huge flames shot out from behind the aircraft, and with them came the familiar gallop, nailing him to the back seat. 170 knots. He slightly pulled back the stick. They were in the sky.

He retracted the landing gear, hearing the knock as they locked up. He turned left and joined the formation ahead. Radio silence. Low height.

Haim Rotem was Number 3 in the interception four-ship formation. This troubled him. In air combat training, he would produce excellent results attacking and downing enemy aircraft, but now, at the deciding moment, due to clumsy aiming work, he found it difficult to score the goal, a bit like a visually impaired person who had trouble threading a needle. Now Banha, and he was second in command.

Is this mission into the heart of the delta, on ground that is controlled by five active air bases, comprised of the best Egyptian interception squadrons made up of the "elected" best pilots? Can only four Sledgehammer jets protect themselves, as well as the strike four-ship formation, in the face of dozens of MiGs that are possibly preparing to attack them?

420 | *FOR HEAVEN'S SAKE*

Here's Ben Eliahu, until recently the Deputy Commander of the Squadron. He was called up urgently by Air Force headquarters to lead an interception four-ship formation. Does Ben Eliahu share all of these questions? Let's assume so. Is the narrow window of time that is left before takeoff enough time to still change personnel or add more aircraft for defense?

This blue is a beautiful color, thought Lt. Avner Naveh, Number 2 in the strike four-ship formation, who was humming songs to himself over the rippling waves of the Mediterranean Sea. Here's the coastline. Here's Port Said. Here's the Nile Delta.

A world of contrasts, Naveh reflected, who flew along with everyone very quickly and very low, the height of the minarets on the mosques. On his way to devastate and destroy, perhaps even fighting for his life, he admired the fishing boats on the water, picturesque villages, and crisscrossing mowed green squares.

What is that? The forward windshield was wrought with the smeared bodies of thousands of flies, joining with the mists of the Delta. *It's almost like a night flight,* Naveh smiled in light of his excessive urgency. He saw Gurion slightly ahead of him and to the left, and he routed his flight according to the "road sign" ahead.

Seven minutes until the pull. Will I be able to identify the target? They continued.

They passed over the Egyptian air base at Tanta. *If Egyptian radar hasn't caught us,* Naveh thought, *these Egyptian pilots definitely are on to us. On the way back they will be waiting for us. But for this very reason, there is an interception four-ship formation, and especially Ben Eliahu.*

"Hail (enemy aircraft)," the controller informed them. *The bastards organized quickly*, Hayun thought, as alert signals increased in number as more Egyptian interception jets took off from the Air Force bases in the Delta.

11:55. Right on time.

"Three, two, one, pull-up," said Talmon, who identified the pull-up waypoint in the leading aircraft back seat of the strike four-ship formation. Gurion pulled up and saw Naveh glued to his tail.

There's the bridge. There's Cairo over there to the side.

Neve executed a wingover maneuver and dove. The flies had disappeared. A perfect view. He released his bombs, and then broke out away from the target, a large explosion behind him. He tilted on his side and saw pieces of asphalt that were torn out of the bridge fly into the air, and a passenger bus that was unable to brake plunged into the water.

Now Numbers 3 and 4, Levy and Koren, knocked out the second bridge. A mushroom, resembling a small atomic bomb, rose from the two bridges. They then heard the air controller shout, "Hail, hail, hail."

We accomplished the mission. We destroyed the bridges. Perfect execution. There is no room for unnecessary entanglements in the backyard of these three air bases, Gurion thought. *If the MiGs will dare to be arrogant, there is Ben Eliahu's four-ship formation as escort. He's a gun magician.*

"Pepper," he ordered the formation, and everyone accelerated a few seconds with their rear burners. 600 knots. "Enough." The throttle levers were set back to their military power range. MIL power is set. 540 knots. At the maximum attainable speed with external drop tanks loaded to the wings and no burner, Ilan Lazar, the navigator in the last fighter of the strike formation, purred contentedly beneath his goggles, and thought, *perfect execution. Now to get out of here ASAP (as soon as possible).*

This is no place for children's games, Naveh thought, stuck on Gurion the leader. He turned his head back and saw that a large distance had opened up between them and Ben Eliahu's interception four-ship formation. *What is going on over there? Why aren't they accelerating with us?*

What's going on with our airspeed? Haim Rotem thought, Number 3 in the interception four-ship formation. He gathered that Ben Eliahu was going slow and opening up a distance between them and the strike four-ship formation. *The task now is getting home, as fast as possible. Why aren't we accelerating and getting out of here? Why is Eitan decreasing the airspeed?*

Hayun, Number 4 in the interception four-ship formation, also did not know what was going on. *They stated specifically in the briefing—if you finish, break contact, as fast as possible. And now Ben Eliahu flew slowly and didn't increase airspeed, and now the MiGs are onto us, all over the Delta.*

If the MiGs head towards the strike four-ship formation, we are too far out to give them immediate assistance, Hayun thought. *If they get there before us, our energy levels will be too low. What is this?*

420 knots.

Flight training, Rotem thought. *The controller is constantly warning us about MiGs, and the whole Delta saw the smoke that the strike formation left behind. Whoever wasn't awake or aware of our arrival, certainly already knows. 420 knots in enemy territory crawling with MiGs is an airspeed that you fly only when you are experiencing a fuel problem, and we don't have that problem. But Eitan is leading. He must know what he is doing.*

In the lead aircraft of the interception four-ship formation, Ben Eliahu was making calculations. *The simplest way would be to fly at 600 knots, stick to the strike four-ship formation, and get out of the Delta as quickly as possible. But our job is to protect them. What happens when MiGs catch up with us when we are going at 600 knots? Our turning radius would be huge and extremely difficult to maneuver, and other MiGs would join the battle and cut through our turning circle, and set on our tails in the middle of our turn. And the fuel. A flight at 600 knots at low altitude results in high fuel consuming. We would have to fight without sufficient fuel for maneuvering. 420 knots is optimal for maneuvering,* Ben Eliahu thought. *If we have to increase airspeed, applying the burners for one second will bring us to 500 knots.* He then noticed MiGs coming down on them. "Break!" he shouted on the radio.

Gurion heard Ben Eliahu's "break" and broke to the left, a low level break. He ended a 90° turn to the west and behind him far away, maybe seven miles, maybe eight. He saw two Sledgehammer jets climbing in the sky and did not understand why. He yelled into the radio, "Stay low!"

Talmon, in the rear cockpit, also wondered what was going on back there with the interception four-ship formation. *Why are they so far from us? What could those two explosions in the air mean?*

On the hot mike in the Number 2 aircraft in the strike four-ship formation, the pilot and the navigator were debating what to do now. Just then, Yoni Ofir announced, "I'm hit," and Avner Naveh saw an aircraft diving to the ground and crashing into a huge shaft of fire. Gurion, leading the strike, got on the radio and announced, "We are continuing north," and everyone, including Naveh and Tamir, the navigator in the rear cockpit, completed their turns and headed out to the Mediterranean.

In Number 3 aircraft of the strike four-ship formation, Eitan Levy, the leader of the rear two-ship formation, decided that the best thing to do was to turn around and aid the escort four-ship formation, and in the midst of a sharp turn around leftward tilt, he pressed the "Panic" Button to jettison all loads.

What's this? The aircraft obtained a huge hit and went into an uncontrollable roll.

"You take it," Levy said, choking in his oxygen mask as it cut off his supply, to Blumi in the rear cockpit.

"I'll take it," Blumi responded.

Stay calm, Eliezer Blumenfeld said to himself. *You've practiced flying. Emergency situations. The pilot is in distress. At the end of flight training, they would give us the controls as a complete surprise, and we were supposed to take control and recover from the extreme situation, manage the radio and join the formation. Right now it's an emergency. Levy is choking in the front seat, and this aircraft is flying so fast and so low. And just a moment ago he executed such a strange accelerated stall.* He examined the wings. *Everything looks normal. No fire, and no warning light is flashing.* Then, as he calmed down and took control of his thoughts, damaged aircraft were filling the sky, and all of them were diving down into the ground. He did not know if they were Phantoms or MiGs, and there were no parachutes in the sky. Blumi completed the turn and tried to identify the location of the other aircraft of his formation. He hoped that the MiGs would leave them alone as he was busy with the flying itself. Particularly, he would like to be at home. Or for Levy to take over control again.

Gurion announced that they were continuing to head north, and Levy said that everything is okay. He took back the control.

Haim Rotem moved his head down to the cockpit to make sure to correctly identify the switch that would jettison the wing fuel tanks, and only them, like Lapidot said. He broke to the left, stayed low, and shifted horizontally, as he always did in training.

I'm not threatened, Rotem thought, sweeping his head from side to side, seeing clear sky. *Wait.* High up in the sky, he saw an aircraft climbing. Rotem accelerated and launched a missile at the MiG he detected up there.

"Break, break, there's a MiG sitting on us," Baruchi the navigator shouted loudly.

He broke wildly. *Damn, I don't have a chance to see if the missile hit.*

A large, billowing cloud of fire and smoke rose from the ground. *Where is Yoni Ofir? Why don't I see any parachutes in the sky?*

The airspeed decreased, as did the altitude. The MiG gave up on Rotem, which eased out of the break and saw Hayun not so far from him. With a MiG-21 closing in on him from behind, he reduced airspeed, and fired at it with his guns.

Hayun broke to the left, while slightly pulling up. Height 4,000. High above him in the sky, he saw a Sledgehammer climb even higher. *Who is that?*

Uri Arad "cleaned" all around, and now he saw two parachutes hanging in the sky. *What is that?* He turned his head to the other side, and his skin tingled. An MiG, so close, and coming in straight for them.

"Break hard, break hard, we have a MiG on our tail," he shouted at Hayun.

Hayun broke to the left as hard as he could, and the MiG slid away from them in a high- angle-off.

"Roll back!" Arad yelled.

Hayun rolled back, banking over to the right.

From the back seat, Arad knew that they were in trouble. The aircraft was slow, lacking energy. They were almost frozen in mid air.

Thump. Something knocked on the airframe.

Arad looked behind and saw burning wings, and in the mirror he saw that the fuselage was on fire and it was quickly getting closer, and in another minute he would be burning inside.

"We're hit, we're hit, jump!" he shouted at Hayun.

"One second," Hayun said.

But Arad knew that there isn't any time, and Hayun did not know what Arad knew about the fire that was threatening to consume them both. He pulled the handle and ejected himself out of the burning aircraft.

Maybe I'll be able to get this aircraft in control in another minute, Hayun thought. He glanced at the three mirrors in the cockpit, seeing a red fireball wrap around the fuselage. He attempted to level the wings, the ailerons were stuck. *That's it.* He pulled the handle.

Maj. Ben Eliahu saw the MiGs inching towards him and enabled an "aileron turn," which allowed him to tighten the turn. He knew that he needed to be precise on the turn—not too fast, as the large turn radius would allow a MiG to sit on his tail, but not too slow, or the aircraft would be "fixed" in the sky. Easy prey.

He then saw a MiG hit Yoni Ofir, his Number 2, who immediately began to burn in the sky.

Damn. He turned to the MiG and sat on his tail.

"Can I continue?" Ben Eliahu asked David.

"Continue, go on," David said eagerly, realizing that they were sandwiched between two MiGs, with the one behind them fixing to settle on their tail. In a situation like this in training, long ago, he would shout at the pilot to shake the MiG out of his tail, no matter what was in front of him in sight. But here and now, it was okay. One Sledgehammer was burning, there were friends hanging on parachutes in the air, over the Fellahin villages of the delta. All he cared about was winning a record for knocking a MiG off of the sky.

A little longer, hold back on alarming Ben Eliahu, he stopped himself, *let him bring down the MiG in front.*

Ben Eliahu placed a finger on the trigger, and in a split second, before squeezing the trigger, he saw an empty MiG canopy. The

Egyptian pilot, terrified at the realization that a Sledgehammer was sitting on his tail, ejected before one round was even fired at him. "Break," David yelled to Ben Eliahu, to get away from the MiG that was behind them. They tried to take him down as well, but they saw hordes of MiGs all over the sky. *Enough. There are moments when you know it's time to give up.*

Ben Eliahu shook the MiGs, headed out to the north, knowing that numbers 2 and 4 were on Egyptian soil, and number 3, Haim Rotem, was right behind him.

* * *

Uri Arad was hanging on his parachute in the sky.

I'm going to be captured, he thought to himself, feeling his rapid pulse and the sudden dryness of his lips. *I'm going to be captured. Bilha was wrong.*

Here are power lines. Just stay out of them. It's a good thing that the lifeboat that's supposed to hang down under the ejection seat failed to open. Here's the ground. A plowed field on the outskirts of a village, carved up by decades of muddy irrigation ditches. *A paratrooper's roll, better than any that I did in parachuting course,* he thought in a small moment of victory. An old man appeared out of nowhere and stood in front of him. Suddenly, more people came and surrounded him.

Everyone was shouting, and the reason for the debate was confusing to him, until he realized that, perhaps, his brown skin color made some of them think that they were dealing with an Egyptian pilot. He joined in their debate and was grateful to the sanity that he still had that kept him sharp and practical, and decided to portray a shocked Egyptian pilot. A mute one, as well. His one-man show held a few fans for a few seconds, until someone pointed out his white undershirt, claiming that it was not what Egyptian pilots wore. Another person agreed and screamed, "*Da mish Masri*" – He is not Egyptian!

Pushing, shouting, and fighting followed. Someone broke his thumb and then landed a blow to his head, and a trickle of blood flowed down his torso. Someone brandished a knife in front of his face. Then came an old man, accompanied by a few young people. He addressed the crowd around him and ordered them to step out of his way. He turned to Ori and said, "*Mah Thafs.*"

Uri knew what the old man said: "Don't be afraid." He calmed down a bit.

They took away his pistol, his g-suit, and tore off his Star of David necklace from his neck and finished by taking his air crewman watch. They then brought him towards a big village house, with a shouting and screaming crowd and the noise surrounding him.

They put him inside the house. He sat in the middle of a large room, surrounded by a group of youths, and thought that they were probably the sons of the old man as they rummaged through his papers from his g-suit. Repeated poundings threatened to break down the door, and it was clear to Ori that it was only a temporary arrangement, as the crowd outside still had not given up on getting their hands on him.

* * *

Hayun knew that it was about survival, just like navigator Yair David from the lead aircraft, who escaped from the Egyptians during the War of Attrition. Hanging on a parachute, he scanned the area beneath him. *Where can I find a cave or a tree or a rock, in the middle of all the swamp down there, something to help me hide from a pursuer?*

"*Whoa!*" A foreign object, huge, fast, terrifying, passed mere centimeters from his head. *Shit. A crazy Egyptian pilot. That's just what I need now, to die in a collision with a MiG.*

Anticipating another crazy pass, he scanned the sky above the Delta. There was no MiG. Far to the left, he saw an orange parachute hanging about. Uri.

Just below him, he saw two rows of houses with a central gravel path winding between them. *Like one of our towns,* Hayun thought, *except these are made of mud and clay, and I'm about to crash into one of them.*

With all of his strength, he pulled the strings to the right, gliding and bumping into the wall of a house in the center of town, and fell backwards into its backyard. Released from the ejection seat, he lowered his helmet and started to run. *The main thing is to get away from here.* However, it was not really possible to run through flooded fields.

His G-suit, life-jacket torso and boots made it even more difficult, and they were not the right mix for a life on the run. *Concentrate. Think. You have to escape from here. The villagers, they're the ones who murdered Goldwasser.*

He fought the mud. He fought for his life. His mind was blank. *Escape, escape.*

He heard voices speaking in Arabic from behind him. Two voices, and they were approaching. Hayun was struggling in heavy mud. *Don't look back, forward, just forward.*

The two voices got stronger. *What do I do?* A small brain cell that was still active told him that they were catching up with him. Freezing on account of the cold and anointed in a cloak of mud, he turned around. Two farmers. *Should I pull out my gun? No.* They peered at him uncertainly, but suddenly found their courage. They grabbed the straps of his torso harness and dragged him in the direction of the village. *Not good. I need to do something, but what?* He passed by the house he fled from. *There's my ejection chair.* An old Arab man, with his back bent, tried to catch up with them. *What does he have in his hand? It's an axe! What is he doing?* The axe was waved furiously at the chair, making sounds like explosions of thunder, sending the old man back a step or two. The three of them debated in the backyard of the house, standing on a paste of mud and excrement, as screeching chickens crossed past them, and there was the old devil once again. Hayun tried to avoid the blunt side of the axe that pounded the scruff of his neck, and he crashed in slow motion into the ground, like in the action films seen at the "Gat" Cinema in Tel Aviv, a city that seemed like a dream to him. The two other men by his side supported him and said something to the old man. It seemed they were convincing him to stop using the axe.

Through the daze that gripped him, he saw that he was in the center of the town, and men, women, and children walked around him. There was a procession of yelling men in shawls and women covered in black, shrieking and wailing. Hayun thought that these were not good signs, and someone behind him hit his shoulder to prove that he was right. That was the cue for a general assault, and everyone beat him on his head, shoulders, arms, and a particularly strong blows landed on his ear, which, began to heat up and beep like the RWR missile warning tone.

How will this end? Hayun shook, while his guards continued dragging him through the village center. Now came the children, who made an attempt to take out whatever was in his plastic pressure suit. Someone, perhaps a child, perhaps an adult, was trying to take off his air crewman watch from his wrist.

Then he saw a big peasant brandishing a pitchfork, like a man about to plunge it into an imaginary box in a pole vault competition. Hayun's functioning brain cells recognized that this was not the peasant's intent, nor was it a pole vaulting competition. This was the middle of a hostile village in the Nile Delta. *Get out, Hayun, run away.* He planted his feet and made a hard jump sideways, falling into a ditch at the side of the road, while dragging his two guards with him.

Waist deep in water, his legs covered in black mud and swampy, he dragged himself out of the ditch. It was too slippery, too deep, and he was too exhausted. *I can't give up, the guy with the pitchfork will get here.*

Clawing on the sides of the crevice, he tried to pull himself up and could not do so.

Something glimmered to his right. A scythe. Hayun threw his body to the opposite of the ditch, and the scythe struck the pressure suit's buckle that was on his foot.

With his consciousness still hazy, he sat, beaten, on the side of the ditch. Just then, out of nowhere, a huge hand, attached to a black body, pulled him out of the ditch. Egypt went dark.

He woke up as he was kneeling on all fours in the central path. The black man, who Hayun was sure was Sudanese, helped him up so that he could stand. He immediately fell to the ground. And again, and again. Finally, the Sudanese man understood that Hayun was too weak, which is what happens when the body of a person, even a pilot, receives countless blows, scythe stabbings and pitchfork proddings. He dragged Hayun behind him, up to the central path.

Again, he fell into darkness. He woke up again. He had difficulty breathing. He was lying on his back, and everything hurt. It was incredibly painful, and he trembled and shook. More breathing difficulties, and it was cold, so cold.

He heard noises around him, and realized that he was in a house. The sound was from the incessant yelling and pounding on the door. Screams. Next to him, he heard the sounds of goats and sheep. *Don't move, stay like this. Just like this.*

Through his squinting eyelids he saw an old woman pass by him, stand by his head, and talk to him. She tried to wake him up. *Don't respond to her, don't respond.* Garlic cloves were then put in his nostrils. No response. She then sprinkled something like perfume on his nose. Still nothing. Suddenly, he felt two thumbs pressing strongly into his eye sockets. The game was over, he knew, and he opened his eyes.

It was dark again. *What's the meaning of all of this shaking? What are these wheezes that are coming from my lungs as I breathe? Keep breathing. Keep breathing. Where am I? What is this? What's lying next to me? Ah, it's a man.*

"Uri?!"

"Kobi?!"

In the dark trunk of a swinging car, they joined hands. For a brief joyous moment, they were overwhelmed by a sense of safety. *We're back together. We'll be fine.*

12:00. *Northern Command*

The Minister of Defense arrived to the Northern Command headquarters in Tel Avital at noon. He was informed by the Chief of Northern Command that the 188th Brigade, under the temporary command of Brigade Commander Ben Hanan, had already crossed the minefields and was continuing the way east. He passed over the attack plan, and said that there was no need to deal with the territory near the front line. Rather, they were to forge ahead by the shortest possible way towards Damascus, even at night. "It is important for every meter taken to be in the direction straight to Damascus," Dayan emphasized.

"We assume that within twenty four hours, it will be possible to begin the counterattack against the Egyptian armored divisions in Sinai," Dayan said. "Therefore, you must prepare for the fact that this is the maximum amount of time that air support will be available."

From there, the Minister of Defense made his way to the forward command post of Rafael (Raful) Eitan's division, to sense the mood among the fighters. "The goal is to reach Damascus," Dayan reiterated to those in division headquarters. "The whole war, even on the Egyptian front, depends more and more on Damascus. Attack in a narrow slice. Pass directly to Damascus."

"How long do I have?" Raful interrupted.

"Thirty-six hours," Dayan said. He continued to Dan Lenner's division, repeating his insights and highlighted to the general, a combat veteran, "Within thirty-six hours, they are supposed to beg us not to enter Damascus."

12:45. The 201st Squadron

"Be calm, they will never kill me," Eitan Ben Eliahu drove the point into Sima Shavit, his favorite operations clerk. "Can you hear me? I will not die in combat." Sima knew that on the morning of October 11, Eitan and the others were heading out on a dangerous mission. In the operations room, on the radio frequency that they share, she heard the screams—"Break right, break left." It was noon. Sima already knew that they once again did not succeed to kill Ben Eliahu, but something bad happened there. Two aircraft from the octet were left behind. She then saw Haim.

Haim was a ginger, and contrary to stereotypes about those with red hair, he was always calm. Very calm. Haim also had a special sense of humor, small, English, mischievous. But now, none of that showed on Capt. (Res.) Haim Rotem, as he got off the bus, face flushed, and with agitated body language.

"Guys, extraordinary success," beamed Sami from Intelligence, meeting the broken Banha team at the Squadron's steps. "They went up in the sky, we can sense them."

Blumi stood in front of him, thrust two fingers up, which Sami was sure were marking a V, and smiled.

Levy, Blumi's pilot, who understood his navigator on the ground as well and also knew the meaning of the two fingers being waved at Sami, asked, "Tell me, was this worth two aircraft and four pilots?"

"I know it's difficult for you," Sami said, turning serious. "It is for me as well. But know that it was worth the price. Um Hashiva is celebrating—they are receiving all wireless communications from the General Staff to the units on the Egyptian front."

In the briefing room, it became clear why the strike four-ship formation did not return to help. "We could not go back due to fuel problems," Gurion explained. "If we insisted on returning, we would become tangled in combat without fuel."

Next, they tried to comprehend the depth of the crisis. Two aircraft were taken down in air combat. Two dead, and two prisoners. The leadership of the interception four-ship formation was flawed, they whispered. Someone in the management did not do his homework. Someone did not consider, did not take in the complexity of the task at Banha. The writing was on the wall.

But above all, the beleaguered group wanted to clarify one issue. Why did the interception four-ship formation escort as they did? After all, it was clear that the MiGs, which had not succeeded in intercepting them on their way in, would wait for them upon their exit, just as they did. Therefore, the most suitable thing would have been to fly away, as fast as possible. Some noticed the large distance that was opened up between the strike four-ship formation and the interception four-ship formation. Others were sure that the interception four-ship formation slowed down. Most of them thought that this was unacceptable on the Delta, in the face of twenty MiGs that were rushing towards them, with a fuel issue that would cause you to have to eject on the way home, as well staff problems since the moment that they received the mission.

Everyone in the briefing room also realized that urge for revenge that comes after not having prevented ejections in air combat is an essential part of the nature of interception pilots. The ethos of the IAF. When the scent of the hunt takes over your nose, you put aside all of the priorities of the mission for which you were sent.

This is particularly true of Eitan Ben Eliahu, who, deep in his heart, is an interception pilot with a knife between his teeth. Therefore, some thought, Eitan was looking for a dogfight, even there, unnecessarily.

No one got up.

Perhaps it was mental fatigue in facing this new blow that has been added to the previous ones, perhaps the dominant personality of Ben Eliahu, their most revered pilot, who never made mistakes in escorting.

They were sitting in their seats, even Haim Rotem, flushed with rage, and silent.

13:00. Chamber of the Head of Central Command

On Thursday morning, Lt. Col. Shimon Lasser, who only a few months prior, passed through command of the Air Control Unit at Mitzpe Ramon and resigned to pursue studies, found himself assigned at the Head Air Command at IAF Headquarters. On the other side of the phone line, directly connected to the control unit at Mount Meron, he began receiving reports from the Air Force in the Golan. They were painful.

A aircraft was shot down. And another. And another.

Lasser took down what he heard. Six aircraft are down.

Maj. Gen. Rafi Bar-Lev, the Intelligence Department Chief, suddenly shouted, "Benny, how many more aircraft do you want to bury in the ground?"

"Up to seven," Benny said, "up to seven."

"Another one is down," Lasser informed his commander and sulked his face towards the ground of the chamber.

"Let them continue to attack," said Benny, who had sworn that he would protect the aircraft. However, the IDF needed to bring the Syrians down to their knees, and not a muscle moved on his face.

15:00. Air Force

Just before 15:00, other aircraft were sent to continue the series of strikes on strategic targets, which was bringing the war to the door of the average Syrian citizen, accelerating the process of breaking and removing Israel's northern enemy from the war circle. Twenty fuel tanks in the large fuel depot at Khan Al-Aysh, east of Damascus, were destroyed. Black smoke covered the sky of the Middle East and darkened the national mood in Syria.

16:00. Northern Command

"We need to get to a situation in which Syria will raise an outcry that the IDF is about to walk into Damascus, so that they request from the Russians, 'get the Jews out of here,'" the Defense Minister reiterated on his visit to the Northern Command Chief, accompanied by the Chief of Staff.

"Pressure to pursue a ceasefire tomorrow is beginning to accumulate," Dayan said, trying to make it clear to the military staff that the hourglass was running out. "Kissinger asked to postpone the meeting of the Security Council by 48 hours, before the shouts of woe come from the Syrians, which would push the Security Council to force a ceasefire. Move quickly. Express train to Damascus."

Night. The 201ˢᵗ Squadron

There was a single aircraft in the sky. Lt. Gil Regev was at the controls. Lt. Itzik Baram, the cool-headed navigator, was in the rear cockpit.

"Wake me when we get close to Sharm," he requested of Regev.

Sharm will come in a moment. The air controller got on the radio, "I see a sea vessel on the water. I will vector you towards it."

Baram was asleep.

In the faint moonlight, Regev identified a trail of waves formed behind two warships.

"Itzik, wake up."

"Let's fire at them," the sleepy navigator volunteered his first conscious thoughts.

Gil knew that for a mission like this, the likes of which he had not practiced, he would need another aircraft that would illuminate the area below with parachute flares. *One doesn't strike after he dispensed his own flares. This can easily result in blinding the eyes and in consequence lead to a vertigo.*

Down in the water, the two warships identified a threatening aircraft, and split their courses among the waves of the bay.

"I am taking the one on the right," Regev said to the controller.

"Fire on them," the controller acknowledged.

Damn. We don't have any bombs. I forgot that we are on a CAP (Combat Air Patrol) mission.

"Then let's strafe with the guns," Baram offered.

Guns? For that, you'd need to make a short-range strafe run. On a night like this?

"*Let's do it*, we'll stick a bunch of rounds in it," Regev said.

Baram called out the altitude. Regev tried to concentrate on aiming. Too short. The rounds did not reach their destination.

They descended more and more into the blackness that surrounded them on all sides, and Baram continued calling out the altitude. Finally, they saw hits and explosions on board, and if they stayed one moment more they would not have made it out of this low pass.

They returned to base for landing.

"We've received reports of a commando attack," said the controller in the tower, "I cannot illuminate the runway."

"Turn them on for a moment," Regev pleaded, "I have no fuel, I need to land and I can't in this darkness."

"It's not allowed," replied the frightened voice on the other end of the channel.

"Do you want us to eject while on top of you?" Regev asked in a casual manner.

"Wait, wait," said the controller in the tower.

"Turning on the lights dimly," the controller returned with an answer.

Dim is a lot better than darkness, Gili thought, knowing that he had enough fuel for just one landing pattern. He extended the arresting hook, and "crashed" onto the runway as if it were an aircraft carrier. He was arrested by the runway's arresting system cable.

Night. Office of the Chief of Staff

In the debate last night, I ordered commanders to attack Syria without consideration of the missiles, Peled recalled. *It is essential that ground forces attack tomorrow with a sense of trust and confidence in the Air Force. I told them. That's how we did it. 330 successful attack sorties, most of the area of the breach. Yet again, I am being charged with high-price fighting. We lost ten more aircraft today, mostly from missiles. 67 altogether. Another 40 or so are being repaired. Slightly progressing. We've lost almost a third of our forces. How much longer can we handle this depletion? When will the airlift finally begin?*

A few minutes after midnight, Lt. Gen. David Elazar invited the IAF Commander to his office.

"It turns out that you can't rely on a promise from the Americans," he said to Peled. "The aircraft that Washington has promised us are not on the horizon."

"We are approaching the red line," Peled said. "If the army is planning major attacks on two fronts, it will be desirable to implement them within the next two days, otherwise it will be difficult to provide the necessary coverage from the air."

Late at Night. The 201st Squadron

Late at night, as he tossed in bed, with images of the battle over Banha passing before his eyes, Haim Rotem discovered that he had lost his hunger to take down aircraft.

Something in the sight of two Sledgehammer jets burning in the sky would not free him from the feeling. *Even in dogfights, we have prisoners? Has the world turned upside down?* It turned and turned over in his mind, and just before he sank into sleep, he understood that the animals that they had been trained to hunt could now remove their skin as well. *Yes. The world is turned upside down. It's a fact.*

October 12

Red Line

Friday started so beautifully, with scents of autumn, chirping birds, and a final victory over the Syrians that looked right at Israel's fingertips.

While the first plumes of light fought to expel the last of the darkness, and despite the dwindling capital that the IAF Commander warned the Chief of Staff about a few hours prior, the Air Force Commander sent his men, for the first time since "Model," to address a few missile batteries in Syria.

"The attacks last night proved that the Syrians have received a new shipment of missiles," the best six men of the 201st Squadron were informed. "The batteries are once again revealing their sharp fangs. We are going out to crush them."

These targets were picked with tweezers, thought Capt. (Res.) Dan Haloutz, leading the three ship formation. *Distant, solitary batteries, and none of them are the threatening SA-6s. The wounds of "Model" still haven't healed.*

They flew low along the Jordan and Hula Valleys. They passed Metula. Haloutz was leading secretly, hidden behind the ridge of

Mount Hermon. They are already gliding down the eastern slopes towards their targets and… the whole sky was filled with black mushroom clouds.

Damned Intelligence, No. 3, the young Lt. Gideon Eilat grumbled. "We identified 20 Gundish AAAs at the target proximity." *Come on. There aren't ten meters in the sky without a black cloud. This isn't 20 that are shooting at us, this is 120.*

At 06:05, the three ship formation pulled up to strike altitude, ignoring the unceasing view of death fired in their direction. In the leading aircraft, Haloutz and Baram identified the target, a missile battery located south Khan Ash-Sheikh, not far off of the main road that connects Quneitra to Damascus. Haloutz executed a wingover maneuver, dove in the direction of the target, aimed, pressed the pickle button, and saw Shalev and Eilat diving in after him. One direct hit, and then another. A third direct hit, and the battery was destroyed. They headed home. *It seems that one really can attack batteries in Syria and return safely.*

"Regev, to the Briefing Room," the operator shouted on the speaker, before he stepped his foot in the building after the end of his night flight that concluded in the adventure in far-away Sharm.

"The Syrians have taken in the lessons of the Six-Day War," they were informed in the briefing room. "The air base that was destroyed is back to functioning status. We are returning to destroy the Damascus International Airport and Hulhula."

Gil Regev shudders. *Damascus. Where Shaniboi and Assael are being tortured with electricity. And Shmueli is my navigator. Wow, Shmueli is young. He's not Itzik, and this is not Sharm.*

At 06:10, the Damascus Airport strike four-ship formation accelerated on the runway, and grouped perfectly in order behind Capt. (Res.) Adi Benaya, the leader.

"Missile switch!" reminded the "Rhino" in the rear cockpit of Number 3.

"OFF," answered Eli Zohar in the forward chamber.

"Switch it to ON," Rhino instructed.

"I'm leaving it on OFF," Zohar said. "Do you remember that story about Melnik launching a missile involuntarily?"

"At least set it to HEAT," the "Rhino" advised from behind.

"We're leaving it in OFF," Zohar ended the debate.

The Lebanese Bekaa. The last turn until Damascus. A cloud screen lay above the surface.

Compound interest, Benaya reflected in the lead aircraft of the formation. *Vapor and hot air mixed with smoke from the fuel that we hit last night.*

"Number 1, pay attention," Number 2, Barnea, reported, "A four-ship formation of MiGs is above us."

"Eye contact," Benaya answered. "We're continuing."

"Descend below the smoke," Benaya ordered in his quiet voice, as if they were in the midst of a bombing exercise on a training range.

Great, Benaya thought in the cockpit of the leading aircraft. *The task was to attack and destroy. We attacked and destroyed. We only left clear skies. We don't have enough fuel to get into dogfights.*

He turned towards home, bringing the formation with him. *Count them. Another one.*

"Number 4, MiG at 12 o'clock," he reported to Gil Regev.

"Gili, break!"

Gil broke. His aircraft was tired. *What happened to the bastard?*

"Gil, break!"

Gil broke. *Damn it, this MiG will catch up with me.*

"*Oish*," Gil Regev sighed in the hot mic. He jettisoned the external drop tanks that were forgotten in the storm of fragility. He smiled as his Sledgehammer returned to normal.

The MiG would not let go. *Wait, you son of a bitch, let me gather some airspeed. Now let's see you,* he smiled below his visor. He let the MiG pass over in front of him, just like Shaniboi taught him. As it passed, Regev sat on its tail, launched a missile, and drove the son of a bitch right into the ground.

Now Benaya came on the radio, saying in his characteristic calm, "Number 4, report position."

Just then, another MiG sat on Regev and started strafing with his guns. Shmueli saw from his rear cockpit and was mesmerized by the white helmet of the pilot that was trying to kill them. He was sure that, any moment, the rounds would penetrate the cockpit, and just like that he would be dead.

"Break, you son of a bitch, break!" Shmueli screamed, copying Yossarian's famous battle cry from *Catch-22*.

"Number 4, what's your position?"

Regev broke, descended low, and gathered airspeed. His mask slipped down his face from the sweat. He remembered that Benaya was waiting for the report on the radio, "Number 4, tangled with MiGs."

Benaya, not understanding Regev's snarl, asked again, "4, what is your position?"

I'm still over Damascus, Regev knew, *and I have to get out of here. In order to do that, I need to break more and disengage the MiGs using my afterburners. But I don't have sufficient fuel for this game.*

Boom.

"Number 4, your position?"

"Number 4 cannot disengage," he said. "tangled with MiGs."

I need to save Number 4, thought Number 3, Maj. Eli Zohar. He galloped with full afterburners, realized that Regev was in a disadvantaged position and attempted to improve his position in the sky. He locked a missile onto the MiG, and pressed. Nothing happened.

"Why isn't the rocket launching?" Zohar gasped on the hot mic.

The "Rhino", who was also fighting the G-maneuvers, and especially a lack of oxygen as a result of the high loads, could not remember anything about the missile arming switches that were remained in their OFF position earlier in the flight. In a hoarse gasp, he let out: "I don't know," and returned to his personal oxygen war.

In the end, the MiG panicked and left Gili alone, and everyone managed to break off and make their way home. Someone reported to Number 4 that the bang that they heard was not imaginary, and the left wing had a hole the size of a bucket.

Hang on, buddy, Gil Regev urged, *hang on.*

At 06:05, during the complications with MiGs over Damascus, another four-ship formation, under the leadership of Amnon Gurion and Yair David, smashed the runways at the air base at Hulhula. For the Sledgehammer jets of the 201ˢᵗ, this was their fourth visit there. They proved to the Syrians that they were dealing with an air force full of bulldogs: tenacious, never stopping until their enemies shouted 'enough'.

Morning-Afternoon. Office of the Chief of Staff and the Senior Command Post

On Friday morning, nothing was really clear to the limited staff meeting in the Chief of Staff's office.

True, the destruction of the 'Third Temple' was no longer on the horizon, and the spirit of Masada was no longer blowing throughout the office. However, the reinforced attack in the Golan failed to break the spirit of the Syrians, and they still had many tanks standing on defensive lines on the outskirts of Damascus. The Iraqis were on their way to join, and would soon have 1,000 on the front, and there was a need to not poke the bear.

"The Syrians haven't collapsed, and it doesn't seem that they will," Dado said, "certainly not in the near term. And since certain achievements have been made in Syria, militarily and territorially, we need to move as quickly as possible to counterattack on the Egyptian front, before the Security Council is able to force a ceasefire and prevent the army to cross. We need to stick an anchor on the west bank of the Canal and create a deterrence of fear, if only partially, in the hearts of the Egyptian forces that invaded our territory."

Everyone knew that, despite repeated assurances by the United States, which claimed that the shipments of weapons and supplies were on their way to Israel "very soon," Israel still had not received any logistical support. Such support would at least have balanced the involvement of the superpowers.

"We may very soon reach the critical point," Maj. Gen. Benny Peled reiterated, announcing his assessment of the situation in the Office of the Chief of Staff. "We have lost 67 aircraft so far. Soon, with the significant lack of air crews in general and Phantom crews in particular, it will no longer be possible for us to launch assistance missions. We will only be able to defend the country's skies."

"In fact, only in the center of the country," he concludes his apocalyptic vision.

At 09:30, Lt. Gen. (Ret.) Haim Bar-Lev, arrived at the Senior Command post in Tel Aviv and presented his plan for a successful operation. Bar-Lev agreed with the Chief of Staff's assessment, and he was able to see the best course of action. "Our best bet is to cross over tomorrow night," he said, "when the bridging equipment arrives. There's no point in waiting for the Egyptian armored forces to begin an operation, push back and destroy it in the Sinai, as the Deputy Chief of Staff suggested. It's possible that we would destroy more tanks, but with the ceasefire, we would be left with large Egyptian forces on our territory, without gaining any territory ourselves."

The Head of Military Intelligence supported the plan of the pair of Chiefs of Staff. Now, it is the IAF Commander's turn. "We would need to cross as soon as possible," said Peled, "as long as the Air Force has the ability to provide coverage and full assistance."

At 12:00, Moshe Dayan joined the discussion.

"If the ceasefire is declared, our forces will have to stand where they are now, which is not a good position for us," he said, and for a moment, it seems as if there was a third side of the Chiefs of Staff triangle that was advocating crossing.

"If the war continues," the Defense Minister predicted, "more reinforcements will flow in: Iraqis, Moroccans, and Jordanians, and it will take months until we accumulate enough strength to decide the battle. I understand that the IDF wants a ceasefire as soon as possible, and sees that the best way to achieve it is by crossing the Canal. I, on the other hand, cannot see a benefit from this attack. In my opinion, it would be best to accelerate progress in the Golan, at any cost, in order to get Damascus within artillery range."

14:30. Office of the Prime Minister

Once again, the War Cabinet convened at the Prime Minister's Office.

Except for a few short bouts of sleep at her home in Ramat Aviv, the Prime Minister spent all of her time in her crowded office, surrounded by the scent of nicotine. A woman of 75 years, a cancer patient, conducted meeting after meeting with a firm hand, a clear head, and a sharp mind. Despite the lack of sleep, the deep despair that shook her throughout the first 24 hours of combat, a terrified Defense Minister, and the IDF not able to fulfill its promises, she was constantly there: a beacon of sanity at the top of the pyramid.

"We've reached a point in which we need a ceasefire," the Chief of Staff said. "Otherwise, we will find ourselves in a war of attrition, with terrible borders, and without the ability to reorganize the army. The best way to accomplish this, is to force Egypt to push for one by crossing into their territory."

"I suggest that we cross, without any delay, as soon as tomorrow, the night of October 13-14," Lt. Gen. (Ret.), Haim Bar-Lev, reinforced the Chief of Staff's statement.

The assessment of the leaders of the country, political and military leaders alike, was that the Egyptians would not agree to a ceasefire in the current scenario. Therefore, the moves proposed by the two Chiefs of Staff were meant as the quickest, most efficient way to force Egypt to request a ceasefire—betting on a bold crossing, significant damage to Egyptian forces west of the Canal, and the undermining of the Egyptian leadership's confidence.

Would it turn out that the crossing operation produces the expected big rewards? On the contrary. Now, it would be the Egyptian's turn to beg for a ceasefire, and our turn to reject it while, at the same time, pursuing and destroying their forces and expanding the enclave in their territory.

"The crossing will involve a tough push of about 10-12 kilometers to get to the Canal," said Deputy Chief of Staff, Maj. Gen. Israel Tal, pouring cold water on the recommendations of a couple of Chiefs of Staff.

"After the breach, the IDF will have to cross, which it is still not ready for, either in terms of equipment or training."

"Considering the stakes, and the risks," Tal continued, "and considering the difficulty in defeating Egyptian infantry forces equipped with anti-tank launchers, there is another option—combat against enemy armor in open territory."

"Another thing," Tal added, "The Egyptians may already anticipate our move and could send two more armored divisions into Sinai. Even before we began, the process would fail."

"Tzvika, your office needs you immediately," Lou Kedar, the Prime Minister's secretary, said as he entered the discussion room. The head of the Mossad left the room.

"Tomorrow, or by Sunday at the latest, we are expecting the Egyptians to send three paratrooper divisions to the area of Bir Gifgafa and Mitla," Zvi Zamir informed the high-ranking forum in the Prime Minister's Office, while adding, "After the Egyptian paratroopers take over and destroy command centers and grab territory and vital crossings, they will send two more armored divisions over the Canal."

"Now, we are going to blow up hundreds of their tanks," Gen. Tal said, jubilantly, seeing that the work of the righteous is done by others.

"You will see soon that the Egyptians will save us," Dayan concluded, his eye sparkling.

Alright, the war cabinet declared, *let's let them come in. We will set up a classic defensive battle. We'll destroy them on our territory. The crossing can wait.*

Afternoon. The 201st Squadron

The partial damage done to Damascus International Airport required a Second Act, and IAF Headquarters decided to send the 201st Squadron to finish the job.

Two hours before the beginning of Shabbat on Friday evening, Capt (Res.) Dani Haloutz found himself leading an operational four-ship formation charged with attacking Damascus International Airport. *Me? Lead the four-ship formation? Damascus? Has someone fallen on their head? I mean, this is something set aside for those of the Generation of Giants: Ben Eliahu, Huldai, Peled, Gurion, and Benaya. And here I am leading Rotem the Ginger, who has more seniority than I do, and Bigelman, a Mirage squadron leader, all the way to Damascus.*

At 15:30, he caressed the black radar radome of the Sledgehammer. *We're friends, remember?* He then immediately took off as the head of a Sledgehammer four-ship formation that was retracting their landing gears in, and in a cloud of black smoke, making their way to attack Damascus International Airport.

It'll be fine, Haloutz reflected. *The lessons from this morning's strike have been learned. Fact. We are on a different route, and right behind us is Bigelman's four-ship formation. If anything goes wrong over Damascus, the Mirages will take care of it.*

Just north of Beirut, they identified the river that cuts through a canyon, and flying low inside of it, they made their way to the Syrian desert north of Damascus. They turned south over the town of Duma, east of the Syrian capital.

They were in the last leg before having to pull up. 30° to the right. The RWR system began to beep.

Avner Naveh's position was at the end of the convoy, with Amnon Tamir in the navigator's seat.

"Did you see that?" Naveh asked, pointing to a missile, apparently launched at them.

"It's not coming towards us," said Tamir, an aeronautical engineer by education, who knew a thing or two about the RWR display and its various indications.

You're right. The missile skipped over them and continued elsewhere. *Wait, it's headed for the Mirages!*

"Mirages, break! Missile!" Tamir shouted on the radio.

Over the Damascus International Airport, the sky was covered with AAA puffs of black smoke, among which the Sledgehammer four-ship formation maneuvered, executed wingovers, dove, released bombs and hit.

Where are the Mirage aircraft? Haloutz wondered. *A bit of artillery and missiles, and they scatter?*

They returned to the wing for a joint debriefing session.

You are heroes. You are crazy. This is what you guys do? You go through this twice a day? Mirage pilots showed glances of admiration for their brothers in the wing, neutralizing the poison arrows that were pointed and prepared to be launched at them.

A great day, Haloutz thought. *I led a four-ship formation, everything ended well, and now, for the masseuse.*

In the room of the 201st Squadron's Deputy Commander, a few of the air crew were entrusting their aching back and neck muscles to the hands of a gorgeous woman. They had to release their muscles, they told her.

Zetelny, taller and sturdier than everyone, discovered that the girl with oil on her hands had a soul, or a heart, or was just created, and she was using all of it on his strongly built body and his woven musculature. He asked himself, *what can I do with this now?* Using willpower to suppress the pleasant tingling, he sailed to other realms of his consciousness, war-like realms. He reviewed in his head the unsuccessful attempt that they made in the morning to destroy the bridge between Lebanon and Syria. He then recalled that Koren and Ami took fire and ejected.

He felt her massaging him and thought, *despite everything, it's best to be a pilot. We die clean, with a beautiful memory and oil on our body.*

14:00-18:00. Syria

On the afternoon of Friday, October 12, the Iraqi expeditionary forces joined the war. Determined and belligerent, 100 tanks attacked the right flank of Dan Lenner's division, which was surprised by the timing, the place, and the power, and withdrew its forces to a new defensive line.

On Friday afternoon, the announcement that "we need to get to Damascus within 48 hours" sounded ridiculous and detached from reality.

The exhausted IDF troops met fierce resistance and persistent fighting. They counted the dozens of their freshly killed, which were joining the long, intolerable list of those killed in containment battles. They failed to reach the line they were meant to arrive at within the first 24 hours.

Now there were these fresh reinforcements from Iraq.

Could the Syrians, with their brothers from the land of the Euphrates and the Tigris, swing the battle once again into their favor?

16:30. Office of the Prime Minister

"Our forces have advanced to within thirty kilometers of Damascus... the outskirts of the city are within artillery range," Mordecai Gazit wrote to Simcha Dinitz, "We are bombing the Al-Mazzah Air base..."

17:30. Office of the Prime Minister

A few minutes after sunset, Mordecai Gazit sent another telegram to Ambassador Dinitz, according to which the government agreed to arrange a ceasefire without any delay.

Dinitz was confused. Ten minutes ago, he sent his reaction to Gazit's joyful telegram to Washington. He quoted Kissinger as saying, "When you get to Damascus, you can use the public transit."

The day before, and on that day as well, he received telegrams from Israel asking him to suspend the ceasefire any way he could, so as to allow the IDF to improve its situation on the ground. The telegram from 16:30 showed that the IDF was indeed on the right path. What was happening now?

The sobering six days of the campaign changed everything that Golda Meir, Israel's Prime Minister thought of the superiority of the IDF. She was informed right then of the surprise Iraqi attack that disrupted the course the IDF forces were breaking through the Golan. She estimated that in the near future, it would not be possible to push the Egyptians back to the west bank of the Canal. She was concerned of potential Soviet intervention, even direct military intervention. She was frustrated in light of the foot-dragging U.S. officials, ignoring the promises that they gave, and despite urgent calls for help, desperately, repeatedly, delaying the supply of tanks and aircraft. She was aware that the army's tanks were going and running out, and strike fighter, which had now become the IDF's best weapon on the ground as well, were nearing the red line, and soon would not be able to offer a helping hand during an attack, having to focus on defensive tasks exclusively. She had taken in the fact that not following through with a ceasefire with the Egyptians in the near future would be followed by a prolonged war of attrition on current lines; this would present Israel with a host of serious new operational and logistical issues, which could necessitate the drafting of teenagers, recruitment of Diaspora Jews, and other apocalyptic steps like those taken during the War of Independence. Weighing all of this, Golda Meir authorized Simcha Dinitz, the ambassador in Washington, to notify US Secretary of State Henry to allow a draft resolution calling for a ceasefire, and preferably during the night.

Evening. The 201ˢᵗ Squadron

As Friday evening turned into Saturday, and a sense of the sacred replaced the everyday, they talked once again about Zemer. *We have an organized squadron leader, paternal, attentive, and with a heart of gold. But that it not enough. It is war now. War. We need a leader. Someone that will push us by the force of his personality and performance. We'll go with blind obedience into the flames and the smoke. Someone else.*

In Nurit and Gil Regev's apartment in the family housing section, Regev hosted his friends, Motti Reder and Amiram Eliasaf.

A glass of red wine and blessings, an everyday ceremony broke the routine of war. Another day that had finished. Sitting in the modest living room sofa set, they listened to Gil, who was counting the MiGs that came out from nowhere in the sky, which almost killed his daily ritual, and Amiram, who was counting the exact number of hits on Hulhula in Syria, and Reder, who said, "You lazy people. One mission, and that's it?" He counted the number of attacks on Syrian military camps in Qatana and the air base in Damiya, and the frightening SA-6, whose launched missile was alerted by the RWR system. The missile was evaded.

As the blood alcohol level increased, they declared, "This is a stupid war." They promised, even swore, that if one of them died, the other two would pay him their respects and would piss on his grave.

Afterwards, Eliasaf cozied up on the bed, on Nurit's side. Regev, and Reder, settled in the living room, could not stop telling jokes. Finally, they fell asleep to their dreams. They were always the same dreams: missiles, aircraft, and a long, long fall, all the way down.

October 13

Ben Eliahu Takes the Lead

Thousands of miles from Moscow, where the Soviet media announced the night before that the USSR could no longer remain indifferent to the crimes of the Israeli army, the Israelis were unaware of the deep concern of the Soviet leadership regarding the fall of the Syrian front and the danger it posed to Damascus. Unaware of the heightened state of readiness that was announced in two of the Soviet military's aerial divisions, the aircrews of the 201st Squadron woke up in the early hours of Saturday to another day of combat.

"The target is the Al-Mazzah Air base, southwest of Damascus," they were told in the briefing room in the morning. "The attack will be carried out by two of our four-ship formations. In addition to the air base, we will also attack the concealed cluster of aircraft underground hangars, located in an orchard near the runways."

"The pull up onto the target will be performed before sunrise, so that we'll avoid being blinded by the sun. We will arrive from the Hermon mountain ridge, which will shield our aircraft from Syrian radar. After we pass through the mountains, approximately ten miles before getting at the air base, we will pull up to 15,000 feet altitude, release the cluster bombs, and turn to go back home."

"One more thing. The choice of a high altitude strike approach is the decision of the IAF HQ, based on intelligence information, indicating that the air base lacks the protection of surface-to-air missiles."

This isn't okay, thought Capt. Amnon Gurion, who led the forward formation. *There are going to be delays, which will make us late for takeoff by 15 minutes. The sun will hit us right in the face.*

05:45. The Hermon mountain ridge. They broke east and climbed to the designated altitude. The blinding light, along with the cloud cover and the morning mists, created a blank wall that prevented any activity all the way to the destination.

This isn't okay, thought Capt. Adi Benaya, who led the second formation. *A weak start.. Gurion took off late, and we went overboard, leaving five minutes after him. We're only left a two-ship formation.*

It's impossible to carry this out, Gurion thought. *The sun is in my eyes, the whole Damascus basin is covered in mist, and we can't see anything. We're returning home.*

If we've made it this far, it's worth a try, thought Yair David, in the rear cockpit. He recalled that only three days ago, despite all of the difficulties, he insisted that the mission was possible, and he and Perry performed excellently in the Delta.

"This is war," Benaya said from the front chamber, neither asking or stating.

"This is war," David answered from the rear cockpit.

"We're continuing," Benaya said, unsure.

"We're going forward," David answered.

"Try to come in at a lower altitude," Gurion suggested, understanding that Benaya was continuing.

He's right, thought Benaya. *That's the only way we can escape the sun.* He lowered his nose and straightened out. Avner Naveh was sticking right behind him.

They passed the camps in Qatana. Every Syrian below them with a weapon pointed at the aircraft and fired in their direction. *I need to break out quickly,* Benaya thought, beginning to zigzag through the sky, with Naveh behind him. That was a mistake. It was dangerous to perform loops with an aircraft that was nearly scraping the ground. They climbed to 2,000 feet, and continued to zigzag with full burners on.

From the navigator's seat, David saw Naveh's aircraft as it passed alongside them, with the trail tracer lit behind him. He maneuvered between them in a sky that was made brighter by the first light of Saturday morning.

We should climb higher, Benaya decided, *before we're taken out by the AAA and all the other shit they're shooting at us. We will strike from above. I should stick to the original plan. Who knows, I might still be able to identify the target.*

Just then, the RWR beeped. In the background of the emerging morning light, Benaya identified "electric poles" with flames were launched into the sky. He understood that the plan needed to be changed. He murmured quietly, "Someone dropped the ball with the intelligence report. What a shame."

The sun was glaring, lighting up the big wheel in the sky, dotted with thousands of AAA puffs of black smoke, and Benaya pulled up, shortening his climb out time. He executed a wingover, dove, set the pipper on the target, and released four tons of bombs. *A good shot.*

BOOM. Something hit the aircraft.

"Fire on the left wing," David reported from the rear cockpit.

Naveh released his load of bombs, glanced in the direction of Number 1, and saw a big fire under the left wing and a cloud of thick, black smoke.

"Number 1, you're on fire," he alerted them on the radio.

They're right, Benaya thought. He saw a long, unfamiliar shadow trailing on the ground, dragging behind a silhouette of a Sledgehammer jet. *The damn gun shell is going to take out my aircraft. I need to leave quickly and at a low altitude so as to avoid getting hit by a missile as well. There's the Damascus River. Excellent! We're out of missile range. It's possible to climb and get away from the flak, and gain altitude in case we need to eject.*

This enduring beast will bring us back home safely, David thought under the acrylic canopy. He saw fire and smoke close to their rear, yet felt that Benaya was still in control of the aircraft. The air controller vectored to Ramat David.

Benaya began banking to the left, towards home, and from the navigator's seat, Yair David noticed that the fire was intensifying and the black smoke was growing longer and longer. Suddenly, he thought that maybe they would not be able to get home, and that despite the aircraft's sturdiness, they would have to eject. *If so,* he thought, *it's preferable to do so over less hostile territory.* With the fingers, he measured on the map the distances to the Mediterranean Sea, and found the shortest route.

"Take two-seven-zero to the sea," he said to Benaya.

"I'm taking it," Benaya replied.

Avner Naveh was concerned. Just a moment ago, he scrambled a rescue helicopter, announcing that Number 1 was on fire, and he was accompanying him all the way. However, he was still concerned. *Fire and electricity do not mix well,* he thought, seeing Benaya's missiles being launched from their launchers uncontrollably.

Seeing fire approaching the Plexiglas canopy, Naveh shouted, "Eject!" *At least we'll get to the coastline,* Benaya thought, though he was not so sure it was possible with stuck flight controls, an unresponsive engine, and an aircraft that was acting as its own master.

Naveh shouted, "Number 1, eject, eject, it's exploding!"

I'm not ejecting, Benaya insisted. That was when he saw the coastline, and felt that the steeply diving Sledgehammer also understood that the mission was completed. Benaya knew that the moment had come; he gained a few more meters over the water, and pulled the handle.

David, the former paratrooper, shouted, "Pull to the west!"

Benaya, who never completed the jump course, did not know how to pull his parachute to the west, and he let things take their course. It is hard for an aircrew member to trust things that are not under his control, but he had no choice. He thought about the date, October 13, and suddenly remembered that the number 13 is considered good for Jews. He then decided that the number only disappointed at the beginning, when the aircraft was hit by a shell, but then recovered and allowed him to get to the Mediterranean, and would provide him a safe landing as well.

The number 13 did not disappoint, and Benaya, who had never been on a parachute before, embraced his beginner's luck.

As they swayed in two orange lifeboats between the waves, Benaya and David heard constant machine gun fire and saw fishing boats on their way to intercept them. They knew that it was not friendly fire, and that this was not a rescue party. Naveh and Eliasaf, who had joined him, acted as two guardian angels, trying to instill fear in the fishing boat hunting party. However, the fishing boats ignored the low-flying Sledgehammer jets, and continued pursuing their targets between the waves as if there was nothing.

After following standard procedures for apprehending "suspects," Naveh and Eliasaf, having understood the life-threatening danger that was heading towards their friends, decided to strike the fishing boats. They destroyed the first boat with gun fire, sending a message to the others, who fled for their lives.

Afterwards, a two-ship formation of Mirages took their place and the rescue helicopter finally arrived. David and Benaya were pulled out of the water and brought to Ramat David, where they were left trembling, bruised, and limping.

07:00. (01:00 Washington Time)

Thousands of miles from Ramat David, on the other side of the Atlantic Ocean, Washington D.C., the capital of the United States of America and of the free world, was asleep and quiet by the Potomac River. Only the lights in the White House were still on.

At 01:00 Eastern Time, US Secretary of Defense James Schlesinger informed Gen. Motta Gur, the Israeli military attaché in Washington, that after a hectic night of discussions, President Nixon ordered the departure of the airlift of supplies to Israel. "The first convoy will leave today with the emergency equipment that you've requested, as well as ten Phantom jets."

"You will continue attacking," Secretary of State Henry Kissinger simultaneously updated Ambassador Dinitz, "We will ensure a regular supply."

The previous twenty-four hours put an end to the illusions under which the US Secretary of State had been operating.

Until the day before, he still believed that he could pursue his policy of non-involvement in the new Middle Eastern conflict. The promises of military assistance that he gave the Israeli Prime Minister were baseless lip service.

On October 13, it became clear to the policy-makers in the White House, headed by Kissinger, that the glasses through which they viewed the future of the Middle East conflict were too rose-colored. The scenario they had envisioned, in which the IDF was about to topple Syria and would soon topple Egypt afterwards, was merely wishful thinking.

Based on his own sources, the Secretary of State knew that the Soviet Union had been providing massive amounts of military assistance to its ally. Now, for the first time, he realized that the Israeli Prime Minister had not been exaggerating: her gloomy theories about the lack of equipment and ammunition were not exaggerations, and her pleas for an airlift were appropriate. Furthermore, he had no doubt that the unilateral support was the source of Israel's problem.

Kissinger knew that US military aid, although promised, had yet to be provided. He was a seasoned politician, and understood that the current situation along the fronts would not lead to a ceasefire with Egypt by purely diplomatic means, and that only a military victory on the battlefield would convince the Arabs to halt fire and sit at the negotiating table. He knew that the military victory would only be possible if Israel's military situation were greatly and immediately improved. He also knew that such an improvement, in light of the situation on the fronts, matched the global interests of the US in the Middle East—the absence of a clear resolution that would increase the parties' dependence on them. For all of these reasons, the US Secretary of State realized that the moment of truth had arrived, and rolled up his sleeves, broke through the hesitation on the banks of the Potomac, and sent his support for the supply airlift.

Morning. The 201st Squadron

Lt. Col. Iftach Zemer felt the murmurs in the air and felt the evasive glances. It was hard on him.

"We are returning to Damascus International," he informed his men, "I will be leading."

Our third trip to this international airport, Regev thought. *This is my second time. The first one wasn't so significant.*

At the runway threshold, maintenance personnel members leaned on the sides of their aircraft, while the "guard" (rescue) radio channel brought the drama of the ejection on the shores of Lebanon to life. Everyone heard that Benaya and David ejected after attacking the Al-Mazzah Air base near Damascus, and they knew that the International Airport was better protected.

The approach route is different, Zetelny reflected in Zemer's back seat. *Someone at headquarters used their head.*

They flew east and crossed the Jordanian border on the northern end of the Dead Sea. They bypassed Amman to the south, and continued east towards the Iraqi border. They headed north, straight into Syria.

What is that? The light of one of the engine generator light was glowing in red.

Maj. Eli Zohar was Number 3, and suddenly he saw that Zemer was signaling with his wings, and understood that the squadron leader was leaving them. *Shit. I'm supposed to take the lead. Until now, I've relied on Zemer, and I didn't bother to follow the map. Let's hope that Romem knows what is going on.*

In the rear cockpit, Capt. Yoram Romem was in a daze. All throughout the flight, he tried unsuccessfully to focus on the map. *Relax,* he told himself, *Zetelny is leading, don't worry.*

"Yoram, are you oriented?"

Silence.

"Yoram?"

"Uh…yes," the drowsy navigator replied. Zohar understood that this response was more or less equivalent to yelling 'No, no I'm not'.

We'll continue north, Zohar thought. *Romem will pull himself together.*

With only a single engine, the heavy, sluggish aircraft was barely able to hold itself in the air, and Zemer insisted that they should not jettison their bombs while over Jordan. *Tossing bombs might cause a war,* he thought, *and we don't need another front. But where is the Dead Sea? There it is.* He pressed the "Panic" Button. *What is this?* The Sledgehammer started going wild, and Zemer felt like a flight course novice, unable to stabilize the aircraft, which upset him and made him nervous. The Sledgehammer continued to go on a rampage and made a sequence of uncontrollable motions. The flight controls were stuck, and the hydraulics were gone. He tried to even out, but to no avail. He lowered the nose down, but there was no response whatsoever. He pulled the stick back—nothing at all.

The flight controls were out of service. It was impossible to lower the nose. *In another moment, we'll stall.* Zemer reached his hand to the handle and pulled.

Zetelny finished rolling on the ridge of a rocky hill in the Judean Desert. He detached the raft and the parachute, felt around his body to make sure that everything was in its place, shot a flare in the air and communicated on his SART

(Search And Rescue Transceiver) with the helicopter that was scrambled to rescue them. *Where is Zemer?*

Zetelny found his commander on the slope of the hill, lying on the ground.

"My back is messed up," Zemer said as his face contorted in pain.

"The helicopter is on its way," Zetelny said encouragingly to Zemer, his commander, the living legend of the pilots. Twelve years older than him and thirty-two classes ahead of him, he belonged to the generation of 'dinosaurs', and there he was, lying at Zetelny's feet, and in pain. The young navigator, Itzchak Zetelny, thought about what was most likely going to happen now, and what would be said about Zemer at the squadron. In the manner of airmen, this burst of emotion was not manifested in any calming caresses or hugs. He simply kept repeating the same line—"The helicopter is on the way."

"Romem, are you oriented?"

"Yes… It'll be alright."

Jabal ad-Druze. There's the orientation.

They crossed the Syrian border, and saw a lazy MiG four-ship formation patrolling ahead of them.

"We're continuing," Zohar said.

"Two, three, pull-up." They pulled up. The MiG four-ship formation was no longer lazy, and Zohar knew that they are waiting for them. He also knew that the wingover point would be right in front of them.

"Jettison all loads, we're going after the MiGs," Zohar said, breaking radio silence.

Like beasts trying to tear out each other's throats, they flew in circles in the sky. The maneuvers made everyone lose altitude. One of the MiG pilots took a second to look behind him, and failed to notice the looming ground in front of him. He was planted on the ground in the midst of a large flame.

"Back to base," Zohar commanded, gnashing his teeth on account of not fulfilling the mission. He knew that there was not enough fuel or weapons for an extended dogfight or for a strike on the air base.

11:35. Sinai

Several minutes earlier, the IDF Chief of Staff landed at the forward command base of Southern Command at Um Hashiva, and he already decided to make his way to Tessa, which housed the regular division headquarters, to meet with Gen. Mandler.

"Notify the division commander that we are on the way," Dado instructed.

"There's no answer," said Gonen, who joined in the helicopter, "I'm afraid that he was hit."

"What's the matter with you, are you crazy?" Dado responded angrily.

However, Gorodish was not crazy. On October 13 at 11:35, the armored personnel carrier commanded by Gen. Albert Mandler, Commander of the Southern Command's Regular Armored Division, suffered a direct hit from a Sagger anti-tank missile. The strike killed everyone inside with the exception of the driver.

Afternoon. Chamber of the Head of the Command Center

"The Americans will not begin the airlift unless we accompany them from Crete or Rhodes," Brig. Gen. Rafi Bar-Lev informed Lt. Col. Oded Erez, Head of the IAF's Defense Branch.

"They are afraid of ambushes."

"That's impossible," Erez said. "The only ones that are able to accompany them for such a distance are Phantoms, and they're too busy. They won't be able to do this mission."

"You've convinced me," Bar-Lev said, "now persuade their air attaché."

"You don't have any security problems until Cyprus," Lt. Col. Erez, in a resolute tone, told Col. Forrester, himself a former pilot who served in Vietnam. "Get to Cyprus, and we will accompany you from there."

"Alright," the colonel nodded his head.

Afternoon. Avi Lanir

In the afternoon, a two-ship formation of Shahak jets from the 101st Squadron, led by Lt. Col. Avi Lanir, the squadron leader, were sent out for a patrol mission in the Galilee. While in the air, the air controller pointed them towards an engagement with MiG-17 aircraft that were attacking Israeli forces in the central section of the Golan Heights.

Lanir could not detect any MiGs. He decided to ignore the updates going around that there was a MiG-17 circling endlessly in the Golan Heights, which was actually a death trap—acting as bait and leading directly to a dense and alert Syrian anti-aircraft array that shot at anything in the sky, without distinguishing between friend and foe. You couldn't find a MiG? You didn't enter into a dogfight? Run for your life. But, unlike others, this is Avi Lanir whom we are discussing.

An officer and a gentleman, Lt. Col. Avi Lanir, the nephew of Eliyahu Lankin, who commanded the naval vessel Altalena, absorbed a prescription of values from infancy, the main components of which were: the homeland, the state, Zionism, vision, mission, and loyalty—as well as the Israeli Air Force, of course.

Once he had received an explicit order, there was no room for exercising discretion. An order from the system was an order from the State, the Torah brought down from Mt. Sinai, and the purpose of everything. Now the State had sent him to catch a MiG, and he still had not caught it.

Thus, in the heart of missile-infested territory at an altitude of 12,000 feet (the altitude favored by missile systems), Lanir decided to locate the MiGs, at any cost. It was then that he was hit.

He ejected from the Mirage fighter not far from a battlefield on which the Raful Tank Division was wrestling with the Syrians, who were defending the road to Damascus. Tanks on both sides saw the open-air parachute hanging in the sky, and they all raced to the pilot. The Syrians won.

It is not known if the Syrians were aware of the top secret information regarding the State of Israel's security to which Lt. Col. Lanir, commander of a Mirage squadron, was privy.

Loyal to the flag, the anthem, and the menorah—symbols of the country for which he fought and would die for, if needed—he was silent when the Syrian thugs upgraded his torture regimen. Perhaps they heard a few fragments of clues concerning the information in his head. They came back to beat him and beat it all out of him, until he could not take any more. His soul left him on the torture table.

Noon. Wing 4 (Hatzor)

"Zemer ejected. He's in the hospital. Go to the squadron and take command. Amos Lapidot will brief you." Plain, simple, to the point, and devoid of emotion, Brig Gen. Peled, the IAF Commander, informed Maj. Ben Eliahu of his new appointment.

Col. Lapidot received him warmly. In the eyes of the Commander of Hatzor Base, Ben Eliahu was the natural choice, one of the squadron's very own. An outstanding pilot and a charismatic leader that always drew people together.

"We still don't know if this will be a two-or-three day position, until Zemer returns, or a permanent appointment," Lapidot said. "Time will tell."

"Another thing, Eitan," the Wing Commander said, giving him a sympathetic look, "I advise that the Squadron be given a day off."

"Absolutely not," Ben Eliahu shot back without delay. "There will be no lull in flights."

"Okay," Lapidot said, "But let's agree that for the next few days, the squadron will receive missions of only second-degree danger and urgency. Now, as for you, Eitan, take a few hours to rest before rushing into the task of commander."

"Amos, I want you to understand me," said Ben Eliahu, his face turning red. "I have no intention of placing the squadron on 'enforced rests', no matter how you try to wrap and present the message to me."

"Oh, well," Lapidot sighed, "Do it your way."

Noon and a Bit After. The 201ˢᵗ Squadron

In the early afternoon, Maj. Eitan Ben Eliahu, 29 years old, who until two months ago was the Deputy Squadron leader for the 201ˢᵗ Squadron, made his way from the chamber of the commander of Wing 4 to his squadron.

He sat in the commander's room and called for Yair David, who was also his age. David, the most senior Phantom navigator of the group, had just returned, still bruised, from his dramatic ejection above the waves of the Mediterranean.

"What do you think about my appointment to squadron leader?" Ben Eliahu shouted in his direction.

"They call you 'Eitan', strong as a cliff" said David. "It's a binding name. It announces that you have confidence. See to it that you take us in the right direction. The squadron needs someone to pull them along."

Afternoon. Morning in Washington

"Britain's ambassador to the United States just received a big hint from me about Israel's willingness to accept a ceasefire," Kissinger informed Foreign Minister Eban and Ambassador Dinitz. "The ambassador was supposed to bring up the proposal at the UN

Security Council. However, the British Foreign Office objected to the initiative and decided to check first with the Egyptian President about his willingness to pursue it."

"This morning, the British ambassador in Cairo approached the Egyptian President and told him of an Israeli proposal for an immediate ceasefire. Sadat refused the proposal," Kissinger concluded.

17:20. The 201ˢᵗ Squadron

Let them calm down, thought Regev, Haloutz's Number 2 in the stand-by interception formation. *A nighttime interception is not my cup of tea*. The siren wailed.

"You're being directed south, MiGs are en route to attack in the area of Um Hashiva," the air controller said.

They made their way to Sinai, and quickly arrived at Um Hashiva. *Wow, a MiG four-ship formation just shot four Atoll missiles head on at us and pulled up. Idiots.*

Regev pulled towards the left, Haloutz chose the right, and both kept eye contact with the MiGs, closing in on them from two directions.

"Number 1, you're all clear," Regev said, guarding Haloutz' tail.

"Copy."

Haloutz launched a missile at the rear MiG of the four-ship formation. *Boom*. The sky was filled with a huge explosion. They turned to the east. *Is it over?*

"There's another four-ship formation in the area," the controller warned, "Keep your eyes open."

The last plumes of light made it difficult to identify anything. *I have to catch one,* Regev thought as adrenaline bubbled within him. He saw a silhouette with swept back wings running close to the gray ground.

"Eye contact," Regev reported to Haloutz.

"Another one is close to the right," reported Ilan Lazar from the rear cockpit.

He left the far one alone, carried out a barrel roll and blew up the nearby one with a missile. *Yes, yes, yes!* They returned to base in the dark. *It's a shame I can't make a buzz and show off to Sima.*

19:30. Jerusalem. Meeting of the Foreign Affairs and Defense Committee

Committee Member Haim Landau asked Aharon Yariv, "Are we recruiting Jewish pilots for the Phantoms?" Yariv came every day to provide the committee with an updated report on security and diplomatic developments.

"I have not been informed about that," answered the bewildered Yariv. He immediately shifted the conversation to the good news. "As of tomorrow, the Phantoms will begin arriving. There will be fourteen of them in the first delivery."

Menacham Begin, Chairman of the Opposition and a member of the committee, was through being impressed by the news. With little delay, he unloaded his frustrations on Yariv, a representative of the defense establishment. "For the last seven days, there has been nothing but babble the likes of which the people of Israel have never encountered. We (Likud members in the Foreign Affairs and Security Committee) have kept our mouths shut, except for our decision to call on the people to stand united behind the fighting army. On Monday afternoon, the people of Israel were victims of a great moral failure. According to reports that we received from the Golan Heights, the Syrian army was broken, and in the South we had already crossed the Canal. I will never forget this moment for the rest of my life. I was so happy that I called to my son in the United States and I said, "Thank God, we're done."

"Yet on the third day of the fighting? No, we didn't break the Syrians, and no, we never crossed the Canal…"

Saturday Evening. The 201ˢᵗ Squadron

As the *kippah* wearers performed the weekly *Havdalah* ceremony, jointly saying the prayer, "Blessed is the separation of the Holy and the Profane," Maj. Eitan Ben Eliahu gathered the members of the 201ˢᵗ Squadron in the briefing room and announced personnel changes in the command structure.

What a great bunch, he thought. *It is my turn to lead them. This is the moment of truth.*

He looked over the ranks and saw his successor to the position of Deputy Squadron leader, Huldai the fiery redhead. He saw "Wild Bull" Eitan, the calm Benaya, Haloutz, who had shot down targets that day, Gurion the veteran and Zohar the fearless. He then peered at the middle ranks, and the young ones. *What a bunch. It will be my task to drive them, lead them into battle, and restore their confidence in the squadron's management and in the headquarters. They have a problem, with him as well.*

For the last two months, Ben Eliahu represented the HQ for them. He and Avihu Ben Nun updated the "Model 5" order, which on Sunday of October 7 had put a severe dent in their confidence. Everyone knew that he was there, in the hours before the mission, with the information and the intelligence. They were certain that the flight route should have been changed for them, because he knew that the Syrians were at the Golan Heights slopes and knew the locations of the barrels and ingress waypoint towers were, as well as the location of Tel Fares and the Rafid Junction.

How could he have let them fly on that damned flight route? Squadron leader Eitan Ben Eliahu would not have approved of what Ben Eliahu, the HQ officer, had approved.

The trauma of Banha was still being felt. Two days ago, as the leader of the interception four-ship formation, he left four of his men on Egyptian soil. Two dead, two prisoners. They could not remember another case in which two blue-and-white aircraft were taken down in a single dogfight—and it happened on his watch.

"This is not the place for unrestrained criticism of the command," he told them. "This is not the time"

"There will be plenty of time to deal with it when this all ends. Discipline is the name of the game," he continued his introduction as Squadron Leader. "Professional discipline, operational discipline, personal and military discipline."

"We will continue to fly," he heard his voice echoing throughout the briefing room. "We will continue to be sent to the most difficult of objectives and destinations, and I will be with you for every mission. Best of luck to us all."

Gil Regev was happy.

Ben Eliahu, the professional, the pedantic, the perfectionist, the one who taught him more than anyone else about the art of flying a

Sledgehammer jet. Someone who knows how to analyze a situation while in the air and to simultaneously perform several actions. A man who can think of the opponent's next step, calculate where he will appear and figure out precisely how to trap him. A man who, while engaged in a two-ship formation dogfight, with all of this occurring, is able to briefly describe his intentions to Number 2 while continuing the operation of his own weapons system. Ben Eliahu is an amazing pilot, a virtuoso. He was not with us for that retreat at Sharm, when a day of combat against Mirages ended in a stinging defeat. The next day, he arrived, brought us all together, asked questions, and boosted everyone's confidence. He spoke about gathering energy and how to turn properly while knowing how to wait patiently. "That is the only thing that will determine the battle," he said. "It's the only way we can win." And so it was. This man is now our commander.

On Saturday evening, October 13, at the end of Ben Eliahu's opening speech, one could hear the sighs of relief throughout the 201st Squadron. Suddenly, all of the anger, unwarranted and unfounded, was pushed little by little into the depths of individual and collective oblivion. Infectious joy took hold of them all. Ben Eliahu was the most worthy pilot for the position.

21:30. Afternoon in Washington

On Saturday night, the second day of Sukkot, a new phase of the superpower's involvement in the Middle Eastern conflict was launched. The United States announced that it was involved, and that Israel was not alone.

As the clocks in Washington, D.C. pointed to 15:30, three US C-5 Galaxy cargo aircraft—enormous monsters—took off with ten Phantoms in their holds, on their way to Israel.

"Some of the aircraft are already in the air, and the rest will depart throughout the day," Ambassador Dinitz reported a half an hour later in a telegram, which upon its arrival in Israel brought about large sighs of relief in the Prime Minister's Bureau.

23:00. *The 201ˢᵗ Squadron*

At the end of a series of nightly meetings in the squadron and in the wing, Ben Eliahu cleared the table, sent his pilots to sleep, and took off on a lone flight with Amnon Tamir in the rear cockpit. At around midnight between Saturday and Sunday, as in the manner of knights moving ahead of a camp, he patrolled alone in the darkened sky, protecting the Refidim base, the Sinai, the State of Israel, and the reputation of the 201ˢᵗ Squadron and their new commander.

OCTOBER 14

Zohar's Private War

The ninth day of combat in the Golan Heights knocked on the door of the exhausted, and especially troubled blue-and-white fighters.

Throughout the entirety of the previous day, they fought a fresh enemy. In the name of Arab brotherhood, an Iraqi armored division joined the cycle of violence. The division constantly attacked IDF forces with determination, sought contact, adhered to its mission, and alongside the Syrian military forces that were entrenched in hardened defensive lines, it began to mark a dark future for the plans of the IDF's Senior Command HQ.

We won't make it to Damascus, the military leaders internalized. *We need to stabilize the defensive line where we have already arrived.*

Seven hundred kilometers away, the guesswork regarding the Egyptian military intentions came to an end. A few minutes after six o'clock in the morning, a heavy artillery barrage began along the entire front. This barrage was accompanied by an aerial attack, with helicopters landing infantry troops, and with half-tracks wandering the sands of Sinai.

06:10. The Refidim Air Control Unit

Half an hour after sunrise, the voice of the air controller from the mountain over Refidim suddenly became silent.

Col. Aharon (Yalo) Shavit, Commander of the Etzion air base, led a formation of Mirage aircraft patrolling in the area. He lowered his wing and saw the air control unit engulfed in fire and smoke.

"Wow, wow, 511 was hit by a Kelt SS missile," he transmitted to the Central Control Center in Tel Aviv.

07:00-15:00. Sinai

Shortly after 07:00 in the morning, the yellow sands of the Sinai Desert hosted one of the greatest tank battles in history—nearly 1,000 Egyptian tanks attempted to breach the defense line, behind which were only about 500 Israeli tanks.

"I bet it was the biggest attack," said the Chief of Staff at 08:00 in the morning.

"This will be the decisive battle," the Deputy Chief of Staff said gleefully, "500 Egyptian tanks will go up in flames."

"It's the best possible situation that we can have," the Defense Minister informed the Prime Minister, "I'm awaiting Egypt's funeral."

Forty hours after their tumultuous meeting on Friday evening, it became clear that their predictions were correct. The Egyptians played into their hands. In a classic defense battle, 250 Egyptian tanks were destroyed, compared to only six Israeli losses.

The joy was considerable in Um Hashiva and at the Senior Command Post in the Kirya military base. Finally, the long-awaited turning point had arrived, as the familiar tune was being played again. Israeli forces had returned and were winning like they always had, evaporating the last traces of the shock that prevailed at the start of hostilities and the terrible days that followed with the burning of Egyptian tanks.

Afternoon. Air Control Unit at Refidim

"Commander, the Head of the Command wants you on the phone."

"Evacuate the female soldiers from the mountain immediately," Maj. Gen. Gorodish barked at Yigal Ziv, Commander of the Air Control Unit.

"I cannot evacuate them," Ziv tried to explain. He had been trying to get the control unit back to operational competency, and was hoping for a sympathetic ear on the other end of the phone line. "The girls play a key role on the mountain. I only have about two hundred soldiers here, and an evacuation will lead to serious operational issues."

Gorodish shouted, "Are you refusing to comply?"

"Wait," the deafened and agitated Ziv replied, getting the Air Force Commander, Maj. Gen. Peled, on the line.

"Listen well," Peled, the man of titanium, told Gorodish, the man of steel, "You do not assign missions to my people, you do not allocate operations and tasks to them, and you do not give them orders."

That was that. The girls stayed.

15:00. *The 201ˢᵗ Squadron*

He took command just the previous day. At 02:00, he got into his bed after finishing a patrol mission on the Canal, and in the morning, he assigned himself another mission. Now he stood on the podium in the briefing room and led the briefing for a mission to attack the Mansoura Airport in Egypt.

"The first two-ship formation is under my lead," Ben Eliahu briefed, "and will carry out an offensive operation to take out the AAA and the missile batteries near the air base. Another six-ship formation, under Eitan Peled's leadership, will execute a pop-up strike immediately after we end."

Amiram Eliasaf was uneasy. *Shlain of all people? The youngest navigator in the Squadron?! He got here only two months ago from the Navigator's Course.* He became operationally qualified just this week, in the crash course that Zetelny gave him. *Why would they place me with an inexperienced navigator for a mission like Mansoura, an air base deep in the Delta, heavily defended by AAAs, missile batteries, and dozens of aircraft patrolling the skies?*

Arik Shlain was uneasy. He saw Eliasaf staring at him strangely and understood that he was dealing with a pilot who was not calm. He thought to himself, *what's gonna happen? After all, I'm not the one holding the stick.*

To be in a cockpit with "Wild Bull" is to be in good company, reflected the "Rhino," Eitan Peled's navigator, who was leading the strike six-ship formation. *Who knows, maybe we'll be able to shoot down an aircraft today.*

"I owe you a MiG," "Wild Bull" said to "Rhino," as though reading his mind.

"This is the arrangement," Peled continued. "Get me there on time, take me to the target, and afterwards, we'll find a MiG for you."

The Bull's confidence is a good thing, thought Rhino. *Yet Mansoura is in the middle of the Delta, in a cultivated plain, with plowed waterways, power lines, huts, and roads. Everything there looks exactly the same; and I'm the lead navigator.*

"Tell me, Rhino," the silent kibbutznik from Ma'agan Michael, a veteran of the Six-Day War and the Phantom squadron, turned to his navigator. "If I bring you a MiG, will you shave off that ridiculous Sancho Panza mustache of yours?"

"It's a deal," said Rhino.

They took off, with Ben Eliahu's loft strike two-ship formation in the lead. The pop-up strike six-ship formation followed a bit behind.

Maj. Ben Eliahu, the lead of the loft strike, identified a formation of MiGs in the distance, engaged in territorial defensive over the air base. *Ignore them. We'll continue to the pull-up waypoint.*

He and Guri Palter, his Number 2, pulled up, and in-conjunction they released their bombs. Ben Eliahu, who once again was itching

486 | <small>For Heaven's Sake</small>

for a take down, continued to the MiGs and pounced on one of them from behind.

"The son of a bitch won't get out of here alive," Ben Eliahu muttered under his helmet. He closed in, sharpened the turn, situated himself behind the MiG with agile maneuvering, and squeezed the trigger. The Egyptian pilot and his aircraft turned into an orange ball of fire, burning in the blue sky.

"Five o'clock, five o'clock[9]," Capt. Amiram Talmon uttered, a number of hisses and groans coming from the back seat in an attempt to warn Ben Eliahu, who heard an incoherent rattle on the ICS. He understood a thing or two about changes in vocal chords when dealing with G-forces, and understood that this particular vocal range, as if taken from a horror film soundtrack, had only one meaning: break, and fast.

He broke into a quick roll. The Egyptian pilot enthusiastically followed, unaware of how close the ground was and what the magician Ben Eliahu had up his sleeve.

"The MiG's been planted in the ground," Talmon reported.

We're done, Ben Eliahu thought as Peled's six-ship formation passed them while en route to strike the air base.

One minute to the pull-up.

External drop tanks glittered in the sky as they fell to the ground. *Not good,* thought "Wild Bull." *Egyptian MiGs saw us and are preparing for an interception.*

Pull-up waypoint.

The "Bull" contemplated. *Should we climb and perform the pop-up strike as planned?*

---

9   I.e., behind and slightly to the right

In the rear compartment, the "Rhino" was also uneasy. *What'll happen with these MiGs, and what's the meaning of that parachute in the sky?*

Yet the "Bull" had already decided, and ignored the MiGs. He pulled up, executed a wingover on the runways, put the sight on the target, focused, pulled the trigger, and released the bombs. Suddenly, silver MiGs headed straight for him from every direction.

Lt. Baruchi Golan, the navigator, shouted, "They're on top of us!"

Itamar Barnea, Number 5 in the strike formation, continued to dive.

Focus on the target, erase everything else. Aim, release, and break hard. The MiG did not stop and was close as it started strafing with its guns.

Dive, man, get down.

An unending series of beeps came on the headsets, and Baruchi threw his mask up and shouted, "Itamar, we're hitting the ground!" Itamar threw his mask up and shouted in return, "It'll be alright, we'll get out of this." *Since when do the Egyptians fly like this?* However, there was no time to wonder now about theoretical issues at that moment. They needed to survive. Barnea rolled from side to side and got rid of the MiGs grasp. They headed out at tree level, and they let out big sighs of relief.

What? Arik Shlain tensed up. *A MiG is on top of us?*

Just then, Amiram Eliasaf, Number 4 in the strike formation, released his bombs. The aircraft shook, and the afternoon sun enveloped the aircraft in an aura of scorching scarlet. The humidity of the Delta created vortexes around the wings, and the sun painted them a little too red. Shlain who was neither familiar with in the Delta nor with it the turbulences, knew that there was a MiG behind them a few moments ago, and it seemed that the aircraft was jerking around with bands of fire all around. "We're hit!" he shouted in the cockpit, "Fire!"

Eliasaf closed the throttles, in an attempt to lower the risk of a conflagration.

"I'm burning," he announced.

Eli Zohar, Number 3 in the formation, attacked the air base's operations bunker, and broke out strongly. He did not see any MiGs, but knew that they were waiting for him nearby.

It was then that he heard Eliasaf yelling that he was on fire, and located him in the sky. He was not on fire, but there were two MiG-21s sitting behind him.

"Number 4, break hard to the left," he yelled to Eliasaf, "they're on top of you!"

What is this? The "Rhino" and the "Bull" tensed as they identified a Phantom flying very low to the north with a MiG on its tail.

They chased after them and yelled, "Sledgehammer heading north, break!"

800, 700, 600. The MiG pilot did not notice them. 500. He noticed. In a great panic, he raised his nose even higher and his airspeed dropped, appearing as though he just stood there in the air.

"The idiot just ended his career," the "Rhino" said gleefully, and understood that his mustache was as good as gone, as Peled unleashed a short burst and blasted the MiG out of the air. Suddenly, a MiG was on their rear. They broke off of the MiG, crossing the Egyptian coast into the Mediterranean, climbing in altitude, and joining into formation.

Where is Zohar?

"Break," Itzik Baram shouted in the rear cockpit. "They're sitting on us!"

Zohar broke, looked behind him, and saw two MiGs launching missiles in his direction.

He pulled the stick to his belly. The missiles missed and the MiGs flew in front of them.

"Break!" Baram shouted again.

Another two-ship formation of MiGs.

Should we escape at a low altitude back to base? The fuel quantity is below the minimum required to safely get back to base with full power. Decide, and quickly. Closer to the ground, it will be more difficult for them to adjust to me, but a few miles from here, there are power lines that will force me to climb, and then we'll get hit.

There's no choice—we need to get rid of them.

"Number 3 is tangled with MiGs," he announced on the radio. He caused the new two-ship formation to pass over in front of him and hoped that someone would come to rescue him.

Another two-ship formation. Zohar sharpened hard the turn in high airspeed. *The MiGs won't be able to keep up with this exercise.*

"Are they still behind us?" he asked Baram.

"Affirmative."

He pulled back even harder.

"Are they still with us?"

"Affirmative," the cool-headed navigator answered from the rear cockpit. "And they are also firing now."

This isn't working, Zohar was frustrated. *The Operations Research Department claimed that a MiG cannot hold these maneuvers at this load. They were wrong. I have to change tactics, and fast.*

He pulled up into a vertical maneuver—setting the aircraft in a straight-up climb; there were a two-ship formation of MiGs again, maybe the same two, and they were unable to hold on to the vertical climb. They could not, but there were others. Another two-ship formation of MiGs waited for him at the top as he levels out of the vertical climb.

Suddenly he recalled something that Avner Slepak, once the best pilot in the Israeli Air Force, said: "When I am completely at a disadvantage, I do some maneuvers that even I will fail in knocking myself out..." The flash of Slepak's battle wisdom shook his hold on the stick, and he pushed it completely forward and goes down, lowering the nose, and vertically dove towards the ground.

At the last possible second, he completed a breathtaking airshow over Mansoura, pulling the stick with all of his might to his belly, and recovered at treetop height.

Calmed down?

Two more MiGs were behind him.

"*Break!*" yelled Baram, who identified missiles that were launched at them. Zohar broke, opened the afterburners and pulled up vertically again. The MiGs failed to hold on, and passed to a position just in front of him.

I'll keep trying with these vertical evading maneuvers until reaching half of the remaining fuel, Zohar decided. *If I fail to disengage,*

I'll level the wings heading north, set the engines to full afterburners, and hope that we'll be able to eject over the sea.

Once again, he chose a piece of clear sky and lowered his nose into a vertical dive, pulling up to treetop height and levels up.

"Clear," Baram said.

"Clear," Zohar said cheerfully in the forward chamber. *What an amazing word!*

They looked around in all directions. Nothing. Not an armed MiG in sight.

They headed towards base, at the lowest altitude possible. *Here are those power lines.*

"Clear," Baram repeated, checking the tail. Zohar briefly rose over the power lines and immediately returned to sticking to the ground.

The fuel was running out. *Do not eject, do not eject. Hold on until landing.*

They crossed the coastline. Several missiles were launched in their direction and fell to the ground half-way to them. *We did it.*

Concerns regarding the fuel quantity indicator soon dwarfed the joy of returning. *700 pounds. It's impossible to make it back to Refidim.*

Bluza or we eject.

"Heading to Bluza," he informed air traffic control, remembering the short and narrow runway adjacent to the wider road, just on the of missile coverage line.

"We're going to Bluza," Barnea and Palter suddenly announced as well.

"Only one aircraft can land at Bluza," the controller responded. "It is a short runway, and it is equipped with an arresting cable."

"I'm going there, I'm the shortest on fuel," declared Barnea, and in a more conciliatory tone said, "Whoever gets there first will land."

"Go to Refidim," Maj. Zohar, a veteran of the Six-Day War and the War of Attrition, ordered the young lieutenant.

"Alright," Barnea said, hearing Zohar's cautionary tone. He understood that there are times in which it is best to remain silent.

"Bluza, can you hear me?" Zohar asked.

"We copy, where are you coming from?" a faint voice on the radio responded. Zohar explained things to him.

He noticed that people and vehicles were moving all around the runway. What's all this? Does the idiot in the tower not understand that he needs to get all of these things out of here? Does he not get that we're flying on petrol fumes?

"Go around," called the controller, as though reading Zohar's mind. "You can't land right now."

He advanced the throttles for a few seconds and went around the field. He prayed that he would not have to eject while right over the airstrip.

"What's the problem here?" Zohar asked.

"You can't land," said the guy from the tower, "The wind direction is opposite to your landing heading."

"Idiot!" Zohar shouted hoarsely. "That's why you had me fly around? Make sure the runway is cleared for landing! I'm landing!"

"The runway is clear," the controller stuttered in the tower, "but the wind direction is the other way…"

The fuel indicator reached zero.

Zohar aligned the aircraft in a final approach suitable for an emergency landing—a steep gliding angle with minimum engine power—and expected to hear the engines shut down during the landing approach. He touched the runway and the engine was still running. He was arrested by means of the arresting cable as the canopy opened and engines shut down. Someone put a ladder next to the aircraft. *Just so long as he doesn't see my knees trembling uncontrollably.* Exterior check: the aircraft was completely intact, as though its plastic covering had just been removed.

"Get in the jeep quickly," they told them. "Yesterday, Egyptian commandos arrived here, and they killed one of our men by the fence."

"Don't mess with my head," Zohar said, furious, "I'll only move from here with the aircraft."

They understood that the man was serious. They towed the aircraft towards the plaza in the front of the landing strip.

He got down from the aircraft, called IAF Headquarters, and reported to them that he landed at Bluza safely. "Send fuel and an External Power Unit (EPU)."

"Wait, we'll send one from Al-Arish," they promised him.

Two hours passed and someone arrived.

At the request of the people at Bluza, Zohar took off and made a low buzz over the airstrip. *Anything you ask*, he thought. Resigned, reminiscing in the cockpit, he was on his way to Hatzor, returning from the hardest sortie of his life.

18:30. Lod Airport

In the early evening on Sunday, a new wind began to blow in the Middle Eastern sky, its huge wings bearing hope for better future for the military of the State of Israel.

Col. Doppler Strobau descended a flight of stairs from the enormous C-5 Galaxy aircraft, the first US supply aircraft to land in Israel, welcomed by female soldiers holding flower bouquets as he opened the wide airlift gates.

21:00. Government Meeting

"I suggest to the committee that we cross to the other side of the canal," said Defense Minister Moshe Dayan, the IDF Chief of Staff in the 1950s. "I am expressing an opinion shared by all of the army commanders. Maj. Gen. Tal, who on October 12 objected to the crossing, has not uttered a different opinion."

"We need to take advantage of the Egyptian army's mistake," said the current IDF Chief of Staff, Lt. Gen. Elazar, who was also invited to the meeting. "Today, they lost 250 tanks. If they return and attack tomorrow, there is a chance that they will lose an even larger number. Yet, I suggest we cross the Canal. This is the only operational move that I see, where we have a chance of getting to a decisive battle. The intention is to carry out the crossing, but it is possible to delay it by 24 hours."

"The Egyptians are returning to their normal selves, and we are returning to ourselves," the Prime Minister was informed by the commander of the Southern Front, Lt. Gen. (Res.) Haim Bar-Lev, over the telephone. Bar-Lev pointed to results from the field and the false reports of senior Egyptian field commanders that were received by the Central Listening Unit.

"I strongly recommend the approval of the crossing operation," he said, completing the third recommendation from the Chiefs of Staff Forum.

Well-experienced and full of doubts in light of earlier promises that were left unfulfilled by military leaders, several ministers were concerned about the fate of the forces that were meant to cross. Some even thought that it would be preferable to avoid crossing the canal altogether. "It is better to contain the Egyptians on the east bank," they said. The IAF was worn out, and would be unable to provide an adequate air defense umbrella for the crossing, and placing IDF forces on the west bank would limit the defensive capabilities in Sinai.

Near midnight, after three hours of heated debate, the Israeli Prime Minister decided to favor the crossing of the Canal, and called for her comrades to accept the recommendation of the three Chiefs of Staff.

Night. The 201st Squadron

"Did you hear that I told you on the radio that 'we are already coming'?" Reder asked Eliasaf, a native of Kfar Shmaryahu.

"When was that?"

"After announcing that you were on fire. The corner market song? 'We're already coming to Kfar Shmaryahu'? Tell me, Amiram, what were you thinking, that we could come and extinguish your fire for you?"

Gil saw that Amiram was not in a joking mood and said, "Actually, we made the strike run and disengaged. We didn't know about your drama back there." All three of them sat down and reconstructed the events that took place over Mansoura, marveling that Eli Zohar made it back alive from his personal war against the Egyptian Air Force. They did not give up on their daily ritual in Nurit and Gil Regev's apartment in the family housing section, drinking a glass of red wine and blessing the life of another day that came to an end.

Late at night, Eliasaf sank into his permanent corner, on Nurit's side. Gil Regev, her new husband, tried to calculate when this would all be over, and Nurit would take Eliasaf's place. Reder continued throwing out jokes from the sofa in the living room, until they all fell asleep.

OCTOBER 15

Preparing for Victory

At midnight, the Israeli government authorized Lt. Gen. David Elazar to implement Operation "Knights of Heart"—the crossing of the Canal between the Egyptian 2nd and 3rd armies, on the northern edge of the Great Bitter Lake.

The failure of the Egyptian attack, a loss of 250 tanks, as well as the American supply airlifts that were beginning to flow regularly and in large quantities, were factors that led to the maturation of Israel's operational capabilities: The IDF would cross the Canal, would seek out and take over a lot of territory, would dissolve the Egyptian achievements, would bring the Egyptian army to its knees, and would win the war.

"Prepare for the crossing," the Chief of Staff announced to the commanders of the Southern Front.

Morning. The 201st Squadron

"Today, the Air Force will continue strategic attacks that should accelerate the Syrian army's surrender," Huldai announced. "We are going to Tartus, on the beach. The target: the fuel tank farms. We will attack with two four-ship formations."

"Hail, hail, hail (enemy aircraft)!" the controller announced, just as the contour of the container farm was visible on the horizon.

"Continuing to the target," Capt. Ben Ami Perry announced in the leading aircraft.

"I'll worry about the MiGs," Ilan Lazar reported from the navigator's seat.

They pulled up and attacked. Once again, the Syrian skies were covered in flames and black ash.

"MiGs, two o'clock," Lazar warned.

"I don't see them."

"I'm pulling," Lazar said.

"I see, I see."

He pressed the pickle button, but the missile failed do launch. "Lock and we'll launch a Sparrow," shouted Perry.

The radar locked on. The Sparrow missile was enslaved and then launched. The missile navigated its way far away from the target and suddenly, without informing Perry and Lazar, it changed direction, a trail of white smoke bursting from its tail, and headed towards the MiG whose pilot was unaware of his own doom. The missile hit in the middle of the aircraft and split the MiG in two.

Perry broke into a victory song that he sang all the way back to the Squadron. "Here the dog is buried, here the dog is buried!"

Afternoon. The 201ˢᵗ Squadron

"Yesterday, Tanta air base was attacked. Today, it is active once again," Ben Eliahu briefed the two four-ship formations meant to repeat the attack.

"Intelligence is reporting that there's a squadron of Libyan Mirages located at the air base. As you know, those are the only aircraft capable of attacking deep within our territory. Yesterday, they successfully attacked targets in the Sinai. Some of them were shot down. It is important that we make their lives difficult. If need be, we will return there again and again."

"Our method of getting the target will be different than usual," Ben Eliahu continued. "Two four-ship formations, one led by myself and the other by Eitan Peled, will fly at more or less the same time."

Tanta is the central interception base of the Egyptian Air Force, thought Gil Regev, the Number 2 in Peled's strike four-ship formation. *Their best pilots. Yesterday, we have almost left Zohar over Mansoura. But today, there are many more of us. Half of the Air Force. The story of the millions of MiGs that surrounded Zohar in the skies will not be repeated.*

We're making a shadow over Egypt, thought Ben Eliahu, smiling contentedly and seeing the sky above the Delta covered with carpets of black smoke coming out from the engine exhaust pipes of other Sledgehammer squadrons.

Two minutes to the pull-up waypoint. A four-ship formation of MiGs was already in the sky. *Obviously they will catch us. The question is, who will it be.* "We'll wait," Peled offered to Ben Eliahu. "The four-ship formation that gets caught will go into a dogfight. The other four-ship formation will strike."

"Break!" Peled shouted, responding to the MiGs' decision to choose his four-ship formation, and the eight aircraft break out.

After all, there was no time for inquiries in the sky as to who the "Bull" was referring when he called to break.

Damn, why do break calls always make me jump? Regev thought angrily, reaching for the "Panic" button. He jettisons everything and breaks.

"Break!" shouted the navigator in the rear cockpit, and Capt. (Res.) Haim Rotem, familiar with the creative communication style of Shimon Noy, who was generally very calm and quiet, understood that it was serious. He broke as much as possible, and then some. *Wow!* An air-to-air missile missed them. *What is that?* Rotem shuddered, as he felt the air the flow into the cockpit.

"Number 1, they are sitting on you, break hard!" Regev shouted to his four-ship formation leader as he saw a MiG dive towards him.

Peled broke and pulled up. Regev was with him. The MiG was with them. *What is happening here*, thought Regev, *our friends in Egypt haven't heard that the Phantom is stronger?* Now they had heard. The MiG could not keep up, and lowered its nose, turning away.

"We're clear," shouted Shmueli from Regev's rear cockpit.

You son of a bitch, in a second you will be under my pipper, Regev thought excitedly. *Hey, what's your rush? Are you insane? What, you dive towards the ground like that before I can shoot you? Why are you suddenly in a blaze of fire? Couldn't you have waited for me to down you like you were supposed to?*

"We're clear," declared Lt. Eliezer "Blumi" Blumenfeld from Ben Eliahu's rear cockpit.

"Bring us back to the pre-planned pull-up waypoint," the squadron leader said.

How in the world am I going to find a turning waypoint for the last leg, Blumi grumbled under his helmet. *We are flying low, so low. And fast, so fast. The minarets are higher than us and the ground is blurring into a stream of colors.*

"When are we turning?" Ben Eliahu inquired.

In the rear cockpit, Lt. Blumenfeld was still struggling with the "identical image" that was the mess of agriculture squares, villages and roads, making calculations that only navigators know.

"When are we turning?" Ben Eliahu urged.

I got it, I got it. Here's a waypoint.

"Turn," he said in a nonchalant tone, hiding the excitedly cheerful heart within him.

At 12:48, bonfires lit up Tanta, and clouds of black smoke covered the sky, hanging over the capital of Egypt's aviation champions. Rotem's cracked aircraft joined the general joy, as it continued the whole flight home.

14:10. Um Hashiva. Sinai

140 minutes of discussions with commanders on the Southern Front came to a conclusion. They began with a brief overview by Gen. Gonen to the Command Post, which was followed by a visit by Generals Sharon and Edan in the war rooms. Dado returned to Um Hashiva, authorized and started to roll out what they prepared in the morning as a "decisive move."

"Knights of Heart," the operation to cross the Canal, was underway.

Night. *The 201ˢᵗ Squadron*

"Well?" asked Ben Eliahu, standing with his legs apart amidst the Squadron's urinals, staring at the wall as men always do.

"Alright," Regev answered.

"And if this continues?"

"That will also be alright."

I'll stay and sleep here tonight, Regev decided, disappointed that the MiG was listed as a squadron victory, and not added to his private collection. *At two in the morning, I need to already be in the sky.*

He took off his shoes and his pressure suit and stretched out on the hard bed. He recalled hearing of a Phantom from their sister squadron being lost over Tanta, and someone seeing parachutes. Suddenly, he forgot about the little disappointment, the private one, and found himself flooded with thoughts about the two who did not return and about others, his friends, who did not return as well.

He then thought about meeting Ben Eliahu in the bathroom. *I said that everything will be fine.*

A moment before he fell asleep, Gil Regev closed the shutters of his private room of concerns with the power of his statement to his commanding officer. He knew that this was a commitment, especially to himself, and he had a feeling that he needed to stand there until the end.

OCTOBER 16

The African Campaign

At 01:25, in the middle of the night, the code word "Aquarium" echoed on the radio receiver in the war room at Um Hashiva. The army ranks, led by Lt. Gen. Elazar, knew that this meant that the inflatable boats, including the vanguard of reservists from the Paratroopers Brigade, had begun to cross the Canal.

Five minutes passed. The name of the Mexican port city "Acapulco" emerged on the walkie-talkie, signaling the arrival of the first paratroopers to the west bank of the Canal.

Morning. The 201st Squadron

Once again, mysterious officers from military intelligence arrived at the squadron.

"Somewhere in between Suez and Cairo, in the middle of the Egyptian missile defenses, at this point just under the sand," they marked a point on an aerial reconnaissance photograph, "the central communications cable passes through."

"Your mission is to hit it, and send all of their communications to the air. At all costs."

This mission sounds a little familiar, thought Avner Naveh. *Like Banha. There, the army said "at any price" as well. But now we're just a two-ship formation. Someone is apparently pretty sure that we can sneak over to the cable without being discovered.*

It's strange, thought Huldai, who was leading the two-ship formation. *We're used to confirming the target with eye contact. We're used to identifying the place where we are releasing our bombs. This time? Sand. How do I find the specific point? The missile array, how do I slip past it? What is the meaning of all of these glances from this guy? It's still too early to eulogize us.*

08:15. Head of the Crossing Bridge in the Sinai

Four hours after fifteen "Crocodile"- type motorized barges arrived at the crossing yard, at the northern end of the Great Bitter Lake, and an hour and a half after the first barge was launched in the water, the reserve battalion commander, Maj. Giora Lev announced to the tense commanders in the war room at Um Hashiva that the paratrooper force would not be alone.

"Ten tanks under my command have moved to the west bank of the channel."

08:25. The 201st Squadron

Lt. Baruchi Golan, the lead navigator, knew that he had a problem. Right then, they were supposed to be on the outskirts of the missile system, and it was by flying below the radar beam that they were protected from it. However, the fog was closing in on them from all sides, and if they did not climb, it would be difficult to identify the pull-up waypoint.

They gained in altitude. *We are moving smoothly,* Huldai thought, *and in another moment, the missiles will start flying. Why in the world is this fog still hanging in the sky?*

In the navigator's seat in Number 2, Lt. Yossi Lev-Ari (Leibo) knew exactly what was going on with Baruchi, and he was not sure if the silent kibbutznik would find their way to the pull-up waypoint. However, he also knew that it did not really matter, because they were the "Number One" squadron, and no one there would give up on locating a pull-up waypoint, especially in a mission.

"Thirty seconds until pull up," said Baruchi, waving his magic wand, breaking the fog and revealing the sands of the desert.

At 08:30, just as planned, they released the bombs.

"Great," the military intelligence officers in the squadron said, "Egyptian communications is now on the air."

10:00. Senior Command Post

After spending 24 hours in Sinai, the Chief of Staff returned to the "Pit" in Tel Aviv with mixed feelings. IDF forces had crossed. On the other side of the Canal, there were 28 tanks and 600 soldiers. It was a good start, but not enough. It was light years away from the plan that was presented to him.

Frustrated, the State of Israel's highest-ranking soldier weighed the inexplicable gaps between what was presented to him the day before with approval of the plans and the situation on the ground.

"…The schedule seems too optimistic to me," he said to Gen. Ariel Sharon 18 hours before, as he overlooked the plans. "It is hard for me to believe that by 23:00 there will be two bridges over the Canal. Yet even if there is only one bridge by the morning, it's still good. I buy it."

Eleven hours later, and Dado still had nothing to buy.

On Monday, October 15, at 20:30, the paratroopers were supposed to cross the Canal. In practice, they crossed five hours afterwards. An hour later, the "crocodiles," the crossing rafts, were supposed to bring the first tanks to the western bank. The first Zionist tank rubbed its tracks on Egyptian soil eight minutes before seven o'clock on Tuesday morning, October 16, a nine and a half hour difference from the original plan. Division forces had to expand the corridor to secure the bridgehead and to allow for uninterrupted movement of heavy trucks in the direction of the crossing point. Oops. The Egyptian Brigade complex, the "Chinese Farm," delayed the establishment of the secure corridor to the crossing point.

Two bridges—barges and cylinders—were to unfold during the night, before midnight. On Tuesday, October 16, at 11:00, there was not a single unfolded bridge, and the arrival of bridges, even then, seemed as though it was an insurmountable peak.

"By dawn on Tuesday morning," said Gen. Sharon, commander of the division responsible for the operation, "two reserve armored divisions, both mine and General Adan's, will be located on the western side of the canal." So he said.

At least there is some good news from the north, the Chief of Staff brightened up. *The Iraqis have lost dozens of tanks.* "Beautiful," he said to Hakah. "Focus on defense. Keep this up."

Afternoon. The 201ˢᵗ Squadron

Senior officers at IAF headquarters decided that Sledgehammer squadrons would be sent to locations where they would be able to disrupt and minimize the will of Egyptian fighter aircraft to fly to the bridgehead. Their air bases, for example.

To this end, it was desirable to increase Sledgehammer control over Egyptian airspace in general, and over the cluster of air bases in the Delta in particular. Therefore, the three missile batteries operating in Port Said, which had survived two attacks and like phoenixes were rehabilitated, needed to be removed once and for all. They had to cease being a nagging thorn in the sides of the aircraft emerging from the north.

At 12:35, four two-ship formations of Sledgehammer jets from the 201ˢᵗ Squadron destroyed the missile batteries in Port Said. "That's it," the intelligence personnel reported, "this time it appears final. It will take a lot of time to rehabilitate it. You have pioneered a safe path."

13:00. Chamber of the Head of the Command Center

"Pass this along to everyone's attention," was written at the top of an urgent telegram that was sent to every IAF squadron and the air control units, "On Tuesday, October 16, 1973, IAF Sledgehammer jets, painted in camouflage colors, which are darker then usual, will appear in the skies of the Middle East."

19:00. The Knesset. Jerusalem

Ten days and a few hours had passed since the outbreak of the war. Encouraged by the news about the southern turnaround and the northern stabilization campaign, Israel's prime minister arose from her self-imposed public silence and daily schedule—which consisted of 18-20 hours of work in her office in the Kirya and a few hours of rest at her home in Ramat Aviv. Shortly before seven o'clock in the evening, she took to the stage of the Knesset in Jerusalem and delivered a speech to the members of the assembly.

Golda summarized the campaign to date, placed the responsibility for the criminal attack on Israel by Egypt and Syria, and explained that there was no need for a vivid imagination to imagine Israel's position prior to the start of the Six-Day War. She repeated and said that the aim of the Arabs was to get to the lines of June 4, 1967, on their way to their main goal: the conquest and destruction of Israel.

Later, she spoke of the full military support efforts that the Soviet Union had provided for its satellites, as shown on October 10, when two giant Antonov aircraft unloaded their cargo to Egypt, end especially in Syria. She then paused, looked up from her text, and said with her voice exposing her repressed rage, "Even at this time, as happened in the dangerous days in the past, we are witnessing the shameful phenomenon of an imposition of an arms embargo on Israel, when we are trying our hardest to defend ourselves. France's embargo remains in effect. Moreover, we warned that the

Mirage jets that France supplies Libya may be used in war against us. They tried to refute our warning, and promised that the Mirages were delivered to Libya under the condition that they would not be transferred to any other country, that they will not be used in war; and here we are. The Mirages that were provided to Libya are participating in the fighting in the Sinai. There cannot be better proof than the IDF shooting them down in flames. This is not to ignore the fact that Britain has also delayed essential shipments for the war effort."

Once again she stopped, looked straight into the camera, and said, "In the face of these phenomena, every peaceful person is entitled to reflect and be concerned about the cynicism and the impartiality of global policy, and to register into their consciousness the account of the selfish, immoral actions waged by the enlightened countries toward a small country, besieged and attacked."

As true, just, exciting, unifying, and powerful as Golda's speech was—and it was—one sentence, problematic and puzzling, was not a moment of improvisation by the 'Queen of the Jews'. The wording was carefully formulated in her office, and without bringing it to the attention of the IDF Chief of Staff or the Minister of Defense, it had been included in the first several minutes. A little phrase. A small nail.

"At this time, as we are gathered here at a meeting in the Knesset, an IDF force is operating on the west bank of the Suez Canal."

On Tuesday at 19:00 in the evening, the Egyptians were still not aware that the crossing operation was underway in the seam between their two militaries, at the northern end of the Great Bitter Lake. Now they knew. Moreover, the prime minister's words were uttered before IDF forces were able to secure a corridor at the crossing point, before bridges were placed, and before the thin bridgehead established by the Paratroopers Brigade was reinforced. That one sentence could have disrupted the entire crossing operation, crushing the dreams of a decisive move.

21:30. Senior Command Post

"What has so far been achieved is nothing more than a raid," Defense Minister Dayan said, throwing a figurative pitcher of cold water on the military leadership. "If, by morning, there are no serious developments—that is, if a bridge is not constructed and the crossing point is not secured—then it will be necessary to evacuate the tanks and the paratroopers that have landed on the same "crocodile" rafts that brought them to the west in the first place."

"However," he continued, "the publicity surrounding the crossing, and especially the prime minister's message to the Knesset, prevents such a move. The immediate return of our forces will be another blow to Israel's prestige, leading to a victorious elation in Egypt. It is only just now known that the crossing occurred, so we cannot retreat all of the sudden. Therefore, we need to make an effort to open up the way to the crossing areas and bridge the Canal."

Nighttime. The 201st Squadron

"So, how is this war?" asked Gidi from the band Kaveret, trying to break the ice.

Silence.

Sima, who was celebrating her birthday, knew that the guys were vying for her favor, and Eliasaf, a native of Kfar Shmaryahu, convinced Sanderson, from the same village, to come. He brought Gidi, Ephraim, Meir, Yoni, Yitzhak and Alon along with him. Yet even the magic of Kaveret, the young rock band loved by all, did not break the cycle of silence.

Then it was Sima's turn to try to break the ice. She was a young girl, who just turned twenty years old. She brought a big cake and divided it up for everyone.

And still, there was this silence.

Danny, Gidi, Ephraim, Meir, Yoni, Yitzhak and Alon, who came to make people happy, continued to sing and played 'Poogy Tales', *Shir HaMakolet* and *Po Kavor Hakelev* from their music album. All around them, the silence persisted.

Suddenly, Sanderson, who knows a thing or two about breaking forced silences, said, "You have a lot of people here."

Sima then thought of all of those who were no longer with them, and could not understand how Sanderson could say such a sentence. Just then, Ben Eliahu said, "Guys, let's sing now, because tomorrow we won't be here."

Finally, everyone laughed.

Then it was the band's turn to wrap themselves in silence.

OCTOBER 17

The Grim Reaper's Scythe

Early Wednesday morning, as the smiling moon hung in the sky and turned the white sands of Sinai into a magical creation, the front positions of Brigade 890 were fired upon. Hundreds of entrenched Egyptians, equipped with dozens of Goryunov machine guns and heavy mortars, turned the sands of Sinai into a slaughterhouse, and for the paratroopers, it seemed as though the sword of Damocles hung over their heads.

"You must scan the two leading central axes for the designed crossing point," they said, "in order to create a safe corridor that will enable the Division to stream in forces, especially for the raft bridges. Based on aerial photographs in our possession, the southern area of 'Chinese Farm' at the edge of your scanning axis, is full of tank hunter cells. Locate them. Destroy them. Open Tirtur up for movement."

In the absence of a single responsible veteran in the field, they were sent on the mission without knowing that in the last twenty four hours, not far from the blood-soaked sands, a desperate battle occurred, during which others tried to break through the corridor as well, from the other side. Furthermore, not a word was spoken about the blows taken by Maj. (Res.) Natan Shonri, Commander of the Paratrooper Reserves Forces, and Col. Amnon Reshef, Commander of the expanded 114th Armored Division, who, in their failed attempt to open the corridor, lost 122 own their own. Only the echo of the grim reaper's scythe was heard in the sands, while it continued and shortened their lives.

Morning. The 201st Squadron

"Maybe you can switch with me?"

Blumi loved Baruchi. How could someone not love the silent, humble navigator and photography enthusiast?

It was difficult to reject his plea, but it was eight o'clock in the morning, and Blumi wanted to sleep. Just sleep. All night long, he was on duty as the Combat Manager. He finished his shift and was assigned the morning sortie. Sleep. Just sleep.

"Don't get angry," he said to Baruchi, "I'm dead tired."

"I'm going to fly with Gadi," Baruch Golan informed Itamar Barnea.

Since the entanglement in the sky over Mansoura, Itamar Barnea felt that something very significant united him and Baruchi. Well beyond the experience, the squadron management seemed to pair them in a permanent placement. *We can't be separated,* Barnea thought, *we can only get through this together.*

"Take care of yourself," he said to Baruchi. "You are my usual partner, remember?"

Baruchi nodded, flashed a little smile and left.

Gadi Samok was not one of the guys. He never had been. He was already alone when he arrived to Israel, a boy of 14 and a Holocaust survivor, and joined the Beit Shemen Youth Village, then the IAF. A fighter pilot. Blonde, big, and strong. There were stories of him being a "decathlon" champion in national sport games.

So they said. They did not hear it from him.

He later took part in the Phantom conversion course and a test pilot course in the United States, which he finished with honors, and upon his return to Israel, he became a test pilot in the aerospace industry. He was assigned as an "emergency placement" to the 201st Squadron. He would occasionally come to maintain their combat fitness. He flew, he performed, he landed. He would close himself off within his four walls, not available for small talk.

Then the war came, and the "mysterious" pilot Samok emerged as a cool-headed, brave fighter who strived for dogfighting engagements. He would stand next to the operations room and sought more and more missions, leaving his colleagues in awe of his performance.

Barnea was not relaxed. *Who will protect Baruchi for me?* He then remembered that Samok was at the controls, and thought to himself, *calm down, idiot. Relax.*

At 10:50, two two-ship formations from the squadron rushed to the bridgehead at the crossing.

What will happen to my damn attacks? Eitan Peled grumbled, seeing the missile battery that he was sent to destroy standing on its place.

"Number 3," he called to Haim Rotem, who was leading the second two-ship formation and was supposed to attack three minutes after him. "Number 3, take note, there are missile launches and lock-on alerts."

At 11:15, the second two-ship formation pulled up. Capt. (Res.) Haim Rotem entered the strike, exited, broke hard out of the way of two SA-6 missiles that were heading right towards him, and looked for Number 4, Maj. Gadi Samok. Just then, Samok was diving towards the battery. He locked on his target, but did not notice the SA-6 missile that was sent after him. He and Baruchi exploded in the sky over Egypt.

17:40. Um Hashiva

"The raft bridge is launched on the water of the Canal, awaiting the first troops to cross," the Defense Minister was informed upon his return from Africa.

"The bridge has been waiting for them to cross since 16:00," Dayan said angrily, "and there are no tanks to cross it!"

Later, they updated him on successes.

"Twenty-two Egyptian tanks were destroyed on the Ismaïlia-Suez Road," they reported to him, and went on to say that the Egyptian 25th Armored Brigade was caught in an ambush and lost almost all of its 100 tanks.

"This Bren is golden," Dado said.

"No excuses, no problems, he carries out everything," Bar-Lev added. "Very professional."

Evening. The 201ˢᵗ Squadron

How many days have passed since this started? Gil Regev reflected. *The guys are disappearing. It's a fact. The briefing room is empty.*

Eitan Ben Eliahu concluded the debriefing, regretting the fall of Golan and Samok, saying, "This is a long war, not like the Six-Day War. We are releasing you for a short vacation, to recharge your batteries."

Regev looked at Ben Eliahu. He then scanned the briefing room, seeing the looks that were directed towards the new commander. *"Model" and Banha are forgotten. Forgiven. In the hundred hours that have passed since the emergency appointment of Ben Eliahu the Righteous, this is all that we know about him: he mended the broken squadron, managed it, and now, when there is no proper time for it, he sends us home. What a commander.*

Night. Kiryat Ono

Sitting around the family living room, the Lev-Ari family guarded over Yosi, their navigator son, who was trying, in exchange, to protect them from the horrors of war, and threw himself into indulging in his mother's delicacies. There was Ariela.

To the side, when no one heard, he told her.

"Tomorrow I'm going on a mission in Egypt."

"Be careful," she said, unsure.

"You're funny," he smiled, "Egypt is a piece of cake."

Nighttime. Chamber of the Head of the Command Center

The Performance Research Officer, Lt. Itzik Ben Israel, entered the room of Lt. Col. Amos Amir, Commander of the Operations Department and the head of the planning team for Operation "Nutcracker 22"—the simultaneous strike of twenty missile batteries between Al-Qantarah and Ismaïlia.

"Amos," he said, "I've just learned that 'Nutcracker 22' is being implemented, and that you've decided to add Skyhawks in the delayed pop-up strike."

"Yes," Amos answered. "Do you have a problem with that?"

"Yes," Ben Israel said. "The Skyhawk has a weak engine, it isn't suitable for a delayed pop-up strike."

"This is how it will be," Amos ruled. "The Skyhawks will participate with everyone else."

"Did you stop him?" Maj. Oded Flum asked, meeting him in the hall as he left.

He knocked at the door again.

"Yes," answered a voice lacking patience.

He entered, holding a portfolio filled with overhead slides in his hand.

From the other side of the door, Lt. Col. Amir jumped up and tore the portfolio from his hands, throwing the slides everywhere, and sent him away furiously, yelling, "I don't care about your slides!"

Late at night, Ben Israel woke Gideon Hoshen, his commander.

"What Amos is going to do is crazy," Ben Israel told Hoshen about the confrontation in the office of the operation commander.

"It's going to be a catastrophe if Skyhawks are involved. Talk to him."

Hoshen later tried, and was thrown out as well.

Late in the night, Lt. Col. Guri Palter, one of the planners of Operation "Nutcracker 22," retired to his home in Neve Monosson.

Palter was the oldest pilot that was stationed in an emergency capacity in the 201st Squadron. A Mirage pilot, he performed the Phantom conversion course and led a two-ship formation. For the past two years, he had been in IAF Headquarters, in the Flight Safety Branch. In April 1973, he received the rank of lieutenant colonel, and with it an appointment as Head of the Education Branch in the IAF Headquarters.

During the afternoon of October 16, he was told to return to the HQ, in order to help plan a major operation.

Impressive, he smiled with satisfaction, relaxing in his bed. *Tomorrow I'll be there with everyone. Planning, and performing. A big celebration.*

OCTOBER 18

Who's Afraid of Missiles?

*W*e are here at the beginning of Simchat Torah Evening, Gil Regev reflected, *and for a few more hours the religious people will dance, be happy, stride in laps and thank God for it is good. Here? There is no joy, and probably no God, or Gadi and Baruchi wouldn't have joined the long list of the dead. Intolerable.*

Rotem saw an explosion, and didn't see parachutes. A kiss of death in the sky. It is better this way. Surely for Gadi, who's only fear was to be lynched by fellahin *pitchforks. Just as well.*

Maybe, in any case, he was reconciling with himself and with God. *Maybe Simchat Torah is a sign to us as well. After dinner, with the final Torah reading, the* Hatan Bereshit, *the one to read the first passage of the Torah, will begin all over again.*

Who knows? Maybe the six who are heading to Egypt in the morning will open a new page for our squadron, as well in the story of this cursed war.

"Now is the moment of truth," said Eitan Ben Eliahu in the briefing room a few minutes after six in the morning. "West of the

Canal is a reserve paratrooper division, and a division or two of tanks. Most of the forces allocated for the crossing are still on the east bank. It is only a matter of time, only a little bit of time, before the Egyptians get their act together, either alone or using Soviet spy satellites, and they will take on our forces on their territory and send fresh armored forces and air strikes."

"In three hours, we are going out to clear out the entire Egyptian missile array in the crossing sector," continued Ben Eliahu, "If we fail, the Skyhawk squadrons will not be able to provide assistance to the army, and that will waste the whole crossing effort."

"Yesterday I was at the general briefing for squadron leaders. At Headquarters, it has been decided to divide the missile array into three. Today, we start the campaign in the north. Al-Qantara. It will be a pop-up strike. Two squadrons of Sledgehammer jets, us along with Squadron 69. We will go in the first wave. Three squadrons of Skyhawks will make up the second wave. We are the ace that can determine the ground battle, and the entire war. Good luck to us all."

06:50. Senior Command Post

"Throughout the night, armored forces flowed, on the raft bridges that broke and were repaired, as well as on the 'crocodiles'," the Minister of Defense was informed by the Commander of the Southern Front, Lt. Gen. (Res.) Bar-Lev. "Three armored divisions are already in Africa, Bren's division crossed the agricultural buffer (a freshwater canal, approximately one kilometer west of the Suez Canal and the shores of the Bitter Lakes, which brings agricultural water from the Nile Delta to the Suez), and is moving ten kilometers west without encountering any resistance."

"Another force," Bar-Lev continued, "moved south and is managing a battle with infantry and anti-tank forces there. The access axis at the top of the bridge ("Spider"), is completely open to traffic, and the Egyptians are still not aware of Bren's progress in the west bank."

"It's going well, if this is the case," Dayan said.

"Yes," said Bar-Lev, "We will know officially within the next forty-eight hours."

"In the history of the Jews, forty-eight hours don't even count," Dayan said, his one eye gleaming.

09:00. The 201ˢᵗ Squadron

"Be careful up there," Pilot Yigal Stavi whispered to his friend, the navigator Itzik Baram. "Keep your eyes in the sky."

"Don't worry," Baram answered.

A girl with her hair down passed among the aircraft with their engines running at the front of the runway. Waving a large cardboard sign, she lingered until the friends under the canopies—those secured in their uniforms, white helmets, dark visors, and hanging oxygen tube—followed her finger and gave her a thumbsup confirming they recorded the changes in radio frequencies. She got into the jeep and returned to the operations room.

The joy is gone, thought the operations clerk, Sima Shavit. *For eighteen months, I have loved them. October's autumn days are unbearable. Love is replaced with concern, so much concern.* Next to the aircraft waiting for takeoff, she realized the fragility of life yet again. *On the one hand, there's the Phantom, the very best aircraft, with the very best pilots. On the other hand, there's Gadi and Baruchi, Yoni, Uri and Dror, who were and are not anymore. What will happen in half an hour? Will someone who just raised his thump up at me burn up in the sky? Will they be executed with pitchforks? Captured? God, protect them for me.*

A few minutes before nine o'clock in the morning, IAF Headquarters initiated Operation "Nutcracker 22."

75 Sledgehammer and Skyhawk jets, a long procession, two by two, headed out on their way to strike and destroy the missile systems in Al-Qantara.

Fifteen minutes until crossing the coastline, Romem thought, sitting in the rear cockpit of Huldai's aircraft. Pictures of his home in Haifa flashed in his mind. Family. Esti. Their togetherness. Then it was the cockpit, instruments, and Ron Huldai, who was lobbing them forward at 600 knots over the Delta.

One minute to the pull-up waypoint. Another six miles, and that's the war.

Huldai shouted, "Birds!" He knew that it was impossible to descend lower than such a low, low height, and pulling up meant early detection by the missiles. However, he needed to do something, and right then, continuing at this altitude would shatter their windshields on a flock of birds, a sure recipe for suicide. He pulled up.

Suddenly, there was something wrong in the cockpit, and they could no longer see the fishing boats and greenery that seemed as if it were from a fairy tale, and all of the displays, lights, and horns began flashing and sounding.

Thirty seconds to the pull up, a giant force shook the aircraft.

"Number 2, we're hit," said Huldai, beginning to pull eastward.

Number 2, Guri Palter, did not need to be updated on the current reality. In his cockpit, as well, the strobes were extending loudly on the RWR display, and Palter said to Baram, "Look around, warn me of any missiles." Just then, he saw a missile explode under Huldai's aircraft.

We'll continue alone.

Missiles! Survive, survive. He broke firmly to the left. The missile exploded behind him. He rolled over to the other side and broke to the right. *Boom.*

In Doron Shalev and Yossi Lev-Ari's cockpit, the atmosphere was cheerful. While the Mediterranean waves swirled beneath them, the two-ship formation in the last combat aircraft in the convoy gathered the best songs of the Zionist repertoire and sang in two out-of-tune voices.

We're the last ones, Lev-Ari thought, *it's good for the Jews. North of us are the missile batteries at Port Said, which died their deaths a few days ago. To the south, Huldai and Palter will be occupied with their own battery. In another moment, we will place the last nail in the coffin of the system at Al-Qantara.*

Damn. We pulled up too far away. We will be approaching the target while flying flat.

8,000 feet. Shalev began a wingover, put the sight on target, released bombs, and started to pull the flight stick back to his belly. "Break, break!" Lev-Ari shouted, seeing a missile roar in their direction. *Boom.*

Palter's aircraft screamed in protest, and the lights on the instrument panel flashed like a Christmas tree. The horn would not stop wailing.

Alright, I don't need you cacophony to understand that we are in trouble, Palter thought, reaching his hand out and stops the screech of the horn.

However, something was still screaming.

Palter took a quick glance around and saw a crack in the cockpit canopy, through which winds pushed through.

He tried to communicate with Baram. The air shriek was increasing. He pulled to the east, heading home. *Boom,* another blow, and the aircraft began to roll to the left. He tried to level the wings. It did not respond. He fixed the stick to the right. *Please level up, level.* The aircraft refused.

He pulled the ejection handle with his left hand. *If there is a God, this seat will work.* The air cut through him at 450 knots, and the rocket under his seat kicked him up. *This is it. Another world. The war for your life. Remember what you learned and taught as the commander of the captivity exercise in Flight Academy.*

He landed on the ground hard, planted in a field flooded with water, sitting in a puddle of mud. His left arm dangled, resting at an unnatural angle behind his body. *But the right is ok,* he cheered to himself.

He pulled out a knife, cut off the life jacket, and blew up the raft. He pulled out the pin of his microphone headset with his teeth, and reported, "Tiger, Number 2 is alright." He saw two Arabs approaching him, one holding a shotgun in his hand, and he reported: "In another moment, they'll take me."

"*Irfa Idik* (Hands in the air)!" they shouted.

He lifted his right arm.

"*Al-Ithnayn* (Both of them)," instructed the one with a gun.

"*Ana majruh* (I'm injured)."

They descended to the flowerbed and yanked the Zionist weed out.

"*Hondi al-Bolis* (Take me to the Police)," Palter requested.

"*Ana bolis* (I am the police)," the Arab with the gun replied.

"*Hondi al-Jaysh* (Take me to the army)," Palter tried again.

"*Mashi* (Okay)," the policeman answered.

Itzik Baram hit muddy ground. He also saw two people with a big gun. *Stop*, they signaled him. Yet they were far away. Being a farmer, he knew mud. He knew that it would be difficult for them to move towards him and reach him. *You run away now, Itzik. Run away right now, just like Yair David in the War of Attrition.*

He went. Stumbled. Stumbled again. He began crawling. He threw everything behind him, leaving his pistol and his SART, trying to move between the bushes that surrounded the waterways. There were voices all around. *They're chasing me.* He jumped into a canal, diving into murky, muddy water. He raised his head to take a breath of air, crossed over to the parallel canal, and plunged in again. *More. More. Hold on.* He took in air in a grateful shriek.

Everyone has disappeared. He pulled himself out of the mud. *Home.* Voices. He hid.

19:00. Total darkness enveloped the swamps of the Delta. He opened his microphone and called. There was no answer. 20:00. Someone called him on the device, and someone else shot at him. He bent over and headed east. They shot, and he evaded. They called him again. *Don't leave me,* he thought, *but they can't hear me.* Suddenly, a burst was fired at him. He entered a deep ditch, and his head bobbed above the water. He tried making a radio contact. Nothing. His friends continued trying to call him. At midnight, he turned off the SART. He had already understood. He came to an area of dense bushes and hides. Fatigue soon overcame the fear. The dawn woke him. *A good place,* he smiled to himself, *a big bush and a cloak of spider webs, protecting me from the Delta mosquitoes. I'll take off my shoes.* He fell asleep again. *What is that?* Soldiers approached him.

When Yosi Lev-Ari awoke from the blackout darkness that engulfed him, he discovered that they were still flying, crossing the Canal at a low altitude, with a large anti-aircraft complex to their right.

"Take a left," he shouted at Doron.

No comment.

"Take a left," he shouted again.

Still no comment.

We can't eject over this compound.

"Take a left!" he screamed.

Just then, the aircraft stalled like an elevator in the sky. Doron shouted, "Leibo, eject! Leibo, eject!"

Are you crazy? I don't want to eject here.

However, Yosi Lev-Ari, whose comrades in the squadron called "Leibo," understood a thing or two about stalling, and knew that the nose would then fall and Doron would surely pull the handle. Doron pulled.

Hanging by his parachute, Leibo desired life. Yet the bullets that whistled around him were not in the recipe for a long life. He pulled on the parachute strings, pleading with those responsible for order in the heavens—*Take me to the east, to the highway, to the border of our forces' sector, to the gates of the Promised Land.* Yet the wind, usually pushing eastward, decided to go the other way that day.

He landed softly and rolled. Soldiers in cream-colored uniforms and strange helmets ran and shot at him, making beams of sand splash at him like a magic fountain. *Hey, my right hand is hit. Run, Leibo, Run. It's only another hundred meters to the road. There is life. Hey.* Another bullet pierced his body. *Don't give up. Run. Here's the road. Here is the road.* Another bullet hit him.

He raised his hands.

Loaded on a jeep, there was Doron.

They drove slowly. Soldiers who tried to hurt them emerged from every pit in the dunes. Then it was their private soldier sitting next to them. He signaled to the watch. Leibo removed his watch and handed it to him. He felt as though his last piece of identification as an airman was taken from him.

The soldier then pointed at his ring. His ring finger nearly tore off in protest as Leibo pulled off his wedding ring, and felt that Ariela and his home had abandoned him as well.

Operation "Nutcracker 22" ended successfully. Out of eight batteries that were attacked, six were destroyed. An anti-radar missile destroyed another, and another was partially damaged. Al-Qantara's array was eliminated, and the sky north of the Canal had been cleaned of missiles.

The price was painful. Six aircraft: two Phantoms, four Skyhawks. One fatality. A crew of five in Egyptian captivity. Four of them were fighters from the 201st Squadron.

There was Amos Amir. He was the Chief Planner. He pushed to perform the plan at all costs, and he knew that perhaps another way was possible, but also knew that all of the inhibitions would be worse in the end. After all, everyone in the Air Force was still influenced by the fiasco of Operation 'Model 5', and no one was prepared to deal with a missile system. At most, they would take out one battery in some backwater here, and another on the fringes there. Until then, when a window of opportunity opened for the Air Force to lift its head. To prove that things could be different. A complete system, the spine of the Egyptian's missile coverage. Just as the IAF practiced all of these years.

Yet the price.

Amos recalled the warnings coming from Ben Israel and Hoshen. He was still not sure if it was necessary. What would happen if future operations will demand the price of six more aircraft? The armored divisions were already in Africa. In the last two days, tank operators had already destroyed batteries with direct laying. It was worth it.

10:30. The 201st Squadron

"We've paid a heavy price," said Ben Eliahu to the group of airmen in the briefing room. "Four prisoners of war, three aircraft. Huldai and Romem managed to land a badly damaged aircraft at Refidim. It's possible that we could use the aircraft later on in the war."

Afterwards he paused, examined his fighters, and added, "Don't forget that we were the first ones. Everything blew up on us. Despite the difficulties and the fire, we destroyed one battery."

"A great success," he continued. "Within thirty minutes, we destroyed seven batteries of the Al-Qantara system. The Egyptian missile array in the northern Canal crossing is out of order."

Someone suddenly let out into the room, "I'm not sure that I saw all four parachutes. It is hard to know who ejected and who didn't. Perhaps the time has come to seriously discuss our ejection method?"

In a Phantom jet, there are two ejection handles. One is located in the pilot's cockpit. The second is with the navigator's cockpit. Whenever the pilot pulls the handle—the initial default option—both aircraft crewmembers are ejected outside of the aircraft. Simple and logical.

However, there is the "gray area" of uncertainty. What happens when a navigator detects an unresponsive pilot, and the aircraft is about to crash? When he pulls the lever in his cockpit when it is set to its normal position, i.e. its vertical setting—he will only eject himself and send the pilot to his death.

This was the reason for the argument: whether to keep the navigator's ejection handle in the vertical position, or to rotate it to the horizontal position, allowing the navigator to eject the pilot as well.

A heated debate took place.

Some of the navigators demanded that it always be in the horizontal position, because otherwise, in the pressure of any series of events, they may forget to turn it to a horizontal position, thereby causing the unconscious pilot to die in the front seat.

Some of the pilots said that, if they keep it in the horizontal position, their fate would be given in advance and would be completely in the hands of the navigator. Situations may occur, they said, in which the internal communications in the aircraft could be disrupted, and the navigator, losing contact with the pilot, might panic and assume that the aircraft might be going down, thus ejecting the both of them, while the situation in the front cockpit, unbeknownst to the navigator, would still be under control.

At the end of the heated debate, they decided to leave the issue to the discretion of the aircraft's crew. Each team would decide independently, "on the ladder," the answer for themselves. A pilot paired with a young, inexperienced navigator, would prefer the lever in the vertical position.

What a squadron, the "Rhino" thought joyfully. *It turns out that in the midst of this structural savagery of ours, we also know how to produce great openness and a culture of conversation when necessary.*

Later, he reviewed "Nutcracker 22." *We preserved the squadron's honor,* he thought to himself. *First of all, Eitan was leading and Amiram was Number 3, who both hit head on. But mainly Naveh and me. Naveh, the brilliant young guy in the pilot's cockpit, who broke with virtuosity from the missile that was launched at us, while almost flying at grass level. He never gave up, and came with force. What a bulls-eye we had on that SA-3 battery. We then returned safely.*

At noon, Ariela Lev-Ari called the Squadron.

"Could I speak with Yosi?"

"He's sleeping," replied the clerk on the other end of the phone line. She did not know how to tell a woman that her husband was apparently being held in Egyptian occupied territory.

"The truth is, if he is sleeping, only you know," Ariela said.

Silence. What could someone say?

Now Ariela knew as well.

Slowly, she put down the phone and looked towards the door, waiting. Soon, they would come to inform her.

10:30. Um Hashiva. Sinai

"I don't understand why Benny went for the missiles," Dayan said, "This really is an error."

Dado, sitting at his side, agreed. "I learned of the attack only when it was already underway."

Is it possible that, with the pressure of the surprise attack that struck Israel on October 1973, and under the influence of the shock and general bewilderment in the first days of the containment defenses, the country's leaders also lost the principle of reporting the truth? The principle upon which on every hierarchical system is based, especially in the military?

After all, here is what we have: A minister of defense claiming that he never knew and was not involved, and a Chief of Staff echoing those sentiments.

Could it be that Maj. Gen. Benny Peled, Commander of the Air Force, initiated "Nutcracker 22," a large-scale operation and the third largest in the war—which involved the participation of a third of the IAF's fighters—without the approval of his superiors?

17:00. A Man Named Epstein

Early in the morning, he left his office at headquarters and headed to another day of work at his Mirage Squadron in Hatzor. *What is going to happen?* Maj. Giora Epstein wondered. *While doing my work at the headquarters, I've already done ten day missions and five night missions. The results? Nothing. At headquarters, they're talking about 220 enemy aircraft, and my friends, most of them in the interception squadrons, are already planted on the ground. What about me? Is this war not going to give me even one enemy take down to put in my file?*

It is not possible to imagine the course of the war in the Canal area were it not for the IAF's successful interception of Egyptian fighters that tried, repeatedly, to attack the bridgehead and the forces west of the Canal.

The deterrence victory of the Israeli Air Force must also be attributed to the scant information held by the enemy, which was caused by a lack of air patrols on their part in the days of Israel's force concentration and bringing the bridging equipment.

In the critical three days of crossing the Canal, October 16-18, the IAF alone shot down thirty-one enemy aircraft and one helicopter in the area of the crossing (six additional helicopters and five aircraft were shot down by anti-aircraft batteries and fire from the armored brigades).

This is already my third sortie today, Giora thought. *At the end, I will land at Refidim and will stay two more days and be part of the on-call group.*

"Engagement," the controller announced and sent them to intercept enemy aircraft attacking the area of the raft bridge.

In light of the flames of a burning half-track, Giora identified a helicopter.

"Authorized," the controller said, "It is not ours."

He turned sharply, reduced airspeed, and was at a distance of 1,100 meters. He aimed a bit ahead, judging the offset deviation. *Boom.* The helicopter crashed in a giant flame.

Maybe this will put an end to all the bad luck?

20:30. Office of the Prime Minister

The six fighter aircraft that were lost today, along with the five from yesterday, brought the total sum to 97. All of this may have been the main reason, despite the fact that the airlifts were running at full steam, for the urgent telegram that was sent from the Prime Minister's Office straight to the Israeli Embassy in Washington, D.C.

"So far, we have lost 52 Skyhawk jets," Gazit wrote to Dinitz, "Seven more are under lengthy repairs. We ordered 80. In the next few days, only 26 will be delivered. The lag is not understandable. Our offensive effort is ultimately weakened in the absence of reinforcements. Moreover, the Skyhawks that have been sent to us are the old model, not the model that we ordered. As for the Sledgehammer aircraft, we are expecting all 32 that we have already been assured."

The Manager of the Prime Minister's Office, senior official Mordecai Gazit, who was familiar with the data and the numbers and knew how to formulate an urgent telegram, was unaware of the "little details," the difficulties of the fighters. For example, he had not been exposed to the captivity gospel of Guri Palter, Itzik Baram, Doron Shalev and Yosi Lev-Ari, who, in those very minutes, were beginning their private war to retain their own sanity.

OCTOBER 19

Circus in the Sky

As the fourteenth day of the war yawned its way to its shift, Soviet advisors informed Alexei Kosygin, their Prime Minister who had been in Cairo for the past three days, that the front had changed.

"We need to have a quick ceasefire," the rulers of the Soviet Union said, "before IDF forces trot their way into Cairo."

No one in the Kremlin knew that the IDF forces were not planning to reach the Egyptian capital. At that time, far away, along the freshwater canal, toward Ismaïlia, Egyptian soldiers were showing courage and determination in the face of IDF soldiers, some of whom, like the tank commander, Lt. Ilan Gidron, had been fighting continuously since the start of the campaign: getting hit, licking their wounds, pulling themselves together, witching tanks, adapting to new crews, changing the framework and moving on.

"Our armored forces are tired," the Chief of Staff told the IAF Commander. "I'm trying to find a way to help them."

"In light of the erosion of my forces," said Maj. Gen. Peled, "I would want to finish one day without losing any aircraft."

13:15. A Man Named Epstein

"Scramble, launch," the air traffic control unit, located on the mountain over Refidim, launched a pair of Mirage pilots, harnessed to their seats and standing by seated in their aircraft as the on-call alert pilots. They had been waiting exactly for this kind of a call.

Epstein led, flying very fast, getting ahead of the Egyptian attack aircraft making their way to the bridgehead. *Great target,* he smiled underneath his helmet, identifying four two-ship formations of Sukhoi-7 jets flying in tandem. *Damn. The closing-in airspeed is too high.*

He pulled 270° to the left over the large lake, and saw the Egyptian octet organizing strikes against concentrations of blue-and-white convoys. He pointed towards the third two-ship formation in the line and launched a missile on the one at the rear. *Bite the dust,* he cheered contentedly, seeing a Sukhoi-7 explodes and falls into the Canal, knowing that that was it, his bad luck was broken.

The second two-ship formation pulled out of the strike. The airspeed was too high to dump the centerline drop tank and clean out the aircraft. *We will fight with what we got,* decided Epstein, and he reduced range to his prey, which initiated a series of sharp breaks. *It's impossible to aim like this,* knew the hunter from Kibbutz Negba. He shot several rounds anyway, and discovered that the adrenaline and the smell of prey swept him far to the west. In another moment, he would be over the missile array territory and it would launch at everyone. *But the son of a bitch must go down.* That was the moment when Epstein "wore" the Mirage. He felt every slight movement on the edge of the wing, he felt the airspeed, and he knew all of the humming noises, every rustle. Enough of thinking about what he wanted, the Mirage would do it for him.

Now he wanted to bring down the bastard that was breaking so desperately in front of him. The Egyptian pilot did not know that one man named Epstein, a veteran hunter and especially determined, put his pipper in front of the Sukhoi-7 along its anticipated flight line, and released a long burst of gun rounds. He broke to the east, dropped a wing to the right, and saw a smashed Sukhoi on the ground, exploded in a huge bonfire.

In the afternoon, he was on-call again.

"A large convoy on its way to attack. Scramble, takeoff!"

Epstein launches off the ground and calls a two-ship formation of Shahak jets that were launched just a bit before him to join him. Bringing in his experience earlier, he restrained his hand from the throttle. *Here is the Canal.* They cross westward. "Join with the CAP from the 201st Squadron. They are flying low over the lake," the air controller said. *Here are the Sledgehammeres.*

What is that? A two-ship formation of unidentified aircraft pulled up from the south, turning to the left towards the west and gaining height. "MiGs," Epstein reported the magic word that sharpened the senses of every interceptor pilot in the sky. He pulled towards them and launched a missile at the one on the right. *Boom.* The aircraft was vaporized in a large explosion. *Sukhoi-20,* thought Epstein. *Resembles the MiG, but not the real thing.*

Wow! Four two-ship formations of Egyptian strike fighter pulled in a left turn for attack. They did not know that Epstein was in the sky.

He chose one, and his finger was on the trigger. *What is that?* Number 3 was pushed between them and announced, "I'm taking him." He let him. Number 3 missed. It was Epstein's turn. *No one will take my prey from me.* 300 meters, a bunch of rounds, and a Sukhoi exploded, turned over, and fell in the lake. In the evening, when Arik Lavie and Yafa Yarkoni came to sing, and Yafa cut cakes that she baked herself and brought from Tel Aviv, they were already pointing at him as the one who had done more than everyone.

17:00. The 201st Squadron

Half an hour before Shabbat would begin, Ron Huldai was sent to lead a proactive interception four-ship formation on patrol in the crossing sector. "Since the morning hours, the Egyptians have been focusing on repeated attempts to attack the bridge," they informed him. "Get out there and protect the ground forces."

"MiGs," Epstein from the Mirage squadron was suddenly heard on the radio. *Where are they?* Suddenly, a Sukhoi-20 was in the sky, and a Mirage was after him. Huldai did not see any other aircraft in the area, so he assumed that the Sukhoi was actually the 'MiG', and he began to pursue it. *Maybe the Mirage will fail?* But it was Epstein there in the sky. *Bad luck for that burning Sukhoi,* thought Huldai, *and for me.*

Alright. A two-ship formation of Sukhoi-7 made their way in a left turn, and Huldai knew that his turn had come. He launched a missile that passed below the rear aircraft of the Sukhoi two-ship formation, but it did not seem to explode.

"Eye contact with the second one," Eli Zohar informed him, sending a missile in the direction of the enemy and blowing him up in the sky.

Huldai went back to the first one. He found it spinning all the way down to the ground. It was hit by the missile after all, in a bright requiem to the two-ship formation that dared come here.

✦ ✦ ✦

24 Hours after "Nutcracker 22" ended, the difficulties returned. Those difficulties that began to bud after "Model 5," sprouted after the loss of Shani and Yaffe, thickened after Hayun and Ofir's aircraft fell, swelled with the fall of Samok and Baruchi, and rooted like a tree planted in a stream of fear after the four last ones were taken prisoner the previous night.

It had only been five days since he received active command of the Squadron, but Ben Eliahu could already recognize all of them: those who went forward come what may, and those who were struggling—they lowered their gears, closed themselves in, and communicated distress in their body language.

He knew how to identify the steps. At first, they stuck next to the stronger ones, trying to gain some inner strength, like they were following a guru. Later, they began to invent faults and issues that needed to be fixed in their aircraft, problems that did not exist. They were trying to find an honorable way to wash away their concerns.

Some of them sought release from missions, claiming excuses of joint pain, tribal code for the males, and especially of the fighter pilot, the pioneer before the camp. He has no way to say "I'm scared."

Just before they really fell apart, they eroded the ceiling of the shrine of heroism and said, "I'm just not happy with this whole 'festival'. I have no hunger to fight."

You must not break them, thought Ben Eliahu, recognizing that this was the final stretch before the crash. He searched for ways to support them, finding them easier missions and allowing them to go back to go back to sheltering themselves in the shrine.

Not everyone.

"I can't do it anymore," they said to their new commander, with their bowed heads proclaiming the control that terror had over them. The final evaporation of their mental strength.

Ben Eliahu debated whether "I cannot" meant "I do not want to," and in the end, he decided that they really cannot.

Nearly their age, and a warrior just like them, he understood that sometimes the shrieking survival instinct is stronger than anything, even their self-respect. There was no reason to push them down even more. After all, their "brothers" in the squadron had already discounted them, and the price tag for cowering would stick with them until their last day. He improvised solutions in an attempt to keep, even a little, lost dignity in their hands.

17:00. Office of the Prime Minister

"We are constantly aware of the possibility that the Egyptians will utilize Soviet surface-to-surface Scud missiles to target our territory," Gazit wrote in a telegram to Dinitz from the Prime Minister's Office.

"In his speech on October 18," Gazit continued, "Sadat threatened the activation of Tafar missiles against targets in Israel; 'Our Tafar missiles, which are able to cross Sinai, are on set up and ready to launch, as soon as the signal is given, deep into Israel. From the first moment of the campaign we were capable of giving the signal and the command, but we recognize the responsibility in using certain types of weapons. We are holding ourselves back from using them. You must remember, incredibly deep'."

"It is unclear whether this is an Egyptian missile, which we do not believe is actually operational, or an Egyptian name for a Scud," Gazit wrote. "Perhaps the possibility has arisen to use missiles activated by the Soviet crew, as Egypt still lacks a trained crew."

"At the same time, we received word from the Americans of the possibility of the Egyptian use of gas. Our sources confirm the existence of such weapons in Egyptian hands, and we know that the Egyptians have used them in Yemen."

"We are under the impression that Sadat has not received an accurate report about what is happening on the front," Gazit continued, "When it becomes clear to him what the real situation is, he is more likely to commit an act of madness and use the missiles or the gas, that is, using an escalatory weapon that he has in his possession."

"We request that you pass all of this information to Kissinger," Gazit concluded, "and to ask him to talk to Dobrynin (the Soviet Ambassador to the United States). We also ask that it be made clear to him that Sadat, who bears heavy responsibility for starting the war in the first place, will be solely responsible, doubly so if this escalates on account of the use of weapons such as missiles or gas—and that Israel will find a way to restore the balance."

22:00. *Senior Command Post*

In the shadow of severe pressures, Soviet leaders exerted pressure on the United States and the UN Security Council to compel Israel to immediately cease fire. Lt. Gen. David Elazar knew that the hourglass was running out, and in the little time that was left, he needed to improve the standing of the IDF forces on the west bank of the Canal, and expand the bridgehead to the north and the south.

"They always ask me how much more time will I need," the Chief of Staff said to Lt. Gen. (Res.) Yigal Yadin, who was with him in the senior command post. "Truthfully, if there is one thing that nags me about this war, it's that we will not succeed, in any way, in pushing them into a total collapse."

"It's because we don't have enough power," Dayan, who was also there, responded. He was weighing a successful day of fighting, in which 23 Egyptian aircraft were shot down, 20 in dogfights, and he was informed by the IAF that, for the first time since the fighting began, the day had finished without a single loss of IAF property or personnel. Nevertheless, he knew that it was just a single, light brush stroke on the wide, grim picture of reality: hundreds of khaki tanks destroyed, a hundred combat aircraft downed, and the hardest news—1,500 killed (actually approaching 1,850 that day, many of them still lying dead on the battlefield at that time).

"What's more, the war is still not over," said Maj. Gen. Tal, as though reading the minister's thoughts. "This is an extremely grave disaster unlike any other for the people of Israel."

OCTOBER 20

A Man Called Zemer

Two weeks had passed since the war erupted. The third Saturday had entered the field of bloodshed, and there was little that could undo the oppressive sense of confusion that was hovering inside the senior command post.

In the past few hours, Dr. Henry Kissinger was summoned urgently to Moscow, and the meaning of the trip was clear—negotiations between the two great powers over the timing of a ceasefire between the vassals under their patronage.

Israel, through its American guardian, wanted to postpone the date in order to expand and strengthen the grip its forces had in "Africa." Egypt, through its representatives, the Soviets, was trying to push it forward, to minimize the damage. Everyone knew that the ceasefire was only a matter of time, just a little time. Everyone also knew that after the ceasefire eventually passed, the negotiation phase would begin; and everyone, especially the group of senior officers gathered in the "Pit," deep underground in Tel Aviv, understood that, when entering negotiations, it is necessary to bring the best cards in hand.

In order for these cards to get in their hands, they would have to "get out of the package," and everyone underground knew that they would not get out on their own. The needed to be taken by force, meaning tanks, pushing to the north, west, and south, crunching and shattering the arrays of fortifications standing in their way, and destroying the missile bases that the IAF had trouble destroying.

They would also avenge the fall of Lt. Ilan Gidron, a simple tank soldier, who for two weeks had fought in the sands of Sinai, had done everything required and even more, until a single machine gun bullet hit his head and added him to the victims of the bloody war that still has no end.

Morning Hours. Chamber of the Head of the Command Center

At the end of the day off that Benny Peled gave to help his fighters recuperate, the IAF aircraft returned and were sent on the missions that they were meant to take the day before: attacking air bases and missile batteries.

"Good hits," his men reported from the field, fanning the flames of joy started by the continuing movement of the 'green' troops inside Egypt. Everyone had their fingers crossed for the crossing of 250 Israeli tanks, which had been sent over since the early morning, in addition to the regular tasks for the tanks in enemy territory: galloping towards missile systems that had not yet been destroyed, turning them once and for all into ruins.

Morning Hours. The 201ˢᵗ Squadron

In The 201ˢᵗ Squadron, the routine operational yawns continued. There were no attacks on air bases, and no destruction of missile batteries. Here was support over the Canal, there was more booby-trapping of axes with cluster bombs. Here and there were offset loft strikes. *We can do more. Are we out of targets?.*

Only the shells and missiles that haunted them in the sky proved that the war was still happening. Contrary to the tradition of the Six-Day War, the Egyptians did not break, and still had a strong fighting spirit. So did the squadron leader, Zemer.

Even in the long-ago days before the war, he suffered from back problems. Now, with the aftermath of his ejection, everything he thought he knew about pain had been radicalized. Bedridden at the hospital at Tel Hashomer. Weights on his legs spaced out his vertebrae, trying to reduce the intensity of the tingling that was shot through his spine and "electrifying" his feet. Col. Iftach Zemer, still the official commander of the 201ˢᵗ Squadron, was fighting a war of his own.

He tried to get up, to walk around—he collapsed. He tried again. Again, he collapsed. However, today, as the sanctity of Shabbat surrounded the inpatient department of Tel Hashomer, it was not a migraine that hurt him, nor his back. Another weight, a huge one, was on his chest.

He called them for seven days, checked up on his fighters, dear to his soul. His favorite "children" in the "Number One" Squadron, and no one came. They left him by himself a half hour's drive away from the squadron.

A week after ejecting, he packed up his aching body, his weight on his chest, returned to his squadron and saw that Eitan Ben Eliahu was the acting commander. Eitan was his deputy, was five years younger, and finished flight course twelve cycles after Zemer—an eternity in IAF terms. Zemer, an officer and a gentleman, thought that he was an excellent choice. He realized that, starting then, he needed to "re-earn" his place in the minds of his fighters. He assigned himself in an AGM-45 (Shrike) air-to-ground guided missile mission in Ismaïlia, and felt that he acquired another enemy, when he requested that Gideon Eilat, the young pilot, settle in the navigator's seat. This was because he was unsure what would happen with his back up there, and he would need to deal with acceleration forces and release the "blue" and "red" rockets to the target. Gideon would not stop lamenting his bitter fate. Zemer did not tell Gideon that, despite his fate in the rear cockpit, the forward chamber was actually bitterer, as he heard the booming whispers in the squadron and noticed the diverted glances. It was very difficult for him in the sky, even in weak g-forces and light maneuvers. His back pain drove him crazy. He once forgot to switch off the ICS in his helmet and screamed at his pain. Gideon asked, "What happened?" Zemer pulled some lie out of his sleeve, as the commander of the squadron cannot display his weakness, and he certainly should not share it.

16:30. A Man Named Epstein

The last forty-eight hours at Refidim, away from the desks at IAF Headquarters, had sharpened Maj. Epstein's hunting senses. At 16:00 precisely, with the onset of a "move and wait" alert, he was sure that the convoy of prey was making its way to the front, as

Egyptians preferred to attack when the sun set to the west, blinding the eyes of the blue-and-white pilots.

Right at 16:30, the voice of Yigal Ziv, the commander of the air control unit at Refidim, was heard on the phone line leading to the alert aircraft. Epstein knew that he was right, and the morning hours, which he wasted wandering around the skies back and forth in level flight, were vanishing.

"Scramble!" said Ziv. *Deir Sawir. The usual place.*

Epstein took off. He wanted more.

Giora Epstein had never given in, to anyone. Ever.

He tried to get draft into the Air Force: heart murmurs made them reject him. He volunteered with the paratroopers. He finished the track, became a class commander, a jump instructor, and returned to the kibbutz for three years, then returned to the military. He proved that heart murmurs would not interfere with skydiving, and he went on to represent Israel in the World Championships. *If I'm good enough to skydive with this murmur, what can the Israeli Air Force complain about?* Seven years after his recruitment into the paratroopers, at the "old" age of 25, the oldest trainee in Air Force history, he began Flight Academy and finished with the highest honors.

"You've been assigned to a helicopter squadron," his commander in Flight Academy told him. He saw the astonished gaze and added, "I understand that you expected to be placed in a fighter squadron, but the corps doctor maintains that your problems will not allow you to deal with the force of acceleration in the jets."

He studied the helicopter, while still dreaming of the combat 'peak', and pressed on. He did not stop pushing.

"Great," Col. Menachem Bar, the greatest base commander in the IAF, told him. "I've heard you, but we have decided that you are more vital here."

He started shouting.

"Calm down, calm down."

"I want to arrange a meeting with Ezer."

He set up the meeting.

"I am staying here in your office until you decide," Lt. Epstein said to Maj. Gen. Ezer Weizman, the commander of all of the pilots.

"Yardena," Ezer called to his secretary on the intercom, "We have a candidate for a cup of tea here."

They finished the tea.

"Go to the squadron," Ezer said, "I will think about what you've told me and let you know."

Epstein returned to Tel Nof.

In the morning, they called him on the phone.

"You piece of shit," the IAF Commander yelled on the other end of the line, "I didn't sleep all night because of you. Now, get your stuff and report back to the OTU, and I don't want to hear from you anymore."

A four-ship formation leapt to the eternal hunting fields.

"Keep going west," said the air controller. Continuing eye contact, a couple of MiGs pulled up from south to north. "Jettison tanks," Epstein ordered. "Pepper," and he immediately pulled to the right with a full afterburner. The three others followed him. What is that? Underneath him was a field of giant puffs of black smoke. However, Epstein knew that puffs do not grow in the sky, nor do they leap in front of combat jets. Twenty MiG-21 jets pulled up heading at his four-ship formation. They worked well, Epstein thought. The first couple that they sent was just a bait. However, he knew that then was not the time to give out scores, and certainly not sympathy. He knew that this was the time and the place to engage in combat. First and foremost, time to blow up the bait.

He descended from the heavens on the first couple, settled on the tail of the rear one, and decided to launch a missile, like he always used to do. From 1,000 meters, he launched a missile that punished the rear MiG for playing with the wrong partner, and blew it out of the air. The Egyptian leader saw the grim reality, and began a series of breaks and descents. Epstein followed. *This guy is good*, thought the Hunter of Negba, seeing the MiG dive towards the ground, gaining momentum, and pulling up at the last moment, with a cloud of dust mixing with the agricultural soil that separated the deserts on both sides of the Canal. *This is going to be interesting.*

He then noticed the pandemonium in the sky, and according to the radio and the glimmers of the delta wings, he understood that another Mirage four-ship formation was involved in a big battle. Everyone was fighting everyone, climbing and diving in a constant roller coaster, and in all of the confusion, Epstein just wanted one thing—to take down the Egyptian that was continuing to break for his life. On the radio, Number 2 announced that he was leaving the scene due to a malfunction, and both Number 3 and Number 4 announced that they had downed all of the MiGs on their own. Epstein was happy about their happiness, but he had a crazy MiG on his mind, and he wanted to take him down more than anything. Just then, he closed in and put the pipper on, and he let out a long burst from the 30mm gun at 300 meters distance. The mad pilot exploded in front of his eyes.

He then turned to the left and heard on the radio that Number 3 was heading home for fuel, and Number 4 did not seem to be in the sky at all. While making a turn, Epstein identified a two-ship formation of MiGs closing in on him from behind at a crazy angle-off. He performed the "yak exercise" for them—rolling under them and letting them pass him and set in front of him. They flew forward like missiles. He turned and sat behind them. It did not matter to him that there were a dozen other MiGs in the sky around him. The only thing that bothered him was the pair of flashes in front of him. It was too late to respond by rolling, and Epstein knew that missiles launched at him head-on at a range of 400 meters are scary, but their chances of success are minimal. Still, he curled up in the cockpit, such an instinctive reaction. The missiles passed over him, as well as the MiGs. He then turned towards the MiGs that launched at him, closing in on the rear one, and began to set the sight on him. He then realized that there was another two-ship formation attacking him from the right. They were already annoying him, and he let them pass him as well, rolling and then sitting on the tail of the rear MiG, setting the sight on him. He squeezed the trigger, and blew him up as well in the reddening sky.

Combat training is like playing poker with matches, Epstein thought.

You lost? An easy insult, a hit to the ego. That is it. No hair is going to fall off your hairline.

Real combat is poker with money. A lot of money.

You lost? You may continue your life in captivity or not at all,
seeing your life pour out with every strike of a pitchfork, axe, knife,
or a sickle.

Under the enemy canopy sits a man. In other circumstances, we
would have been friends, sharing the love of flying despite language,
national anthem, customs, flags, and particularly the leaders that
send us to kill one another. Now they have sent us, and only one of
us will return home safely. It had better be me.

Epstein made a turn in the sky, and another two-ship formation
of MiGs flew towards him. He did not know if they were new pilots
or if they already had a taste of aerial encounters, and it did not really
interest him. He climbed after them as they climbed in a loop. He
let the rear MiG reach inverted flight at the top of the loop, settled
under it, and caught it in his sight. He shot a short burst, and saw
the rounds crack the cockpit. The MiG lowered its nose in slow
motion, and Epstein saw it dive uncontrollably into the ground,
marking its death with a surge of fire. He broke clean, and stuck
his head around, looking right, left, behind, forward. The sky was
clear. No more MiGs. No parachutes. Nothing. He did not have
much fuel left and only about 30 rounds left in each of the guns.
He decided that, with four MiGs downed in one battle, it was fine
to end things. He turned east, crossing the Suez Canal and pulling
towards Refidim. At the underground hangar, his body betrayed
his story. His muscles were trembling, his legs were seemingly cast
in lead weights, and only two determined technicians managed to
pull him out of his seat.

A few hours afterwards, he was stabilized at IAF Headquarters
in the Kirya, where he found that his battle achievements had
resulted in nine Egyptian aircraft shot down in the last 48 hours.

Benny Peled, the toughest of them all, the commander of all of the pilots, pounced on him with kisses and hugs.

He made Epstein feel embarrassed.

18:00. Office of the Prime Minister

"Today was good," Dayan reported to Golda. "However, it is still a slow and heavy issue. Israeli forces took control of the Fayed air base. Thousands of Egyptian vehicles, probably the supply and administration ranks, were seen fleeing on the roads from Suez towards Cairo. Ariel Sharon is a stone's throw from Ismaïlia. If there won't be any particular difficulties, we will take the Hermon in the north and the territory between Suez and Ismaïlia in the south."

23:00. Office of the Chief of Staff

"The Egyptian Air Force is in a difficult situation," Benny Peled reported. "Two hundred of their aircraft have been shot down. Yesterday, we took down twenty of them. Today, they lost eighteen, twelve of them in dogfights. By today, while the Egyptians have been receiving replacement aircraft from the Soviet airlifts, their air force is missing pilots in general and pilots skilled in these aircraft types in particular. This is the reason that they used their Delphine aircraft to attack our forces, for the first time. A jet trainer is not supposed to participate in combat."

"The Syrian Air Force has lost close to one hundred and twenty aircraft," Peled continued. "The Syrians have not received any new aircraft, and they are suffering from a significant lack of air crews. The action that they performed today—two Sukhoi-20 aircraft arrived to the refineries in Haifa and dropped a firebomb into the water near Acre—is an act of desperation. The Syrians are trying to prove to themselves, and their army, that they are still in the picture."

Night. The 201ˢᵗ Squadron

The shape of our behavior, of all of us, is a mirror of the soul, Regev thought, recalling that Zemer returned and did not intervene with Ben Eliahu's management of the squadron. *What a man. What a huge soul.*

Afterwards, he skimmed the day's events in his mind, and concluded that things were beginning to calm down. He was reminded of a sentence that the man with the black patch said in a television interview, "We can withstand this war, and every additional day is in our favor."

What did you mean by "in our favor," Honorable Defense Minister? The growth of outposts in Egypt and Syria? Just that? What about the death toll and the squadron's prisoners, Mr. Minister, sir? Can you guarantee that every additional day will be in our favor here, as well?

OCTOBER 21

At Any Cost

*T*his is surreal, Gil Regev thought, indulging in the in the smells of Prosper's kitchen.

At three in the morning, they woke me up. Briefing room. Attack formation. Over half an hour ago, I launched AGM-45 (Shrike) missiles on missile batteries in Egypt.

Back and forth, black and white. This is the mission that we were raised on, that we've practiced. Take off and land, take off and land. This is our reality, all second nature to a fighter pilot. This routine built our mental resilience. But now, this war. It pushes me into the maw of real combat, where everyone, everyone, is trying to kill me. Only me.

Breaking away from the plush armchairs in the clubroom, the quiet whisper of the air conditioner, from the bunches of grapes, the bag of chocolate milk, cookies, a cup of coffee, Prosper's food, God, how he makes me so happy with his omelets with onion and parsley, soft bed, new sheets, clean underwear, spotless toilet, art performances—to leave all that for this boom. Damascus. Delta. Again and again. On every trip, doing it all over again.

True, I am a pampered fighter pilot. I live in a bubble, cut off
from the shrieks of the wounded, the wheezing of the dying, the spurts
of blood, mangled limbs, body odor drifting all around, the terrible
cries, the calls, "Mom, I don't want to die."

Yet I have my own struggles. Going back and forth demands
endless reservoirs of self-control and mental strength. I also know that
if something goes wrong, I will be left all alone, in the heart of enemy
territory; without a team, a department, or a company to assist me,
to support me, or to rescue me. Just alone by myself.

I still do not know which is better: to be a soldier on land, cut off
entirely from the tranquility of the safe world, calm, and surrounded
by conveniences; or to be required, each time, to collect myself and
take myself away from the good life straight to the flames of hell, and
realize that I am alone, always alone.

Here's Barnea and Eliasaf. It's good to have friends with whom
I can share difficulties. To hold on to life. Here is Eliel.

"Regev," he said, "This is exactly why we got the squadron
air crew's glasses, watch, and jacket." Afterwards he smiled his
enchanting smile and added, "War is such fun."

08:00. Office of the Defense Minister in the Kirya

On Sunday morning, two weeks and a day since the outbreak
of war, the Minister of Defense arranged a discussion in his office.

A few hours earlier, aware that the upcoming ceasefire would
interrupt the IDF's progress in the west bank of the Suez Canal,
Lt. Gen. Elazar ordered the commanders of the armored forces in
Africa to run towards the south, and to make every effort to reach

the city of Suez, which would completely encircle the Egyptian Third Army.

"The arrival of a ceasefire agreement is imminent," Dayan said to those present in his office, as if they were not already aware.

"One more thing," he added, staring with his one eye directly at a group of generals—three of whom were retired generals, who came to help at the onset of the war, when they saw that a black flag hanging over the state's continued existence. "A ceasefire agreement will include, among other things, the return of all prisoners."

10:15. Senior Command Post

"'Operation Dessert', meant to conquer the Hermon range, is scheduled to begin this evening," Maj. Gen. Yitzhak Hofi informed the IDF Chief of Staff on a telephone conversation. The regular Golani Brigade and Paratrooper Brigade 317 reservists, in cooperation with helicopters, armor, and artillery, would coordinate to regain control of the country's eyes.

Noon. The 201st Squadron

Lt. Iftach Zemer, the 34-year-old squadron leader, was very fond of Lt. Yitzhak Zetelny, a 23-year-old navigator.

When everyone was sent for instruction at the Flight Academy or placed in IAF Headquarters, he kept him along, coveting the tall navigator, with his rapid approach and the most original thinking in the squadron.

Zetelny entered Zemer's room, and with considerable discomfort, requested to speak with him. "There are quite a few fighters in the squadron who do not think that you deserve to be squadron leader," the young navigator said.

* * *

On Sunday morning, two weeks and a day since the outbreak of "this thing," Lt. Itamar Barnea was unaware of the things that Zetelny told Zemer, nor aware of the issue of prisoners brought up by the Minister of Defense.

The war is about to end, he grumbled to himself, *and this slipped through my fingers. I ran a lot of missions. I performed all of the tasks. Except this one.*

True, I didn't have any opportunities. Nevertheless, Ben Eliahu, Huldai, Zohar, Peled, Haloutz, Perry and even young Regev have already downed some. What about me?

Right, there is one MiG to my name. The end of 1972, a dogfight in Syria. So what? I need a downed aircraft now, in the real thing, and this war is about to end.

Still, should I give up on myself? Here's Avner Naveh, a young pilot, outstanding in training battles, and he keeps telling me—'Itamar, leave the MiGs, forget it. I haven't downed any either. It's all nonsense. What is real is the attack. That is our mission that we do all the time, farther and better than anyone'.

Downing an enemy aircraft entitles the pilot, or the crew, to an exciting meeting with the IAF Commander, champagne toasts and a place on the special plaque board bearing the names of the pilots next to other boards in the squadron clubroom. It is a great honor, a place in the Hall of Fame.

It is good that it is like this. After all, most of the training for the combat squadrons in the IAF focuses on dogfights, and here the bill is paid, and the one holding it deserves respect.

Yet on the way to the stage, other heroes are forgotten, as well as other tasks, that some would say are more important, and more dangerous.

A dedicated interception pilot clings to his country's border, sometimes skipping lightly across the frontlines, sometimes accompanying an attack formation deep into enemy territory. He waits for the cherry on top—confrontations with enemy aircraft. It is a game with predictable results. And fame, lots of fame, comes with the final whistle.

A strike pilot is always in enemy territory. Again and again, he pushes through the opposition posed by AAA and missiles that try to take him out, and he does the wingover and dives into the target, puts his sight on it, and is oblivious to everything fired at him. He knows that, if he is hit, he is so far away from home. He will eject, either into captivity, or to death.

And he continues. Time after time, again and again.

Okay, Barnea nodded, and Naveh thought that, finally, some sense has entered the mind of Barnea the hothead, and he did not know that it had not occurred. Barnea continued to think only about the enemy aircraft that would come and enter his sight. *I need to close this issue. Naveh can say whatever he says.*

Here's Gil Haran, my interception standby alert navigator. Just yesterday, he returned from a vacation in the United States, and this morning, he's already made two missions into Egypt, trying to catch up with the rest of us. Poor guy. He's missed the whole war. Maybe he'll catch an interesting mission or two. If only they scramble, just scramble us.

"The war is concluding today," said the "Rhino," the leading navigator for the on-alert interception two-ship formation.

Barnea nodded, thinking again about a MiG in his crosshairs. Now he saw Eitan Peled, "Wild Bull," the leader, Number 1 in the interception two-ship formation, who, in this war, had brought down two helicopters and two MiGs. Barnea thought of everything he would give to be in his situation; even just one MiG. He then thought about how life throws surprises at us, as this was the same "Wild Bull" who, during training, would make so many mistakes and made so much nonsense that it is hard to believe that an experienced pilot would do, and who was the squadron's idol. A man who is not afraid of anything. He is professional, down to earth, relaxed, poised, cool headed, and brave. The man most suited to war. All of the navigators wanted to fly with him. All of the young pilots did, as well. A few days earlier, when everything was much more difficult, he heard him speaking with the young navigators. "It's always hard in wars," he said to them in a monotone voice. "We'll come out of it, just like in the Six-Day War. We hold the stakes, we'll take the air, and then we will win."

14:00. Sirens. *Yes. Don't disappoint me*, Barnea whispered to his aircraft, observing its silhouette, touching it lightly. He climbed up, harnessed himself in, and started the engines.

Itamar Barnea did not know it, but most of the Israeli Air Force on Sunday afternoon, October 21, was concentrated in the north and was devoted almost entirely to support and to soften up resistance for Operation "Dessert." Dozens of sequential Skyhawk flyovers headed to the Hermon and the Golan Heights. Cries for help in Arabic were answered by the Syrian Air Force, sent to disrupt the Skyhawk's strike, and get in turn blue-and-white aircraft sent to intercept them.

The on-duty interception two-ship formation in the 201st Squadron, for instance.

They flew north.

While in the air, the air controller cancelled the interception mission.

Damn. Someone beat us to it, probably the sister squadron at Ramat David.

"Stay on patrol above the Sea of Galilee," the controller said. "General heading, north - south."

Yes! Barnea was cheerful, identifying a two-ship formation of MiGs high in the sky on his left.

"I'm taking them," he said to the leader. He left his position in the formation and made a sharp turn.

What? There's another two-ship formation of MiGs in the sky. And another one.

"A lot of MiGs are arriving," the controller reported. As if they did not already know.

Now, now. A Syrian MiG-21 ran for his life, one poor MiG. *Eliminate it. Immediately.*

In the rear cockpit, Haran was delaying with locking on. *Damn,* grumbled Barnea, *Gil is still rusty. My hit has escaped.*

"Look back," he told him, "I'm locking on." He pressed the pickle button, and a missile was launched. *Fall, you son of a bitch, fall.* The MiG broke sharply, exiting the sight. He evaded the missile. Short ranges, wild breaks, Barnea closed in, the Syrian responded in time and evaded, and the both of them were losing altitude and airspeed. Damascus was in front of the nose, and it was clear to Barnea that the Syrian was returning home, and now, for the first time, he was not so sure that he would succeed in taking the Syrian down. They passed each other head-on, and Barnea shot with his gun. Nothing.

Damascus was in his peripheral vision and missiles were launched towards him. Suddenly the MiG pulled up, and Barnea knew that the stubborn and worthy Syrian opponent was trying to gain energy, and he glanced at his indicators and saw that he hardly had any fuel left in the aircraft, maybe not even enough to land at Ramat David. So he understood that this is it, no other choice. He lowered his nose firmly, leaving the fighting scene and his dream with it. He glanced behind him… a MiG was sitting on his tail.

Eitan Peled jettisoned his external drop tank and called Barnea to return. No answer. Now a MiG four-ship formation came towards him, and he let them pass forward, lingered a bit, and allowed the next four-ship formation to pass forward as well.

"MiG to the right," the "Rhino" shouted, and "Wild Bull" broke to the right, climbed a bit, and set on his nose. He shot a missile that failed to hit, and the MiG tried to sit on their tail. A lone Sledgehammer zigzagged and broke among the MiGs, and more MiGs and four-ship formations came towards them on all sides. In the rear cockpit, the "Rhino" knew that they were fighting the battle for their lives, and he was not so sure who would win it.

An explosion in Barnea's aircraft, and suddenly the nose fell down, the controls did not respond, and all of the indicators flashed and screamed, as the ground was getting closer. Hanging in the sky, swinging on his parachute, Barnea remembered a story about Icarus the Reckless in Greek mythology, whose enthusiasm did not take into account the rules of the game, and he got too close to the sun until it melted his wings. The sense of insult overwhelmed him. *I, Itamar Barnea, I was knocked out of the air. I, Itamar Barnea, I brought it all on Gil, who is hanging in the sky next to me.*

What is this? A falling leaf in the silent, Syrian autumn wind, Barnea curled up in his parachute cords and reported on his SART that MiGs were strafing at him.

"Wild Bull" Peled heard Barnea report that he was in the air, meaning on the parachute. Peled looked towards Damascus and saw a big fire of a burning Phantom on the ground, and the air controller told him to head home. Peled, who broke off from his personal MiGs, said that he was staying to take care of Number 2, who had just ejected. He approached Barnea and asked how he was. Barnea said, "I'm still in the air," and then reports that MiGs were shooting at him. Then, the radio connection interrupted.

I'm still alive, Barnea thought, celebrating his temporary victory. He noticed that he was about to land inside a large military compound in which hundreds of soldiers were running around. They all fired in his direction.

Ouch. Blood gushed, flowed and ran down his right thigh. He then noticed the holes in his parachute, which explained his speed gliding towards the ground. *Damn!* His right thigh was shattered.

He threw his pistol so they would not think that he came to fight, sat up, and a thought continued going through his mind— *Everything will be fine, Itamar, everything will be okay.*

However, a hundred Syrian soldiers stood on the hill opposite from him. All of them shot at him, approached, and stopped. They aimed at the broken figure, and shot again, drilling into his flesh.

They reached him. A meter away from him, maybe a meter and a half, he saw someone with shoulder stripes and another with stripes on his sleeves. The one with stripes on his sleeves pulled out a gun. *This is a movie,* Itamar thought, *this can't be real.* Yet it was not a movie, and the one with sleeve stripes aimed his gun at Barnea's chest and squeezed the trigger. Barnea fell back in slow motion, like in Western films, and saw 'shoulder stripes' gesturing at 'sleeve stripes': *Enough, he's dead.*

Except that he was not dead, and though his body was pierced and bleeding, he felt them pick him up and throw him into the back of a pickup truck. During the short trip, 'shoulder stripes' turned around and removed Barnea's watch. Barnea came to terms with the situation, and understood that sometimes, life is short. He envisioned the face of Tali, whom he married only a little over a year ago, before him. Very emotional, he imagined breaking up with her, asking that she not be angry at him. Then it was his parents, ending it with them too. A great silence fell on him, a great sadness, and completion.

They stopped. In the twilight of his consciousness, he felt something being thrown at him. It was Gil. The way Gil leaned on his shoulder, motionless, breathless, it was clear that he was dead. Barnea was angry again, so very angry.

"Wild Bull" landed. He taxied to the underground hangar.

In the rear cockpit, the "Rhino" was not able to rise from his seat. He did not know if it was because his life was almost taken above Syria, or because of Itamar, his friend. He simply stayed in his place, and cried. He just sat there and cried.

15:15. Missouri Complex, Sinai

On Sunday morning, Maj. Gen. (Res.) Ariel Sharon, commander of one of the armored divisions in the Sinai sector, was instructed to send the 600th Brigade to attack 'Missouri', the Egyptian compound on the northern flank of the bridgehead.

Col. Tuvia Raviv was the brigade commander. "I'm not sure my forces can break deep into their infantry," he said to Sharon. "I'd prefer to continue the slow, systematic breakdown we have been doing the last few days."

"Attacking Missouri is a mistake," Sharon said to Gonen and Bar-Lev. "Instead, it is better to conquer or besiege Ismaïlia. It would have a tremendous effect."

"We are attacking Missouri," Dado said, "That is an order."

At 15:15, the 600th Armored Brigade, with its remaining thirty-six tanks and the reinforcement of five others, started a two-headed attack on the Missouri compound.

The force that was coming from the east ran into a minefield, halting their progress and dealing with self-rescue attempts under constant artillery fire. The second force, moving on the west axis to the compound, was caught in an ambush between infantry pits armed with anti-tank weapons. A few minutes before sunset on the first day of the third week of the war, the saga of the 600th Brigade, unable to occupy the complex, came to an end, with a loss of twenty-two tanks and mourning twenty-four dead and missing.

19:00. Office of the Prime Minister

"At this very moment, our forces are beginning the campaign to bring the Hermon under Israeli control," the Minister of Defense reported to the Prime Minister. "During the night, we hope to be able to re-hoist the Israeli flag over the mountain."

Two hours passed, and it was the Prime Minister's turn to update the Minister of Defense.

"This is the wording agreed upon by the two superpowers, and it will be brought to the Security Council within the next few hours," she told him, and she read the telegram that was in front of her: "The Security Council calls on all parties involved in the fighting to cease fire and to end all military operations no later than twelve hours after receiving this decision."

"It seems that the Security Council will adopt the decision at 03:00 Israel time," Golda said.

22:30. Office of the Defense Minister

"They won't stand on us with a stopwatch in hand," Dayan said to the group of officers gathered in his office. "I suppose," he continued, "it will be possible to take advantage of the whole next day and continue with the military momentum to increase our accomplishments on the ground. First of all, we need to finish conquering the Hermon by morning. In Egypt, Bren's division will continue southward to reach the city of Suez and complete the separation of the Third Army."

Midnight. Senior Command Post

"The Pitulim Post is in the hands of the paratroopers," Hakah reported. "The lower cable car was taken by Golani. A Givati Brigade force and a 188th Armored Brigade force that joined them on the way to the Israeli Hermon Outpost encountered heavy resistance."

Midnight. Chamber of the Head of the Command Center

"The depth of the IDF's progress in Egypt has put them in a panic," they smiled at the IAF Control Post. "Suicide waves, you cannot define it differently. Again and again, Egyptian aircraft were sent to disrupt the movement of our forces. Again and again, they were shot down. Nineteen aircraft."

"Three of ours fell as well," someone mentioned, "two of them in dogfights."

A Mirage in Sinai. A Phantom in Syria. Perhaps the crew from the Phantom landed safely. Someone spoke on the radio with the pilot.

Midnight. The 201st Squadron

What is going to happen? Regev thought. *We thought this was all over. Just today Itamar and Gil both went.* Side by side, they curled up on mattresses spread out in the clubroom, the tent, and surrounding rooms. Some fell asleep right away, fleeing into unconsciousness. Others did not close an eye all night. Lying there with their eyes open, they remained silent on the mattresses in the dark.

And only Eliel could not stop laughing.

OCTOBER 22

A Ceasefire?

As Sunday moved into Monday, members of the Israeli Government gathered and were brought up to date about the political affairs of the last few days.

At the end of her speech, the Prime Minister read the text of the resolution calling for a ceasefire between Egypt, Syria, and Israel, as was accepted by representatives of the two great powers—against the wishes of Israel, and in violation of clear assurances on the part of Dr. Kissinger.

Immediately after her speech, the Minister of Defense took the floor and updated the ministers on the situation on the fronts. He then discussed the military strike to conquer positions at Hermon, which began that night and would apparently continue into the early morning hours. He said, with his one eye glinting, "Although the proposal for a ceasefire will arrive at the table of the Security Council in approximately three hours, I see no problem with timetables for conquering 'the eyes of the country'. This is due to the fact that even if the proposal is approved at three o'clock (Israel time), it will still take twelve hours for it to enter into effect."

At 01:20, the crowded conference room received an urgent message from the President of the United States, who had been informed about Israel's great anger over Kissinger's agreement with the Soviets.

"The decision that was sent to the UN Security Council is an accomplishment for the United States and for Israel," Nixon wrote, "...there is no mention of a withdrawal. Troops will remain in place."

"Furthermore," the President continued, "it was agreed that the two major powers would support the opening of direct talks between the parties, without preconditions, and utilizing all of their weight to bring an immediate exchange of prisoners."

"I regret that, due to a lack of time, we could not consult with you before we passed the final version to the Security Council desk," Richard Nixon concluded. "I hope the Prime Minister and her cabinet will accept and support the decision."

At 01:45, a letter from the US Secretary of State arrived, which emphasized what was already known before: "The agreed-upon resolution references UN Resolution 242."

"The reference is minimal," Kissinger wrote, "and it is not possible to add to or subtract from it."

Resolution 242 was approved by the UN Security council on November 22 1967 and came to regulate the new situation in the Middle East, with the end of the Six Day War. The problematic clause in the proposal dealt with the scope of the withdrawal. The text of this proposal in this section was vague, and called for withdrawal from territories, and not from the territories, leaving a bone of contention, open to multiple interpretations. The State of Israel had argued that the agreement did not call for a withdrawal from all territories occupied in the Six-Day War, but rather, allowed for the creation of new, secure and recognized borders. In contrast, the Arab countries argued that Resolution 242 called for a full Israeli withdrawal from all territories conquered in June 1967.

On August 4, 1970, the Israeli government decided to accept the peace initiative of US Secretary of State William Rogers, according to which, peace would be established in the Middle East, beginning with a ceasefire agreement between Israel and Egypt, and continued in accordance with Resolution 242.

In the dispatch passed on to the Americans and in her speech in the Knesset that day, Prime Minister Golda Meir repeated and interpreted Resolution 242 as Israel viewed it—a withdrawal from "territories," not "**all the territories.**" Speaking before the Knesset, the Prime Minister said, "Israel said publicly that pursuant to its right to secure, defensible borders, it will not return to the borders of June 4, 1967, which expose the country to the temptations of aggression, and provide—in different sectors—decisive advantages to aggressor. The ceasefire lines can be placed only within secure, recognized borders agreed upon and determined by a peace treaty."

Talks were held with Dr. Kissinger before his trip to Moscow, in which the Israeli Prime Minister asked that any agreement of understanding with the Soviets regarding a ceasefire would not reference Resolution 242. Yet afterwards, Kissinger pretended as though he did not know, and had not heard nor seen this information, and was prepared to sacrifice one of the Jewish State's inalienable assets in one dismissive stroke of a letter, in the name of US or even personal interests.

Golda was upset.

Why 242? It's a decision that belongs in another era, another reality. Another war. Mentioning it will reward the aggressive Arabs. You promised to try and prevent it. Since August 1970, we have had a mutual understanding regarding our interpretation of the proposal. What happened now?

Time constraints did not allow you to send the Israeli government the final draft that was received in Moscow?

Come on, really. Before his trip to Moscow, US Secretary of State, Dr. Henry Kissinger, you promised that we would not stand in a fait accompli.

Like the Russians are the supporters of the Arab states, you Americans are supposed to represent Israel. You've stumbled. You promised that every agreement with the Soviets would be done in coordination with us. And what is this? The text of the proposal that's been passed to the UN Security Council threatens to keep us from our planned military objectives, deals with the vital interests of the existence of the State of Israel, and you cannot find the time to provide us with a draft for review?

The Israeli Prime Minister gritted her teeth in badly-concealed anger. "Breaking a promise leaves me with a heavy feeling," she said to the ministers meeting in her office.

However, Golda Meir was a sober woman.

Even with seeds of anger and wrath, as legitimate as it may be, the Prime Minister did not lose touch with reality: Israel was bound with steel ties to Uncle Sam, and there was nothing else like it.

"Despite all the anger, Israel cannot say no to the American proposal for a ceasefire," Golda said. "Our nation has two things that characterize its people: unsurpassed courage, and an inability to bear losses. When there is no choice, there is no choice, and everyone understands that. Yet if there is a choice, you cannot say no. The only country from which we are able to receive arms from is the United States. Had the terms of the ceasefire been impossible for us, then we would refuse. But if we refuse, we automatically cease receiving weapons."

"I would like to remind the members of this government that the IDF is in the midst of an attack, and it is assumed that the situation will improve in the coming two days, not worsen," said the Chief of Staff, who was also sitting in the meeting. "A brief pause would be disastrous for us. In a respite of a week or ten days, and the Egyptians will enhance their missile system, so that once again, we will have limited aerial freedom of movement and action. The Syrians will receive a substantial build-up of weapons from the Soviet Union, plus fresh armored forces from Iraq and Jordan."

"Therefore," Lt. Gen. Elazar said, "Fighting cannot resume after the short pause. Also, we should tie Israeli agreement with the ceasefire with a condition for a solid American promise to supply arms to Israel."

With characteristic army terseness, which was perhaps inappropriate, Lt. Gen. Elazar tried to clarify for those present that the IDF, which he commanded, had the advantage at that moment. The IDF was initiating, the IDF was pursuing, and since the State of Israel was about to enter into a ceasefire while Egyptian forces were present in territory in Sinai, it was important to find a counterbalance to their weight there. A heavy weight would be the conquest of a larger area, more specifically, towards the city of Suez. Therefore, a formula needed to be found that would allow Israeli forces another day, or two preferably, of military action. A formula of a "ceasefire and a wink," in which it was clear that it would break open again within a week or two, would not help. It would, in fact, be the opposite. "Therefore, if you are going to send us to war again in a week or two, forget it. Allow me to complete the war here and now. This is the only way that we can reap the fruits of the spree of our military's momentum; complete the encirclement of the Third Army; reach Suez; give the Egyptians a sense that we have defeated them; and cause them to abandon any thought about renewing combat in the near future, when the knife of our armor is raised to their neck all the way to Cairo."

The discussion ended at 04:00. The Israeli Government decided, following the request of the United States and the personal message from President Nixon, that it was willing to accept the Security Council resolution calling for a ceasefire with Egypt and Syria, if it will also ensure the exchange of prisoners.

At 06:20, following the agreed-upon text formulated through the night between the Americans and the Soviets, the UN Security Council approved Resolution 338.

At 07:00 a call was made by the Security Council, which indicated that within twelve hours, by 18:52, there is a ceasefire on all fronts; just as the Minister of Defense expected.

Without delay, Israel announced that it accepted. Israel's UN Ambassador, Yosef Tekoah, informed of Israel's interest in strengthening its grasp on Egyptian territory, and reported to the Prime Minister's Office that Resolution 338 did not establish any mechanism for observers to determine the positions of the two sides on the ground, thus leaving open many possibilities to maneuver. Just as the Chief of Staff wanted.

While Resolution 338 was activated, the Prime Minister's Office receives a telegram, this time from the Israeli Ambassador in Washington. "The US Secretary of State should leave Moscow at 10:00," Dinitz wrote, "and he plans to land in Israel for a short round of meetings for a few hours."

Morning. Hermon Outpost

At 10:35, after seven bloody hours, soldiers in the Golani Brigade, accompanied by some in the Paratroopers 317th Reservist Brigade, climbed onto the roof of the Hermon Outpost and raise the flag of the State of Israel.

At 10:38, Major Katz opened the Brigade radio channel, and in an excited voice, said, "For the attention of every station in the world, the flag is raised."

Maj. David Katz did not mention the brigade commander and the battalion commander who were injured during the take-over of the mountain, nor the 77 others. Nor Hill 16, or Hill 17, of the tank bend. Nor the 56 fatalities, 53 of which were from the Golani Brigade. One artillery gunner, one combat engineer, and Yossi Weisbrot, a "boy" with an eternal smile always on hand, a tank commander in the 188th Brigade, who had survived all of the defensive and breakthrough battles of the war.

As the UN Security Council announced Resolution 338 in the UN building in New York, calling for a ceasefire between all parties, a single bullet shattered Yossi's forehead, leaving an impression of dark blood, flowing non-stop onto the rocks of the "Eyes of the Country," and painting the war's very last painting.

Noon. Iftach Zemer

"In the situation that has been created, you need to clear your place," the IAF Commander spouted off at Lt. Col. Zemer, who initiated a personal meeting with the commander.

"I am ready to change command as soon as you decide."

"In a week or two we'll conduct the replacement ceremony," Peled said. "Do you find it acceptable that we leave Eitan Ben Eliahu as the permanent squadron leader?"

"Yes," Zemer replied, "I strongly support the appointment."

13:30. Henry Kissinger

As the gates of command in the 201st Squadron closed for Iftach Zemer, the US Secretary of State of the United States landed in Israel.

"The Egyptians are willing to ceasefire at six in the evening (19:00 Israel time)," Kissinger reported to those present in the Prime Minister's Office, after finishing talks in Moscow.

"The Soviets explicitly demanded withdrawal to the 1967 borders," Kissinger added, awakening Golda's sensitivity to UN Resolution 242. "Of course, we rejected it out of hand."

"The two superpowers have pledged to release prisoners," he added, informing that "the airlift will continue for another three weeks." The Secretary of State continued his reassurance campaign, trying to be attentive to the telegram that the Prime Minister's Office released in the early morning hours. "In any case, the air lift will not stop as long as the Soviet airlift to Arab countries goes on." He continued, "You should know, the President has pledged to replace all of your equipment losses."

"One more thing," he said before departing. He led the Prime Minister to understand that, if there were urgent military concerns, it would be possible to maneuver a bit and improve the Israeli position in the south even after the ceasefire went into effect. "I'll be on the aircraft when you progress. When I get to Washington, I will submit a statement of protest."

14:45. Moshe Dayan

"Push south," the Minister of Defense instructed the Chief of Staff, upon hearing from Kissinger that the President of Egypt agreed to a ceasefire. "Use all of your force to push further south."

"I'm in constant contact with the troops," Dado said. "I talk to them every fifteen minutes. That's exactly what we are doing. Pushing south."

16:00. Kissinger and IDF Generals

At the request of the US Secretary of State, the Chief of Staff, the Chief of Military Intelligence, and the Commander of the Air Force were summoned to review the situation on the fronts.

"Today, the Egyptian air defenses have been wiped out," the IAF Commander reported, knowing that his aircraft have carried out a record of raids on the Egyptian front, 570, of which 440 were assistance mission to ground forces.

"Also today, we have cleared the last active missile system to the south of the Gulf of Suez," Peled continued, "The Syrians still have 16-17 active batteries. Most of them are SA-6s. The Egyptian Air Force has lost 254 aircraft since the beginning of the war, the Syrians have lost 205, and we have lost 102 aircraft."

"It's not just that the ceasefire goes against the interests of the IDF," said the IDF Chief of Staff to the Secretary of State, "but it saves the Egyptians from even heavier blows."

"What do you attribute to the IDF's victory in this war?" Kissinger asked.

"There is still a significant gap between the IDF and Arab militaries in terms of leadership and the quality of individual fighters. This gap is affording us the ability to overcome their superior numbers," Dado said.

17:00. Office of the Defense Minister

"The ceasefire goes into effect at 18:52," the Defense Minister again informed the Chief of Staff. He continued, "Bren can continue to progress to the south along the Little Bitter Lake, on the way to Suez, even after 18:52."

At 18:15, an order was distributed from the Headquarters of the Operations Branch, informing all forces on the Egyptian front that the ceasefire would begin at 18:52. "I am telling you," Dado instructed Bar-Lev on the telephone with the guiding spirit of the Minister of Defense, "all of those that are still on the move are able to finish their movements."

22:00. Governmental Meeting

"The Egyptians are firing as if there is no ceasefire," the Minister of Defense informed the other governmental ministers. "If they will continue shooting in the morning, we will want to continue the operation that we were not able to complete."

"Are you suggesting a major operation?" the Prime Minister asked Dayan.

"I am speaking of the operation that we have already begun," said Dayan, revealing a secret paper of his and Dado's.

"Yes, it will be a big operation," Dado said, who was also present at the meeting. "If the Egyptians will continue to shoot in the morning, we will want to clear the whole area."

If Egypt would not accept the ceasefire in practice, and would continue firing on Israeli troops in the combat zone, the IDF would retaliate, and therefore the government reached a decision at midnight. If the Egyptians continued fighting, the IDF would be authorized, simultaneously with the fighting, to complete the task of connecting the Canal with the southern part of the Great Bitter Lake and to the south towards Suez. Right into the hands of Dayan and Dado.

Night. The 201ˢᵗ Squadron

We were laying low today, Regev thought, *only 37 missions. Assisting ground forces, tanks, trucks, nothing serious. Nothing heroic. Maybe just Ben Eliahu's three ship formation, sent out an hour ago before sunset to close a personal account with the Third Army commander and his staff deputy. There are camouflaged bunkers there. The intelligence people said that they put a lot of effort into them. It could be hard to find them.*

They returned to the Squadron disappointed. They said that they didn't see anything tangible destroyed or ignited. Then came the intelligence reports, and it turns out that the obituary of the performance was premature. The communications bunker was completely destroyed. Injuries were reported in the Command Bunker. According to the intelligence report, the Third Army Commander walked twenty kilometers to the alternate headquarters. The guy's in good shape.

It's wonderful that everyone is thinking about us. They brought a masseuse who has fallen in love with Zetelny's broad shoulders. It's exciting that countless packages are delivered here, full of underwear and cigarettes from the ladies at Ha Vaada Lema'an Hahayal *(The Committee for the Wellbeing of the Soldier). It's nice that there are still films in the wing cinema. But how on Earth can we find consolation in this war?* Regev thought. *What happened to Itamar and Gil yesterday? How are Shaniboi and Assael holding up? What about all the others? And if what they say is true, is the war really ending today?*

Just before he fell sleep, he suddenly thought about Motti Reder, the guy who no one was really enthusiastic about when he arrived from the Super Mystére squadrons. Throughout the war, when everyone walked around with grim faces, he would subject them to his gallows humor, and in the most stressful moments, in the briefings in the early days of the fighting, he would shout with pathos, "I will kill Arabs! For every one of you!" and everyone would fall to the floor.

And now 'everyone' *is less than half of the squadron,* Regev thought as he fell asleep.

October 23

A Predetermined Chronicle

"The Egyptians, around the territory of the Third Army, have violated the ceasefire throughout the whole night," the IDF Chief of Staff informed Israel's Minister of Defense. "They have destroyed nine of our tanks and attempted to kidnap soldiers in various places. Give me permission to continue to make progress here in full swing."

"Go for it," Dayan replied.

09:00. Office of the Prime Minister

"While he was here, Kissinger whispered to me that if we had attacked first on October 6, we would not have received anything, not even a screw or a nail," Golda shared her little secret from the night before with Dayan, and her face turned serious. "It took them time to take in the fact that we didn't begin the fighting. In the first reports they received, their sources indicated that we instigated hostilities."

"The Egyptians are violating the ceasefire along the front with the Third Army," the Minister of Defense informed her for her consideration.

"This needs to be reported to the Americans immediately, and the IDF Spokesperson needs to put out a message, emphasizing the repeated violations of the ceasefire on the part of the Egyptians." They both agreed.

09:45. The 201st Squadron

There is something to this intensity, Ben Eliahu thought, thrilled, as his 19 fighters followed him from the briefing room to the buses that took them to their aircraft's underground hangars.

Quality is a key ingredient, thought Huldai, *but that intensity is impressive, very impressive.* He glanced around him and saw a formation of 10 giant Sledgehammer jets all around him taxiing along the taxiway to the takeoff runway.

I wonder if the Syrians will get the big hint that we will leave them, and they will finally deign to lay down their weapons, Ben Eliahu reflected in his cockpit. He was leading the strike six-ship formation to the underground fuel containers farm in Khan Ayish, northeast of Damascus.

I wonder if I can grab a few more downs just before this war ends, Huldai thought in his cockpit, leading the violent CAP four-ship formation. Their task was to act as a diversion to draw MiGs away from Ben Eliahu and his aircraft, so the enemy would not interfere with the attack. *Just so long as the four ship formation of Shahaks don't steal from us all the dogfights. And the glory.*

As always, Ben Eliahu thought, *the same pattern—a low flight over the water, we pass Sidon and then Beirut with the estuary of Ibrahim river (wadi), and east to Lebanese territory.*

Zetelny was in the rear cockpit, watching the Land of the Cedars pass under them and he saw the beautiful Wadi, which reminded him of the area around Montfort. *If there is ever peace, this is a place that he will have to visit,* he thought to himself. Yet it was not the time, as they were already in Syrian territory, very low among the mountains.

10:15. "Three, two, one, pull up," Zetelny said, and Ben Eliahu pulled, obstructed by a mountain. It seemed as though no war-monger could find them.

Strange, Ben Eliahu thought, *this is the first time that I've attacked an underground target, nevertheless, there were indications above-ground pointing to its location.* Everyone attacked. There were several hits, and some others hit near the target. A giant mushroom rose upwards, igniting the sky of the Middle East.

A minute before the designated attack time for Ben Eliahu's six-ship formation, and a little to the west of them, Ron Huldai pulled-up to the sky, with Rotem, Haloutz, and Stavi behind him.

If the Syrians are serious, their radar will find us, Huldai thought.

They were serious. Two minutes after pulling up, a rain of external drop tanks rolled down in the air, and the Sledgehammeres four-ship formation was followed by an emerging four-ship formation of MiGs.

The first two-ship formation of MiGs closed in on Huldai, and he allowed them to pass in front of him.

"Another two-ship formation," warned Romem in the rear cockpit.

Huldai broke and performed a "scissors" maneuver with one of the enemy aircraft. The MiG, which struggled to hold its altitude, hit the ground and crashed.

Haim Rotem settled on the rear MiG of the two-ship formation that attacked Huldai, and Amnon Tamir, in the rear cockpit, locked on. They launched an AIM-9 Sidewinder missile, which exploded behind the MiG, who had just broken out and escaped. They moved over to the MiG in the front. They launched. Nothing. Now another two-ship formation came. *I give up on the missiles*, Rotem decided, switching to guns. Smoke. *Great. What is that? The MiG is flying like bullets never hit his left wing.*

"The Phantom currently heading north, get out of the way," Haloutz shouted, seeing a Phantom that failed to hit. He did not know that it was Rotem, who three times in the last minute came to the opening of the Promised Land and didn't pass through the gates, and Haloutz wanted to down a MiG and for no one to interfere. Rotem got out of his way, and from a range of 600 meters, Haloutz launched a Sidewinder, which "screamed" the whole way to the MiG, which was promptly turned into a giant blaze.

"Release, release the nose down, get more energy," the "Rhino" shouted from the rear cockpit, and Haloutz did what the "Rhino" asked of him, and pulled out of the dogfight a bit, lowered the nose, added 150 knots to his airspeed, and returned to the heart of the dogfight. He saw another MiG a bit ahead of him. *This is not the way you down an aircraft, but the MiG is halted with low airspeed, so maybe we can down him.* Haloutz went into a sharp right turn, with a slight raise of the nose towards the MiG. Just then, the air controller pressed to disengage, but the "Rhino" secured a lock and said, "We have a lock-on. Switchover to radar." The range was 1,500 meters and the angle-off was 45°. This was not an optimal situation, but Haloutz wanted to take him down, and the "Rhino" said that everything was okay. He launched a Sparrow (AIM-7E-2) missile, which was headed to the left after launch, in the wrong direction. They were confident that the missile would not hit the target, but the smart missile had other plans. It cut and changed direction, moving right and hitting the center of the MiG. Haloutz thought to himself, *I didn't know that the "Rhino" could shout so loud when he's happy*, and he joined the happiness, in a calmer tone. Only one Syrian pilot teetered on a parachute high in the sky, and everyone was guiding each other by referring to the guy hanging below the parachute—"under the parachute," "above the parachute."

They directed Yigal Stavi just like that. He detected a MiG below the paratrooper, followed after him, sent a Sidewinder and cut the MiGs tail. A moment later, another parachute was in the sky, while the MiG crashed into the ground in a big flame.

"Let's go home," Huldai said.

Stavi, of all people, the gentle Jerusalemite, did not hold back his feelings about his first MiG. He buzzed low over the squadron, and broke above the top of an eucalyptus tree. *A fitting end*, thought Shmueli in the rear cockpit.

Noon. The 201st Squadron

Adi Benaya and Amnon Gurion were two four-ship formation leaders, eight links in a chained puzzle of 350 strike sorties that the IAF was sending in a concentrated effort, probably the last, on the Third Army system.

Phantoms, and especially Skyhawks, struck repeatedly at tent camps, headquarters, artillery batteries, tanks, and vehicles that were trying to flee for their lives.

The Egyptian missile array is destroyed. We are once again the kings of the sky, Gurion thought. He was sent to bomb a military camp near Adabiya, and while Zetelny was directing him to the target, he identified Egyptian soldiers running for their lives, desperately seeking shelter from the flying angel of death. For a moment, it was hard for him to cope with the unfairness. However, then he remembered the early days of the war, and all at once, with a load of bombs traveling behind the panicked crowd below, his mercy was cut out of his heart.

17:45. Senior Command Post

"Bren's forces are on the outskirts of Suez," stated the report from Southern Command. "There is no organized resistance by the enemy, but there are no plans to enter the city at night. We'll wait for the morning, and we'll see what tomorrow brings."

Five minutes passed, and the Minister of Defense called the Southern Command's Forward Command Unit at Um Hashiva and instructed Gen. Gonen to continue to operate all night, regardless of the ceasefire.

The Chief of Staff, who also came on the line, added, "We need to continue and fight as hard as the ammunition and fuel supplies permit."

18:00. Washington

In the Oval Office of the President of the United States, Gen. Brent Scowcroft, Kissinger's senior aide, called the Israeli Ambassador to the United States. He noted that the US Secretary of State was also in the room, and he told Simcha Dinitz that he urged Israel to cease fire immediately.

"You cannot expect IDF troops to be used as live targets for the Egyptians," the ambassador replied, "they will respond to those that fire on them constantly."

"We've understood," they answered him, "So at least make sure that the IDF will refrain from offensive operations."

18:05. The Prime Minister and the Knesset in Jerusalem

Only one week had passed since the Prime Minister left her chambers in Tel Aviv, traveled up to Jerusalem and updated the Knesset about the history of the war that was pushed on the State of Israel. Today, she went once again.

"On the Syrian front, our situation is better than it was before the outbreak of violence," Golda revealed to the representatives of the people. "Not only is the whole area back in our hands," she said, "but our situation is much better. We are now holding more positions on the ridges of Mount Hermon, as well as on the eastern front line."

"While the Egyptians had early victories across the Canal," Golda continued, "a bold counter-attack by the IDF managed to push our forces to regain control of the Canal on the eastern line and even a large space west of the Canal line, territory that now opens up possibilities for defensive and offensive maneuvers alike. This arrangement has taken away the ability of the Egyptian Army to threaten the Sinai and Israel. IDF forces west of the Canal are a strong basis for engaging in further operational initiatives, should they be required."

20:05. Senior Command Post

"By the end of the night, the whole southern sector of the west bank of the Canal will be in our hands, including the gulf coast near Attaka," the Chief of Staff reported to the Minister of Defense, putting into practice what the Prime Minister stated in her speech.

Night. The 201ˢᵗ Squadron

Gil Regev did not know that the Egyptian Air Force hardly attacked today, concentrating their efforts in intercepting the Israeli Air Force aircraft that were continuing to crush the foundation of the Third Army. He also did not know that the Egyptians lost eleven aircraft in desperate attempts to defend their forces. However, he did know that another day had passed without IAF losses in aircraft or personnel. He also knew about the nine Syrian loses. After all, he was with Ben Eliahu, on the attack of the fuel containers farm. Afterwards, he had heard from Huldai all of the tales of the interception four-ship formation. A nine-branched *menorah*.

It's respectable, thought Regev, relaxing in his bed, with Eliasaf to his side. *We are striking targets and downing aircraft. The fact that the Egyptian and Syrian Air Forces, throughout the war, have hardly hit our ground forces, is because they have spent most of their time guarding the home front and placing their aircraft in defensive missions. That is entirely because of us. It is due to the hundreds of sorties of the four Phantom squadrons that struck in the home front in Egypt and Syria, as well as the air superiority of the Phantoms and Mirages when entering dogfights. How many aircraft were downed in this war? Someone said more than 330. And another 100 were shot down by anti-aircraft fire from the ground. Quite a few.*

Then, after not thinking of her for a lot of time, just before sleep's protective blanket wrapped around him, she reappeared.

"Nurit," he whispered quietly, so Eliasaf won't hear, "It will be fine. In a moment, it will be over."

OCTOBER 24

The Apocalypse at Suez

Something has to be changed.
The Israeli stew is about to flow over Egyptian troops. The Egyptian leadership in Cairo internalized the updated situation of the problematic battlefield west of the Canal, especially the movement of Israeli tanks to the Suez-Cairo road. They were afraid of the Zionist revenge galloping all the way to the pyramids. They cried desperate cries for help from their patrons.

In Moscow, the decoded calls of help showed a real crisis, especially for the Soviet Union, which faced the possibility of losing its largest client state in the Middle East.

In Washington, cheerful updates were received from the southern front. Dr. Henry Kissinger, Secretary of State of the United States and a big opportunist in regional affairs, smelled a one-time opportunity to get a foothold in the country of the Pharaohs.

In Africa, IDF armored forces continued to advance westward and to the south, ignoring the warnings of the Americans and the Russians. *We didn't initiate this*, the Israelis argued, *we are just responding*, and they were hoping to finish the fiery dance just before the two superpowers would stop it, and achieve the complete encirclement of the Third Army in the air, the sea, and on land.

At 01:00 Jerusalem time, the UN Security Council approved the text of Resolution 339, submitted by the Soviet Union with U.S. support, which stated that the armed forces of the two warring sides would return to positions held on Monday, October 22, at 18:52. It also empowered the UN Secretary-General to pursue all necessary measures in order to observe the fulfillment of the ceasefire, calling for the immediate posting of a compound for observer forces embedded within the positions of both sides.

03:00. Office of the Prime Minister

"Kissinger has a solution," Golda informed Dayan. "He suggests that we make a symbolic withdrawal, only a few hundred meters. Just one hill."

"Forget it," she said.

"It's out of the question," Dayan said, supporting her. "If we withdraw even a little, it will indicate to everyone that we are receptive to Kissinger's principle. It will be the beginning of a bigger withdrawal. The Egyptians, the Russians, and the Americans will pressure us to finish what we've started. They will come to us with photographs, they will push us farther and farther, until we lose everything that we have accomplished in the last thirty-six hours. We have to say loud and clear—we will not go backwards, even if the United States will work against us."

"Kissinger yelled at me on the telephone," Golda continued, "He and Nixon are unwilling to accept our position. They say that we are violating the ceasefire agreement, while continuing to make progress on the ground. Of course, I told them that they were wrong, and after the conversation was over, I entrusted Dinitz to repeat to them that we agree to a ceasefire where we stand, with a condition of reciprocity."

03:20. Senior Command Post

As the Minister of Defense informed the Chief of Staff about the details of UN Resolution 339 and the discussions that he shared with the Prime Minister, the Israeli Liaison Officer to the UN received a message. According to the message, Finnish General Ensio Siilasvuo, one of the Senior Middle East Officers in the UN, received an order from New York to send UN observers to the Egyptian front line, in order to monitor the implementation of the ceasefire resolution.

"We are ready for that," Dayan said, offering a renewed ceasefire beginning at 07:00.

03:00. Office of the Prime Minister

"We will not succumb to the pressure to retreat from the current lines," the War Cabinet strengthened Dayan and Golda's decision, and decided to recommend it strongly to the government.

"After the encirclement of the Third Army, heavy international pressure is expected to fall on Israel," Minister Galili said, "We need to make a maximum effort to reach an understanding with the United States, but without giving up what we have achieved."

The Cabinet agreed with Dayan's position that Israel agree to a ceasefire at 07:00, though only where the lines stood at that hour, and with express Egyptian agreement.

05:50. IDF Operations Branch

A few minutes after sunrise, the IDF General Staff Headquarters distributed an order to its forces indicating that the Southern Command was to stabilize the line everywhere Israeli troops were present, so that all access roads and high ground would be under Israeli control. Combat operations would continue until 07:00, including IAF assistance operations and air strikes against Egyptian troops in the east bank of the Canal.

In any case of Egyptian violation of the ceasefire after 07:00, it would be necessary to respond and operate freely in the area that did not respect the ceasefire.

06:00. The 201st Squadron

There is permission to attack until 07:00, the command chamber of the IAF is informed. They then prepared hasty mission orders to Wing 4. They sent four formations—one Super Mystére and three Phantom formations—to perform final strikes on forces of the Egyptian Army.

"Everyone that can organize and find an aircraft is authorized to join the formation leaders," they told the Squadron. They sent eleven aircraft to strike the forces of the Third Army on the side of the road ("Lexicon Highway"), east of the Canal.

Yigal Stavi led the last formation. *Here's the road. It's five minutes to seven, just don't miss the final beat. Where the hell are the targets?* "Baby Face" Stavi was bothered. *How could the Egyptians disguise themselves so well?*

"Dragon Formation, hurry!" he heard the rush on the radio.

What are they thinking? That we are playing around?

"Number 1, I see embankments with many non-armored vehicles in the East," Gil Regev said on the radio, rolling his R's.

At 07:00 on the nose, the Dragon Formation's last bomb fell perfectly on Egyptian forces in the sands of Sinai.

At 07:30, Regev felt that this time, the war really was over. On the bus, the whole way from the underground hangar to the squadron building, the song "To Love Life" played in his head. He began to sing, weak at first, then stronger, and finally, very loudly: "...Like in the legends, I've stayed alive..."

07:00-14:15. The City of Suez

As the last bomb of the Dragon Formation made its way to the sands of Sinai, and Gil Regev celebrated the gift of life, at least until the next war, IDF artillery began a heavy bombardment of the city of Suez.

On Monday, October 22, the State of Israel rolled up its sleeves and decided to play in the big leagues. New rules. Gone were the days of *Srulik*[10], the disciplined student in the Middle East classroom, whose main interest was a high score for good behavior.

---

10 A popular 20th century illustrated character symbolizing the State of Israel.

On Monday, October 22, without an agreement between them and without a declaration of the new protocol, the country's leaders, and especially those who held the reins of the country's security, decided that, from now on, they will do only what was good for the Jews. And if it was necessary, they would lie. To everyone else. Just like everyone else.

We will not preach to you, and we will not speak to you about hypocrisy and double standards. We will simply "fib" and we will say that we are the best in the world, and that everything is because of the Egyptians. They're the ones who started this. We are responding. We know that this isn't the case, but we have no other choice. We really don't. We are speaking here of our national assets. In just a moment, when negotiations will begin, it will just be us in front of the Egyptians. We are the only ones that will be asked to give up territory, just us. Therefore, we will continue now and we will move to the west and more to the south. Although the ceasefire that we agreed on is in effect, we need to produce the necessary balance of fear in front of the Egyptian President and his Cult of Generals. If we need to complete the encirclement of the Third Army to do so, so be it. If we need to continue with air strikes and further break down their forces, so be it. And if we need to conquer the city of Suez and complete a naval blockade, so be it.

So, on Wednesday, October 24, the Israeli leadership continued to claim that the Egyptians were breaking the ceasefire and that they were merely reacting. They understood that this was the last chance to take Suez, the largest city along the Canal and the third largest in Egypt, and to cut off supplies, water, and shelter that the city was still able to send to the forces of the Third Army on the east bank of the Canal. Before the observers arrived; and before the US knew what was happening.

08:45—Col. Paddy Hogan, Siilasvuo's Deputy, made an emergency call to Dayan, informing him that he received Egypt's response regarding the ceasefire: "Agree, agree, agree."

"Did the Egyptians really repeat it three times?" Dayan asked, jokingly.

"Four times," Hogan replied.

09:30—As though Col. Hogan never said a word, IDF forces entered the main street of the city of Suez, located at the confluence of the southern end of the Canal and the northern end of the Gulf. "The Egyptians are collapsing. A quick rush of tanks and APCs on the main streets, and it's a ghost town," they reported, "There isn't a real threat, mostly a commando battalion. A fast sweep."

Lt. Aviram Barkai, a young tank commander, returned to the battlefield just two days earlier after recovering from an injury. He growled in frustration. *Why didn't they choose us?* He watched with despairing eyes as twenty tanks from the sister brigade, chosen to play the last chord of glory in the war, hauled behind them bored paratroopers riding in half-tracks, and other armored vehicles. Most of them, like on a field trip, were in a convoy of buses and trucks.

09:50—Inside the city of Suez, the main transfer station for pilgrims from Egypt to the Arabian Peninsula, loud, constant gunshots were heard. *The guys are meeting resistance*, thought Barkai. *I wonder who the fool is who still dares to pick up a Kalashnikov in front of them.*

There was not a single idiot. The IDF forces that took over the main road in Suez City faced resistance from populist militia men with many skilled snipers and tank hunting squads in their midst. They injured commanders on the move who were exposed to turrets, and they destroyed the armored column.

It was as though nothing had been learned from eighteen days of fighting.

10:00—"Fighting rages in the City of Suez, things are going wrong. We have many casualties and wounded," commanders of the paratroopers and tank forces informed the division commander. He passed the reports to the senior command post.

"Activate the Air Force again," instructed the IAF Commander, whose aircraft had been grounded since 07:00. "I want immediate assistance to the forces in Suez City, as well as other missions aimed at all areas of the Third Army."

"Use all of your available force," Dado said. "For us, the ceasefire is over."

At midday, Dayan decided that a picture was worth a thousand reports, and traveled by helicopter to visit his forces in Africa.

"The Egyptians have started attacking our forces," the Defense Minister updated the Prime Minister from the field. "Due to this, the Chief of Staff ordered the use of aircraft and artillery."
Not a word was spoken regarding Suez.

It was right there, in the outskirts of the large city, that they returned. One half-track, then another, and another. Combat veteran paratroopers shouted in the direction of Lt. Barkai, "Hurry, hurry," but he did not understand what the rush was about. *There's no need to hurry.* He helped to set up long lines of stretchers, upon which dead paratroopers were placed, with their tall combat boots, with their treaded soles and reddish-brown leather, poking through the scratchy wool blankets.

14:15—"The Egyptians are continuing to break the ceasefire... I've ordered the Air Force to attack enemy aircraft," Dado informed Dayan, who was still at the Forward Command Post of Bren's division.

"Perhaps they aren't stopping because we aren't stopping?" Dayan suggested.

15:45. *The 201st Squadron*

As the fighting continued in the City of Suez, the 201st Squadron finished its last mission for the Yom Kippur War. A four-ship formation of Sledgehammer jets, led by Adi Benaya and Yoram Romem, located Egyptian tanks hidden in the sands of Sinai. They blew up five of them, and damaged a few others. There were no missiles and no AAAs. Suddenly, the air controller got on the radio and announced that there was no authorization to continue the attack. This time, they thought that this was it—really, truly. The war had ended. Benaya reflected and thought to himself, *what a coincidence. I was the first one in the sky when this all started, and here I am now, turning off the lights.* On the way home, the tension that was stored within him for 18 days under the Plexiglas canopies began crumbling, and he started celebrating by singing songs and screaming in joy. *So sentimental...*

16:00. Office of the Prime Minister

"I have just received a report from Kissinger," the Prime Minister informed the War Cabinet, "according to which, Sadat has reached out to the United States and has urgently pleaded that the Americans send troops to Egypt to protect against Israeli aggression. Kissinger told me that the request came in response to our continued fighting initiative and the further progress our troops have made in the field."

"This is very clever of Sadat," Golda said, and suggested that the Israeli Air Force be immediately halted.

"The IDF is only fighting back when they attack us," the Defense Minister and the Chief of Staff argued.

"Get me Dinitz," Dayan requested.

"Simcha," the Defense Minister said to the Israeli Ambassador in Washington, who is on the other end of the phone line, "Tell Kissinger that all of the Israeli activity in Egyptian territory is a response to Egyptian provocations. Reassure him that 'with a hand on the Bible', we have no intention to progress towards Cairo, but also not to turn back east over the Canal in the area of the Third Army."

A few minutes after the end of the political-security consultation, the Minister of Defense called Lt. Gen. (Res.) Haim Bar-Lev, Commander of the Southern Front, and informed him that they were boiling over in Washington about the fact that the 'business' was not yet concluded.

"Is it possible to make a giant push in order to prevent further shooting?" Dayan asked.

"The battle between the Egyptian commando force and IDF soldiers in Suez has been raging for hours," Bar-Lev reported.

600 | For Heaven's Sake

"Washington isn't hearing about that fighting," Dayan responded.

"The IAF has been plowing the two Egyptian divisions trapped on the east bank of the Canal," Bar-Lev informed Dayan.

"This has to stop," Dayan said. Aware of the Americans' anger, he realized that it was no longer possible to stretch this out.

17:00. A Man Named Epstein

In the afternoon, Giora Epstein was assigned to the on-call interception group in his squadron. Two two-ship formations. Four veteran four-ship formation leaders, who could together count 30 downed enemy aircraft.

Four days earlier, Epstein returned to IAF Headquarters, armed with the record accomplishment of nine enemy bails in one war. After he received a reception reserved for record-breakers, he realized that the ceasefire was only a short time away. *The store is closed, over and done-with.*

One thing was still missing: the war atmosphere in the Mirage squadron. Not the Refidim Alert Wing, but the squadron itself, for which he was Deputy Commander three months ago.

On Monday evening, when the IAF Headquarters again began to blow the winds of war, senior staff members estimated that the ceasefire was a dead horse. The next day, aircraft were again sent to strike enemy forces. Epstein realized that this really was the last chance.

"I am leaving to join up with the Squadron," he reported half-heartedly. "I'll stay there until the end of hostilities."

A mistake, he grumbled to himself for the next two days. *A mistake. The squadron, of course, is the womb of combat that we all emerged from. It has its typical smells, sounds, atmosphere and tradition. This is important. It's fun. But downing enemies is more important, and to shoot them down, I should be at Refidim. It's a fact. The Refidim Alert section keeps downing aircraft, and I've just been "holding level altitude" for the last two days, hot on the trigger of this great aircraft with no equals.*

In April 1962, the first Mirage landed in Israel. Everyone fell in love at first sight. The hot French piece was perfect, and they caressed it like they had never caressed before.

They went up in the cockpit, sat down on a "Martin Baker Mark 4"—the best seat in the world—with an adjustable cushion, which adapts itself to your back's personal curves. It felt like the perfect suit was stitched around them. They took a pilot, sat him down, and built an aircraft around him.

Everything in the cockpit was so simple, so friendly. A few indicators, three switches, and in the most user-friendly positions. And the stick grip. *Oh, the stick grip.* It was like a Stradivarius violin.

They took it into the sky, and it took them wherever they wanted. Smoother, faster, and more natural than anything else that they had known. stick and throttle, and the perfect flight experience.

After four years of matrimony, they learned that not everything was perfect. What could you expect from a hot French chick? The engine would shut itself down in the air, the tires exploded at during landing touchdowns, and malfunction followed malfunction. A dissonance between the beauty and the integrity of its operation and the maintenance problems. Yet all this did not detract from their love for the aircraft, it only sharpened their vigilance.

Then he began to meet MiGs. On Thursday, July 14, 1966, he also started knocking them out of the sky. The Mirage's first take-down in the world, and the MiG-21's first bail. The Mirage continued to run and take down enemies. It did not stop. By October 1973, the Mirage claimed about 200 downed aircraft, and another 220 in the 18 days of war. More than 400 enemy downed aircraft on the one hand and only 10 Mirage downed on the other, and that was the whole story.

"Takeoff," the controller said. "Switch with the four-ship formation on PAC over the Canal."

They flew economically. They needed to save fuel for the patrol that would end with sundown.

"Get ready to get in," the controller instructed Epstein.

"Engagement, heading two-two-zero," the controller yelled to the formation that was supposed to be leaving back home. He was sending the others right into the only purpose for what Giora Epstein was in the sky.

"What about us?" Epstein asked.

"Keep the channel clear and continue the patrol," the controller answered.

Yet it was Epstein on the other end of the line, and for him, as with every interception pilot, the "engagement" was the highlight of his professional life. Epstein felt a light dryness in his throat, and understood that he had made the right decision. He knew that the next few minutes would again be a reflection and essence of all of his years of training.

"You continue," he answered the controller, "I'm going to battle." He already turned to the heading of the MiGs. "Give me more data," he asked.

The shocked controller, the operational arm of the IAF Commander in the field, refused to participate in the illegal game played by Epstein, the insolent major from Kibbutz Negba, and chose to remain silent.

We'll get along without him, Epstein decided.

"Jettison," he ordered on the radio, and the whole formation dropped their external drop fuel tanks from their wings and accelerated towards Jabal Obaiyed.

Southwest of the Great Bitter Lake, he saw two explosions in the sky, and shortly afterwards, three large explosions on the ground. Now it was clear to him in which heading he needed to fly. It really was the right place, because MiGs and Mirages were chasing each other everywhere, and to the outside observer, it looked like a game of tag. However, Epstein had no time to wonder about what someone thought from the side. He only wanted one thing: to down enemy aircraft. *Here's a two-ship formation of MiGs.* He rushed towards them and launched a missile towards the one in the rear, and it explodes next to the MiG. The MiG continued to fly, dragging a trail of smoke behind him. *There's no time to whine,* Epstein thought, short-cutting the way and closing-in to guns' range. The smart Egyptian pilot saw that there was a Mirage sitting on him from 500 meters away, and even without knowing Epstein, he knew what was going to happen. It was a shame for him. Epstein lifted the trigger guard and squeezed, releasing a long burst from two 30mm guns. An ejection seat was fired to the sky, and Epstein said, "Thank you," on the radio, though unsure to who he said it, or why. Yet as he had already said it, he looked for one last glance as the MiG continued flying, unmanned, drawing a straight line in the sky. However, time was short, and there was more to be done. It was just another MiG hanging 'free' in the sky, and the pilot did not know the greatness of the hunters is now after him.

Epstein tightened up his turn, closed in, launched a missile while diving and "in exchange," he experienced an engine compressor stall (surge). He shut down the engine, because that was the way to restore the spirit of this uncooperative French lady, and restarted it. Everything was fine. He then saw the MiG, which actually looked like a burning iron mixture in the sky. He had no time for self-congratulation, as the battle was yet to be concluded. He pulled up and found another MiG passing from one side to the other, and a Mirage was tailing him. The MiG kept flying and the Mirage left him alone. Epstein did not understand why the Mirage would not simply take him down. He asked the pilot on the radio, "What happened? Why didn't you take him out?" The pilot replied, "It's a MiG without a pilot." He approached and saw that there really was not pilot, nor a canopy over the cockpit. He thought that perhaps it was actually his first MiG. But he then saw another two-ship formation of MiGs in the sky, and he still wanted to down enemy aircraft. After some sharp maneuvers, he closed in on one of them and he hit him with the guns. It was suddenly quiet, and Epstein was alone in the sky: no Mirages, no MiGs, just the stunned controller, who did not understand what this crazy pilot, who stayed last in the combat arena, wanted from him. Epstein wanted more, and asked the controller to find him more targets. The controller responded that there were no more targets—that was it. Epstein understood that this time, it really seemed over, and he returned to Hatzor in total darkness. Amos Lapidot, the wing commander, heard from him that he took down three enemies, the rest of the formation took another three, and that the second four-ship formation took some down as well. "All in all, the score is 12:0 in our favor," he said.

Lapidot then replied, "Giora, this time it's final. The war is over."

17:30. Office of the Prime Minister

While Epstein was juggling in the sky, Simcha Dinitz called the Prime Minister's Office and reported that he passed on the explanations of the Prime Minister and the Minister of Defense regarding the continued fighting on the Egyptian front along to Kissinger. "An hour earlier," Dinitz told them, "General Alexander Haig, President Nixon's White House Chief of Staff, called. He snapped angrily at me on account of the renewed fighting, and demanded that it stop immediately. Otherwise, he will consider breaking away from Israel."

"'Our forces have not advanced at all,' I replied to him. 'They are operating according to strict orders to limit themselves only to responding to enemy fire and blocking Egyptian attempts to progress on the territory'. I also said that that, 'according to my information, the fighting is dying down. Please let the President know that Israel will not put him in an uncomfortable position'. Haig came back to me and said that he informed the President, who was relieved, but reiterated that he would have to take drastic steps, including breaking away from Israel, if the developments change course."

17:50. Office of the Defense Minister

"We have stopped the operation of the Air Force," Lt. Gen. (Res.) Bar-Lev said, "Though I would still be happy if you would allow one last mission to aid in finishing the conquest of Suez City."

"Impossible," Dayan said. "Relations with the United States are very tense, and the Secretary of State received an explicit promise from us that we will not renew the fighting."

20:00. Senior Command Post

"It's quiet in the South," the Chief of Staff was informed upon returning from a meeting in the Defense Minister's office. "Only paratrooper rescue operations are still ongoing in the City of Suez."

"Since 10:00, we've sent out 300 flights," the IAF Commander informed him. "We hit the ports of Suez City, we destroyed tanks, infantry pillboxes and artillery batteries. We also hit fuel containers south of the Canal. We continued to crush everything that moved on the Suez-Cairo road. The Egyptians tried to stop us, and it cost them 14 aircraft. There were no casualties among our forces."

"We have finished the current phase," said Lt. Gen. Elazar. "In all likelihood, tomorrow will be quiet on both fronts. We must compel the Third Army to withdraw to the west bank, and thus create symmetry. They hold territory of ours on the east side of the Canal, and we hold territory of theirs on the west side."

"We need to completely encircle them, from the land, air, and sea," the Chief of Staff instructed the General Staff.

"We are getting ready to return to prior competency in three phases," Lt. Gen. Elazar continued, listing three steps. He then announced, "Starting tomorrow, October 25, the General Staff will return to regular work, as it was before the war."

"One more thing," Israel's top soldier added, as something in his face betrayed his inner turmoil, "There is to be no release of the reserve forces. Did you hear me? No release of the reserves The whole army, regulars and reserves, will remain on standby for immediate combat."

THE LAST DAYS OF OCTOBER

A World in Turmoil

At dawn on Thursday, October 25, the war in the Middle East threatened to take the world by storm. It all began with an emotional appeal from the Soviets, who called on the United States to join them in sending a joint statement to the United Nations. The message would state that in light of Israel's repeated ceasefire violations, and following the frantic call from the Egyptian President, who requested that both superpowers support the return of IDF forces to the October 22 armistice lines, both superpowers decided to station a joint expeditionary force in Egypt to enforce UN Resolutions 338 and 339.

The Americans, who did not know how to deal with what they had been served, began a series of internal discussions and consultations while postponing an answer.

"If our demands are not met," warned Leonid Brezhnev, the Soviet Union's strongest man, "then we will be left with no choice but to send an independent military force to Egypt, one that consists entirely of our armed forces."

As the two superpowers found themselves in the midst of a crisis that threatened to escalate to a point of no return, dragging both countries into the conflict between their satellites, the history books marked the 29th anniversary of the first Japanese kamikaze attack on the US expeditionary forces in the Pacific Ocean.

Not knowing that they were part of an ironic 'celebration', in the minutes before sunrise, the last of the IDF forces extracted themselves from their own 'suicide' mission in Suez City. Almost 24 hours after the second ceasefire, 20 hours after having entered to "restore order," the conquest attempt ended in a resounding failure. 80 deaths, and 120 wounded. Four tanks were left behind, one of them with the tank crew itself.

"We completely reject the idea of sending a joint force to Egypt," the President of the United States explained to his Soviet counterpart. "The United States has no information about any ceasefire violations. We are in constant contact with the Israeli government to ensure the implementation of the ceasefire. I assume that you are maintaining such contact with the Egyptians."

"Let's strengthen the UN observer system," Richard Nixon suggested, "and include within it observers from both of our countries."

"This is a time to act in harmony, and not unilaterally," the President continued, "and therefore, the United States cannot, under any circumstances, agree to a unilateral Soviet intervention in the region. Such an action on your part would be a breach of the principles that we have agreed to in the 1972 Summit in Moscow, as well as agreements intended to prevent nuclear war," President Nixon cautioned Brezhnev. Much like President John F. Kennedy in his management of the Cuban Missile Crisis in 1962 he showed that at the moment of truth, the US would not accept threats from anyone, nor would it be the first to blink in the confrontation that was forced upon it.

At 10:15, as though the world was not seething and threatening to blow itself up and Israel with it, as the one that "brought" the world to this, the IDF's Senior Command Post ceased to operate in emergency mode, to which it had grown accustomed since the war began. The Chief of Staff and his assistants left the "Pit" and returned to their staffs and chambers.

Fifteen minutes later, unaware of the changes in the IDF's emergency preparedness, Kissinger updated Dinitz regarding the Middle Eastern situation picture as it was perceived by the United States. "Israel should prepare to fight the Egyptians and the Soviets," he warned. "It is our assumption that, starting tomorrow, the Soviets may land around 4,500 soldiers. Furthermore, It may continue like that every day."

"We're not going to leave you alone," the US Secretary of State made it clear to the Israeli Ambassador. "The Sixth Fleet was ordered to begin moving in Egypt's direction, and all of our armored forces and paratroopers stationed outside the United States were put on alert. We suggest that you not renew the fighting on the day that the Soviets land in Cairo, but instead, wait for the next day. This way, and only this way, it will be made clear to the whole world that Soviet expeditionary forces landed in Cairo with the explicit intention of fighting alongside the Egyptians."

"The Soviets have not fought in a country that does not border the Soviet Union since World War II," Dinitz said.

"There's a first time for everything," Kissinger replied.

* * *

On Friday, October 26, the leader of the Western world proved yet again that no one should blink nor panic in the face of false threats from the Russians. The masters of diplomacy in the White House gave the Kremlin's top brass the rope they needed in order to descend the tall tree that they climbed. The Soviets backed down on their declaration to send an expeditionary force to Egypt, and thus allowed the world to remain intact.

The political kettle was still seething.

"The United States is aware that the fighting that was continued after the ceasefire went into effect on October 22 was not initiated by Israel," Kissinger said to Dinitz, "However, we do not understand your insistence on the issue of the Third Army. Sadat's calls for help are again impairing the delicate fabric of the agreement reached last night between us and the Soviet Union. It could bring the situation to a boiling point."

"Israel is playing a dangerous game," Kissinger continued, "and could lose all of its achievements entirely due to its insistence to refrain from lifting the siege imposed on the Third Army."

"Why do you refuse to allow the Third Army to return to Cairo, with all of their equipment?" Kissinger wondered. "The Soviets will provide new tanks to Egypt in any case."

"I am not aware of a single instance in history in which a country set a beleaguered army free, with all of its equipment, after it came to attack the country," Dinitz said.

"I'm also unaware of any case in history in which a small country caused a severe confrontation between two superpowers," Kissinger shot back.

* * *

It was just after dawn, Saturday morning, October 27.

"The Russians called me on the red line," Kissinger updated Dinitz. "They have asked, on behalf of Sadat, that we turn to you and ask that you allow the passage of non-military supplies to the Third Army. During the conversation, I made it clear to the Russians that we will accept a delay of one more day in order to resolve the issue before appropriate action is taken. We feel that this time, unlike with the threats from two days ago, they mean what they say. They are determined not to allow the Third Army to starve. If you do not remove the blockade, they are ready to launch a military operation with planes. Just lift the blockade."

"Look, Simcha," Kissinger said to the Ambassador, with a cautionary tone in his voice, "we are not going to risk war with the Russians over food for the Third Army."

"One more thing," Kissinger concluded, "Just know that I still have not passed on the Soviets' message to the President. I do not assume that you expect his reaction to be the same as it was two days ago (when he responded firmly to the USSR, and did not require Israel's withdrawal)."

At 05:30, an hour after the end of the briefing with Kissinger, Dinitz called Israel and reported that President Nixon wanted to make it clear that he would not permit the destruction of the Third Army, which was encircled after the implementation of the ceasefire. "By 14:00," Dinitz said, "The Americans want to hear from us to know if Israel will allow the delivery of food, water, and medicine to the Third Army. Kissinger has threatened that a negative response will force the United States to vote against Israel in the UN."

Dr. Henry Kissinger walked with virtuosity along the tightrope of diplomacy and the double game—on the one hand, he was demanding a partial Israeli withdrawal, but on the other hand, he had expressed his enthusiasm that the Third Army was encircled, despite it occurring after the ceasefire was enabled; on the one hand, he has strongly criticized Israel for the continued fighting, and on the other, he inquired how long Israel would need to eliminate the Third Army, before Soviet intervention would put the region in a whole new situation. This juggling came to an end in the wake of the Russian saber rattling.

At the end of the worldwide talks with Russian, Egyptian, Israeli and US officials, Kissinger understood that the world was a moment away from a fatal confrontation between the superpowers. He realized that the time had come to bend the Israeli hand, and, as always, he found a decent dividend in the developing scenario a unique opportunity for the United States to be seen as Egypt's great savior and to reap immediate foreign policy profits in the land of the Pharaohs.

Once again, Israel was made to pay the price. On its own. As always.

"Israel is being punished, not due to its actions, but due to its size and the fact that it is alone," Golda Meir wrote in an angry and assertive message to Kissinger, encapsulating the whole issue.

On Saturday, October 27, at 14:00, the Israeli government announced that it would permit convoys with food and water for a period of 48 hours. It announced this while aware of the US ultimatum, aware that no one else in the entire world would stand alongside it, internalizing the fact that the ceasefire could end, and while knowing that the flames of conflict would return and rise higher

At midday on Sunday, October 28, as the IDF held an area of 1,600 square kilometers west of the Suez Canal, and the Egyptians held an area of 1,200 square kilometers in Sinai, the first convoy of humanitarian supplies was on its way. The convoy's departure eradicated the IDF's ability to overwhelm the Third Army, paved the way for the arrival of other convoys, and severed the fuse from the Russian powder keg.

* * *

As the dunes of the Sinai received reports of a supply convoy making its way with numerous cries of *"Allahu Akbar,"* the former commander of the 201st Squadron stood in the place that was his home for the last two and a half years.

"Would you mind if, until the date of the replacement ceremony, I used my room in the meantime?" Zemer asked Ben Eliahu, his first deputy nearly the whole way.

"No problem," said the squadron's acting commander.

They made some small talk, and Zemer made it clear to his former deputy that he had no intention to intervene in the command of the squadron. He only came to take care of the families of the POWs and the missing persons, and then to personally say goodbye to his staff.

Zemer gathered his staff and looked proudly at his "children." He asked about how things were and how the war was, tried to find some way into the hearts of these men, some sort of connection. However, it was painful for him, so painful, to see that the men standing in front of him lacked even a modicum of compassion and kindness towards him. Zemer was being sympathetic and generous, but the situation just made him unhappy. He had no anger towards them. Zemer was not an angry man.

On Monday morning, October 29, the 17th anniversary of the Sinai Campaign, the blitz that also contributed a modest amount to the State of Israel's loss of senses, Col. Iftach Zemer began his project with the families.

He left with Yoel, his dedicated driver, to visit everyone: Kobi's Dafna, Haim's Fany, Uri's Havah, Meri's Daniela, Itzik's Ilana, Yosi's

Ariela, Guri's Aviva, and Itamar's Tali. They also visited the families of the bachelors and the MIAs.

All of them, unaware of commander Zemer's personal tragedy, showed him love and kindness. They spoke to one another, and all agreed that the man who came to their houses was an angel in human form.

During the nights, he returned to his home at the squadron, told Eitan about his experiences, and headed back to his private quarters in the family housing section. There, and only there, while curled up alone in his bed, when no one was looking, he released a heavy sigh into the air of his room.

* * *

On Tuesday morning, October 30, the Foreign Affairs and Security Committee was situated at Hatzor.

"You are all standing in Wing 4, one of the Air Force's combat wings," Col. Lapidot said, beginning the visit of the guests. "I will describe the activities of the wing during the war for you. I will leave time for questions at the end, and afterwards, we will take a tour of the wing and finish with a visit to the Phantom squadron."

"During the war, the Phantom squadron carried out the most difficult and most complicated missions," Lapidot said. He went on to describe the F-4 Phantom's various capabilities and its technological superiority to the committee members. "Despite all of the measures, the Phantom squadrons paid the price. The IAF lost 30 Phantoms during the war, and those of us here have sustained a large part of those loses. We lost fourteen out of the thirty total aircraft."

"In the meantime, we have received reinforcements," Lapidot said to the stunned committee members. "We have replaced our equipment loses, but not our loses in terms of personnel. The 201st Squadron lost 40% of its combat personnel. 21 air crewmen were killed, captured, or are still missing."

Everyone in the 201st Squadron eagerly awaited the committee's arrival. This was the opportunity that they had been waiting for, and they was no chance they would miss it. Two days earlier, the Israeli government allowed a pathway for humanitarian supplies for the besieged Third Army. They knew that the government was deciding whether to continue allowing convoys through or to make the ordeal a one-time affair, and the public debate that was heating up made its way into the Squadron building.

What is this nonsense, the air crewmen raged. *For what did we fight this war? For what have we lost friends? Give us the opportunity to end things properly, with no mercy or sentiment, to bring them to their knees, and choke them until they've had enough. Let us teach them a lesson so that they'll never want to come back, ever.*

"The 201st for the Third Army," they wrote on a big poster board that was hung in the squadron's clubroom. "Save every flight." "Improve your appearance before the soldiers in the Third Army!" Beneath the poster, they arranged an exhibition that indicated to the committee members how a package of supplies intended for the soldiers of the Third Army should look like. They painted a television, coupled with candy, chewing gum and bags of water— everything possible to ease the lives of the life of the besieged soldier. Someone added condoms. After all, it would be unethical to prevent an Egyptian soldier from continuing to practice safe sex.

"See what the fighters think," Begin said to his colleagues in the committee, "Learn from them what the government's decision should be."

"I would like to thank you for the tour and the comprehensive review," the head of the committee, MK Haim Zadok, said to his host, Col. Lapidot, just before returning to the Knesset in Jerusalem.

"Before we part, I would just like to say one thing. I want you to inform the pilots on our behalf that there is nothing more important to us or closer to our hearts than the release of the POWs. Every effort is being made to get them released as quickly as possible."

The Battle is Over, but Not the War

A gain with the screaming? He did not think a human being could scream like a trapped pig.

He curled up in a fetal position on the concrete floor. *Stop, please stop, those are my friends.*

The latch turned and the door opened. There were two guards with black hoods on their heads. *It's my turn. In another moment, I'll be wailing like that.* They dragged him and another door opened as he started shaking. *Control yourself.* Someone spoke in Arabic, while someone else translated his words into broken Hebrew, "What squadron are you?"

"The 201st."

"What is this? Is everyone here from 201?" the interrogator asked as he started to laugh. *A good start, I think.*

"Give me names of crew members in squadron," the interrogator quietly requested.

Volunteer false information. This was what he learned in captivity training. He recited the names of the Maccabi-Tel Aviv football and basketball players. "*Kadheb* (lying)," the interrogator shouted, and a giant hand struck his hooded head. "Tell truth," the interrogator offered, "save yourself the pain."

Don't break. Continue with the same plan. He recited the names of administrators in the squadron.

The interrogator shouted, "Kadheb!" Suddenly, he was lifted and suspended upside down with his feet tied together, like a piece of meat at the butcher shop. *Ouch!* A torrent of blows threatened to crumble his kneecaps, shaking him on the rope. *Please, please, enough. No one prepared me for such a beating. So much pain...*

"I ask again," the interrogator said, "What are names of the crewmembers in squadron?" *Do not break, stay strong, and confuse the bastard. Chat him up until he is persuaded.* He recited the names of his classmates in grade school. "Kadheb!" *Ouch! It feels like he's driving an electrified nail into my balls!*

"Last time," the interrogator said, and through the uncontrollable shaking, he understood that he meant it.

The same question was asked. *You will not break, understand? You will not break!* A few stuttered words left his mouth.

"*Kadheb!!*" OUCH! The current from the strike felt as though it hit his brain cells, and felt as though threatening to scatter them into a thousand shards of pain on the floor.

They took him down. *I won,* he thought. *They realized that I'm unbreakable.*

Wait, are you crazy? Why are you stuffing me in a tire? The lashes continued.

He yelled and screamed. Though he heard the screams, it did not sound like his own voice at all. *It's not me at all.*

Darkness. *What is this? It's so wet.* Water had been poured on him to wake him up, and as they recognized the moment he awoke, they asked the same question. *Enough, you've held up well. The other prisoners must have told them. Otherwise, they wouldn't know that I was lying.* He told them. They really did know. They even knew that Rotem was a ginger, and Huldai was the commander's replacement. *Maybe now they'll leave me alone.*

"What are numbers of combat squadrons in Air Force?" He told them about the squadrons at Hatzor. "What about the others?"

"I only know those at my base," he said. A bad answer.

Something was being dragged across the floor. He quivered under the bag on his head. "You should tell the truth," the translator said.

"That is the truth," he said, and his whole body shook uncontrollably. OUCH! In the middle of the scream, the likes of which he had never heard before, he realized that both of his ears were getting shocked with electricity. All of his hairs stood on end, and his brain felt as though it was melting and dripping on the floor. *Stop, please stop. I can't take anymore. God, please let me lose consciousness. I should have fasted on Yom Kippur...*

"Okay, okay, I'll tell you."

"Great," said the interrogator. "Now tell us about the types of smart bombs there are for Phantom."

"Airmen are less familiar with the smart bombs. This is the Technical Division's specialization. We just drop them."

The interrogator shouted, "*Kadheb!*" Someone pulled down his pants, as a sour smell spread in the room. He peed. They laughed, and he prayed that it was not what he thought it was. Ahhhh! His body felt as though trying to break out of his skin. As he slipped out of consciousness, he understood that this was the "pig" scream that he had heard before, and that perhaps another comrade was curled up in his cell at that moment. He was terrified, so terrified. *I'm out of control.* He trembled, shaking so hard

"More electricity?" the translator asked.

I don't want anymore. Please, no more.

The solitary confinement cell. This was his home. A concrete floor, a tarp, two itchy blankets and a light bulb that was lit 24 hours a day. This was it. He rolled over from his stomach to his back. His whole body hurt. He had no idea that it could hurt so badly. He put a rag on his eyes. *I don't want to see the light. Just darkness.* He figured out the hours of the day based on the calls of the muezzin and the guards switching shifts. Each shift was about two hours, maybe three. Time flowed like a clock in a Dali painting, and every second felt like an hour, perhaps two.

I'm cold. Through a crack in the wall, he saw Syrian jail guards wearing thick wool coats as they played with snowballs, while he was in there in his underwear, curled up in blankets and shivering. He shook constantly. He took olive pits, drilled holes in the blankets, and slipped some shoelaces through. *Now I have a sleeping bag. It's a small victory.* He turned his tank top undershirts into socks. Another victory, and yet, it was still cold. He jumped on the floor. Day and night, he jumped on the floor, and ran around clockwise around the cell. He would get tired and would pause. Then he would move counterclockwise. He counted the number of laps, and improved his results. He warmed up. *It's cold again. So cold, and the shivering never ends.*

Two pita breads with a slice of cheese and a few olives in the morning, rice or bulgur at noon, and sometimes a piece of bone with some remaining beef, half an orange, and tea in the evening. That was it. He would divide the orange half into servings to make it through the evening, and would eat the skin.

I'm so thirsty. He banged on the door. He shouted, "Toilet, toilet!" He just needed to drink. *So what if the hose in the bathroom is coated with shit. I don't care.* All he cared about was that the guard would come soon to get him. Today, the guard did not feel like it, as it was a lot of work: opening the door, closing it again, putting a blindfold over his eyes, leading him, waiting, and then returning. He restrained himself. Then his bladder felt as though it was on the verge of exploding.. *I can't do it anymore.* He urinated on the plastic food plate, and drank his own urine. *It stinks, but I'm not thirsty anymore.*

He built his own world. He started with his underwear. *I have two, one without rubber.* He moved the rubber from one pair to the other. Hour by hour. A day, then another day. A surprise—he received plaid pajamas. He tore off the pocket. There, a chessboard. He made orange and white soldiers from the orange skins and hid his board, so they would not interrupt his games.

He fell on Sunday, October 7. He painted a calendar on the wall, and scratched another line each day.. At the end of each week, he scratched a horizontal line through all of them. Another week had passed. By his count, it was Hanukkah. *My birthday.* Lighting candles in his mind, he sat in his cell and sang a traditional Hanukkah song, and someone joined him from the neighboring cell. His cell door opened, and the guard started beating him. *Let him hit me. My birthday has been celebrated.*

Sirens went off in the background, as the Israeli Air Force flew over Damascus. They were punished, and were forced to stand for a week—it was forbidden for them to sit or lie down. They could only stand, for 24 hours. Every few minutes, someone would appear, randomly and suddenly. They would open the latch on the door, catching him as his swollen feet, with their falling toenails, failed him as he collapsed in the corner of the room. The lashes then returned once more.

How long will this last?! He felt like falling asleep and waking up in a few more months. Out of desperation, he constructed a chart leading to the day that he would meet with the other prisoners. He established deadlines. Another month until the joint meeting. A week passed, and another one, and a third passed by as well. At the end of the last week, he moved the deadline by another month. *I won't allow this meeting to be cancelled.*

He was dropped alone in a cell, locked inside 24 hours a day. There was no one with whom he could share his fears, his pain, and his anxiety. He just felt as though he was nothing, if not less than nothing, knowing nothing and worth nothing. *Hang in there, you hear? Keep your head up. You're an air crewman. Hang in there. Do it for yourself, for what people think of you. Sanity, man, sanity! Don't let the madness possess you. Fly home on the wings of imagination. That anchor will keep you sane.* He thought of home all of the time. Even in his dreams. Home, just home. He thought of conversations with his wife, with his son, and reminisced about the trip they took in the summer before the war. Day after day, minute after minute. Again, and again. He missed it all so much.

He remembered his father, a Holocaust survivor. *They murdered his wife and two children, and he went on to survive and build a family. What is this stupid captivity compared to what he went through? Keep your head up! Do you understand? Raise your head! This will end one day. Maybe the Sayeret Matkal special forces will take over the prison and bring you home. I won't break. I'm going back home from this. This will be over, understand? It will be over.*

November 5, 1973

The 201st Squadron cleaned itself up ahead of the commander replacement ceremony. Lt. Col. Iftach Zemer, the outgoing commander, and Maj. Ben Eliahu, the incoming commander, said what was always said in these ceremonies, and wished each other success in their new endeavors. Zemer said, "May we see all the prisoners back with us soon." They shook hands, and all members of the squadron, fighters, technicians, and administrators, sat down together at a shared dinner party.

Late in the night, Lt. Col. Iftach Zemer retired to his house in the family housing section. He realized that that was it, as things were brought to a conclusion. Only a happy ending was missing.

November 16, 1973

True to its word not to allow further convoys to the Third Army unless Egypt released all of the IDF prisoners, the Israeli government was pleased to inform the general public and concerned families about the prisoner swap with Egypt, which went underway that very day. 233 prisoners made their way to Israel, including nine prisoners from the War of Attrition. The 201st Squadron prepared an exciting welcome for the first returnees—two veterans of the War of Attrition, Itzik Fier and Menacham Eini, along with two prisoners of the Yom Kippur War, Guri Palter and Kobi Hayun, both of whom were injured.

Yair David brought the board from the briefing room with Fier's request. It was on that board that the pilot wrote on June

30, 1970, "Do not erase until I get back!" David presented it and told him, "There, now you can erase it."

November 21, 1973

Waves of public protest slowly increased as the country mourned its 2,222 casualties, demanded explanations for the failure and called for the resignation of the political leadership, headed by Meir and Dayan. Attentive to the growing public call, the Israeli government announced the establishment of a commission of inquiry headed by Supreme Court Chief Justice Shimon Agranat. The commission was charged with investigating the circumstances surrounding the eruption of the Yom Kippur War and the measures taken from the defensive containment operations through the failed counter-offensive on October 8.

As the committee received its mandate and began to organize the schedule for the appearances of their first witnesses, prisoners continued to arrive from Egypt. Uri Arad and Yosi Lev-Ari were the first to come, and Doron Shalev and Itzik Baram two days later.

Only Yoni Ofir, Eran Cohen, Baruchi Golan and Gadi Samok were not among the returnees, and their burial places remain unknown.

January 18, 1974

In the largest tent compound at the 101st kilometer on the Suez-Cairo road, Lt. Gen. David Elazar, the IDF Chief of Staff, shook hands with Field Marshal Mohamed Abdel Ghani el-Gamasy, the new Egyptian Chief of Staff. The two military leaders presented the Disengagement Agreement reached between the two countries before in front of the international news media that gathered at the compound at a tent opening. The IDF would withdraw from both banks of the Suez Canal, and its forces would be stationed at a distance of 20 kilometers away from the Canal. The Egyptian military would withdraw 90% of its forces stationed on the east bank of the Canal.

The ceasefire between Israel and Syria, which had previously been declared on October 24, 1973, lasted only a few days. In December 1973, as wintry weather intensified and covered the basalt rocks of the Golan Heights with snow not seen since Roman times, the Syrians launched routine artillery bombardments on IDF forces in the "Enclave" (an area that the IDF seized in Syria beyond the Purple Line). They did so in mild dosages, in a "considerate" manner.

No more.

Realizing the consequences of Israel's Disengagement Agreement with Egypt, and knowing a thing or two about the rules of negotiations in the Middle East, the Syrian leadership decided to come to the negotiating table with the strongest starting position, and instructed its army to begin a real war of attrition.

February 1974

The US Secretary of State shuttled between Jerusalem and Damascus, marking the start of indirect talks between the two countries.

The Syrians announced that they did not intend to settle for the withdrawal of IDF forces merely to the borders of the Purple Line. "We want a more concrete compensation, a realistic territorial accomplishment, like our brothers in Egypt."

* * *

The latch opened again, and a reeking rag was tied over his eyes, but in a different, unfamiliar way. *Please, just no more torture. Please, God, just no torture.* The door opened and they removed his head covering.

There was a large room with bunk beds. A group of young men were cramped up in the corner. Bearded and thin, very thin. Some stared. Others trembled. *From where did they bring me a group of Holocaust survivors?*

Suddenly, he shuddered. *These are my friends! These are my friends!*

Twenty-three officers. Nineteen pilots, two tank crewmen, a doctor, and an intelligence officer. Mattresses were arranged in a circle. They sat, silently, looking at each other in amazement. Someone started talking and said, "Today is our second birthday. If we're all together, it's a sign that something good is brewing." Someone who had counted the days, like he did, stated the date according to his calendar: Wednesday, February 20, 1974. Everyone talked without stopping all night, and the next day, and then the next night.

Beginning of March 1, 1974

Not far from the prison in Al-Mazzah, and a few days after the prisoners were united and the snow began to thaw, the Syrians escalated the war of attrition that they imposed on Israel. They carried out repeated attempts to gain control over the peaks of Mount Hermon, which were accompanied by incessant rocket attacks directed towards the towns in the Golan Heights and towards IDF forces.

April 1, 1974

After 140 meetings with 58 key witnesses, the Agranat Commission presented its interim report to the Israeli government. The commission held that the IDF Directorate of Military Intelligence, and especially Maj. Gen. Eli Zeira and his Deputy, Brig. Gen. Aryeh Shalev, were directly responsible for the failure in warning about the war. The Directorate of Military Intelligence had accumulated considerable alarming information about an upcoming war, but the incorrect use of information and the fixated way of thought (the "conception") brought about a significant failure. Maj. Gen. Shmuel Gonen ("Gorodish") did not spread his forces effectively to avert the Egyptian attack. Lastly, Lt. Gen. David Elazar bore overall responsibility for the intelligence and operational failures that took place before the outbreak of the war.

April 3, 1974

Lt. Gen. David Elazar submitted his letter of resignation to the government, which accepted it. Maj. Gen. Zeira, Maj. Gen.

Gonen, and Brig. Gen. Shalev disregarded the commission's serious findings, which ascribed the failure of the war first and foremost to their personal performance, and decided to continue their service in the IDF.

April 11, 1974

Israel's Prime Minister, a leader and a lady, did not flaunt the conclusions of the Agranat Committee, which absolved her of any responsibility, and even praised her actions. She decided that the cost of the losses, the failures, the national rift and the protest movements that urged her to leave office necessitated action on her part.

At an emergency session of the Knesset, Golda Meir announced her resignation and, with it, brought about the resignation of the Israeli government.

April 18, 1974

For the first time since the armistice agreement of October 24, the Syrian Air Force sprang into action. In the late afternoon, eight MiG-17s attacked IDF positions on the highest mountain in the country.

* * *

On the evening of Thursday, April 18, Yigal Stavi, from the 201st Squadron—who participated in the war that had just ended, and was awarded the rank of captain earlier than expected after his commanders decided that he excelled in every task —arrived at Sima Shavit's home in Afeka. He missed her, as did everyone.

In October 1973, several days after the ceasefire agreements were signed with Syria and Egypt, she finished her service as the operational clerk of the 201st Squadron, her service in the Israeli Air Force, and her service in the IDF. She moved to Jerusalem, and turned a new leaf. She was a first year university student in literature and philosophy. On weekends, she went back to her home, which served as a pilgrimage site to the members of the squadron. They would sit and talk, watch a film or go to a restaurant on occasion, before returning.

And then, there was Yigal, the handsome youth from Jerusalem.

"How are you, Sima?" he asked shyly, surrounded by her stormy presence.

"Come on, we're going to a movie," she said. Not a word about the war.

Shortly after midnight, she accompanied him to his car.

"Tomorrow we're getting back at the Syrians," he said, sounding apologetic.

"Switch out," she told him, "Switch, it's already late."

"I can't," he said, a smiling half-moon hanging on his face.

"Leave a little later," she almost begged.

"It's impossible," he said with that smile again, made even brighter by a street lamp.

On Friday, April 19, 1974, IAF aircraft were sent to strike targets in Syria - 308 sorties. Capt. Yigal Stavi's aircraft was one of them.

"Our mission is to attack an isolated SA-6 battery on the front line, on the slopes of Mount Hermon, at the Israel-Syria border," briefed Lt. Col. Eitan Ben Eliahu, the leader of the formation and the squadron leader.

Four headed out, two two-ship formations in intervals. Ben Eliahu led and Gil Regev was with him. Eli Zohar and Yigal Stavi were right behind them. *There's Arbel Cliff.* Kiryati was amazed in the navigator's chamber behind Stavi. This mountain is always beautiful. They descended low over the groves of the Galilee Panhandle, sneaking to Mount Dov, and circling around the Hermon from the west.

"Three, two, one, pull up," said "Rhino" to Ben Eliahu. They pulled up, dove, and released. Gil Regev was behind them. "Target destroyed," they both reported.

"We can go to the launchers," Ben Eliahu said. They entered.

"The missile threat area is insanely hot," Kiryati grumbled nervously in front of the annoying RWR warning tones.

"We'll finish off the SA-6 launchers and then go back," Stavi said. "We'll finish and return."

They made a wingover, dove, and released their bombs, as the RWR kept on screaming.

They broke to the right, with Damascus in the corner of their eyes.

"Identifying Strelas," Stavi reported on the UHF (Ultra High Frequency) radio.

"Missiles from the left!" Kiryati shouted on the ICS.

Boom. The stick refused to respond. Stavi pulled—nothing. Kiryati tried, but the stick remained free in is hand. "What do we do? What do we do?" Stavi did not answer. "We're going to crash into the mountain!" Kiryati set the ejection select lever to the horizontal position and pulled.

At the 201st Squadron, the news was received in astonishment. *Let's say that they didn't take them,* Shmidko thought, tossing and turning in bed, unable to sleep. *How would they survive this insane cold, in the snow, without a blanket?* Suddenly he remembered that Stavi, very much loved by all, apologized to him over the fact that it was his fault that a downing from the helicopter sortie that took place on the first day of the war had not been listed. He wanted to go back in time so very much and tell him, *It's really not important, Yigal. It really doesn't matter. Just come back safely.*

On Sunday, Sima returned to her studies in Jerusalem. On the way, she stopped at the Stavi family home.

"There is hope, they still don't know what happened to the crew," she told Yigal's parents. Yigal, who just two days ago, was looking at her with his calm, boy-next-door eyes.

There was a knock on the door.

Col. Lapidot, who was her Wing Commander until she finished her service in October, took a hesitant step inside, sat down, and said, "I'm sorry, I'm so sorry."

"It can't be," Sima said, "It just can't be…"

May 31, 1974

At the southwestern tip of Lake Geneva, in Switzerland's second-largest city of the same name, military representatives from Israel and Syria signed the Disengagement Agreement.

Recognizing the State of Israel's sensitivity to the fate of its 62 prisoners, and seeing their 386 captives as a worthless package, the Syrians refused to pass over the list of IDF POWs and placed conditions on their transfer. They agreed to release the prisoners, on the condition that Israel agreed to make territorial concessions in addition to the release of the Syrian prisoners.

The Israeli representatives agreed, as though a gun was put to their heads.

June 1, 1974

246 days after they switched from an almighty aircraft, a soft bed and a luxurious clubroom to the Syrian prison and a reality that proved harsher than their darkest nightmares, the injured four—Abraham Assael, Itamar Barnea, Avikam Leif and prison rookie Kiryati—began their journey to Israel.

June 5, 1974

The State of Israel, as the clear winner of the war, which held 400 square kilometers in Syria and just 40 kilometers from Damascus, ratified the agreement between the military leaderships of the two countries. Israel was required to withdraw its troops back to the Purple Line and was forced to accept the border adjustments, in which Syria was given back the town of Quneitra, the Rafid Triangle, and several hills in the southern Golan Heights.

June 6, 1974

On Thursday, 251 days after they fell captive, Haim Ram, Gilad Graber, Yitzhak Yahav, Ori Shahak and Shaniboi got onto a polished bus in the prison compound and made their way home, dealing with the critical question of how to escape a kiss from the parched lips of the Prime Minister.

At 10:00, they landed at Lod Airport, where there was a surprise. "Please remain in your seats, the Prime Minister will get on this plane to welcome you himself." *Himself? It's true, Golda's kind of manly, but still…* Then came Yitzhak Rabin, the Chief of Staff of the Six-Day War, and they began to realize that some things had happened in their small country while they were far away from it. They had no energy for a speech by Israel's new Prime Minister. They wanted to see their family and friends, who were waiting for them behind barriers.

The wait was hard for the families as well, especially for Haim Ram's wife, Fany. She did not care when a solemn military policeman told her, "Miss, please wait like everyone else." She insisted on passing through, but the MP insisted as well. However, Fany wanted her Haim at that instance. *Right now, after 251 days.* So she resorted to biting, freeing herself from the grip of the MP's hand and rushed towards the plane in fashionable bellbottom pants flapping in the wind, the whole way to her *Haimke.*

In the reception hall, Haim, Gilad, Itzik, Uri, and Shaniboi met Blumi, who said, "What a great war we had. Steaks, good food. You missed it all." Motti Reder added, "Yes, truly a wonderful war, and wonderful fucks."

* * *

In June 1974, the 201ˢᵗ Squadron finally witnessed the war coming to a conclusion. Disengagement agreements were signed. There was a deafening silence on the borders. The story of the Yom Kippur War was over and completed.

"Wild Bull"—"When you fall at the Hermon, remember me"—removed his long johns from his jumpsuit.

"Rhino"—who shaved off his trademark mustache—decided that since it was all over, he could go back to growing a mustache. From the beginning.

Eitan Shmueli would climb into his aircraft the way he felt like climbing. He stopped insisting on putting his right foot first, and also stopped spitting to the left before closing the canopy.

Motti Reder searched for a way to fulfill the many promises that he gave to young ladies, who required his repayment in the form of wedding bells.

Yossi Eliel no longer wrote "Welcome" in illuminating Arabic letters on the board, and stopped pressuring his comrades to improve their Ishmaelite vocabulary, because, after all, it did not look like the Arabs were coming anyway, and they did not have to welcome them graciously. He even stopped referring to Sima, the student in Jerusalem, as Fatima, and he explained to her in her home in Afeka that there was no longer any reason to prepare for a conquest.

Every last one of them found the ladder to let them climb down from the black humor tree, and stopped telling each other "See you in Al-Mazzah," or even "See you on the Guard."

Lastly, Peri stopped writing poems.

In the family housing area, Gil Regev hugged Nurit strongly and told her again about the war that ended. "The squadron did what it had to do, without excuses and evasions, and without complaints such as 'This hurts,' or 'That's hard.'"

"On Sunday afternoon, about twenty hours after the war started, we already had seven POWs. Can you wrap your mind around that? Seven airmen in a Syrian prison. Boom. In an instant. There were two others who bailed over Israel. We lost four aircraft for nothing, but we continued to fight, and didn't give up on a single mission. Then we suffered more loses. Especially in Egypt. But we never said no. We were ordered and we flew, anywhere, anytime, no matter what happened before. Today, we know that we took down more aircraft than any other Phantom squadron, which is amazing. Despite all of the losses, with fewer aircraft and fewer staff, we shot down the most. It proves that we were always at the forefront of battle."

"Listen to me," he said as his gaze softened, "We went above and beyond. And even more than that."

"But the price, Nurit. The price. How is it that we, the 201st, the first ones and the most experienced, how can it be that we lost seven crew members and fourteen others were captured? And now Stavi and Kiryati?"

"How did it happen to us, Nurit? We started with twenty-seven airplanes, and finished with thirteen. Do you understand? It doesn't make sense. It's unacceptable."

"Maybe we hit our heads against the wall a bit, Nurit. Maybe."

"Maybe the burden placed on us was like a bridge too far. Maybe." Again, he held her tightly and said, "I'm tired, Nurit. I'm so tired."

"Oh, Gilush," she told him. "My Gilush…"

He curled up on her lap, and dreamt the dream that came back every night. There was the Phantom again, and he was taxiing it, full of bombs, through the streets of an unfamiliar city, being careful not to rub his wingtip on a home, a car, or a light pole. He searched for a section straight and wide enough for him to take off. He found it. He opened his burners, accelerated, and again found an obstacle in the distance that could interfere with the takeoff. He debated whether to keep taking off or if he should stop, and at the last moment, when the aircraft nearly lifted up to the air, he realized that he would not succeed. He slammed on the brakes, and stopped just before crashing.

He taxied around again, and searched once more for a street long and wide enough so that he could take off, all throughout the night.

STAND AND BE ACKNOWLEDGED

A huge thank you to Lt. Col. (Res,) Ziv, the Commander of the Skyhawk and F-16 Squadrons, who has flown in all of the Israeli Air Force's fighter aircraft (except for the IAI Kfir), and accumulated hundreds of hours flying as the Second Deputy Squadron leader on the wings of the hero of our story—the F-4 *Sledgehammer*.

"He's the right man," the tight-lipped IAF veterans told me about him. They were right. Ziv performed Sisyphean detective work for this book and found all of the concepts that required a "linguistic makeover" and turned an aviator's language—which borders on foreign to most of us—into a language that fits (almost) everyone.

The professional appendix at the end of the book is his handiwork.

A big thank you goes out to the three people that first put me on the right track for this book. To Lt. Col. (Res.) Dr. Ido Amber, former Head of the Israeli Air Force's History Branch, who opened the first hatch for me. To Lt. Gen. (Res.) Dani Haloutz, who was a young reservist pilot in the 201st Squadron, a warm and humble person and right for any job, who further opened the hatch. Lastly, to Brig. Gen. (Res.) Ran Pecker, the Commander of the Tel Nof air base during the Yom Kippur War, a "revered commander" in the eyes of most of the combat pilots in the 1960s and 1970s, who, in moments of my own indecision, helped me choose the right path.

Heartfelt thanks go to Dr. Haggai Tzoref, the Head of Documentation and Commemoration in the Israeli State Archives, whose wisdom, sensitivity, and inexhaustible knowledge were of great help to me.

Thank you to the staff at the IDF Archive—Director Ilana Alon, Avi Tzadok, the Director of the Documentation and Catalog Department, and Iris Sardes, a clerk in the Archive, who were attentive collaborators and were always ready to help.

Thanks to Lt. Col. (Res.) Ze'ev Lachish, Director of the Palmach House, former Head of the IAF's History Branch, who received the material relating to Air Force's decisions in the first 24 hours of the war and added helpful comments.

Thank you to Professor Uri Bar-Joseph, a renaissance man, whose books and insights were extremely helpful to me.

Thanks to Professor Eyal Zisser, Head of the Moshe Dayan Center for Middle Eastern and African Studies, who greatly helped me in an important and unique section of the book.

Thank you to the staff of the IDF Military Censorship, led by Deputy Censor Col. Ron Karnieli, who knew how to delineate the boundaries of security information with vigor, wisdom, sense and sensibility.

Thanks to Jackie Shaporen, Chairman of the Israeli Air Force Association, who helped to locate missing people.

Thanks to Meir Amitai, a staff member in the Israeli Air Force History Wing in the 1990s, for his great comments.

Thanks to Lt. Col. Motti Habkuk, Commander of the IAF's History and Information Wing, who helped me at the outset.

Thanks to Nitzan Shapiro, a man of common sense and inexhaustible knowledge. He was always there for me, and helped locate things that no one else could.

Thank you to all of the interviewees—without whom, this book would have been impossible.

Thank you to the staff of the Kinneret Zamora-Bitan Publishing House, who labored day and night working on the Hebrew version of this book, and especially the owners, Eran Zamora and Yoram Rose, who were reliable, kind, supportive, and always in a positive mood. Thanks as well to literary editor Tami Chapnik, who proved that the sky is not the limit.

Finally, I want to thank Tami, the woman of my life, who, in the midst of urgent treatments at the clinic and turbulent management meetings, found, as with my previous books, the windows of opportunity to go over the current book as well. Through her intelligence, sensitivity, and her love of reading, she knew how to comment, enlighten, and create a better book from the masses of drafts.

Warriors of the 201st Squadron
Pilots
Regulars

Name	Rank Before the War	Position in the Squadron	Final Rank	Final Position	Business Today
Iftach Zemer	Lieutenant Colonel	Squadron leader	Lieutenant Colonel	Head Instructor in the Flight School	Retiree of the Israeli Air Force and of El Al Airlines
Ron Huldai	Major	First Deputy Squadron leader (Acting Squadron leader, October 6-8)	Brigadier General	Hatzor Base Commander	Mayor of Tel Aviv
Amnon Gurion	Captain	Second Deputy Squadron leader	Colonel	Head of the Training Department/ Air Force Headquarters	Marketing Consultant
Haim Ram	Captain	Fighter Pilot	Lieutenant Colonel	Involved with IAI's Lavi Project	Electronic and Infrastructure Simulation Engineer
Ori Shahak	Captain	Fighter Pilot	Major	Head of Strike Assistance in the Operations Department/IAF Headquarters	Flight instructor
Eitan Levy	Captain	Fighter Pilot	Major	Section Head of Fighter Aircraft in the Weapons Department/IAF Headquarters	Lawyer and Notary; Air Conditioning Specialist Engineer
Moshe Koren	Captain	Fighter Pilot	Lieutenant Colonel	Section Head of Accident Investigations in the Department of Quality Control/IAF Headquarters	Partner and CEO of a cosmetics factory
Motti Reder (deceased)	Captain	Fighter Pilot	Major	Fighter Pilot and Test Pilot for the 201st Squadron	Died of illness after the Yom Kippur War
Gil Regev	Captain	Fighter Pilot	General	Head of Human Resources in the General Staff Headquarters of the IDF	Organizational Consultant for Medical Systems

643

Yossi Eliel (deceased)	Captain	Fighter Pilot	Lieutenant Colonel	F-16 Squadron leader	Killed in a training exercise after the Yom Kippur War
Doron Shalev (deceased)	Captain	Fighter Pilot	Major	Fighter pilot in Squadron 101	Killed in a training exercise after the Yom Kippur War
Gideon Eilat	Captain	Fighter Pilot	Brigadier General	Head of the Intelligence Group/ IAF Headquarters	Pilot in El Al Airlines

Emergency Placements

Name	Rank Before the War	Position in the Squadron	Final Rank	Final Position	Business Today
Eitan Ben Eliahu	Major	Active Squadron leader From October 13	General	IAF Commander	Chairman of the Diaspora Museum. Chairman of Aeronautics Ltd. Chairman of the Academic Center for Business and Law. Chairman of Aerial Photonics.
Guri Palter	Lieutenant Colonel	Fighter Pilot	Lieutenant Colonel	Head of Accident Investigations in the Quality Control Department/ IAF Headquarters	Israeli Air Force retiree and El Al Airlines
Levy Zur	Major	Fighter Pilot	Colonel	IDF Attaché in Venezuela	An IDF retiree; Businessman
Eitan Peled	Major	Fighter Pilot	Colonel	Head of MAFAT Branch (Administration and Weapons Technology Development and Infrastructure)	Retiree of the IDF, Law student
Gadi Samok (deceased)	Major	Fighter Pilot	Major	Test Pilot	Killed in the Yom Kippur War
Eli Zohar	Major	Fighter Pilot	Lieutenant Colonel	Head of the Joint Branch/IAF Headquarters	Entrepreneur in Israel and abroad
Uri Sheani (deceased)	Major	Fighter Pilot	Major	Division Commander in the Flight School	Killed in the Yom Kippur War
Amiram Shaked (deceased)	Captain	Fighter Pilot	Major	Test Pilot	Killed in a training exercise after the Yom Kippur War
Meir Shani	Captain	Fighter Pilot	Major	Fighter Pilot in Nesher Squadron	Captain in El Al Airlines
Yonatan Ofir (deceased)	Captain	Fighter Pilot	Major	Instructor at the Flight School	Killed in the Yom Kippur War
Yigal Stavi (deceased)	Lieutenant	Fighter Pilot	Captain	Instructor in the Flight School	Killed in the War of Attrition in Syria after the Yom Kippur War

Itamar Barnea	Lieutenant	Fighter Pilot	Colonel	Head of the Casualties Department in the IDF General Staff Headquarters	Doctor of Clinical Psychology. Head Psychologist at NATAL
Amiram Eliasaf	Lieutenant	Fighter Pilot	Brigadier General	Hatzor Base Commander	Businessman and aviation consultant
Kobi Hayun	Lieutenant	Fighter Pilot	Colonel	Head of the Review Division in the Security System Comptroller's Office	Businessman dealing with coffee shops and food retail

Reserves

Name	Rank Before the War	Position in the Squadron	Final Rank	Final Position	Business Today
Adi Benaya	Captain	Fighter Pilot	Lieutenant Colonel	Second Deputy Squadron leader, the 201st Squadron	Pilot for El Al Airlines
Haim Rotem	Captain	Fighter Pilot	Lieutenant Colonel	Aerial Fighter in the 201st Squadron	Industrial physicist in the MRI field
Dani Haloutz	Captain	Fighter Pilot	Lieutenant General	IDF Chief of General Staff	Businessman; Chairman of the Etgarim non-profit organization
Ben-Ami Peri (deceased)	Captain	Fighter Pilot	Lieutenant Colonel	Head of the Behavioral Sciences Branch	Died of illness after the Yom Kippur War

Flight Qualifiers

Name	Rank Before the War	Position in the Squadron	Final Rank	Final Position	Business Today
Rafi Har-Lev (deceased)	Brigadier General	Fighter Pilot	Brigadier General	Head of the Intelligence Group	Died of illness after the Yom Kippur War
Amos Lapidot	Colonel	Fighter Pilot	General	IAF Commander	An IAF retiree

Navigators
Regulars

Name	Rank Before the War	Position in the Squadron	Final Rank	Final Position	Business Today
Amiram Talmon	Captain	Aerial Fighter (On unpaid leave)	Colonel	Chief of the Integrated Training Department in the General Staff HQ	Developer of science teaching aids for educational institutions
Paltiel Barak	Lieutenant	Aerial Fighter (Reserves in a Permanent Position)	Major	Navigator and Officer in F-16 Barak Squadron	Software engineer
Eliezer Blumenfeld (Bar-El)	Lieutenant	Fighter Pilot	Major	Deputy Commander of the Recruitment Bureau	An IDF retiree. Tour guide
Yitzhak Yahav (deceased)	Lieutenant	Fighter Pilot	Lieutenant Colonel	Branch Head at IDF Headquarters	Died of Illness in July 2013
Itzchak Zetelny (Amitay)	Lieutenant	Fighter Pilot	Brigadier General	Head of Human Resources/ IAF Headquarters	Aerospace and defense consultant
Benjamin Kiryati	Lieutenant	Fighter Pilot	Colonel	Legal Consultant Officer at the Military Advocate General Headquarters	Chairman of the Children of Israel Foundation (Keren Yeldai Israel); Head of a law firm
Shimon Tzror	Lieutenant	Fighter Pilot	Lieutenant	Instructor at the Flight School	

Dror Yaffe (deceased)	Second Lieutenant	Fighter Pilot	Lieutenant	Fighter in the Squadron	Killed in the Yom Kippur War
Gilad Graber (Regev)	Second Lieutenant	Fighter Pilot	Major	Group Leader in 201st Squadron, Boxing Officer	Instructor and translator of technical literature
Eitan Shmueli	Second Lieutenant	Fighter Pilot	Captain	Instructor at the Flight School	Owner of a law firm
Arik Shlain	Second Lieutenant	Fighter Pilot	Major	Fighter in the Squadron	Business developer
Nimrod Amami	Second Lieutenant	Fighter Pilot	Lieutenant Colonel	Head of the Planning and Organization Department/ IAF Headquarters	Department manager in a credit company

Emergency Placements

Name	Rank Before the War	Position in the Squadron	Final Rank	Final Position	Business Today
Oded Erez	Lieutenant Colonel	Fighter Pilot	Brigadier General	Head of the Intelligence Group/IAF Headquarters	Director of public companies. An IDF retiree
Uri Talmor (deceased)	Lieutenant Colonel	Fighter Pilot	Brigadier General	Head of Human Resources/ IAF Headquarters	Died of illness
Yigal Bar Shalom	Lieutenant Colonel	Fighter Pilot	Colonel	Head of the IAF "Pit"	An IDF retiree
Shimon Noy	Major	Fighter Pilot	Lieutenant Colonel	Aerial Coordination Officer for Joint Operations	
Yair David	Captain	Fighter Pilot	Lieutenant Colonel	Head Test Engineer in the Flight Test Center	Patent attorney and doctoral law student
Gil Haran (deceased)	Lieutenant	Fighter Pilot	Captain	Instruction Department/ IAF Headquarters	Killed in the Yom Kippur War
Yitzhak Baram (deceased)	Lieutenant	Fighter Pilot	Captain	Instructor at the Flight School	Killed in a training flight after the Yom Kippur War
Eitan Barush	Lieutenant	Fighter Pilot	Captain	Fighter in the Squadron	Tour guide abroad
Yehoar Gal	Lieutenant	Fighter Pilot	Colonel	F-15 Navigator	Businesses in dental health
Abraham Assael	Lieutenant	Fighter Pilot	Brigadier General	IDF Attaché in France, Spain, and Portugal	Retired. IDF Attaché Trainer
Yosi Lev-Ari	Lieutenant	Fighter Pilot	Colonel	Unit Commander in the Computer Department in the IAF	An IDF retiree
Avikam Leif	Lieutenant	Fighter Pilot	Major	Fighter in the Squadron	General and business consultant
Baruch Golan (deceased)	Lieutenant	Fighter Pilot	Lieutenant	Instructor at the Flight School	Killed in the Yom Kippur War

Reserves

Name	Rank Before the War	Position in the Squadron	Final Rank	Final Position	Business Today
Yoram Romem	Lieutenant	Fighter Pilot	Colonel	Unit Commander in the Computer Department in the IAF	A consultant for high-tech companies. Holds a Doctorate in Philosophy of Science
Uzi Shamir	Lieutenant	Fighter Pilot	Lieutenant Colonel	Head of MAFAT (Administration for the Development of Weapons and Technological Infrastructure)	Bank worker
Ilan Lazar	Lieutenant	Fighter Pilot	Lieutenant Colonel	Branch Commander in IAF Headquarters	Importer of Scania trucks and buses

Glossary of Terms

Accelerated Stall: A momentary control loss of the aircraft, resulted from over-pitching to an extreme AOA (Angle-Of-Attack), which is usually expressed as a quick, unpredictable roll to the side of the stalled wing. Accelerated stall occurs when the pilot pulls back to sharpen the aircraft's turn beyond the AOA limit, and as a result, the aircraft promptly sharpens the maneuver and performs a snap roll.

Afterburner: A system installed in the rear section of the engines at aircraft tail. Its purpose is to ignite a mixture of fuel and gases propelled from the engine and thus generate substantial extra thrust. The system consumes a lot of fuel in a very short time, and due to its waste, it is only activated in short intervals in which ultra-high airspeed is required (during interception) or a sharp maneuver is needed (dogfight or pop-up strike). In twin-engine jets, there are two afterburners, one per each engine.

Ailerons Sewing (Turn) Maneuver: An aerial maneuver generally used in dogfights. Its purpose is to gain an advantage over the enemy aircraft. During the maneuver, the interceptor aircraft dives sharply, rolls and turns towards the opponent's heading, and then recovers the dive straight towards the tail of the opponent. This maneuver got its name because of the ailerons special operation on which it relies.

Air Force Base: A military air base from which squadrons and other units operate.

Air Intake: The front of the jet engine. Its purpose is to provide a means for the air to flow into the jet engine, where it is compressed, mixed with fuel and then combusted to generate thrust.

651

Aircraft Oscillation: A cyclical, uncontrollable motion, which the aircraft encountered due to a technical failure or a faulty operation. Oscillation is usually expressed in the repeated, rapid and uncontrollable pitch changes.

Ait: The IAF nickname for the A4 Skyhawk, a US-made strike fighter aircraft, developed based on lessons learned in the Korean War. It is used primarily to support ground forces.

Alert 5: An alert in which teams need to be ready to takeoff within five minutes or less from the moment they are scrambled. During this alert, they need to be dressed in their flight equipment (overall, shoes, and g-suit) at all times, and stay in close proximity to their alert aircraft.

Alert 15: An alert for when the teams need to be ready to takeoff within 15 minutes from the moment they are scrambled.

Alert 60: An alert indicating that air crews must not leave far from the squadron or the base, defined by a designated distance in which they can takeoff within 60 minutes from the moment they are scrambled.

Angle-Off: The difference, measured in degrees, between the chase aircraft heading and the enemy's. This angle tells the relative fuselage alignment. For example, if the angle-off were 0 degrees, the chase aircraft would be on a parallel heading with the enemy and the chase aircraft fuselages would be aligned; if the angle-off were 90 degrees, the chase aircraft fuselage would be perpendicular to that of the enemy. This respective angle is different from the **aspect angle**, which is the number of degrees measured from the tail of the enemy to the chase aircraft. Aspect angle is important because it tells the pilot how far away he is in degrees from the target's stern, which is the desired position.

Angle-Off (In Dogfights): Angle-off is the difference, measured in degrees, between the heading of the strike fighter's at the back and the bandit's aircraft in front. This angle indicates the relative fuselage alignment. For example, if the angle-off were 0 degrees, the rear aircraft would be on a parallel heading with the one in front, and the aircraft fuselages would be aligned, and if the angle-off were 90 degrees, the fuselage of the rear aircraft would be perpendicular to the aircraft in front in the dogfight. For this matter the rear aircraft sits on the tail of the one in front hence he has an advantage over it.

Anti-Aircraft Artillery (AAA): Either mobile or fixed, including several barrels, it is utilized for quick and continuous fire of hundreds of anti-aircraft rounds to down intruding aircraft. It is deployed to protect air bases, essential military facilities, or accompanies ground forces on the front line. Because of the multiple gun barrels and the ability to densely cover a given airspace, AAA were regarded a serious threat to IAF aircraft that attempted to strike enemy air bases and at the front line vicinity.

Aviation Squadron Leader: An air crew officer with the rank of lieutenant colonel, who serves as the base commander's deputy. The aviation squadron leader is also in charge of the aviation management unit of the base, which supports the flight squadrons activities, including command over the base's central command operations post, the control tower, the runways, intelligence, fire fighting units, etc.

Banking Over: A change in the direction of the turn of the aircraft by rolling over and tilting bank angle to the other side. Generally, a banking over maneuver is utilized to avoid surface-to-air missiles, as well in a "full disadvantage," situation wherein the aircraft is threatened by an enemy aircraft that is on the tail in gun fire position a few hundred meters behind.

Barrel Roll: A diagonal, half-vertical maneuver, combining a loop and a roll, which makes the aircraft appear to loop along the inside of a barrel, while rolling along its longitudinal axis. This maneuver is generally used in dogfights.

Blips: The return of an echo of a detected object on a radar display in the air control unit or on the aircraft instrument panel. "Blips" appear as yellow dots on the radar display in the air control unit or as a green dot on the aircraft's radar display. Their display on the screen to indicate the presence of aircraft in the air. Based on the "blip" movement on the display an experienced air controller knows how to identify the speed and the heading of the tracked aircraft.

Braids: A horizontal zigzag maneuver done in coordination with the wingmen in the two-ship formation, while exiting the strike run. The two fighters maneuver left and right, one against the other, scissoring wide while flying forward and diving to lower height.

Chaff: Metal fibers stored in cartridges, which are dispensed by the aircraft into the air (or fired from cannons) in order to deceive enemy radar by masking its display. During the Yom Kippur War, the Sledgehammer jets used chaff during air-to-ground missions only. A cartridge of chaff stored in the air brakes was sufficient for a one-time use.

Clean (Air-to-Air Configuration): An aircraft configuration in which all external loads are not installed (external drop tanks or bombs). Its purpose is to reduce the aircraft drag and weight hence to decrease the fuel flow while significantly improving the aircraft's available maneuverability. Clean configuration is the preferable for dogfights. It is also possible to obtain a clean configuration if the aircraft is already airborne by pressing the "Panic" button hence jettisoning all external loads (see Panic).

Close Pass: A close passing (hundreds or tens of meters) between two or more aircraft. Generally, the event is unintentional, and is indicative of poor aerial picture perception and a lack of eye contact between the aircraft acting in the same airspace.

Cluster Bomb: A large number of miniature bombs backed in one container, designed to hit large areas where military forces are concentrated or to hit exposed facilities.

Combat Manager: A squadron airman assigned by the squadron leader to replace him on the ground and handle all squadron warfare activities from within the operation (OPS) room. This task was limited to only few of the squadron veteran formation leaders, senior navigators (WSOs), or pilots from the squadron command staff e.g., squadron leader or deputy squadron leader.

Compressor Stall: A compressor surge which is a complete disruption of the flow through the engine's compressor that is caused by pressure differences in the engine's air intake, preventing the engine from providing the essential thrust for flight. A compressor stall is accompanied by a characteristic noise. In most cases, the only way to recover a stalled engine is to shut it down and restart it again.

Control Officer: In various control centers as the HQ and Wing Command and Control Centers, the control officer carries out routine work, and in fact, operates the Air Force or wing—they receive and pass along messages, distribute telegrams and mission orders, etc.

Usually, they are not actually officers but rather sergeants, who left one of the training courses (e.g., flight course or the air controller course) and became control officers. Their nickname during the Yom Kippur War was "The kids."

Delayed Pop-Up Strike: One of the forms of pop-up strikes, in which the climb up to the wingover execution point starts earlier than usual and is performed on a shallower dive angle. This type of pop-up strike exposes the aircraft to longer duration hence increasing the risk for the aircraft to be hit.

Nevertheless, the delayed pop-up strike provides the crew with more time to detect and identify the target, and to gain more altitude for obtaining an even shallower strike angle.

Direct: A bombs release method in which the bombs are released manually. This method is used as a backup release option should a malfunction or failure occurs in the avionics system's weapon release computers. The bombs are released as soon as the weapon release button (pickle) is pressed. The probability of hitting the target using the direct release method highly depends on the release conditions as well as on the pilot's skills..

Disadvantage: An aerial position where the aircraft faces a disadvantage position with respect to another aircraft, and should the pilot neglect to take defensive actions, the odds are that it will be hit or downed by its opponent. A full disadvantage is considered a situation where the aircraft is highly threatened by another aircraft, which is in gun firing position on its tail.

Dive Bombing: A strike maneuver also designated DTOS (Dive Toss) in which the pilot makes a diving path at a pitch-down angle of approximately 40° to the ground, during which he presses the Pickle button to release the bombs. The computer then releases the bombs provided that all conditions are met for the bombs to hit the target. The bombs then continue on a ballistic trajectory towards the target. Typically, the computer will prevent bombs from being released at either too steep or too shallow an angle.

Drag Chute: During every landing, the Phantom pilot deploys a drag chute attached to the tail of the aircraft. Its purpose is to decrease the aircraft speed during the landing run until it reaches the taxi speed (from approximately 100 knots until complete stopping, the pilot uses the brakes as well).

During his taxi on the runway, the pilot releases the drag chute. It is then picked up by the runway crew, which returns it to the squadron that reuse it on its aircraft.

Drogue (Flag) Strafe: Aerial gun fire training. The trainee pilot fires from his aircraft's guns (one gun only is installed on the Sledgehammer) at a drogue, which is towed by another aircraft several hundred feet behind. The training aircraft are loaded with combustion-free training bullets that are painted in color to enable to distinguish the hits of the particular aircraft from other aircraft participating in the training sortie. After landing, the number of holes in the drogue fabric are counted and the hits are attributed to the pilots by the color of their bullets. According to the number of rounds fired and the number of hits, the pilot's "gunnery level" can be determined.

Drop a Wing: An expression that states the act of rolling the aircraft to a 90° bank angle about its longitudinal axis without actually turning to either side. The purpose of the wing drop maneuver is to provide the crew with a clear view of what was obstructed just below the aircraft (such as other aircraft during a dogfight, a target on the ground, etc.).

Drop Tank: An external fuel tank. During the Yom Kippur War, the IAF's three leading fighters (F4 Phantom, Mirage III, and A4 Skyhawk) were provided with the option to load such fuel tanks – one per each wing station and one on the centerline station pylon. This type of fuel tank may be jettisoned or released from the aircraft airframe. The purpose of the fuel tank jettison system is to reduce the aircraft's gross weight, hence improving its aerodynamic performance. This action is usually performed prior to commencing an air to air engagements or when the aircraft is threatened by missiles, and the crew wishes to reduce extra load to enable high maneuverability.

"Eject" Light: A warning light on the side-wall of the navigator's cockpit. It is illuminated when the pilot presses the respective button in his cockpit.

The light's purpose is to signal to the navigator to get ready for an immediate ejection, in case that the ICS have malfunctioned or in emergency. At the beginning of each mission, the pilot presses the button to test the system. The navigator should verify and announce that the light is illuminated.

Ejection Seat: The pilot and navigator seats are designed from the outset to be able to become ejection seats, should the need arise for abandoning the aircraft. By pulling the ejection handle, the cockpit canopies are blown off, and the seats are jettisoned by means of rockets out of the cockpit immediately afterwards.

The seats come with pre-installed parachutes, harnessed to the torsos of the pilot and the navigator. The seat is separated from the crewmember during the ejection process, and each of the crewmembers remains hanging below the parachute's canopy with a rescue raft, which is attached to the parachute by a rope hanging between their legs.

Electronic Intelligence: Such intelligence, especially in the Air Force, allows for the detection of enemy aircraft, even before they show up on the radar screens. Electronic intelligence units existed during the Yom Kippur War, embedded in several local air control units, or as separate units in the field.

Electronic Warfare (EW): The use of electronic and electromagnetic technology to mask enemy radars, jam radio communications, and mislead Surface-to-Air Missile (SAM) systems.

Emergency Placements: Every airman serving in a permanent placement in IAF Headquarters or as an instructor in the IAF Flight School is assigned to an operational squadron, in the event of an emergency situation. They come to train during peacetime, usually once per week. During wartime, most qualified airmen are scattered from the Headquarters and Flight School and return to their operational squadrons to reinforce the regular personnel of the squadron.

End-of-Training Season Party: During the 70's, a year would be divided into three training seasons of four months each. Every training season was followed by a party at its end, to which all members of the squadron were invited. There were usually humorous shows, and there was always great anticipation for the event. The task of organizing the party was usually assigned to one of the regular pilots in the squadron.

Engagement (for dogfighting): An order obtained on the radio from the air controller that vectors the formation towards enemy aircraft, with the intention to intercept them and engaged in a dogfight.

Energy: An expression of the level of the aircraft's ability to maneuver versus its opponent in the next few moments when it is engaged in a dogfight. The level of energy is a combination of both altitude and airspeed:

A higher aircraft with a high airspeed - high energy level.

A lower aircraft with a low airspeed - low energy level.

When acting over enemy territory, the aircraft should possess a high level of energy, i.e., a combination of high altitude and airspeed that can provide the pilot with the option to sharply maneuver the aircraft as required.

EW (Electronic Warfare) Pod: An external rectangular or oval-shaped pod loaded on the center line station of the aircraft. It enables the use of electromagnetic transmissions on frequencies that jam capabilities of SAM battery radars, hence disabling their ability to detect and track aircraft.

Final: The last edge of the landing pattern, where the aircraft aligns with the runway centerline, descends along the glide-slope, and extends its flap and landing gear for landing.

First-Line Squadron: A squadron equipped with the most advanced combat aircraft used by the Israeli Air Force and is considered the spear-head of the corps. Sledgehammer squadrons in the Yom Kippur War were considered first-line squadrons.

Flap: An extendable control surface installed at the wing's trailing edge at the wing root, next to the fuselage, which increase the wing lift when extended, hence enabling operation in lower airspeeds. The flap system is employed at low airspeeds for takeoff and for landing.

Flare Illumination: Flares are dispensed from an aircraft in order to illuminate a certain area on the ground during darkness. These flares are equipped with parachutes and burn for several minutes, long enough to provide sufficient lighting to distinguish between targets on the ground in order to attack them at night, or during search and rescue operation for detection of the searched object.

Flight Qualifiers: The fighters are assigned to a squadron for the purpose of maintaining their flight qualifications despite the fact that they are assigned in emergency to maintain their HQ special duties, hence they will not join to enforce the squadron should a war erupt. Therefore, the flight qualifiers join the squadron's training flights, but perform fewer sorties, just enough to keep their flight qualifications.

Foe: A definition of an airborne enemy aircraft (one of the Fs in IFF. The I stands for Identification and other F stands for Friend.)

Formation Flying: The disciplined flight of two or more aircraft under the command of a flight leader in the front. Formation flying is usually done in either a two-ship formation or four-ship formation. The four-ship formation has a leader (Number 1) and a sub-leader (Number 3).

Four-Ship Formation: Four aircraft, consisting of two-ship formations, each with its own leader, but under the command of the lead element's leader, who is designated "flight lead." The flight is usually led by the most experienced pilot who was qualified and authorized by squadron leader to lead a four-ship formation.

Friend (*Amit*): Air Force jargon for friendly forces (also used in the term IFF – Friend or Foe, which refers to other aircraft detected in the vicinity).

Frog (PK52 Luna-M): A Soviet-made Surface-to-Surface medium-distance missile. Used in the Syrian army.

Full Burner ("Firewall"): Full activation of the afterburner, and not partial activation ("reduced burner"). The maximum forward setting of the throttle is also referred to as "firewall" position in pilots lingo.

Furrow (Decoy UAV): A modified BQM-74A (Chukar) target drone, the size of a jettisonable fuel tank on a fighter jet, manufactured by Northrop Grumman. The purpose of the furrow was to deceive the radar systems of enemy missile batteries—so it would appear on their screens as a full size strike fighter, causing them to launch their missiles and revealing their location for the real IAF strike fighters, as well as to empty their launchers, enabling the first wave of strike fighter come in and strike these batteries.

G-load: A unit of measurement that expresses the force of gravity, with +1 representing the Earth's standard gravitational force. Maneuvering the aircraft changes the magnitude of gravity's load applied on the aircraft and crew.

Ground Echo: A faulty radar mask generated when a radar emitted beam return from the ground and is received by the aircraft's radar. When the aircraft radar is set to lock on a target, the pilot needs to verify that the radar has not shifted to lock on an undesired ground echo.

Ground Steering: A system installed on the nose landing gear. It provides the pilot with the option to steer the aircraft while taxiing on the ground and in the initial stages of the takeoff run until the aircraft has sufficient airspeed to control the yaw with the rudder, as it becomes effective. Steering is performed by operating the foot pedals, while simultaneously pressing the ground steering button located on the stick grip.

Ground-Air Control Officer: A representative of the intelligence agencies in the squadron, whose duty is to provide the squadron fighters with the intelligence information that they need to execute their missions, with respect to and in coordination with the ground forces.

G-suit/Pressure Suit/Tightly-fitting Trousers: A suit that is an integral part of the pilot's flight equipment, and is worn as a sort of trousers from the ankles to the hips. In the trousers is an interconnected system of air bags that are supplied with air by means of a quick-disconnect hose in the cockpit, provided with air pressure from the engine compressors. During ejection, the hose is disconnected to allow a safe separation of the pilot from aircraft.

When performing high-G maneuvers, the bags inflate, applying pressure to the legs and abdomen, reducing the amount of blood that is able to deplete from the head and upper body hence pooling in the lower body. This assists the crewman with maintaining consciousness throughout the high-G maneuver.

Guard: A stress radio channel, which is used by the pilot should the aircraft encounter a serious problem or if the crew had to eject. During operational actions, the channel is kept open for reception by all IAF airborne aircraft, control units, control towers, and the HQ control chamber.

Throughout this book, when "Guard" is mentioned, it refers to cases where the crew needed to eject from an aircraft. A mobile radio transceiver designated SART, which is an integral part of the safety and rescue equipment that the pilot and navigator wear over their G-suit torso, is calibrated for transmitting and receiving over the Guard channel.

Gundish (ZSU-23-4): A Soviet made Anti-Aircraft Artillery (AAA) equipped with four barrels, which is mobilized by means of an armored track vehicle, and is equipped with a detection and fire control radar. The Gundish gun was proven its efficiency during the Yom Kippur War, primarily due to its radar, and especially for targeting aircraft at an altitude of range of up to 7,000 feet.

Hail: A code word used by air control operators during the Yom Kippur War, to alert their pilots of enemy aircraft in their proximity.

Head-on: A situation in which one aircraft flies past another in opposite directions i.e., at heading angle of 180° (head-to-head).

Heat: A missile selection mode set by a switch located in the cockpit, which provides the pilot with the option to switch between the various available types of air-to-air missiles. When "HEAT" position is selected, the infrared ("hot") homing missile is ready to sense heat emitting aircraft and home on them.

H-Hour: The mandatory reference time for joint forces operation. Used for comprehensive syncing. It is according to this time that the rest of the times of an operation are derived, and each of the participating formations set their time according to it, so their ETA (Estimated Time of Arrival) at target will be properly synchronized.

Hot Mic: The operational setting of the ICS (Intercom System) on a two-seat aircraft, which allows constant communication (hot-line) between the pilot and the navigator. This is in contrast to a "Cold Mic," in which the crewmember has to press and hold a button in order to speak on the ICS.

Immediate Alert: An alert in which crews are seated in their aircraft at the underground hangar, with the engines not started, but are in standby for start and scramble as they get the order. The alert is usually carried out in the hangars next to the runway, to minimize the time required to taxi to the runway.

Inertial Navigation System (INS): A computerized navigation system that the navigator operates. The INS is a self-contained system that does not rely on external navigation aids like VOR, ADF, DME, GPS etc. and provides the crew with aircraft present position, which is used for navigation. The INS utilizes gyros, sensors, and accelerators, which cause the system to drift and accumulate position errors. In state-of-the art systems, these errors are corrected by GPS inputs, which were not available in 1973.

"Ingress Waypoint" Tower: A tall metallic construction tower colored in either red and white or black and white stripes, which are positioned at a fixed and noticeable projecting points format the proximity of the border lines. Towers were utilized for the purpose of providing crews with a vector point for the last strike leg to targets using the heading and time to target method (the leg in which the "heading and time to destination" method is applied).

Intelligence Technology Service: An IAF Intelligence-related technical unit. Its main purpose is to make use of aerial photographs and identify targets, and pass the results over to HQ operational quarters that prepare target sheets for attacks by Israeli aircraft.

Jumpsuit: A flight outfit with many pockets, made from flame-retardant materials.

Kelt (Raduga KSR-2): An aircraft-sized Surface-to-Air cruise missile manufactured by the Soviet Union. Launched by large bombers, its rocket motor can be detected at a distance, and is capable of reaching a range of 200 kilometers. In the Yom Kippur War, the Egyptians launched 25 missiles of this type at Israeli targets. Twenty of them were intercepted by the IAF and Israeli anti-aircraft defense forces, and three did not reach their targets for various reasons. Two hit Israeli targets: one hit the air control unit at Ofir, and the other hit the regional control unit over Refidim.

Sledgehammer: The IAF nickname for the Phantom jet. A two-seater fighter aircraft, the American-made twin-engine, multi-mission aircraft designated the F-4E. The aircraft is equipped with a radar, and one of its primary advantages is its high thrust, thanks to twin J-79 engines.

The Sledgehammer was used for interception, strikes, and bombings. It was capable of all-weather operation, and excelled at long-range missions.

Landing Gear: A shock absorber installed on each wing and under the nose. It supports the aircraft's respective wheel, on which the brake assembly (main landing gear), ground steering (nose wheel), and dampers are installed.

Last Chance: A final maintenance exterior check of an aircraft, performed just before takeoff, wherein the senior technician crew checks the aircraft for any liquid leakage or other abnormal indications that would deteriorate the aircraft serviceability.

Leg: A section of the navigation route to the target whose two ends serve as reference waypoints for navigation. Each leg starts with a new heading that the navigator calls for the pilot to turn to shortly before the aircraft gets there. For example, "Next leg is heading zero-eight-four, 20 miles long." In some cases, a leg-head waypoint includes a change in height and airspeed.

Lock On: A situation in which the aircraft's radar locks on to the echo-returns of the target. Lock-on target is a mandatory step prior to the launch of a radar guided missile.

On the Phantom, lock-on is usually performed by the navigator. In the Yom Kippur War, the radar lock-on was also required for Air-to-Surface strikes, designated DTOS (Dive Toss).

Loft (Weapon Release): A bomb release method in which the aircraft's final strike run is performed in a very low altitude, in a manner similar to that used in minimum exposure weapon delivery.

The aircraft performs a high-G pull-up to a steep climb angle with leveled wings at a pre-determined point. During climb, the bombs are automatically released and start their ballistic trajectory towards the target. After the bomb-aircraft separation, the aircraft sharply breaks away to either side, and dives back to low altitude to gain distance away from the target area. This type of delivery is considered safer because the weapon release is executed in offset, i.e., a relatively larger distance from the target, which is followed by a breakaway to either side, ensuring that the aircraft will not enter the threatened target zone.

Map Room/Navigation Room: A room in the operations complex of the squadron, in which the squadron's assigned mission commands are converted into operational mission plans drawn on maps and aerial photographs.

Master Caution (MC) Light: A primary warning light illuminated in a bright amber light. The MC light is in installed on both instrument panels at a prominent location. Its purpose is to draw the crew's attention to any malfunction that just occurred in the aircraft. As a direct result of the Master Caution's "warning call", the pilot can find the respective caution light on the caution panel that was the cause for the MC light illumination, and can urge the crew to initiate a set of actions as directed in the Emergency Checklist's respective page. By pressing on the MC light (i.e., resetting the MC light), the light is extinguished, hence it is set to standby mode and is ready to illuminate again should another caution light turn on.

Master Map (or simply "Master"): The original map created for an operational order. The map is drawn by the senior (lead) navigator, and then the junior navigators make second original copies of the map for the remaining formation crews.

The method used for second original map creation is attaching three additional maps to the original map with carbon papers placed in between two each maps, and then tracing all the illustrations and texts on the original to pass it over to the remaining copies.

Master Order: A binder of general operational attack plans for a particular enemy front, which are pre-planned, recorded, and distributed to the respective squadrons during peacetime, which will be converted into the actual Mission Order should conflict erupt in that front, such as a Master Order planned for an attack of Syrian air bases.

MiG-17: A swept wing single-seater fighter aircraft manufactured by the Soviet Union and used by Egypt and Syria during the Yom Kippur War. At low speeds, it has excellent maneuverability, hence IAF pilots were instructed to avoid engaging a dogfights at airspeeds lower than 400 knots.

MiG-21: A supersonic, single-seater fighter aircraft manufactured by the Soviet Union, with maneuverability equivalent to that of the Mirage 3. It was the leading Egyptian and Syrian aircraft during the Yom Kippur War.

Military (MIL) Power Setting: An engine setting where the throttle is advanced to full military (MIL) thrust however without employment of the afterburner. This setting is used any time the pilot wishes to accelerate to maximum possible airspeed without employing the afterburner. As the throttle is set to MIL the aircraft airspeed and fuel flow increase and reach levels that prevent a continuous operation in this setting.

Mirage 3: See Shahak.

Mirage 5: A supersonic aircraft manufactured by the French company Dassault. The IAF ordered this model type in 1966, but due to the French arms embargo, the aircraft were never supplied to Israel. Libyan Mirage 5 aircraft were used on the Egyptian front of the Yom Kippur War.

My Course: An extremely meaningful term for every fighter who successfully graduated the flight course and became a pilot or navigator. Members of a course become like a close-knit family by its conclusion, accompanying their fellow coursemates over the years. Their course number becomes an additional family name and a label marking the air airman's seniority and experience.

Napalm: A firebomb consisting of flammable liquids used for hitting and clearing out wide open spaces.

NAV On: An announcement made by the navigator upon completing the alignment process of the INS (Inertial Navigation System), setting the switch to NAV position and clearing the pilot for taxiing to the pre-takeoff hold station.

Negative G: During every maneuver in which the nose is pushed sharply down, the pilot will sense a decrease in the force of gravity, a sense of weightlessness, like a roller coaster suddenly plummeting downward at the top of the hill. The pilot is lifted up, against his harnesses and upward to the canopy. Anything not tied down or secured in the cockpit will float in the cabin during negative G.

Nesher: The first fighter aircraft manufactured by Israel, based on the Mirage 5 designs. The primary differences compared to a Mirage 3 are a greater range and improved weapon loading capacity.

Nozzle Flaps: An item that is checked during takeoff checks and called out in the cockpit. The pilot check the position of the nozzle flaps, which are installed at the end of the engine exhaust pipes. Upon the activation of the afterburner, the pilot checks the condition of the nozzle flaps to ensure proper operation. Proper operation of the nozzle flaps indicates the serviceability of the engines and afterburners.

"On the Ladder": An expression that refers to the last moment before the airman actually climbs into the cockpit to perform a mission. As long as the crew is next to the ladder, it is still possible and relatively easy to change or update the details of the mission and take decisions as required. However, once the canopy is locked down, and with the ticking of the clock, mission changes becomes more complicated.

Operations (OPS) Room: The heart of the squadron, which also has the designation "00" for the crews when they wish to consult with the squadron from the air. All of the squadron's activities are controlled from the OPS room. The OPS room houses the Combat Manager, the Operations Officer, and the operations sergeants, as well as all communication equipment (telephone and telegraph hub, etc.).

Mission Orders are received from the HQ at the Operations Room, and all mission related information is handed from the room to the mission planning teams and to the formation leads, mission aircrews assigning is determined, as well as weapon loading orders handed to the maintenance chiefs.

OTU (Operational Training Unit): Where an operational training course is held. All flight academy graduates attend this Flight Academy course as fighter pilots. It is where they study and practice the fundamentals of operational flight and combat doctrines of the Israeli Air Force for interception, dogfights, and various types of attacks. At the end of the course, graduates are assigned into the operational squadrons.

Panic Button: A button located in the cockpit, which is activated when the aircraft is engaged in a dogfight or in an emergency (i.e., a failure or damage to the aircraft that demands a clean configuration). Pressing the panic button results in the jettisoning of the external drop tanks, as well as the bombs and pylons that were loaded under the aircraft's wings and centerline stations. The purpose of the load jettison is to reduce the weight and drag and set the aircraft into a clean configuration, which significantly improves its ability to accelerate and to maneuver.

Pepper: An alias for the afterburner (the significance of "Full Pepper" is "set the afterburners to full thrust or 'firewall' position").

Phantom: See Sledgehammer.

Pickle: A weapon-release button located on the stick grip. When pressed, the aircraft releases bombs or launches an air-to-air missile.

Pipper ("Predicted Impact Point"): Refers to a dot at the sight center, which serves as the aiming point.

"Pipper On": The Sledgehammer' sight pipper consists of several circles and a dot in the center—the "piper." When a heat-seeking missile is launched at a target, the piper should be placed on the tail of the enemy aircraft; for gun strafe, the piper should be placed on the enemy aircraft's fuselage; and for bombing, the piper should be placed right on the target.

Placard: A small plastic board, with a magnet attached to its back, which is attached to the board in the operations room.

The name of the airman assigned to the mission is recorded on one of the placards, and the aircraft tail-number allocated for each crew (i.e., pilot and navigator), the weapons and the fuel load configuration is recorded on the other placard.

Pod Formation: A strike method that was primarily used by the U.S. military. In essence, it is a strike formation configuration executed at a high altitude, with the EW pods activated when required. This method was supposed to provide the strike formation with immunity from Surface-to-Air missiles. It was only attempted once during the War of Attrition, and was discontinued due to its failure.

Pop-Up Strike: A method of strike, in which the formation arrives at target vicinity at a low altitude to avoid being detected by defense radar systems (i.e., Surface-to-Air missiles and AAA). At target proximity, each aircraft executes a tight pull-up maneuver for the purpose of climbing fast to the attack altitude, then identifying the target, executing a wingover towards it and diving at the target to make a bombing run and to release bombs. Immediately after the bombs are released, the aircraft disengage and get away as fast as they can from the target area. This type of strike is considered dangerous, because it requires the air crew to get at the target proximity, and during the strike run recovery, they actually are passing over the target, thus exposing themselves to AAA barrels defending the target.

Positive G: During every turning maneuver, the pilot will sense an increase in the force of acceleration, just like on a roller coaster in a loop. In this case, the pilot is pressed hard into his seat.

In fighters, the load of acceleration can be increased up to 7-8G, and in exceptional cases, even to more than 10g. Acceleration's increased pull is sensed by the airmen as an increase of their weight. For example, if the pilot's helmet weighs two kilograms on the ground at 1G, a maneuver of 5G will increase the helmet weight to 10 kilograms loading the airmen heads. This figure also affects the airmen's body in a similar manner. At higher levels of G, it becomes more difficult for the pilot to function and may result in a black out, caused by the blood pooling in the lower part of the body when under acceleration causing a temporary loss of vision or even G-LOC (Loss Of Consciousness).

Preventive Enemy Infrastructure Attack: A tactical (bombing) assault, usually carried out deep in enemy territory, with the purpose of preventing the movement of enemy reinforcements or supplies to the front lines.

Pulling Sharply: Pulling on the stick harder during a turn, hence increasing the G-load imposed on the aircraft, sharpening the turn and reducing the turn radius as a result.

Pull-up: In this book, pull-up is referred to the pre-planned waypoint on the final strike leg in which the pilot is ordered by the navigator to pull up and climb to the attack run.

Pull-up Waypoint: A geographic point located on the navigation route's final leg a short distance before target and a slightly in offset. Pulling up on that waypoint will provide the pilot with the best position to execute the optimal strike run on target.

Radar Beam: A beam of electrons that is emitted from a radar antenna and covers an area that is limited in both azimuth (traverse) and in elevation. Thus, it is essential that the radar beam will be precisely aimed at target the area.

Radar Warning Receiver (RWR): A passive system installed in the aircraft, with an RWR display indicator on the instrument panel. It detects radar emitter activity of enemy SA batteries, identifies the type of missile according to the received parameters, and determines the approximate distance from the aircraft, as well as its flight stage, i.e., detection, tracking, lock-on, or launch. This state is indicated by means of an audible signal and a display on the RWR indicator in the cockpit. The RWR installed in the F4 aircraft had also the option to detect the older versions of aerial radars, which were mostly limited for range finding and were installed in the MiG-21 and Libyan Mirage aircraft models.

The RWR warns the pilot of a threat by means of indicator lights, a green indicator, lines or strobes and audible signals. The audible signal frequency, its cyclic repeating and strobes length provided pilots with the combined indication as to the intensity level of the threat.

Radio: Nickname for the communications system on the aircraft. The Phantom fighter had three radio sets installed: "Green" UHF (Ultra High Frequency) #1 radio set used for communication with the air controller, "Red" UHF #2 radio set used for communication with other formation aircraft, and a "Blue" radio set used for reception only, without the option to transmit.

Readiness Officer: An aircrew officer who serves as a regular pilot in the squadron. In addition to flying aircraft, he is also in charge of the preparation of mission order archives, updating and developing combat doctrine, and other operational issues.

Rudder: A vertical control surface installed on the aircraft's tail and is part of the vertical stabilizer. Its purpose is to maintain the aircraft's stability in the air about the yaw and roll axes.

SA: Surface to Air. Refers to the ground-launched anti-aircraft missiles (see SAM).

Sa'ar (Storm): An Israeli Air Force nickname for the upgraded Super Mystére, which was modified and upgraded when its engine was replaced with the Pratt & Whitney J52 engine that originally was installed on the Skyhawk.

SAM: An acronym for a Surface-to-Air Missile. Most are in a battery array of different types of missiles, designed to protect high-profile targets or wider swathes of territory.

SART (Search And-Rescue Transceiver): A mobile radio transceiver , which is an integral part of the life jacket equipment (nicknamed Mae West) that the pilot and navigator wear over their G-suit torso. With this transceiver channel automatically set to "Guard," the pilot can call for a rescue helicopter after ejecting from his aircraft.

Scud: A Soviet-built Surface-to-Surface missile used by the Arab countries, with a range of hundreds of kilometers.

Second-Line Squadron: Squadrons of the IAF that operate older types of aircraft and are therefore assigned to missions deemed less complicated than those assigned to the first-line squadrons (especially close support to forces in the front line and less deep sorties into anti-aircraft threatened enemy territories). Skyhawk and Super Mystére squadrons were considered second-line squadrons in the Yom Kippur War.

Set Switches to "ARM": A radio call ordering all aircraft in the formation to set the armament system switches to the "ARM" position, in which every press on the Pickle button will result in releasing the respective selected weapon.

Shafrir 2: An Air-to-Air, heat-seeking missile from the Python Air-to-Air missiles family, developed by Rafael Advanced Defense Systems, and designed to hit targets when aimed to the tail of the opponent aircraft. Despite the fact that the previous model (Shafrir 1) was not successful and caused distrust among the pilots, the Shafrir 2 earned respect in the Yom Kippur War thanks to its successful performance (in its service time in the IAF, the Shafrir 2 took down 106 enemy aircraft). This missile is not carried by the Sledgehammer.

Shahak: The IAF nickname for the Mirage 3 fighter, which participated in the Six-Day War, the War of Attrition, and was utilized as the primary interception aircraft during the Yom Kippur War.

"Shoulder" EW System: A codename given to helicopters equipped with an EW system. An array of "Shoulder"-equipped helicopters operated in offset from remote over Israeli-controlled territory during massive fighter strikes beyond enemy lines with the purpose of jamming all enemy radars.

Shrike (AGM-45 Punch Missile): An Air-to-Surface missile used against general ground-based radars and typically used against AAA fire control radar systems. The missile homes on the microwave energy emitted by the radar transmitter.

Sidewinder AIM9D: An Air-to-Air missile that homes in on the heat emitted from the enemy aircraft's jet engine, hence it can hit target only if launched from its rear sector.

Skyhawk: See Ait.

Sparrow (AIM-7E-2) Missile: A U.S.-made Air-to-Air radar-guided missile that was supplied to the IAF with the Sledgehammer aircraft and was considered innovative during the Yom Kippur War. The uniqueness of the Sparrow missile is that it can be launched at targets beyond the visual range, rather than only at the rear sector of the target.

Spin: A spin is a situation where the pilot loses all control over the aircraft due to its autorotational move, caused by the loss of lift on its wings following a stall (see Stall). During a spin, the aircraft experiences a high yawing rate to either side while losing altitude rapidly due to the lack of lift on its wings. In most cases, an unintentional spin is a result of a sharp maneuver attempt made by the pilot in a low airspeed condition.

Stall: A situation in which the aircraft's airspeed is too low, and the air flow over the wings is not sufficient to produce the lift necessary to continue staying airborne. In this situation, the aircraft loses altitude and becomes uncontrollable (and is, in fact, falling down). A stall can result in the aircraft crashing into the ground, unless the pilot finds a way to increase speed. In most cases, pushing the stick forward will result in airspeed buildup, provided that there is sufficient altitude for the recovery.

Start-and-Hold Alert: An alert when air crews are already seated harnessed in their aircraft at the underground hangar with the engines running and awaiting to be scrambled. This type of alert was usually carried out in hangars located at the proximity of the runway, shortening the time required to taxi to the runway. The Start-and-Hold alert is at the highest level of all alert types, and the time required from scramble to takeoff is approximately one to two minutes.

Stick: A flight control means used by the pilot to control the control surface angles, hence changing the aircraft's flight attitude. The stick controls the ailerons for roll and the elevators for pitch. Other flight controls are the pedals that control the rudder, and throttles that control the engines' thrust.

Strafe: A flat diving strike run executed at a 20° dive angle towards the ground. During strafe dive, the pilot fires rounds at the target from the aircraft guns. When strafe is performed during a dogfight, it is designated either "firing guns" or "guns run."

Strela AA Missile: A shoulder-launched Surface to Air (SA) missile, which is employed by enemy ground forces. The SA-7 is equipped with a passive seeker, which only receives the heat radiated from its target aircraft, hence the target has no early warning when that type of missile is launched at it. The SA-7 is considered a serious threat in areas where ground forces are deployed, due to its availability, the ease of its operation, and the lack of threat warning in the cockpit as it is launched. Because of the missile's shape, some of the air crews nicknamed it "the cigarette."

Strobes: Lines displayed in colors on the aircraft's RWR display when enemy radar is active—when it is tracking, locks on to or launches missiles at the aircraft. These lines start emerging at the display center and extend outboard, and their respective length represents the approximate distance from the emitting source of the beam.

Sukhoi 7: A medium-range strike fighter produced by the Soviet Union. It served the Egyptian and Syrian air forces during the Yom Kippur War.

Sukhoi 20: A jet strike fighter produced by the Soviet Union. It served the Egyptian air forces during the Yom Kippur War. This is an upgraded Sukhoi 7, capable of carrying larger loads and taking off from half the length of a runway.

Super Mystére (Model SMB2): An upgraded version of the Mystére model fighter. It was upgraded by the IAF by replacing its engine and by modifying the shape of the wing. These improvements enabled the aircraft to reach a supersonic speed in a level flight, as well as improved its maneuverability.

Surface-to-Air (SA) Missile Battery: A missile array whose purpose is to shoot down enemy aircraft. It includes a fire control center, detection and fire control radar, several launchers, missiles, and logistical areas. Also designated a SAM (SA Missiles) battery.

Surface-to-Surface (SS) Missile Battery: A missile array whose purpose is to hit essential enemy facilities from remote, and employs long-range missiles.

Technical Division: An essential and integral part of the squadron, which is in charge of maintaining the squadron aircraft and preparing them for flight during the turnaround. This includes refueling, checking their serviceability and loading them with weapons according to the loading plan received from the squadron's operations room, which obtains the mission orders from its superiors,(i.e., the on-duty Combat Manager, the Flight Division Commander, or the Squadron Commander). The Technical Division is also in charge of repairing aircraft damaged during combat (either by its own personnel or by referring to higher maintenance levels, either in the base or in other bases).

Technical Officer: An officer, usually the rank of major, who is in command of the Technical Division. The technical officer is an integral part of the commanding staff of the squadron and reports directly to the squadron leader.

Temperatures: One of the engine parameters checked during takeoff, upon which is a condition for the afterburners activation. The pilot calls out "*Temperatures*" after ensuring that the engines' exhaust temperature indicators on the instrument panel have reached desired satisfactory indication.

Territorial Defense: A CAP (Combat Air Patrol) held over a pre-defined territory, which is considered tactical or strategic, such as an air force base, a town, or a sensitive military facility. The CAP is usually performed by either a four-ship or two-ship formation, patrolling above the designated area at an intermediate altitude of 10,000 to 15,000 feet, which are allocated to protect this area from enemy aircraft attack.

Three-Hundred (300) Feet: Approximately 100 meters AGL (Above Ground Level). This height is considered a very low flight altitude, which in many cases, allows for the penetration of enemy territory without detection by enemy radar systems. In the Yom Kippur War, Sledgehammer aircraft even got lower than that to heights of 100 feet (approximately 30 meters), sometimes even less, in almost all of the sorties executed in threatened areas.

Throttle: Part of the phrase "Stick and Throttle," expressing the two essential means for flying the aircraft—the control stick, and the lever that controls the engine's power.

Throttles: A pair of levers on the left console of the cockpit, with which the pilot controls the engines' power setting and activates the afterburners. An almost identical set of levers is installed in the navigator cockpit's left console as well.

Time-Map-Terrain Navigation: A manual navigation method (also designated Contact-Nav). This was the common method before the INS era for low flight in visible conditions where the navigator or pilot have the pre-planned route illustrated on the map with all essential marks including legs heading, fuel quantity at leg start, waypoints, and accumulated time along the route marked by ticks. The navigator observes the passing terrain below, and has to identify landmarks along the route, check the aircraft's present position against the route on the map, and take corrective actions in heading and/or airspeed to return to the pre-planned leg or make a shortcut as required to a designated waypoint along the route. This navigation method is used as a backup to the INS should it fail, and is useful for changes of destination that were not pre-programmed in the navigation computer. It is also useful for visual verification of a pre-programmed route navigation.

Torso/Harness: A life jacket consisting of straps, buckles, and other survival equipment incorporated in the flight equipment, which is essential for the pilot and the navigator. An integral part of the harness is the safety and rescue equipment stored in the life jacket pockets. The life jacket is harnessed to a parachute, which is attached to the ejection seat.

Training Season: Every year was divided into three training seasons, each one lasting four months. Every season was considered a training cycle, during which the various training plans were executed in the IAF, starting with the Flight Academy and continuing with the general training plans for all IAF operational squadrons.

Tupolev (Tu-16): A Soviet-made twin-engine jet bomber used by the Egyptians in the Yom Kippur War to launch Kelt missiles at various targets in Israel.

Tupolev 22 (Tu-22): A bomber and supersonic patrol jet manufactured by the Soviet Union. Some were converted for reconnaissance purposes, as well as to be used as EW aircraft for jamming enemy radar or for ELINT purposes.

There was no regular supply of this aircraft in the Egyptian or Syrian air forces. However, Syria was sent one aircraft of this model, prior to the outbreak of the Yom Kippur War, to support the Syrian Air Force's electronic warfare array.

UAV: An Unmanned Aerial Vehicle, normally used for aerial photography and gathering intelligence behind enemy lines. During the Yom Kippur

War, the IAF operated the Teledyne Ryan model 124I UAV, which was designated back then as an RPV (Remotely Piloted Vehicle). The 124I UAV was a jet aircraft that had low-altitude flight capability for 500 feet photography and a high-altitude cruise flight capability up to 56,000 feet with still image cameras.

Vertigo: A spatial disorientation. This physiologic phenomenon may occur primarily in limited flight conditions e.g., dark night, clouds, twilight time, or dawn. In many occasions, vertigo is likely to develop over the water, where the sea color mixes with the sky color, without a clear horizon line that may be referred to for aircraft attitude control.

Visor: A transparent piece of plastic that is installed on the front of the pilot and navigator helmets, allowing them to see through. The visor's purpose is to protect the aviator's face in general, and the eyes in particular, from the wind blowing during an ejection and from being hit by objects should the canopy jettisons. The visor is installed on a rail, hence it may be raised or lowered at required.

Weapon Match for Target: Selection of the appropriate weapon to destroy a certain target with distinctive properties. For example, concrete penetration weaponry is selected for fortifications, or cluster bombs (CBU) for dumps of non-armored vehicles and soldiers.

Weapons Systems Officer: An airman serving as a regular pilot in the squadron who, in addition to flying, is also in charge of the process of accepting a new weapon in the squadron, including training and publishing the properties related to it. The weapons systems officer is also in charge of handling the upgrade of existing weapons systems in conjunction with the HQ Weapons Systems branches, and takes all necessary actions to ensure their readiness for testing during the next combat drill.

Wing: A name designated to a military air base within the hierarchy tree of the IAF, which hosts aircraft operating squadrons only (e.g., Hatzor air base).

Wingover: A maneuver in which an aircraft pulls up, makes a steep climb, followed by a turn towards the target at the top of the climb. The maneuver ends with a dive at the target, flying in another direction from which the maneuver began. This maneuver provides the pilot with a constant eye-contact with the target from the pull-up moment to the weapon release moment.

In Air-to-Surface: Turning sharply while setting the nose down at the target.

WSO: An abbreviation for Weapon Systems Operator, which is an airman who occupies the rear cockpit of a fighter aircraft, and is simply designated navigator in the IAF. The WSO's duties are navigation, weapon systems operation, participating in dogfights by tracking enemy aircraft and locking the radar on them, as well as recovering the aircraft should the pilot become injured or fails to control the aircraft.

BIBLIOGRAPHY

Personal Interviews

Air Force Headquarters

Brigadier General David Ivry—Head of the Air Division (Deputy Air Force Commander)

Major Dan Alon—Head of the Office of the Air Force Commander

Colonel Giora Furman (Ram)—Head of the Operations Department

Colonel Amos Amir—Replacement as the Head of the Operations Department

Lieutenant Colonel Oded Erez—Head of the Defensive Branch/Operations Department

Major Aryeh Barkol—Head of Electronic Warfare Section/Defensive Branch

Lieutenant Colonel Aviahu Ben Nun—Head of the Attack Branch/Operations Department

Major Eitan Ben Eliahu—Head of the Combat Section/Attack Branch/From October 13th, Active Commander of the 201st Phantom Squadron

Major Giora Epstein—Head of the Photography Section/Attack Branch

Lieutenant Yossi Boles—Officer in the Photography Section/Attack Branch

Captain Ido Amber—Head of the Special Operations Section/ Integrated Branch/Operations Department

Captain Shmuel Natanel—Head of the Control Officer's Section/ Coordinated Operations Branch/Operations Department

Lieutenant Colonel Ami Ayalon—Head of the Command Branch and Acting Command and Control Officer

Lieutenant Colonel Shimon Lasser—Emergency Placement in the Command and Control Officer's Command Center

Major Tzvika Yammai—Commander of the Central Control Unit 333/Officer in Air Control and Command

Lieutenant Colonel Gideon Hoshen—Head of Operations Research/ Weapons Department

Lieutenant Yitzhak Ben Yisrael—Operational Research Branch Officer

Lieutenant Levy Zur—Air Force Headquarters

Colonel Oded Marom—Head of the Instruction Department

Lieutenant Colonel Haim Neve (z"l)—Assistant to the Head of the Intelligence Department

Lieutenant Colonel Yehuda Porat (Porty)—Head of the Research Branch/Intelligence Department

Major Yoav Dayagi—Assistant to the Head of the Research Branch/ Intelligence Department

Major Avner Yofi—Section Head of the Egyptian Air Force Activities Department/Research Branch

Captain Aharon Ze'evi Farkash—Section Head of Egyptian Air Defense/Research Branch

Lieutenant Yonatan Lerner—Section Head of the Superpowers/ Research Branch

Lieutenant Colonel Giora Ben Nir—Head of the Collections Section/ Intelligence Division

Major Avraham Benedek (Pat)—Head of Early Alert Section/ Collection Branch

Captain Danny Shimel (Shacham)—Deputy Head of Early Alert Section/Collection Branch

Lieutenant Colonel Reuven Eyal—Head of the Technical Branch/Intelligence Department

Major Oded Flum—Section Head of Aerial Operations Department/Pre-Mission Intelligence/Intelligence Department

Second Lieutenant Yoram Yaron—Officer of the Aerial Operations Department/Pre-Mission Intelligence

Major Yossi Aboudi—Head of the Air Force History Branch/Planning and Organization Department

Wing/Base/Squadron leaders

Colonel (Res.) Yaakov Agassi—Acting Commander of Wing 1/Ramat David

Lieutenant Colonel Arik Ezuz—Commander of Aviation Squadron Wing 1/Ramat David

Major Yitzhak David—Commander of the 109th Skyhawk Squadron/Ramat David

Lieutenant Colonel Tzvika Hess (Hed)—Commander of the 110th Skyhawk Squadron/Ramat David

Major Avraham Vilan—First Deputy of the 110th Skyhawk Squadron/Ramat David

Lieutenant Colonel Yehuda Koren— Commander of the 117th Mirage Squadron/Ramat David

Lieutenant Colonel Yoram Agmon—Commander of the 69th Phantom Squadron/Ramat David

Major Aviam Selah—First Deputy Commander the 69th Phantom Squadron/Ramat David

Captain Yitzhak Gat—Second Deputy Commander the 69th Phantom Squadron/Ramat David

Colonel Ran Pecker—Commander of Air Force Base 8/Tal Nof

Lieutenant Colonel Eliezer (Liezik) Prigat—Commander of the 119th Phantom Squadron/Tel Nof

Major Arnon Lavoshin—First Deputy Commander of the 119th Phantom Squadron/Tel Nof

Major Giora Ram—Commander of the 115th Skyhawk Squadron/Tel Nof

Major Shmulik Ben Ram—Acting Commander of the 116th Skyhawk Squadron/Tel Nof

Major Nachum Marchavi—First Deputy Commander of the 116th Skyhawk Squadron /Tel Nof

Colonel Amos Lapidot—Commander of Wing 4/Hatzor

Lieutenant Colonel Iftach Zemer—Commander of the 201st Phantom Squadron/Hatzor

Major Ron Huldai—Acting Commander of the 201st Phantom Squadron/Hatzor (Until October 9)

Major Shlomo Shapira—Commander of the 105th Dassault Super Mystére Squadron/Hatzor

Lieutenant Colonel Yaakov Bigelman (Gal)—Commander of the 113th Mirage Squadron 113/Hatzor

Major Yisrael Baharav—Acting Commander of the 101st Mirage Squadron/Hatzor

Colonel Amichai (Shumi) Shmueli—Commander of Air Force Base 6/Hatzerim

Lieutenant Yiftach Spector—Commander of the 107th Phantom Squadron/Hatzerim

Major Shlomo Egozi—First Deputy Commander of the 107th Phantom Squadron/Hatzerim

Major Uri Shahar—Commander of the 102nd Skyhawk Squadron/Hatzerim

Major Menachem Sharon—Commander of the 144th Mirage Squadron/Etzion

Major Danny Pesach—Commander of the 140th Skyhawk Squadron/ Etzion

Other Various Air Crewmen
Lieutenant Yaakov (Yankee) Yardani/The 110th Squadron
Lieutenant Roni Moses/The 110th Squadron
Lieutenant Alon Givoni/The 109th Squadron
Captain Gideon Sheffer/The 119th Squadron
Major (Res.) Yitzhak Galnatz/The 115th Squadron
Major Yisrael Baharav/The 101st Squadron
Major (Res.) Eitan Carmi/The 101st Squadron
Captain Gidi Levani/The 101st Squadron
Captain Mickey Katz/The 101st Squadron
Lieutenant Yehoshua Shalen/The 101st Squadron
Captain Amir Nachumi/The 107th Squadron

The 201st Squadron
Fighters of "The One" Squadron in the Yom Kippur War (see separate list on page)
Captain Benzi Nahal—Technical Officer
Sima Shavit (Kadmon)—Operations Clerk
Zivit Kvodi (Segoli)—Operations Clerk

Others
Captain Motti Kimmelman (Carmel)—Senior Air Force Representative in Intelligence Unit 848 at Mount Canaan ("Ararat")

Lieutenant Dudi Yaron—Air Force Representative in Intelligence Unit 848 at Um Hashiva ("Babylon")

Lieutenant Yossi Benvenishti—Senior Air Force Representative in Intelligence Unit 848 at Ofira ("Yaakov")

Lieutenant Colonel Oded Sagi—Regional Control Unit Commander at Mount Meron

Captain Yair Kafri—Senior Control Officer in the Regional Control Unit at Mount Meron

Sergeant Ora Fabian (Gilboa)—Sergeant of Electronic Intelligence in the Regional Control Unit at Mount Meron

Major Yigal Ziv—Commander of the Sinai Regional Control Unit

Major Avraham Albo—Commander of the Mitzpe Ramon Regional Control Unit

Captain Avi Amitai—Commander of the Ofir Control Unit

Major Shlomo Nir—Commander of the 200th Squadron

Lieutenant Aharon Shohat—Operations Officer of the 200th Squadron

Lieutenant Yehoshua Oren—Commander of the Dalton Unit of the 200th Squadron

Colonel Rafi Savron—Commander of the Northern Air Command Post

Staff Sergeant (Res.) Meir Azuri—Northern Air Command Post

Staff Sergeant (Res.) Ofer Sharabi (Shadeh)—Northern Air Command Post

Lieutenant Colonel Yigal Bar Shalom (Barshi)—Aviation Consultant in Dan Lenner's Division in Northern Command

Colonel (Res.) Yoske Naor—Head of the Electronics Section during the War of Attrition

Sources Outside of the Air Force

Zvi Zamir—Head of the Mossad

Lieutenant Colonel Avner Shalev—Head of the Office of Chief of Staff David Elazar

Colonel Aharon Levren—Assistant to the Head of the Operational Research Department in the Intelligence Division

Colonel Gideon Gera—Assistant to the Head of the Operational Research Department in the Intelligence Division

Lieutenant Colonel Zosia (Zizi) Kniajer—Head of the Jordan Branch in the Research Department of the Intelligence Division

Major Yaakov (Yankle) Rosenfeld—Head of the Egyptian Army Section, Branch 6, Research Department of the Intelligence Division

Major Amos Gilboa—Research Department of the Intelligence Division

Lieutenant Colonel Ephraim Lapid—Deputy Head of the Collections Department in the Intelligence Division

Lieutenant Colonel Sammy Nahmias—Head of the Special Operations Branch in the Collections Department

Lieutenant Colonel Aryeh Bentov—Deputy Commander of the Central Collection Unit 848 (8200)

Lieutenant Colonel Reuven Yardor—Head of the "Code Breakers" Branch in the Central Collection Unit 848

Major Noam Shapira—Head of the Egyptian Section in the Central Collection Unit 848

Major Eliz Noi—Head of the SELA Section in the Central Collection Unit 848

Captain Pesach Melubani—Head of the "Shofar" Section in the Central Collection Unit 848

Captain (Res.) Sefi Ben Yosef—Intelligence Deciphering Officer at Um Hashiva/"Babylon"

Lieutenant David David—Officer of the Central Collection Unit 848 at Um Hashiva/"Babylon"

Lieutenant Colonel Yossi Langotsky—Technical Unit Commander in the Intelligence Corps

Civilian Engineer Nachum (Chumi) Yaakovi—Electronics Branch of the Technical Unit in the Intelligence Corps

Captain Yair Ravitz (Ravid)—Unit 154 (504)

Lieutenant Colonel Avraham Bar David—Artillery Commander in Northern Command

Gideon Samet—Editor of the *Haaretz* Newspaper

Books

- IDF **Archives**—Various documents dealing with IDF activities in the Yom Kippur War, particularly **Yom Kippur War/the course of the war/the containment defense phase**, Operations Branch, Training Department, History Nov. 77, Research Crew of the Northern High Command Post.

- **Israel National Archives**—The minutes of Government and Foreign and Security Committee meetings, telegram exchanges between the Prime Minister and the Embassy in Washington before and during the war.

- **Air Force Participation in Land Warfare in the Yom Kippur War**, History Branch of the Air Force.

- Meir Amitai, **201 The One**, with the assistance of Zmora-Bitan Publishing.

- **The One, the Yom Kippur War**—A collection of flights and stories of Squadron 201 in the Yom Kippur War.

- **The One: 30ᵗʰ Anniversary of the Yom Kippur War—The Stories Behind the War** (CD)

- Lt. Col. (Res.) Dr. Elhanan Oren, **The History of the Yom Kippur War**, Headquarters Division—Training and Doctrine, Department of History

- **The Syrians on the Fences: Northern Command in the Yom Kippur War**. Editor: Danny Asher. Tel Aviv: Maarachot, 2008.

- Danny Asher, **Breaking the Concept**, Tel Aviv: Maarachot, 2003.

▫ Yoel Ben Porat, **Locking**, Tel Aviv: Edanim, 1991.

▫ Aryeh Braun, **Moshe Dayan in the Yom Kippur War**, Tel Aviv: Edanim, 1993.

▫ Hanoch Bartov, **Dado**, Tel Aviv: Dvir, 2002.

▫ Uri Bar-Joseph, **The Watchman Fell Asleep**, Lod: Zmora-Bitan, 2001.

▫ Uri Bar-Joseph, **The Angel**, Or Yehuda: Zmora-Bitan, 2010.

▫ Shmuel Gordon, **30 Hours in October**, Tel Aviv: Maariv Library, 2008.

▫ Moshe Dayan, **Milestones**, Jerusalem: Edanim and Dvir, 1976.

▫ Zvi Zamir, **Eyes Wide Open**, Or Yehuda: Kinneret, Zmora-Bitan, 2010.

▫ Eli Zeira, **Myth vs Reality**, Tel Aviv: Mishkal, 2004.

▫ Eliezer Cohen, **The Sky is Not the Limit**, Tel Aviv: Maariv Library, 1990.

▫ Binyamin Peled, **Days of the Account**, Ben Shemen: Modan, 2004.

▫ Yigal Kipnis, **1973—The Road to War**, Or Yehuda: Dvir, 2012.

▫ Ze'ev Schiff, **Earthquake in October**, Tel Aviv: Zmora-Bitan-Modan, 1974.

▫ Yosef Eshkol, Yitzhak Livni, Mordecai Naor, "Interview with Lt. Gen. David Elazar," **Bamahane**, Eve of Rosh Hashanah, 1973.

▫ **Haaretz**, 14 September 1973.

▫ **Yedioth Ahronoth**, 7 October 1973.

▫ **Maariv**, 23 June 1971.

Made in the USA
Middletown, DE
28 October 2018